SACRAMENTAL PRESENCE
IN A POSTMODERN CONTEXT

BIBLIOTHECA EPHEMERIDUM THEOLOGICARUM LOVANIENSIUM

CLX

SACRAMENTAL PRESENCE
IN A POSTMODERN CONTEXT

EDITED BY

L. BOEVE AND L. LEIJSSEN

LEUVEN
UNIVERSITY PRESS

UITGEVERIJ PEETERS
LEUVEN – PARIS – STERLING, VA

2001

ISBN 90-5867-186-0 (Leuven University Press)
D/2001/1869/92

ISBN 90-429-1067-4 (Peeters Leuven)
ISBN 2-87723-597-1 (Peeters France)
D/2001/0602/89

Library of Congress Cataloging-in-Publication Data

The presence of transcendence: thinking 'sacrament' in a postmodern age / edited by
Lieven Boeve and John C. Ries.
    p. cm. -- (Annua nuntia Lovaniensia; 42)
  Includes bibliographical references.
  ISBN 9042910828
    1. God--Omnipresence. 2. Presence of God. 3. Transcendence of God. 4. Sacraments.
I. Boeve, L. (Lieven) II. Ries, John. III. Series.

BT132 .P74 2001
231'.4--dc21   2001052388

Leuven University Press / Presses Universitaires de Louvain
Universitaire Pers Leuven
Blijde-Inkomststraat 5, B-3000 Leuven (Belgium)

© 2001 – Peeters, Bondgenotenlaan 153, B-3000 Leuven (Belgium)

PREFACE

In 1997, LEST I dealt with Christology in a context of religious pluralism, in *The Myriad Christ: Plurality and the Quest for Unity in Contemporary Christology*. LEST II started from a fundamental theological and sacramentological question, as reflected in its title: how to think *Sacramental Presence in a Postmodern Context?*

Where can we think God appearing in a so-called postmodern setting, in which no foundation seems given? In what way is it possible to signify reflexively the presence of God, which is confessed to in faith? Moreover, how can we understand sacramental presence after the (supposed) end of metaphysics, the traditional philosophical tool for sacramental theological thinking? From November 3 to 6, 1999, an international group of about 250 scholars, primarily in the fields of fundamental and dogmatic theology, philosophy of religion, and sacramental theology, gathered in the second biannual congress of the *Leuven Encounters in Systematic Theology* (LEST) to deal with these questions.

The congress was an initiative of the project-research group *Postmodern Sacramento-theology*, in which, from 1996 on, Lambert Leijssen, Georges De Schrijver s.j. and Lieven Boeve joined their efforts. The project concerned an investigation into the possibility of a contemporary coping with the sacred, from the Christian tradition, in the light of a redefinition of the transcendent in the postmodern context. This endeavour received substantial project grants (FWO-V – K.U.Leuven Research Fund) for the period 1997-2000. So it was made possible to enlarge the team with two scientific collaborators, Stijn Van den Bossche, and Jeffrey Bloechl (1997-1999), succeeded by John Ries (2000). In 1998 the project also has been accepted as one of the four research subjects for co-operation between the Leuven Faculty of Theology and the Netherlands School for Advanced Studies in Theology and Religion (NOSTER).

The texts of the main lectures, responses and a selection of fundamental theological papers which were offered at the congress, are included in this volume[1].

1. Three volumes of *Questions liturgiques/Studies in Liturgy* contain papers from the fields of sacramentology and liturgy (vol. 81, 2000, nr. 3-4, and another one dedicated to the work of L.-M. Chauvet, vol. 82, 2001, nr. 1). A collection of thematically ordered papers from the junior scholar's conference, preceding the congress on November 3, 1999, together with some other papers of the main conference are published in the *Annua Nuntia Lovaniensia* series (Faculty of Theology – Peeters Press).

The present volume includes, first, the "Opening Address" by God-fried Cardinal Danneels, Archbishop of Brussels-Malines, Great-Chancellor of the K.U.Leuven and its former professor of sacramentology at the Faculty of Theology. Then Lieven Boeve presents the state of the question which engaged the project research as well as the congress: "Thinking Sacramental Presence in a Postmodern Context: A Playground for Theological Renewal". He also introduces the other contributions. First of all, this regards the seven main lectures, five of which were commented upon by respondents. The second part of the volume gathers a selection of offered papers, dealing with the congress theme from a fundamental-theological angle.

We take the opportunity to express our gratitude to all those who contributed to the success of LEST II. First, we thank all contributors and participants for generously sharing with us their expertise and friendship. Secondly, we owe special thanks to the Fund for Scientific Research – Flanders (FWO-V), the Research Fund of the K.U.Leuven, and the Netherlands School for Advanced Studies in Theology and Religion (NOSTER) for their financial support. We appreciated very much the help of many professors, assistants and doctoral students of the Leuven Faculty of theology in the preparation and the course of the congress. Running the risk of forgetting to many people, we mention only Christopher Robinson whose contribution was crucial. This present volume is also the fruit of much editorial work after the conference, for which we received valuable assistance of Johan Ardui, Christophe Brabant and John Ries. In this regard we owe thanks as well to the editor of the BETL Series and Peeters Press for their willing assistance. Last, but not least, we want to thank our colleagues in the project, who assisted from the beginning up to the end in the organisation of the congress and the editing of the proceedings: Georges De Schrijver, Jeff Bloechl, Stijn Van den Bossche and John Ries.

Lieven BOEVE
Lambert LEIJSSEN

CONTENTS

OFFERED PAPERS

INDEX

OPENING ADDRESS

It does not fall to me to sketch the program for the work of the coming days. That is something you all have with you already. It is also not for me to outline the problematic of sacramentology in our day, or at any rate not to identify the direction where we are to seek the solutions for this crisis in the sacraments, in which the Church and its pastoral work turns.

But you will excuse a pastor and ex-sacramentologist for being unable to completely resist the urge to lay a few problems before such an eminent panel of specialists. You will forgive me for – in that capacity – laying before you a sort of "catalogue of difficulties", knowing full well that one Conference can certainly not be charged with the task of dealing with all of them. The sacraments pose problems for thinking and acting in the Church.

The main problem is that of the core of Christianity itself: its incarnational character. How can God – transcendent, ahistorical, and pure Spirit – enter into a geographical and historical context, reveal Himself physically, and thus take up into Himself all the servitudes of finitude? The sacraments stand at the heart of this question: how can God mediate divine salvation through flesh? Tertullian's expression *"Caro cardo salutis"* remains essential for the problematic of the sacraments. This problem weighs particularly heavily on our contemporaries, precisely because of their Manicheistic thinking: they can not place the "historicity" and "situatedness" of God's appearance.

The sacramentologist will also have to raise questions about the rationality of the blind spot that prevents our contemporaries from perceiving the invisible world. This will require penetrating cultural-historical research. This can seem far-removed from the properly sacramental problematic, but in fact it is thoroughly embedded there: so long as one remains blind to the invisible, it is impossible to enter the world of the sacraments. Is the current scientific-technological thinking of our contemporaries compatible with belief in the sacraments? Why not? And what are we to do about this?

A quite different question asks about the status of sacramental reality. What the sacrament produces is neither of the physical order nor of the psychological order, but of a very specific sacramental order. This is exceptionally important for, among other things, the status of the "*realis praesentia*" in the Eucharist. Our contemporaries seem to have no idea whatsoever about how to conceive of the status of such a reality: for them, presence is physical or psychological. Metaphysics is alien to them. Hence their difficulty situating real presence and hence, too, their incomprehension of, for example, the efficacy of the entire liturgy: the latter is appreciated only for its psychological effects or to the degree that it advances social cohesion. It goes without saying that, with regard to the Eucharist, it is insufficient for a theologian to say that transubstantiation, transfinalisation, and transignification and so forth are merely deficient theological constructions. But then which concept is admissible for contemporary thinking?

A related question concerns the entire structure of sacramental causality: how do the sacraments bring forth their effects? Classical theologians have worked out a wide array of theories in response to this question, but most of them are extremely difficult to uphold today. It remains a task for sacramental theology that it investigates this terrain: what is the specific causality of the sacrament, and how does it function?

A great deal of recent research into the anthropology of the symbol has rightly become a new domain within sacramentology. The specific causality of the symbol may well be the best approach to thinking about the sacrament. But this touches on a wide field of research which has only just opened up, leaving much work still to be done. Still, important results may indeed be expected from this area.

This brings us to another problem: the inter-disciplinarity of studies on the sacraments. The contemporary sacramentologist faces an almost impossible assignment: competence in many different domains – Scripture, Patristics, the history of liturgy, anthropology, ethnology, the phenomenology of symbol, cultural-historical analysis, and philosophy. No one can manage this alone. There is no theological discipline that demands more inter-disciplinary co-operation than this. This broad scope of fields of research and thus also methods is both the cross and the joy of the sacramentologist.

We come next to the problem of the phenomenon of the rite. There is still a great deal of ritual ingrained in our contemporaries, yet they are inaccessible to church rituals. The stark, impoverished and repetitive character of liturgical ritual does not appeal to them. This makes it a duty of sacramentology to investigate the function of the rite in the formation of community and the cohesion of the group.

This raises the question of the proper specificity of the rite in Christian liturgy. Considered within the whole of the immense arsenal of rituals in religions and cultures, what is the originality of the sacramental rite in Christianity? In an age when the media brings everyone into contact with rituals from all over the world, and when the contemporary ritual of Celts and Germans knows its second entry into modernity, what do Christians have to say about ritual?

Liturgical language also presents a problem: this is generally a matter of the inadequacy of liturgical use of language with respect to modern sensibility; the vocabulary and the idiom of the liturgy does not appeal to modern people. There must be a new adjustment. But is this really the main problem? On closer inspection, it seems that this has to do with much more than a problem of form. It is neither the vocabulary nor the idiom, but the faith-content that they transmit which creates difficulties. What remains incomprehensible is also, in fact, impossible to believe. It is the content of the message that meets with resistance: the language-problem is only a preliminary skirmish.

There is also considerable research into the proper language wielded by the sacrament as such, and which is sometimes rightly called "performative". What is the proper status of performative language as one genre alongside, for example, informative, narrative, and *sapiential* language genres? This, of course, is closely related to the question of the original form of sacramental causality.

Finally, there is still a great pastoral problem which does not directly concern the sacramentologist alone, but which he or she, as "ecclesial figure", simply can not escape. This is the problem of sacramental discipline in the Church, and the conditions for initiation in the sacraments. The point where this is felt most sharply is with marriage, and by extension with baptism. In these instances, the only rituals available to people are those of the Church. Civil marriages involve only a very weak, skeletal ritual. The same goes for baptism: there is no civil ritual at hand, and this bestows a hereditary burden on request for baptism by parents who are practically unbelieving; they come as much or more to celebrate the birth to natural life as to celebrate the birth to divine life.

This poses a problem for pastors: confusion rules. Some admit everyone to the sacraments, but on minimal conditions, while others practice rigourism. In cases of marriage between baptised partners who are in fact without faith, this can lead to irresolvable problems in the later case of divorce: was such a marriage with little or no faith in the sacrament and yet for baptised in fact a marriage at all? And how would one determine the minimum degree of faith necessary for a marriage to have been valid?

There is thus a great deal of work to be done. I can only lay these, my concerns before you, and wish you much energy and pleasure in your labours during these days in Leuven. But I thank you already in advance for the work that all of you, as theologians – both here and elsewhere – carry out for the benefit of the Church.

November 3, 1999   + Godfried Card. DANNEELS
                                   Archbishop of Mechelen-Brussels

INTRODUCTION

THINKING SACRAMENTAL PRESENCE
IN A POSTMODERN CONTEXT

A PLAYGROUND FOR THEOLOGICAL RENEWAL

In his *Opening Address*, Godfried Cardinal Danneels, presented to the congress's participants eleven challenges to reflect upon – in his words: "a catalogue of difficulties". These challenges varied from fundamental questions to more concrete problems for reflection. How is it today possible to think the very incarnational character of Christianity, implying the discussion whether God can mediate divine salvation through the flesh? Why does our contemporary culture and society seem to have lost to a certain degree the potential 'for perceiving the invisible world'? What about the structure of sacramental causality? What is the role of cultural anthropology in sacramentological reflection? In what way are sacraments rites functioning in the formation and cohesion of communities? Is the language used in liturgy still adequate to reach people with modern sensibilities? How can people in a detraditionalised Western society be initiated into the practice of Christian sacraments? And so on. In the present volume, particularly the first range of questions is dealt with.

During the last few years, theologising about sacramentality has become an important item for scholarly discussion. This theme became important also outside the circle of sacramentologists and specialists in ritual and liturgical studies. Philosophers of religion and fundamental theologians have shown their interest in the subject, using it as their main focus for reconceptualising the relation between transcendence and immanence, or the mediation of the divine. Moreover, the vocabulary and major themes of sacramentology have become key-concepts pervading other philosophical and theological disciplines. While, generally speaking, the 1960s showed a special interest in eschatology, and – due to Vatican II at least in Catholic circles – in ecclesiology, the 1970s in christology, the 1980s and 1990s in the doctrine of God and the Trinity, the years around the millennium seem attracted to doing theology starting from a sacramentological or liturgical angle. Accordingly, its questions, methodology, and terminology of sacramentology seem to have moved towards the centre of theology.

I. POSTMODERN 'SACRAMENTO-THEOLOGY' AND THE CHALLENGE OF THINKING SACRAMENTAL PRESENCE

In 1996 the project "Postmodern Sacramento-theology" started in Leuven. The neologism "sacramento-theology" was meant to indicate the basic sacramental structure of religious life, thinking and activity as a point of departure for theology. Such theology does not envisage the construction of a new "sacramental theology" or "theology of the sacraments" but a specific perspective from which to theologise as such. Every expression about God, whether in word or deed, needs to be understood as sacramental and thus submitted to sacramento-theological reflection to the degree that it is inscribed in and gives form to the mutual involvement of human beings and God. Thus considered, every theology is sacramento-theology, and sacramentology is no longer only, or mainly, a single theological discipline, but an essential feature of the fundamental or systematic theology to be set forth momentarily[1].

The term "postmodern" indicates the resolute contextual footing from which this theology stems, rooted in the conviction that Christian faith, and the Christian tradition, always bear a context from which they can never be extracted. It is only thanks to a context that Christian faith could have and still can take form and be handed down through the centuries. Tradition, as movement through time, can be described as a process of recontextualisation which must be renewed in each shift of context [Schillebeeckx speaks of "horizons of understanding"[2]]. Often when contextual sensibilities shift, the dominant form of tradition loses plausibility, bringing forth experiences of alienation. It is only by seeking a new relation between the received tradition and the changed context – resulting in a new form for tradition – that lost authenticity can be regained[3].

---

1. In line with the programme of this project, I ventured an exploration into a postmodern sacramento-theology in *Post-Modern Sacramento-Theology: Retelling the Christian Story*, in *ETL* 74 (1998) 326-343. Parts of this study are reworked in the present contribution.

2. E. SCHILLEBEECKX, *Mensen als verhaal van God*, Baarn, Nelissen, 1989, p. 35; for the development of tradition as a "fusion of horizons", see pp. 59-63; E.T. by J. Bowden: *Church: The Human Story of God*, London, SCM, 1990, 40-45. Schillebeeckx owes this theory to H.-G. Gadamer (*Wahrheit und Methode: Grundzüge einer philosophischen Hermeneutik*, Tübingen, Mohr, 1960).

3. For the issue of tradition, see L. BOEVE, *Onderbroken traditie: heeft het christelijke verhaal nog toekomst?*, Kapellen, Pelckmans, 1999, part 1. An English translation of this study is in preparation.

From such a perspective, the adage *philosophia ancilla theologiae* remains valuable today for a theology which understands itself as *fides quaerens intellectum*. As the reflective clarification of a general contemporary sensibility, philosophy (and the human sciences) provides theology with contextually plausible models, patterns and strategies for thought, and a vocabulary for recontextualisation. As the critical consciousness of a context, philosophy is often of particular value for clarifying the experiences and effects of alienation which accompany a paradigm shift[4]. This is certainly the case for what is sometimes called *postmodern* critical consciousness[5].

Thinking sacramental presence – as one of the major themes in sacramento-theology to reflect upon the relation between transcendence and immanence –, therefore, sets new challenges for the theological agenda. In what follows, I first explore the basic structure by which theologians have until now articulated the sacramentality of existence. This must include some attention to the integration of modern sensibility in recent decades. I will then turn to the postmodern critique of the modern master narratives, which to a significant degree also applies to the Christian narrative. After an analysis of postmodern critical consciousness, I will sketch some major questions for a recontextualisation of the theological reflection on the sacramentality of life. Finally, from this framework, I will situate and present the contributions made at the LEST-congress, which are included in this volume.

1. *The Shift from a Premodern to a Modern Outline of (Sacramental) Theology*

a) *The Persistence of the Premodern Sacramento-Theological Structure*

Notwithstanding of the reception of modern elements into theology and Christian praxis, especially after Vatican II[6], the prevalent

---

4. For the notion of "paradigm shift", see Hans Küng's reception of T. Kuhn, in H. KÜNG & D. TRACY (eds.), *Theologie – wohin? Auf dem Weg zu einem neuen Paradigma*, Gütersloh, Verlagshaus Gerd Mohn, 1984; ID. (eds.), *Das neue Paradigma von Theologie. Strukturen und Dimensionen*, Gütersloh, Verlagshaus Gerd Mohn, 1986; E.T.: *Paradigm Change in Theology. A Symposium for the Future*, Edinburgh, Clark, 1989; and in H. KÜNG, *Theologie im Aufbruch. Eine ökumenische Grundlegung*, München – Zürich, Piper, 1987.

5. Cf. L. BOEVE, *Bearing Witness to the Differend. A Model for "Postmodern" Theologizing*, in *Louvain Studies* 20 (1995) 362-379, esp. pp. 363-368; and *Critical Consciousness in the Postmodern Condition. A New Opportunity for Theology?*, in *Philosophy and Theology* 10 (1997) 449-468.

6. In order to regain the theoretical credibility and practical relevance of Christianity in Modern times, theologians have often sought a rapprochement with a range of modern

sacramentological interpretation of symbols and rituals used in the celebration of the Christian sacraments has remained virtually premodern. The underlying notion was that the holy or the sacred constituted a realm of its own, transcending the mundane, and that this source of wholeness is accessible to us through the enactment of ritual gestures, images, and words.

An unspoken but defining feature of this sacramentology, or more generally, sacramento-theology, is a neo-Platonic cosmology, or onto(theo)logy. According to the latter, all creatures are ordered by the quality of their being, and can thus be located on a continuum flowing from God (*proodos/exitus*) and returning to God (*epistrophè/reditus*). The fundamental idea here is that of the *analogia entis*, a consequence of the emanation of beings from an original being. Although mediaeval theologians highly nuanced this neo-Platonic scheme (e.g. from the perspective of a theology of creation stressing the *creatio ex nihilo*), it remained the basic paradigm for understanding the relation between God and the world[7]. In theological epistemology, this neo-Platonic framework formed the foundation of theological knowledge. It is in light of this scheme that Thomas Aquinas' perspective on analogy has been generally received. According to Aquinas, we can justly attribute to God such "simple perfections" as goodness, wisdom..... which are attributes borrowed from human experience and expression, because these perfections, according to the *analogia entis*, exist preeminently in God already before creation: "Whatever is said both of God and creatures is said in virtue of the order that creatures have to God as to their source and cause in which all the perfections of things pre-exist transcendently"[8]. To be sure, negative theology does nuance the pretensions of this claim, but within the neo-Platonic scheme this does not change the definition of the onto(theo)logical foundation it implies. The logical order which human experience discovers to be discontinuous, because there is no univocity in speech about God, nonetheless reaches God,

---

ideas. Generally speaking, they have tended to reshape theology in accord with the modern turn to a subject-centered worldview. Concretely, this has meant leaving behind more Scholastic thought-patterns, and entering into dialogue with Kant and Hegel, existentialism and personalism, Marxism and neo-Marxism. The systematic theologies of Bernard Lonergan, Karl Rahner, Edward Schillebeeckx, Johann Baptist Metz, and Hans Küng are the offspring of such endeavours.

7. That this could be the case for Thomas Aquinas, follows from the study of F. O'ROURKE, *Pseudo-Dionysius and the Metaphysics of Aquinas*, Leiden, Brill, 1992.

8. T. AQUINAS, *Summa theologiae*, Ia, q. 13, art. 5 (ed. Blackfriars in conjunction with London, Eyre & Spottiswoode – New York, McGraw-Hill, Vol. 3, trans. H. McCabe, 1964, p. 53).

because that discontinuous *logical* order rests on a continuous *ontological* order. Within a neo-Platonic framework, the being of that which is caused depends first on the being of the cause, or source: hence, understood from the neo-Platonic basic paradigm, there is a background "logic of the same"; ultimately theology is necessarily a homology. In this perspective, theological truth is supported by ontology. This same principle also holds for sacramentology:

> The sacramental event can be understood in neo-Platonic terms as the illumination of the single hidden origin in the 'being, living and thinking' of contingent beings, an illumination through which these same beings become transparent to the primordial ground which shines through them[9].

More specifically, sacraments function as events which bring believers into harmony with this origin, and do so in a reality which possesses a general sacramental structure because of the driving force which extends from the God-origin to beings, and therefore the transparency of those beings towards the God-origin. In such a context, sacramental grace is defined according to a causality-scheme: sacraments institute harmony with the origin. Sacraments, as means of divine salvation for humankind, are not only the signs (*signum*) of grace but also what exercise or realise it (*causa*). It is in the sacrament itself, which "causes/realises what it signifies", that grace comes to us[10]. Sacraments stand in the *exitus* from God and they lead back toward God (*reditus*). According to Thomas Aquinas, God is the *causa principalis* of the grace which occurs in and through the sacraments (which can thus be defined as *causae instrumentales*). Only God, he says, can produce grace — "as fire warms by virtue of its own heat". "For grace," he concludes, "is nothing else than a certain shared similitude to the divine nature"[11]. As

---

9. G. DE SCHRIJVER, *Experiencing the Sacramental Character of Existence: Transitions from Premodernity to Modernity, Postmodernity, and the Rediscovery of the Cosmos*, in J. LAMBERTS (ed.), *Current Issues in Sacramental Theology*, Leuven, Abdij Keizersberg – Faculteit Godgeleerdheid, 1994, 12-27, p. 13 = *Questions Liturgiques/Studies in Liturgy*, 75 (1994) 12-27.

10. This point is worked out in L.-M. CHAUVET, *Symbole et sacrement. Une relecture sacramentelle de l'existence chrétienne*, Paris, Cerf, 1990, esp. pp. 13-49 (chapter 1: "Critique des présupposés onto-théologiques de la sacramentaire classique"); E.T.: *Symbol and Sacrament: a Sacramental Reinterpretation of Christian Existence*, Collegeville, Liturgical Press, 1995, 7-45.

11. T. AQUINAS, *Summa theologiae*, III, q. 62, art. 1 (cf. n. 6, Vol. 56, trans. D. Bourke, 1975, p. 53). See also art. 2: "considered in itself grace perfects the essence of the soul in virtue of the fact that this participates, by way of a kind of likeness, in the divine being. And just as it is from the essence of the soul that its powers flow, so too it is from grace that there flow into the powers of the soul certain perfections called the virtues and gifts, by which those powers are perfected so as to achieve a further fulfillment in the acts

instruments, sacraments are those by means of which God produces grace[12]. Their original impetus comes forth from God.

As I have already mentioned, such premodern thought patterns continue to determine much sacramentology and, more broadly, theology even after Vatican II. I refer, for example, to the theology of Hans Urs von Balthasar[13], and in this regard to the insightful study by Georges De Schrijver, on the crucial role played by *analogia entis* in von Balthasar's thought[14]. The same principle is also operative in the theology of Joseph Ratzinger[15]. For Ratzinger is convinced that the dialogue between Judeo-Christian biblical faith and Hellenistic (neo-Platonic) philosophy has been providential. Greek thinking has an eternal value for Christianity because it helped to establish and maintain its original form. Ratzinger's neo-Platonic Augustinian vision of the world took shape during his early study of Augustine and Bonaventure: reality possesses a binary, polar, structure which is fundamentally asymmetrical and hierarchical[16]. The world radiates from a more real and more intelligible reality remaining beyond the world, from which the world came forth and to which it returns. Our world is said to be sacramentally structured in the sense that it points transparently to the eternal. In this connection, Ratzinger speaks of the "sacramental grounding of human existence": "in the illumination of the world towards its eternal basic foundation, the human person also experiences who he or she really is: someone called by and to God". Sacraments aim consequently at the "Einfügung in den durchgottete Kosmos"[17].

---

proper to them" (p. 58). Thomas continues that *sacramental* grace adds something over and above the grace of the virtues and the gifts, "namely a special kind of divine assistance to help in attaining the end of the sacrament concerned" (p. 59).

12. Cf. *ibid.*, pp. 53-54: "this is the way in which the sacraments of the New Law cause grace. For it is by divine institution that they are conferred upon man for the precise purpose of causing grace in and through them.... Now the term "instrument" in its true sense is applied to that through which someone produces an effect".

13. H.U. VON BALTHASAR, *Herrlichkeit. Eine theologische Ästhetik. Fächer der Stile*, Einsiedeln, Johannes, 1962; *Herrlichkeit. Eine theologische Ästhetik. Im Raum von Metaphysik*, Einsiedeln, Johannes, 1965.

14. G. DE SCHRIJVER, *Le merveilleux accord de l'homme et de Dieu. Étude de l'analogie de l'être chez Hans Urs von Balthasar* (BETL, 63), Leuven, Peeters Press, 1983.

15. See, e.g., J. RATZINGER, *Theologische Prinzipienlehre. Bausteine zur Fundamentaltheologie*, München, Wewel, 1982.

16. See L. BOEVE, *Kerk, theologie en heilswaarheid. De klare visie van Joseph Ratzinger*, in *Tijdschrift voor theologie* 33 (1993) 139-165 (with a summary in English), esp. pp. 147-149 and 160.

17. J. RATZINGER, *Die sakramentale Begründung christlicher Existenz* (Mietinger Kleinschriften), Freising, ²1967, pp. 18-19 (translation mine).

b) *The Integration of Modern Sensibilities*

Many modern theologians have reacted against this "transcendence" of the holy and have rejected its premodern dualistic, static, and ahistorical conceptions, seeking instead approaches more attentive to modern sensibilities. Yet here too, and despite modern accents, there often is an important, implicit neo-Platonically structured onto-theological premise. Methodologically, many theologians in one way or another enter into dialogue with contemporary philosophy and human sciences. The anthropological foundation of the sacraments is one of the most prominent outcomes of this endeavour: they are often explained as rituals pregnant with individual as well as collective meaning. But the theological legitimation of this move is frequently carried out by recourse to classic, albeit rejuvenated, ontological schemes.

The theology of Karl Rahner, for example, which undertakes a unique and successful dialogue with modern philosophy and anthropology[18], rests precisely on such a classically structured basic scheme. Rahner's transcendental theology presents a dynamised and subjectified (or personalised) reflection on the relation between God and humans in a fundamental way, thus opening a place for both the human experience of freedom and the sacramental event[19]. Still, the self-communication of God as grace-filled presence appearing to a fundamental human autonomy must be understood within the framework of neo-Platonic onto-theology: attempting to conceptualise the ontological essence of the self-communicating God, Rahner writes:

> that in this self-communication, God in his absolute being is related to the created existent in the mode of formal causality [in contrast with the efficient causality in which something caused is distinguished from the cause], that is, that he does not originally cause and produce something different from himself in the creature, but rather that he communicates his own divine reality and makes it a constitutive element in the fulfillment of the creature[20].

18. Cf., e.g., K. RAHNER, *Foundations of Christian Faith. An Introduction to the Idea of Christianity*, trans. W.V. Dych, New York, Crossroad, 1984, pp. 24-25, on "The Interlocking of Philosophy and Theology"; E.T. of *Grundkurs des Glaubens. Einführung in den Begriff des Christentums*, Freiburg – Basel – Wien, Herder, 1976, 35-36.

19. For a concise account of Rahner's sacramentology and its promise, see L. LEIJSSEN, *Rahner's Contribution to the Renewal of Sacramentology*, in *Philosophy & Theology* 9 (1995) 201-222.

20. K. RAHNER, *Foundations of Christian Faith* (n 16), p. 121. In the next paragraph Rahner situates the ontological foundation and legitimation in the transcendental experience of the order of every finite being toward the absolute being and mystery of God. As such, transcendence, in a first movement toward the creature, underpins the transcendental movement toward transcendence.

God's self-communication, God's grace, is for Rahner an inner, constitutive principle of humanity given freely by God. Wherever people open
themselves fully to God, the sacramentality of the whole of existence –
the self-communication of God to the whole of existence – comes to
light. In this connection, the sacraments are "nothing else but God's effi-
cacious word to man, the word in which God offers himself to man and
thereby liberates man's freedom to accept God's self-communication by
his own act"[21]. Hence Rahner's modern sacramentological approach is
carried out against a background which remains primarily classic.

Somewhat stronger accents of modernity can be found in the work of
theologians who no longer focus on the human subject as such, but
instead begin from its social and radical-historical rootedness. Still more
than others, these theologians see rituals and symbols no longer as
merely rendering the holy present in its salvific immediacy, but, in line
with the modern conception of time, as the germinal break-through of a
fullness that is yet to come – this is the full realisation of God, humans,
history and the world respectively: in short, the advent of the reign of
God on earth, whether or not tempered by an eschatological proviso. As
opposed to what may be considered the de-historicised and spiritualised
concept of grace in more traditional theologies, these late modern theologians stress the this-worldliness, historicity and materiality of Christian salvation.

One of the most important theologians in this respect, Edward Schillebeeckx[22], points out:

> modern believers can trace a forerunner of divine salvation in freedom
> which is realised in socio-political action. Here the divine reality proves

---

21. *Ibid.*, p. 390. On the sacrament as "real symbol", see *Überlegungen zum person-
alen Vollzug des sakramentalen Geschehens*, in *Schriften zur Theologie*, Bd. X, Einsiedeln – Zürich – Köln, Benziger Verlag, 1972, 405-429, esp. pp. 422-423 (translation:
Considerations on the Active Role of the Person in the Sacramental Event, in *Theological
Investigations*, vol. 14, trans. D. Bourke, London, Darton, Longman & Todd, 1976, 161-
184, esp. pp. 177-178). Rahner here attempts to revise the causality-model in which the
sacraments have been conceived ("sacraments cause what they signify"): the grace for
which the sacrament stands is distinguished precisely where the individual person takes
up the freedom and free choice which God has bequeathed to him or her, such that he or
she is thus brought to the fullness of human personhood.
22. This applies especially to Schillebeeckx's later writings, beginning in the 1970s,
and not to his first sacramentological writings. Recently, Schillebeeckx wrote an article in
which he drew the lines of a new approach into sacramentology and announced the publication of his new monography on the topic. See E. SCHILLEBEECKX, *Naar een herontdekking van de christelijke sacramenten: Ritualisering van religieuze momenten in het
alledaagse leven*, in *Tijdschrift voor theologie* 40 (2000) 164-187 (wit a summary in English). The provisional title of Schillebeekx' new sacramentology: *Sacramenten – Jezus'
visioen en zijn weg naar het rijk Gods: Zin- en contrastervaringen tot ritueel gelouterd.*

itself to be a *reality*, as the one who wills good and opposes evil, the liberator from alienation. Thus the history of human liberation can become a "disclosure" in which man learns to recognise God as the one who wills the *complete* liberation of man[23].

In this sense, "orthopractic" human love "becomes the *sacrament* of God's redemptive love". Rather than leading immediately to harmony, this love leaves us restless "so long as salvation is not realised universally and completely for each and every individual"[24]. But despite this restlessness, already in today's experiences of human love and liberation, even in conditions of suffering, guilt, and death, there appear fragments of eschatological joy. From this perspective, guided by a commitment to the broad and history-bound sacramentality of liberating human action, Schillebeeckx situates the sacraments as "anticipatory, mediating signs of salvation, that is, healed and reconciled life"[25]. The sacraments and the liturgy are essential elements in the living relationship to hope for eternal salvation and redemption. They are prophetic forms of protest against the unredeemed character of history and they call for a praxis of liberation. Schillebeeckx continues:

> So if it is rightly performed, there is in Christian sacramental symbolic action a powerful symbolic potential which can integrate politics and mystics (albeit in secular forms). In remembrance of the passion of Jesus Christ which was brought to a triumphal conclusion by God – as promise for us all – in their liturgy, Christians celebrate their particular connection with this Jesus and in it the possibility of creative liberation and reconciliation in our human history[26].

Another authority, Johann Baptist Metz, relies on the commemorative-narrative dimension of the sacraments. For him, they are the privileged locus of the narrative tradition concerning the *memoria passionis, mortis et resurrectionis Jesu Christi*. By means of their narrativity, sacraments enable people to participate in dangerous and subversive but at the same time liberating memories of the fact that there is hope and a future for all. In this way, they also mobilise energy for acts of liberation[27].

23. E. SCHILLEBEECKX, *Christ. The Experience of Jesus as Lord*, trans. J. Bowden, New York, Crossroad, 1989, p. 814 (E.T. of *Gerechtigheid en liefde. Genade en bevrijding*, Bloemendaal, Nelissen, 1977).

24. *Ibid.*, p. 834.

25. *Ibid.*, p. 836.

26. *Ibid.* In his recent article, *Naar een herontdekking van de christelijke sacramenten*, these modern ethico-political accents – e.g. the importance of contrast experiences as experience of God – are still prominently present (see pp. 182-183).

27. See also F. SCHUPP, *Glaube – Kultur – Symbol. Versuch einer kritischen Theorie sakramentaler Praxis*, Düsseldorf, Patmos, 1974, esp. p. 258 ff. (Teil 2: "IV. Symbol und

Perhaps the ceremonial-ritualistic aspect in the sacrament does not elucidate clearly enough that sacraments are also macro-signs of salvation narratives... It is probably of major importance to elaborate more explicitly
the basic narrative structure of the sacrament – not only with a view to
theological clarification of the relation between word and sacrament, but
especially also with a view to Christian praxis itself: in this way the sacrament can possibly be related to narratives of life and suffering and in them
be explained as salvation narrative[28].

Yet despite their attempts to embrace modernity, the approaches of
Schillebeeckx and Metz have their weaknesses. It has been argued, for
example, that Schillebeeckx has failed to distance himself from a premodern conception of reality. In a study on the theological premises of
Schillebeeckx, Georges De Schrijver points to such ambivalence in his
thinking. While Schillebeeckx does recontextualise ethical praxis in line
with modern developments, this seems not to have occurred on the level
of theory. Despite his modern hermeneutical perspective, he ultimately
maintains a worldview in which God is still the highest being. This leads
De Schrijver to point out:

Schillebeeckx's vision of our processes of experience and explanation of
the world is directed ultimately to the experience and recognition of a God
who makes himself known to us as the God of salvation by means of a salvation history. God is the highest "object" of human experience, however
much His immediate inclination toward us is comprehended only according
to the medium (or means) of our creaturely dependence[29].

Aufklärung"). Schupp enters into dialogue with Kant's "Critique of Judgment" and representatives of the Frankfurt School on the possibility of rehabilitating symbols and
sacraments (the biblical-symbolic potential of reconciliation) anamnetic-anticipatorally in
the light of a social praxis.

28. J.B. METZ, *Glaube in Geschichte und Gesellschaft. Studien zu einer praktischen
Fundamentaltheologie*, Mainz, Matthias Grünewald, 1977, p. 185; E.T.: *Faith in History
and Society. Towards a Practical Fundamental Theology*, trans. D. Smith, New York,
Seabury Press, 1980, p. 208 (translation corrected).

29. G. DE SCHRIJVER, *Hertaling van het Christus-gebeuren: een onmogelijke
opgave?*, in E. KUYPERS (ed.), *Volgens Edward Schillebeeckx*, Leuven – Apeldoorn,
Garant, 1991, 53-90, esp. p. 82 (my translation). Where Schillebeeckx "concerns himself
with the mutual relationship between God and the world", De Schrijver feels compelled
to raise questions: "In my opinion, such points reveal a style of thought taking very little
account of the Enlightenment legacy of a cleft between old and new religious world-
views... A revision of the manner in which God, person and world relate to one another,
and with which modern cosmology and philosophy are occupied, is apparently not on
[Schillebeeckx's] agenda. Still, one might wonder how meaningful many Christians of
today will find a God who is the primordial source of the world outside of the world, and
who lets himself be known only as gracious presence and creative power. Some might
well propose that the old philosophical theism must now be considered untenable in an
age when many have begun to discover a world-immanent piety far removed from classical theism" (pp. 78-79) (my translation).

For his part, Metz, at least after 1985[30] and in accord with his resolute option for a narrative-practical approach, seems to have left no room for posing classic metaphysical questions. On a more reflective-theoretical level, he goes no further than an affirmation that the history of suffering comprises dangerous memories which, when spoken out, recall to us God's universal salvific will (which would then underpin the subjectivity of all). Instead of elaborating a truly systematic theology, Metz contents himself with presenting challenging theological intuitions (such as, e.g., "interruption")[31].

Perhaps for reasons to be explained within modernity itself, a sacramento-theological recontextualisation in full discussion with modernity has not yet been fully completed. Nevertheless, a number of modern accents have been introduced including: historicity, this-worldliness, the primacy of praxis, futurity, attention to suffering, all of which have been remarkably promising stimuli for fruitful theologising. Nonetheless,

From his outline of a new sacramentological approach (see *Naar een herontdekking van de christelijke sacramenten* (n. 22)), it is not immediately clear whether Schillebeeckx could overcome De Schrijver's criticism. Informed by the broad field of ritual studies, Schillebeeckx tightly links the anthropological and theological dimensions in the Christian sacraments. "For Christians the totality of the ritual as such is already God's mediation of grace, as this realises itself in and through the proper performative power, on the levels of cognition, emotion, and esthetics, of the liturgical performance inspired by Christian faith". When it comes to elaborating the theological dimension, he adds: "[S]acraments are an existential-emotive encounter with God in Jesus Christ", and "In the Christian sacraments the encounter with God occurs in a special way" (p. 184-5, my translations). While he has warned that a merely anthropological explanation of the sacraments misses their theological focus, it seems that, for a in-depth theological reflection upon the structure of this sacramental encounter with God, we must await Schillebeeckx' monograph.

30. Cf. J.B. METZ, *Unterwegs zu einer nachidealistischen Theologie*, in J.B. BAUER (ed.), *Entwürfe der Theologie*, Graz – Wien – Köln, Styria, 1985, 209-233.

31. Cf. J.B. METZ, *Unterbrechungen. Theologisch-politische Perspektiven und Profile*, Gütersloh, Verlagshaus Gerd Mohn, 1981. Elsewhere I have pointed out how Metz's intuitions in fact stand in need of further reflective clarification – as would become clear were he to enter into dialogue with the critical voices of postmodern thought. Cf. L. BOEVE, *Lyotard's Critique of Master Narratives: Paving the Way for a Postmodern Political Theology?*, in G. DE SCHRIJVER (ed.), *Liberation Theologies on Shifting Ground* (BETL, 135), Leuven, Peeters Press, 1998, 296-314; and *Postmoderne politieke theologie? Johann Baptist Metz in gesprek met het actuele kritische bewustzijn*, in *Tijdschrift voor theologie* 39 (1999) 244-264. One dialogue partner certainly promising considerable insight and stimulus would be the postmodern, language-pragmatic philosophy of Lyotard. But Metz is resolute in his refusal of all such dialogues. Cf. J.B. METZ, *Wohin ist Gott, wohin denn der Mensch?*, in F.-X. KAUFMANN – J.B. METZ, *Zukunftsfähigkeit. Suchbewegungen im Christentum*, Freiburg – Basel – Wien, Herder, 1987, 124-147, p. 141; and *Die Verantwortung der Theologie in der gegenwärtigen Krise der Geisteswissenschaften*, in H.-P. MÜLLER (ed.), *Wissen als Verantwortung. Ethische Konsequenzen des Erkennens*, Stuttgart – Berlin – Köln, Kohlhammer, 1991, 113-126, p. 122.

theologians remaining firm and explicit in their commitment to a pre-modern sacramental structure ignore or rule out these modern intuitions. The result is a stark divide in the theological landscape between modern and antimodern approaches[32].

2. *The Postmodern Context: Modern Master Narratives and Contemporary Critical Consciousness*

Our definition of "postmodernity" focuses on the manifest loss of plausibility of the so-called modern master narratives (as well as the erosion of the reactionary antimodern narratives). According to Jean-François Lyotard[33], this is due to the emergence of "counter-examples" which have made it clear that modernity could not fulfil its own promises. Moreover, such examples often support the idea that those promises themselves have stood in our way[34]. Lyotard analyses master narratives under either of two main types. On the one hand, he identifies narratives of rationality and technology which aim at complete transparency and thereby at an unlimited mastery and use of reality. On the other hand, he examines master narratives of emancipation which promote a utopic image of some human fulfilment, then on that basis developing a critical relation to (the past and) the present, and finally unfolding a strategy for realising utopia. An example of the first type is Hegelian idealism which would legitimate all knowledge of nature, society and state by situating it in the development of the life of the Spirit (*Geist*), and also scientific positivism, with its many and diverse

32. For an overview of these theological positions, cf. D. TRACY, *On Naming the Present*, in *Concilium* 25 (1990) 1:66-85. Tracy distinguishes modern, antimodern and postmodern theologies, and then sketches the first two positions in contrast to one another.

33. Cf., e.g., J.-F. LYOTARD, *La condition postmoderne. Rapport sur le savoir*, Paris, Minuit, 1979; *Le différend*, Paris, Minuit, 1983; *Le postmoderne expliqué aux enfants: Correspondance 1982-1985*, Paris, Galilée, 1986. E.T.: *The Postmodern Condition: A Report on Knowledge*, trans. G. Bennington, Manchester, University Press, 1984; *The Differend: Phrases in Dispute*, trans. G. Van den Abbeele, Manchester, University Press, 1988; *The Postmodern Explained: Correspondence 1982-1985*, trans. D. Barry, Minneapolis, University of Minnesota Press, 1993.

34. Cf. LYOTARD, *Le différend*, pp. 257-258, nr. 257. As Lyotard points out: the speculative principle that all that is rational is real and vice versa (Hegel) has since been refuted by Auschwitz; the Marxist historical-materialist teaching that every proletarian is a communist and vice versa was discredited in Berlin (1953), Budapest (1956), Czechoslovakia (1968), and Poland (1980); the liberal parliamentarian ideal of democracy of the people, for the people and by the people was struck a blow by the events of May 1968 in Paris; the different versions of economic liberalism arguing that the free market of supply and demand could insure general welfare were contested by the economic crises of 1911, 1929 and 1974-1979. The alleged fulfillment of all these promises has brought us nothing but blood and misery.

reductionisms (evolutionism, sociobiologism....), all of which offer us a conclusive explanation and an efficient course of action. Illustrations of the second type of master narrative include the different societal ideologies from the 19th and 20th centuries that reflect what is considered to be the ultimate aim of the human person and society: individual freedom for liberalism, complete solidarity for communism, or general welfare for capitalism, etc. Master narratives display absolute, universal and cognitive pretensions, and reduce everything in a hegemonic way to the inner definition of a single narrative[35]. And it is precisely these pretensions that appear false. Insofar as premodern narratives also remain active in modernity, they share in these characteristics. Premodern narratives have likewise reduced everything into what is defined solely or ultimately according to a single master narrative.

The loss of plausibility in master narratives is coupled with a growing consciousness of: (1) the fundamental plurality of the postmodern condition, (2) the radical particularity and contextuality of one's own narrative, and (3) the irreducible heterogeneity which emerges in the midst of that plurality and which precipitates a specific contemporary critical consciousness[36].

The fundamental plurality of the postmodern condition follows from the experience that each perspective seems to have equal legitimacy and worth, even if they are nonetheless incompatible. This basic experience presents itself across an extremely diverse range of domains in the human life-world: politics, economy, leisure, forms of personal and communal relationships, art, education, science, etc. There is no longer a universal perspective, no all-encompassing patterns of integration possessing universal and objectively determinable validity. Each claim to universality and totality is unmasked as the absolutisation of what is in reality a particular point of view. "Henceforth truth, justice and humanity are plural"[37].

---

35. From Lyotard's perspective, all of this can also be said of the Christian narrative. Consider the following summary list of master narratives: "the Christian narrative of redemption of the Adamic fault (la faute) by love, the Aufklärer narrative of emancipation from ignorance and servitude by understanding and egalitarianism, the speculative narrative of the realisation of the universal Idea by the dialectic of the concrete, the Marxist narrative of emancipation from exploitation and alienation by the socialisation of labor, the capitalist narrative of emancipation from poverty by techno-industrial advancement" (Le postmoderne expliqué aux enfants, p. 47; my translation).

36. I have elaborated on these considerations in Critical Consciousness in the Postmodern Condition (n. 5).

37. W. WELSCH, Unsere postmoderne Moderne, Weinheim, VCH Weinheim, 1987, p. 5 (my translation).

Insight into the fundamental plurality of our postmodern condition simultaneously reveals that all discourses and narratives are necessarily particular and contingent. This holds even for our "founding" narratives in which we ourselves, our community, and our history are described and redescribed. Not even a narrative of plurality exceeds the limits of a specific context. There is thus no universal perpective, no fixed kernel, no irreducible substrate of truth to be expressed, not even if one were to grant that such a claim would always have to be renewed or revised with each new shift or change in context[38].

The decline of master narratives, however, does not mean the end of narratives that institute and support the integration of individual and collective identity. Narratives continue to be told, and identity is still established. But insofar as they are conscious of plurality and contingency, these narratives can no longer maintain their former pretensions to complete transparency and unqualified pursuit of clarification and mastery. They no longer present themselves as founded in reality or somehow representing what "really is". Their plausibility means *contextual* plausibility. The multiplicity of particular narratives relativises the possible pretensions of each narrative, but without leading to radical relativism – for this standpoint still lays claim to the position of general observer. Since we can not abstract from our own narrative, it must be that all other narratives will *not* hold equal worth to us. We are always rooted in a context, and our reflectivity is contextually horizoned: we take distance in the midst of our attachments and rootedness.

Consciousness of both irreducible plurality and undeniable particularity arise from our confrontation with irreducible otherness, and thus from the experience of conflict, since plurality necessarily entails conflict. In the encounter with another discourse or narrative, which by definition constantly resists reduction to our own discourse or narrative, there appears an unconquerable fundamental heterogeneity which in turn points inexorably to the limits of our own narrative. It is a sensitivity to this experience and what it implies that prevents us from falling back into hegemony once again, or at least keeps us vigilant against the constant tendency of all narratives to do so. This sensitivity can also motivate a critical evaluation of contemporary hegemonic narratives, which forget or ignore otherness, either by enclosing it in a single narrative or by excluding it entirely.

---

38. An incisive account of this particularity and contextuality can be found in the work of Richard RORTY, particularly in *Contingency, Irony, and Solidarity*, Cambridge, University Press, 1989.

Insofar as plausibility must be necessarily contextual plausibility, then the present Christian narrative may no longer be capable of offering orientation and integration in a plausible way. Up until now, this narrative has most often answered the challenges of our condition by grafting itself onto modern master narratives of emancipation (which have now become implausible), or by hardening itself into an antimodern Christian narrative still embedded in premodern frameworks. According to the first response, Christian love is identified with striving for human freedom and liberation; according to the second, we rather meet an ontologically secured hegemonic Christian narrative of absolute truth. But both narratives suffer from a loss of plausibility since they too easily maintain a pretension to universality, cognitivist description, and hegemony. Because of their lack of unconditional openness for otherness, they fail to conceive of themselves as radically particular and contextual narratives figured on the field of irreducible plurality.

3. *Towards a Postmodern Sacramento-theology*

Still, this need not mean the end of the Christian narrative as such. A shift in context does imply a complete loss of plausibility, but it represents a challenge to renew the effort of recontextualisation, to look for a new relation between the received tradition and the changed context. In postmodern cultural-philosophical reflection, it may happen that the theologian finds a new impetus to interpret the Christian tradition in such a way that within a context of plurality it again inspires people who are searching for integration and orientation, but now without falling prey to the hegemonic schemes of master narratives. This implies that the Christian narrative become reflectively aware of its own particularity and contextuality, and that it reconceptualises its claims to universality and comprehensiveness. This leads us to the following considerations: (1) first I intend to deepen the sense of the critical thought-patterns specific to our new context and thus available for theological recontextualisation; (2-3) then I will sketch the outline of such a recontextualisation.

(1) As I have noted, the postmodern consciousness of radical plurality has led diverse authors (for example, Lyotard, Derrida, Levinas, Foucault[39]) towards an increased sensitivity to "alterity", "otherness", and "heterogeneity", to what is "different", or "that which cannot be made one's own without negating it". In Lyotard's vocabulary, this is

---

39. All of whom, insofar as they privilege difference over identity, side with Heidegger against Hegel.

designated by the "differend"[40] and, in the aesthetic realm, the "sublime"[41]. A reflection which takes as its point of departure this sharpened sensitivity to "heterogeneity", if it is consistent, inevitably comes to the understanding of its own particularity, limitedness, and contingency. The plot of a narrative of difference and otherness becomes itself interrupted by an irreducible heterogeneity. In his "language pragmatics" in which he considers human existence as grasped in language, Lyotard presents us with a schematic representation of this situation. A brief look at it gives a vivid illustration of much of what is involved in a thinking of radical heterogeneity and alterity.

For Lyotard, multiplicity is not a static but a dynamic reality. He attempts to clarify this by examining what takes place during the act and process of speaking where one sentence follows another. This sequence does not simply transpire by design. After a certain sentence "A" (already belonging to a specific order of sentences: descriptive, imperative, interrogative, exclamatory, etc.) numerous sentences can, in principle, follow, and all according to the nature of the discourse-type which regulates the "linking" of the sentences. Examples of such discourse-types include narrative, argument, prayer, education, and humor. What is specific to plurality, according to Lyotard, consists in the fact that the many discourse-types are heterogeneous and incommensurable with one another without any single one of them enjoying any special privilege. All discourse-types possess an equal right to provide the conditions for linking one sentence to the next. All that is assured is *that* a sentence always follows (even silence is a sentence) but not *which* sentence follows. This means that a moment of indeterminacy always occurs between two sentences. Every sentence arouses an immediate expectation; every new sentence implies an "event". The nature of the new sentence which is to fulfill the expectation aroused by the former sentence is always contingent. Two sentences are thus separated by an elusive moment of relative nothingness. This, however, can just as well be called absolute fullness in the sense of a moment of irrecuperable heterogeneity, or difference: unutterable, inexpressible, irreducible – in short, an "event".

Understood in this way, plurality implies conflict, irreconciliation, even irreconcilability. Regardless of how it may be considered, each

40. Cf. LYOTARD, *Le différend* (n. 33) and *Judicieux dans le différend*, in IDEM et. al., *La faculté de juger*, Paris, Minuit, 1985, 195-236.
41. J. LYOTARD, *L'inhumain. Causeries sur le temps*, Paris, Galilée, 1988; *Leçons de l'analytique du sublime*, Paris, Galilée, 1991. ET: *The Inhuman. Reflections on Time*, trans. G. Bennington, Cambridge, Polity Press, 1991; *Lessons on the Analytic of the Sublime*, trans. E. Rottenberg, Stanford, University Press, 1994.

choice for a specific sentence to establish a link unjustly resolves a conflict (a "differend"), at least insofar as other, diverse but equally legitimate possibilities are also at hand. In other words, the link established between a previous sentence and this specific new one prevents a link actualising other, no less justified possibilities. In the absence of a meta-language or an all-encompassing discourse-type, it is therefore impossible to adequately fill-in the created expectation. No single sentence succeeds in totally expressing the multiplicity of possible linking sentences, or better still, the moment of indeterminacy, of heterogeneity. Here we see the postmodern disavowal of the modern ideal of self-grounding thought worked out in a theory of language: according to Lyotard, no single sentence is capable of pronouncing at the same time its own being-event. The feeling of "it happens" cannot be contained in words, in a sentence. Nor can it be mastered hegemonically. What Lyotard evokes as the "sensibility for the impossible sentence", can itself not be stated, but only referred to. One can only bear witness to it; or better still, one *must* bear witness to it. The sense of the event demands witnessing. Moreover, it mobilises action against any hegemonic, totalising discourse that proclaims itself to be the privileged master of all links between sentences. Such a pretense weakens, forgets or even rejects the event as event.

For Lyotard, it is the task of philosophy to bear witness to the event of heterogeneity[42]. Contemporary philosophy would then need to fashion its discourse so that its structure expresses an openness to otherness, though of course the particularity of any philosophy always threatens to close it again. For in its attempt to express the inexpressible (or the fact that there is something inexpressible), philosophy necessarily reduces or betrays it. On the other hand, this is also precisely the moment in which

---

42. Lyotard himself does so in a two-fold manner. We have just illustrated his language-pragmatic approach; in addition to this, he also develops a postmodern aesthetic of the sublime, in which the sublime is conceptualised as an analogue to the event of heterogeneity. Essential for a postmodern aesthetic is the irresolvable tension between the impossibility of rendering the un-presentable in sentences, colors, sounds, and images and the strong sense that this must nonetheless be done. On this, see, among many others, *Réponse à la question: qu'est-ce que c'est le postmoderne?*, *Post-scriptum à la terreur et au sublime*, and *Note sur les sens de "post"*, in *Le postmoderne expliqué aux enfants*, resp. 11-34, 105-115, and 117-126; and also *Réécrire la modernité, L'instant, Newman, Le sublime et l'avant-garde, Quelque chose comme: "communication... sans communication"*, *Représentation, présentation, imprésentable*, and *Après le sublime, état de l'esthétique*, in *L'inhumain*, resp. 33-55, 89-99, 101-117, 119-129, 131-139, en 147-155; as well as *Anima minima*, in *Moralités postmodernes*, Paris, Galilée, 1993, 199-210. A specific, partial study of Kant (on the *Critique of Judgment*, paragraphs 23-29) can be found in *Leçons sur l'Analytique du sublime*.

philosophy comes up against its own particularity and thereby points beyond it, to the fact that something always escapes it. Lyotard adds that it is certainly conceivable that other discourses might also carry out this task of bearing witness[43].

In short, a particular narrative can not fully present the fundamental heterogeneity accompanying it (the ultimate which cannot be mastered or grasped), while at the same time heterogeneity can only be referred to within the limits of this particularity. Even though heterogeneity constantly escapes particular speech, it is only within this speech that the "other" can be spoken about. Heterogeneity, then, can no longer be referred to in terms of 'presence', but only in terms of a 'present absence'. Heterogeneity can not become present in thinking, language, signification, symbol or ritual, but it also can not be postulated as simply absent. It can be evoked only as absence made present. In this regard, the "other" and the "self" cannot find each other in a higher identity; heterogeneity is in fact precisely that which in principle makes such identity impossible.

(2) Such a dynamic thought pattern, characteristic of postmodern critical consciousness, offers opportunities for a recontextualisation of theology. The tension created by the constant and inevitable escape of heterogeneity from each particular attempt to give it expression can serve as the basis for a reconceptualisation of the dialectical relationship between transcendence and immanence, a relationship that is fundamental for the Christian tradition. The interwovenness of transcendence and immanence comes to expression in the dynamic interplay between the event breaking up the narrative and the narrative's witness to that event. The transcendent event repeatedly breaks open the immanence of the narrative, while precisely that immanence can, in the effort of bearing witness, define itself in view of that event. Accordingly, the relation between transcendence and immanence is not bi-polar, i.e. considered to be two opposed layers into which all of reality is divided. Instead, transcendence is clarified as an ineffable moment of disruption or interruption in the midst of the immanent reality (of language).

43. Lyotard himself claims that one such discourse would be "Jewish thought"; cf. *L'inhumain*, p. 86. For his understanding of what he calls "Jewish thought", cf. *Heidegger et "les juifs"*, Paris, Minuit, 1988 (ET: *Heidegger and The Jews*, trans. M. Andreas, Minneapolis, University of Minnesota Press, 1990) and *La terre n'a pas de chemins par elle-même* (in *Moralités postmodernes*, 95-102). In both of these texts he calls "Jewish" that which is conscious of the (often forgotten) alterity breaking into one's own autonomous projects.

This way of understanding transcendence is theologically fruitful and can prevent theology from becoming hegemonic. It dispossesses theological reflection of the possible pretense that it has made God comprehensible and given a place within the immanence of reality. God is revealed anew in every event of heterogeneity – an event which, for theology, can be defined as the event of grace – but without implying a localisation of God. The framework of postmodern reflection no longer permits us to think of God as occupying a localised position or site. In the grace-event, God becomes known as un-represented, hidden, ungraspable and incomprehensible, always other, at the same time opening up an expectation of a God who will come as the limit of, and break into, (worldly) time[44]. In this way, theology takes leave of the classical pattern of "homology".

Reconceptualising the relationship of transcendence and immanence is not only promising where it points to a new theological epistemology, but also where one attempts to recontextualise reflection on the sacramentality of life. Here, too, transcendence no longer denotes a premodern, neo-Platonic "presence" or a modern, as it were Hegelian, "identity". In the postmodern context of plurality, transcendence is conceived of in accordance with the event of heterogeneity which confronts us with the particularity and contingency of our own (Christian) engagement with reality. Transcendence, as event, interrupts and disturbs the ongoing particular narrative, challenging this narrative to open itself to the heterogeneity which breaks through in that event. The religiously experienced and interpreted relationship to the transcendent can thus no longer be conceived as premodern "participation" in salvific presence, or as modern "anticipation" of the ultimate identity. The Christian narrative which has become conscious of its own particularity and contingency can only adequately relate to the transcendent when it (1) *opens itself up*, cultivating a sort of contemplative openness into which the transcendent as interruptive event can enter, and (2) *bears witness* in a non-hegemonic way to the transcendent with the help of its own, always fragmentary words, images, stories, symbols and rituals[45]. The sacra-

---

44. Cf. BOEVE, *Critical Consciousness in the Postmodern Condition* (n. 5).

45. The radicality of negative theology functions as the methodical presupposition of all speech about God. Negative theology functions not purely as supplement to positive speech about God which it then submits to criticism and thus correction. In principle, negative theology problematises (with an eye to God's excess) all speech about God, in a sense preceding it and encompassing it. On this, see L. BOEVE, *Postmodernism and Negative Theology. The A/Theology of the "Open Narrative*, in *Bijdragen* 58 (1997) 407-425; also K. HART, *The Trespass of the Sign. Deconstruction, Theology and Philosophy*, Cambridge, University Press, ²2000.

mentality of existence does not offer us insight into some underlying foundational order, legitimating the existing narrative. Nor does it provide the redemption manifestly lacking in an unredeemed world. On the contrary, it opens up precisely that unredeemedness, that moment of interruption, to which no hegemonic narrative does justice. This sacramentality points toward neither an ahistorical ontological depth inviting human similitude, nor a history whose fulfillment is insured through a process of maturation, but instead the undermining of such self-assuring human constructions.

In this respect, the postmodern sacramental perception of time no longer reflects a premodern eternal continuum, in which the actual "now" ceases to be. Nor is sacramental time embedded in a modern perspective of progress that cancels the "now" in function of the future. Rather, sacramental time is the time of the interruptive, apocalyptic "now-moment" ("kairos"), the event which opens up the particular and contingent, placing it in the perspective of the transcendent God, but without nullifying or cancelling its particularity and contingency. The event of grace, or the grace of the event, consists in precisely this: self-enclosed narratives are opened up, and this openness is remembered, experienced and celebrated. Living by this openness to what happens, narratives lose their hegemonic characteristics and become truly "open narratives".

(3) When "sacramentality" is understood in such terms, that is to say as the interplay of contemplative openness for the event of heterogeneity and the evocative bearing witness to it, then being a Christian can be most adequately described in terms of "sacramental life and thought", and theology as sacramento-theology, in a double sense: as reflection on sacramental life and thought on the one hand, and itself as expression of this sacramental (life and) thought, on the other. Theology, too, then reconstructs itself along the lines of an open narrative, standing in the contemplative openness for what happens and bearing witness to this interruptive event. More specifically, a postmodern sacramento-theology is then aware of the 'interruption' or 'disturbance' of the particular narrative through a confrontation with the open non-hegemonic Jesus-narrative. Christian praxis as "imitatio Christi" will in this regard be focused on the option for the other, especially the excluded other, as a concrete incarnation of the Other[46].

---

46. In this regard, a postmodern theology of the "open narrative" can be considered an authentic recontextualisation of late-modern political theology (see n. 31).

Sacramental celebrations, as moments of condensation of sacramental life and thought, are ritual gatherings where the fundamental faith convictions and insights of the Christian tradition are articulated metaphorically and expressed in symbols and symbolic actions. The basic metaphors of Christianity which concern both creation and the incarnation, crucifixion and resurrection of Jesus Christ, are actualised in a testimonial and narrative way as the interruption and claim by God, summoning us towards conversion, openness and bearing witness. In a Christian perspective, the incarnation stands as the concrete marker of God's active involvement in the history of humankind. The paschal mystery (crucifixion, death and resurrection) forms the ground of hope for wholeness on behalf of a saving God, even in the experiences of unredeemedness, the hiddeness of God and God's "present absence". In each of the sacraments, in a particular way, this 'dangerous memory' is commemorated.

4. *Conclusion*

In the postmodern context the Christian narrative can regain contextual plausibility only by recontextualising and reconstructing itself as an open narrative. In this regard, it must be able to take distance from premodern and modern ontological foundations, as well as from the modes of legitimation offered by modern philosophies of history. The sacramentality of life, clarified and celebrated in the sacraments, is no longer considered as participation in a divine being, nor anticipation of a self-fulfilling development, but as being involved in the tension arising from the irruption of the divine Other into our human narratives, to which the Christian narrative testifies from of old. Sacramental living and acting thus presuppose the cultivation of a contemplative openness, and testify in word and deed to that which reveals itself in this openness as a trace of God. It goes without saying that such recontextualisation will have serious consequences for Christian self-awareness, and that such a sacramento-theological structuring of human existence has implications which go beyond a theology of the sacraments.

II. MAIN CONTRIBUTIONS OF LEST II

I now briefly present the contributions engaging the challenge of thinking sacramental presence in the postmodern context. The definitions of 'postmodern' used by the authors are diverse although they all imply elements of the one presented here. In addition, especially Heidegger's analysis of onto-theology, and its radicalisation in deconstruction are considered most often a common background. The way in which postmodern sensibilities and reflections are evaluated, and the way in which theology should relate to them, however, is very divergent.

The first text *Postmodernity and the Withdrawal of the Divine: A Challenge for Theology,* is by Georges De Schrijver s.j., emeritus professor of fundamental theology (K.U.Leuven) and co-promoter of the research project Postmodern Sacramento-theology. At first, De Schrijver gives an illustrated account of the shift from modernity to postmodernity, this in reference to the uprisings of European political and third World liberation theologies perceived as late-modern reactions to distortions in the processes and ideological legitimations of modernity. The 'fall of the Berlin Wall', one of the best illustrations of Jean-François Lyotard's quote that in the postmodern condition the grand narratives have lost their credibility, confronted these theologians with a criticism which challenged more deeply the still modern presuppositions of their theologies[47]. On the level of speculative thinking, this shift has been reflected upon in terms of the collapse of metaphysics as ontotheology (Heidegger), and, beyond Heidegger, in terms of difference and differ*a*nce (Derrida). More sociological approaches into the postmodern context accentuate the existential insecurity resulting from detraditonalisation and differentiation, which might offer new opportunities for religion. Neo-orthodox revivals could serve as an example here. Others attempt to retrieve the sacramentality of life, although often in abstract speculation (Marion, Milbank), starting, in reaction to secular nihilism, from a theological nihilism, by 'deconstructing closed circularities of thinking'. However, De Schrijver remarks, where does the question of justice arise here? Do such approaches not too easily introduce an unworldly exalted concept of love, which misses the ability to develop sensitivities for social antagonisms? Sacramentality therefore seems to be truncated here. Although maybe the contrary is the case: "sacramental contact with an asymmetrical God prompts one to take seriously asymmetrical relations in society and to act accordingly, in solidarity with the dispossessed".

---

47. Georges De Schrijver, until October 2000 co-ordinator of the Leuven Centre for Liberation Theology, has elaborated further on this theme in *Liberation Theologies on Shifting Grounds. A Clash of Socio-Economic and Cultural Paradigms* (BETL, 135), Leuven, Peeters Press, 1998.

The Brazilian theologian Maria Clara Luchetti Bingemer (Catholic University of Rio de Janeiro) investigates in her paper *Postmodernity and Sacramentality: Two Challenges to Speaking about God*, the experiential locus for naming God today. It seems that in the wake of modernity, after decades of continued secularisation, religious experience is on its way back ('retour du sacré'). This religious resurgence, however, does not seem to have a lot in common with Christianity. The new religiosity seems foremost concerned with – what the modern mind would call – magical beliefs and practices, or a vague involvement in rather holistic and immanentist anonymous powers or energy. This divergence challenges theology with some crucial questions, e.g. about the nature of transcendence in Christianity, the role of religious experience and its relation to community and tradition. Answering these questions however, is necessary, for Christianity is essentially incarnational, it must also look today for an new synthesis in and for the present context. Doing so, theology is challenged not only with criticisms of anthropocentrism, patriarchism, racism, etc. but particularly with inter-religious dialogue. Bingemer suggests in this regard that this dialogue inspires theologians, first, to take a more theocentric approach, highlighting mystical experience as experience of God as starting point of their reflections. Secondly, theology should reduce the christological accents in favour of pneumatological entries to discuss this experience. The result of such reflection ventures, after the proclaimed death of God, a rediscovery of God as the Other, whom one desires to experience (which necessitates, certainly in our post-christian contexts, a pedagogy of the experience of God). Thinking this experience may start from fundamental anthropological dimensions as gratuity and desire, and is inherently connected to an ethical praxis (in Christianity a praxis of love in favour of the poor and marginalised). In her conclusion Bingemer pays attention to the vulnerability of reason in theology, due to the inherent vulnerability of religious experience itself, which is framed from the relation to the Other. Because of this, theological projects remain in principle unfinished.

Terrence Merrigan, specialist in the theology of interreligious dialogue (K.U.Leuven), responds first to Bingemer's appeal to religious experience, and afterwards to her account of the specificity of the Christian understanding of God. In reference to the theology of Hick, who defends similar starting points he asks her in this regard two questions. First he doubts whether the category of religious experience, viewed from a theocentric perspective on the plurality of religions, really helps us to come closer to the God of Christianity. Perhaps to the contrary,

such move – as is the case in Hick's real-centrism – forces us ultimately
to make abstraction of Christianity-like conceptuality in thinking transcendence. Secondly, in connection with this, Merrigan wonders – noting that Bingemer differs from Hick's views about incarnation as a myth
or metaphor – whether holding to the literal doctrine of incarnation is
necessary for establishing Christianity as a religion of love and Jesus as
the unique mediator of salvation.

The contribution of Paul Moyaert, professor of philosophical anthropology at the Institute of Philosophy in Leuven, focuses on the significance of the Church teaching about the Eucharist at the Council of
Trent: *Incarnation of Meaning and the Sense for Symbols: Phenomenological Remarks on a Theological Debate*. The starting point of Moyaert
is the presumption that the core of religion (i.e. its *sine qua non*) entails
the human sensibility for symbols. This sensibility is a fact of human
existence, which cannot be reduced or traced back to something else[48].
Moyaert's study therefore concerns the power inherent in symbolicity,
and in this regard, for example the question in what way the link
between 'symbolic sign' and 'symbolised reality' should be thought.
From this perspective, he develops the position that the dogma of Trent
on transubstantiation intends to safeguard an authentic and correct view
on what is at stake in symbolic praxis. The question therefore at stake is:
how to understand the 'is-relation' in 'this is my body'? To make this
claim Moyaert first, in referring to Polanyi, distinguishes between signs
as indicators, and as symbols. This difference consists in the fact that the
former have an extrinsic relation to the signified while the latter are
characterised by an intrinsic one. Signs as symbols have strongly incarnated meanings, as is for instance the case with a flag or relic. Here the
incarnans (sign) and the *incarnatum* (the signified) slide into one
another. Symbols in a way take part in what they symbolise; there is an
objective relation between the two, which transcends human involvement, creativity and interpretation. One could say that objects having
become symbols therefore have 'transubstantiated'. Intellectualist doctrines of symbols fall short in understanding what is really at stake
here, because symbols are considered as (interchangeable) means to
direct a person to a content. They cannot get hold of the 'peculiar role
that the *incarnans* plays in the *Faktum* of symbolic praxis'. Trent's dogmas of 'realis presentia' and *transsubstantiatio*, although often in danger

---

48. Moyaert elaborates this point further in his monograph: *De mateloosheid van het
christendom: Over naastenliefde, betekenisincarnatie en mystieke liefde*, Nijmegen,
S.U.N., 1998.

of being 'dragged into a speculative metaphysical discussion', are in essence not theories to explain or justify symbolic praxis, but indicate the limits of rational theology, invoking theologians to a *theologia orans*. As a dogma, *transsubstantiatio* becomes a limit-concept, intending to protect the eucharistic symbolic praxis from scientific curiosity and speculative reason. The dogma in a way is what it signifies – becomes symbolic itself. However, Moyaert adds, Trent was maybe too explicit in its protection of the sensibility for symbols, because a too literal interpretation may prove contra-productive as well.

Moyaert's respondent, Fergus Kerr (Blackfriars – University of Oxford, U.K.) agrees with his criticism on the inadequacy of intellectualist sign theories to deal with symbolic praxis, and 'translated' his phenomenological account in a Wittgensteinian analysis. He adds, though, that Moyaert's non-metaphysical position, in line with Catherine Pickstock's thinking, needs to be complemented with a theo-ontology, i.e. a Christian ontology which does not ground symbolic praxis, but 'brings out the ontological implications *post factum*'.

The contribution of David N. Power, o.m.i., teaching at the Catholic University of America (Washington, D.C.), is entitled *The Language of Sacramental Memorial: Rupture, Excess and Abundance*. Herein, Power highlights some of the main concerns and claims of his recent book *Sacrament: The Language of God's Giving*[49]. For Power, the shift from modernity to postmodernity had affected extensively sacramental celebrations and sacramental theology. Postmodern sensibilities first of all include disillusionment about the bankruptcy of modern projects, often fuelled by horrendous memories. On the other hand, the chains of modern totalising projects been broken, postmodernity offers opportunities for the resurgence of creative powers. This creativity does not destroy modern achievements, but deconstructs these to undo of their exclusions in heeding otherness, 'to keep signification open'. Some theologians, including Power, have become sensitive to these expressive powers of language, which enable not only retrieving a repressed past but also the criticising and remedy of the exclusions and marginalisations of the present. The postmodern condition has made theologians, in considering liturgical traditions, attentive to 'the polysemy of rites, symbols and texts, and the circumstances and processes of their ongoing interpretation'. Perceiving sacraments heuristically as language events, which redescribe reality in light of the Christ event, Power shows how in sacramental celebration and reflection the breakdown of traditional meaning

49. New York, Crossroad, 1999.

and its creative re-appropriation are simultaneously at work. Most adequate herein seem the categories of 'rupture' (sacrament is an 'open sign', breaking open totalising narratives and rituals), 'excess' (in which language empties itself before the inexpressible God), and 'abundance of gift' (overcoming, but not annulling, the distance between the giver and the gifted). To conclude using the thought of Stanislas Breton, Power refers, to a sacramental 'meontology' as an opportunity to exploit the linguistic turn in sacramental theology without falling back into metaphysics: not as 'a rejection of ontology but [setting] its limits and [marking] the point where poetic and metaphoric language take over in naming the ineffable'.

Responding to Power, Werner G. Jeanrond (professor of systematic theology, Lund, Sweden) illustrates some preconditions for legitimately developing such sacramental theology. Among other things, Jeanrond asks criteria for theologically assessing liturgical creativity in order to also preserve continuity with the Christian tradition. In line with this first comment, he pleads for a hermeneutics of suspicion, towards not only the modern project but also the postmodern condition. Striving for expressivity and poetic transformation can become totalising as well. Jeanrond also wonders whether a foremost linguistic approach runs the risk of reducing liturgical praxis, forgetting about the non-verbal nature of liturgical action. Finally, he warns against a current tendency to isolate the cross from the Christian memory, which involves the complete Jesus-narrative up until the resurrection.

In *The Church as the Erotic Community*, Graham Ward develops a position which is in close connection with the premises developed in *Radical Orthodoxy*[50]. This movement only supports postmodern criticisms of modernity insofar as this enables one 'to reclaim the world theologically'. The thinking patterns available to do so are inspired by Augustine and hold that by participation the finite receives its integrity from the infinite. In an archaeology of presence Ward shows first that only from early modern theology on (with Calvin and the council of Trent as examples) did 'presence' become thought of as atomised, reified and commodified. Postmodern critical accounts of presence 'only fetishises the now even more', presenting it as the unpresentable, the

---

50. Graham Ward is professor in Contextual Theology and Ethics at the University of Manchester (U.K.). He is mostly know from his *Barth, Derrida and the Language of Theology* (Cambridge, Cambridge University Press, 1995). He is the editor of *The Postmodern God: A Theological Reader* (Blackwell Readings in Modern Theology, Oxford, Blackwell, 1998) and of *Radical Orthodoxy: A New Theology*, which he co-edited with Catherine Pickstock and John Milbank (London – New York, Blackwell, 1999).

indecideable, or the sublime, and depicting it from within an economy of desire kept going on by 'lack'. In pre-modern times 'the present' never was characterised as a distinct entity and time as an endless series of distinctive 'now'-s, but – as in Augustine – perceived as participating in eternity, holding together and engaging past and future. A contemporary theology, therefore, should reflect upon eucharistic presence in terms of 'participation in a temporal plenitude', not driven by an economy of lack but of excess, of love. Whereas the first atomises and reifies difference, difference in the latter is relational, and desire not oriented to what is absent, but to what is all too present. Our love participates in the divine Trinitarian love, 'reaching beyond and forgetting itself, but in that very activity loving itself most truly'.

In his response, Kevin Hart criticises Ward's too facile refutation of deconstruction, after having used it to dismantle modern thinking of presence. To the contrary, when carefully viewed, deconstruction might well be present in the very heart of Christianity itself[51]. Modernity has been too easily evaluated by Ward (and his fellow theologians of *Radical Orthodoxy*) as nihilism, which theologians should overcome. They tend to forget 'to diagnose the nihilism at work within theology itself' and end up in a neo-platonic, Augustinian grand narrative of Christianity. Instead of (harmonious) 'participation', Hart suggests that being a Christian rather involves a 'belonging' to Christ which interrupts our lives. Finally, he remarks that 'one does not necessarily get closer to God by pushing one's Christology ever upward', running the risk of becoming insensible for God's love 'disturbing the immanence of our lives, helping to fight misery and oppression, even when they stem from ourselves'.

In his contribution *Présence et affection*, Jean-Yves Lacoste[52] presents a phenomenological reflection which is quite characteristic for the tendencies which Janicaud defined (and criticised) as 'the theological turn in French phenomenology'[53]. As is the case in the work of Jean-Luc Marion[54], Lacoste attempts to reflect philosophically about the Christian way-of-being, not as a particular ontic mode of what Heidegger ontologically

51. This is one of the claims Kevin Hart defends in his monograph *The Trespass of the Sign: Deconstruction, Theology and Philosophy* (Cambridge, Cambridge University Press, 1989, ²2000).

52. Jean-Yves Lacoste is the author of *Expérience et absolu: Questions disputées sur l'humanité de l'homme* (Épiméthée: essais philosophiques), Paris, P.U.F., 1994 and editor of *Dictionnaire critique de théologie*, Paris, P.U.F., 1998.

53. See D. JANICAUD, *Le tournant théologique de la phénoménologie française*, Combas, Éclat, 1991.

54. Cf. e.g. J.-L. MARION, *Dieu sans l'être*, Paris, Communio – Fayard, 1982.

coined as *Dasein*, but through and beyond Heidegger. He analyses the
latter's atheistic being-in-the-world as closure, imprisonment in and ruled
by the conditions of the world. He opposes this to the liturgical attitude,
which is characterised by an interrupting openness wherein the absolute
is encountered. In his lecture Lacoste at first distinguished, with Heidegger, between objects (*des objets*) and things (*des choses*). 'Things',
according to Heidegger using the example of a jar, are unlike 'objects'
not reducible to their objective content. They bear a multitude of interpretations, developed within a broader horizon of significations, the
'game of earth and heaven, gods and mortals', *das Geviert*. Their presence therefore cannot be objectified, reified. Presence, here, as well as
absence are rather caught in a game which is not played without us, but
neither thanks to us. Presence is advent, *acte de présence*, never to be
hypostasised, thus an event bound to particular places and times. According to Lacoste, Heidegger's thinking may provide a conceptual framework for a theology of the Eucharist to approach reflexively 'eucharistic
presence'. The language of things indeed is the language of liturgy. Nevertheless, in Heidegger, liturgy remains 'a celebration of the immanent',
never stepping outside 'the horizon of an atheistic existence'. Seeing
things in their truth implies that in liturgy things are played to manifest
their theological meaning, as gift of presence. Of importance here is the
eschatological setting of this gift, received in this world but not to be
reduced to it. In faith 'we open the liturgical non-place', and 'we consent
to the liturgical non-experience', although we remain caught in the
embrace of the world. In this world, God gives God's presence pre-escha-
tologically as a foretaste of what is to come. Ultimately, the very significance of liturgy is bound to this riff between a faithful existence in the
world and the ultimate fulfilment in the Parousia. Lacoste ends his exposition asking whether there is as well a role for affectivity (with cognitive
value!) in receiving sacramental presence. The affect of 'being-in-peace'
is according to Lacoste a good candidate. On a deeper level, 'sensing
oneself as being-in-peace is knowing that one exists in the mode of the
being-in-alliance [*être-en-alliance*]', the pre-requisite of living according
to the mode 'being-before-God'.

Responding to Lacoste, Ignace Verhack, professor of philosophy of
religion (K.U.Leuven), especially questions his endeavour to go, with the
use of Heideggerian notions and thinking patterns, beyond Heidegger.
Verhack first of all wonders whether 'being-in-peace' is completely analogous to the Heideggerian notion of *Befindlichkeit*. Is this affect the condition of being touched by divine presence, as in Heidegger *Befindlichkeit* is constituted by the fact of being touched by Being and beings?

Or is this effect rather the product of the symbolic subversions necessary to open the liturgical non-place? And can this 'presence', even as eschatological reality, be thought of in a liturgical 'non-place'? Does this not necessitate to postulate a liturgical 'place', where the liturgical *chose* can give itself? In the same vain a second question concerns the way in which Lacoste attempts to think sacramental presence, first, through the notion of facticity, and, secondly, with the notion of *chose*: 'Which is the precise relation between the gift of Being which is played in the thing as work of gathering [*rassemblement*] and the gift of divine presence in the eucharistic thing?' Where does the theological (trans)signification show up? How is it enacted?

The last text of the main papers is by Louis-Marie Chauvet, professor at the Institut Catholique in Paris (France): *The Broken Bread as Theological Figure of Eucharistic Presence*. In difference from Lacoste's thinking sacramental presence through and beyond Heidegger, Chauvet's attempt goes along with Heidegger, following a 'homologous' path. The Christian symbolic universe does not supersede Heidegger's 'atheistic horizon of meaning', but is to be situated next to it, as another way of being-in-the-world[55]. For his sacramentological reflections, Chauvet retains from the latter also the critique of onto-theology, and therefore rejects all thinking of sacramentality in terms of causality. Determining the truth today is no longer a matter of metaphysics, although the 'meta-' as 'thinking beyond' should be left in place. It should, however, rather be grasped in the 'triangle' of this 'méta-function', hermeneutics, and phenomenology. Concerning eucharistic presence this 'meta' of the truth of the eucharist can only be thought of by following the long way of hermeneutics and attempting to express its mystery phenomenologically. Chauvet's hermeneutical study of the intention and context of the scholastic doctrine of transubstantiation shows that it poses two challenges to contemporary theology: how to think the radicality of the Church's belief, and what about the relation between liturgy and theology? The main limit of this doctrine is the forgetting of the relational aspect (because thinking in terms of being [*esse*], and not in terms of being-for [*adesse*]), and thus also the link between Eucharist and Church as communion. In his phenomenological considerations, going into the fracture-liturgy of the bread, Chauvet develops however the claim that the *adesse* is constitutive for the sacramental *esse*. Sacramental presence inscribes in the very materiality of

---

55. In a masterful way, Chauvet elaborated his position in *Symbole et sacrement. Une relecture sacramentelle de l'existence chrétienne*, Paris, Cerf, 1987.

bread and wine God's absolute otherness. Conceptually presence there-fore always involves absence, is 'advent' or 'coming-into-presence'. Precisely this is shown in the fracture-liturgy, in which bread is already bread-in-action, bread broken and shared: at this very instance the essence of bread is manifested, creating symbolically an open space (for others). Theological discourse, of course, cannot be reduced to these thoughts, but, in its difference, confesses that this bread has become Christ himself. The open space of bread broken and shared 'becomes the great sacramental figure of Christ's presence'.

At the congress, the main lectures alternated with paper sessions in which 30 scholars from a variety of universities and countries presented their research. A selection of these papers is presented here. It concerns papers which thematically fit in the present volume, reflecting the fun-damental-theological debate which is going on. Herein the same variety in evaluating the present condition for theology is found once again.

Robert Barron's *Thomas Aquinas: Postmodern* endeavours to demon-strate that 'Thomas account of God and the creature assuages both the modern fear of a domineering and competitive supreme being and the postmodern anxiety concerning the aggressive and self-important sub-ject'. Concerning the first claim, although on first sight confusion is pos-sible, Thomas distances clearly himself from any univocal understand-ing of the divine 'to-be' and creation's, which is characteristic for so-called classical theism, in fact already present in Duns Scotus and continued in late Scholasticism (Suarez) and modern philosophy. A close reading of *De potentia* shows that, according to Thomas, there is no common framework in which God and the world can be situated. Therefore, competition between the two is impossible. This insight may well serve as a major hermeneutical key for understanding the whole of Thomas' theology, Barron adds, and is of main importance for Aquinas perspective on creation as *creatio ex nihilo*. From the perspective of the creature, creation designating a relation to the creator, makes up the 'to-be' of the creature: i.e. there is not first a creature which then has a rela-tion to God. Rather than an ego clinging to its independent ontological status, i.e. a supreme being, the creature is a 'supreme letting-be'. Bar-ron concludes that the main problem of both modern and postmodern criticism is 'substantiality', first of God, secondly of the subject, result-ing in violence and conflict.

In *Incarnation and Imagination*, Anthony Godzieba (Villanova Uni-versity, PA) observes that Heidegger's critique of onto-theology appeals to Catholic theologians in two ways. On one hand they are challenged to evaluate whether their theologising is still metaphysical; on the other, standing in their specific theological tradition, they must be careful not to adopt too easily Heidegger's all too protestant views on theology as faith seeking understanding. Godzieba also dismisses theological projects growing out of the desire – in line with certain trends in postmodern thinking – to overthrow the whole of modernity – and religion in modernity – at once, and those ending up in radically decontructive apophasis. With Metz he reminds us that a practical, narrative and memorative theological approach can provide an outcome, resulting in a thoroughly hermeneutical theo-logy which is aware of its particar bounds to place and time. Here the apophatic resides, as modelled in the dynamics of incarnation, within the kataphatic, inviting to 'imagine the world otherwise' (R. Kearny) – as Jesus did with the imaginary of the Kingdom of God.

Laurence Hemming (Heythrop College, London, UK) situates his reflections on transubstantiation 'after Heidegger'. First he reminds us that in Thomas Aquinas' definition transubstantiation is not a 'rupture of physics', but involves the 'redemption of the physical': Aristotelian physics is 'both preserved and disrupted', 'transubstantiation stands as the refusal of a saturation of the cosmos with the Christian God'. Moreover, for Thomas 'the real transubstantiation is enacted in the intellect of the believer' who came to know this because of God's power. Theologians, as Chauvet, seek to overcome the embarrassment transubstantiation provokes by using Heidegger's elaborations on the fourfold to give meaning to what is at stake in the Eucharist. In the mean time, the term appeared also outside the theological discourse, exploiting the embarrassment which goes along with it. This leads Hemming to affirm – against theologians seeking for a non-embarrassing explanation – that the real issue of transubstantiation is not about the bread and wine, but about the person on whom a change is effected by his *knowing* a change has taken place in the thing of which is said to be transubstantiated. 'The being of the bread and the wine is eventuated [...] in a particular way which must entail and effect a change in me'.

In *The Concept of 'Sacramental Anxiety': A Kierkegaardian Locus of Transcendence?* John Ries (K.U.Leuven) engages the labyrinthine nature of Kierkegaard's work, and observes that much of his writing is permeated by a concern for circumscribing a 'locus of transcendence', a place wherein grace might break into one's existence. One way of understanding such a Kierkegaardian locus of transcendence is through 'sacramental anxiety', a concept that Ries develops through reading Kierkegaard's *The Concept of Anxiety* and *Three Discourses on Imagined Occasions*. The

first, written pseudonymously, unravels the concept of anxiety, unfolding
a kind of philosophical anthropology which makes room for faith; the
second, written in his own name, muses upon three sacramental occasions (a confession, a wedding, and at a graveside), reflecting a theological anthropology which also makes room for faith, but in a significantly
different way. The concept of 'sacramental anxiety' thereby indicates the
point, or better the 'moment,' wherein transcendence might break into
human existence. Insofar as the concept of 'sacramental anxiety' can
delineate the conditions of (existential) religious possibility, it is surely
fundamental to theology, although he finds that it likewise creates a profound challenge to any theologizing, since it is also inextricably occasional.

Stijn Van den Bossche (K.T.U. Utrecht, The Netherlands – K.U.Leu-
ven) explores the contribution of Jean-Luc Marion to the conference's
theme. Although Marion, together with Louis-Marie Chauvet, may be
considered as a protagonist of a post-metaphysical fundamental-sacramental theology, and had been invited as a keynote-speaker, he could
unfortunately not attend the conference. Yet his thought, and especially
his recent 'essay on a phenomenology of givenness'[56] adds a very challenging perspective to the discussion. According to Van den Bossche,
Marion offers nothing less than a new first philosophy to theology.
Within phenomenality Marion points to an invisible but phenomenally
assignable dimension of 'givenness', that precedes 'object' and 'being'.
There is shown that reality gives itself, before any differentiating gaze
interferes. In this dimension of givenness, the Christian may observe the
immanence of God, be it that this dimension also keeps upright for the
non-believer. Moreover, by analysing the Biblical witness of Christ,
Marion is able to demonstrate that Jesus Christ – within the framework
of this phenomenology – is the historical paradigm of the phenomenon
of revelation. After having outlined the main features of this phenomenology, Van den Bossche reflects upon some of its theological consequences.

In *A Genealogy of Presence*, Vincent Miller (Georgetown University,
USA) warns theologians against too idealist, abstract and speculative
approaches of thinking presence. He refers them back to a cultural
analysis of the broad cultural experience of presence, its material infrastructure, and the power relations involved in it, to start their reflections
from. For popular culture and religiosity is almost never really a *locus*

---

56. J.-L. MARION, *Étant donné. Essai d'une phénoménologie de la donation*, Paris,
1997, 452 pp. An English translation is in preparation.

theologicus, taken up in discussions about 'sacramental imagination', but often instrumentalised and recuperated. In an analysis of the power dynamics within Catholic cultural production (focusing on imaginative agency and cultural capital) Miller shows that the Catholic reform after Trent sought to control the meaning of rituals, gestures and images of popular religiosity 'to contain their polysemy within the bounds of orthodoxy'. The same is true for the Liturgical Renewal which not only introduced a theologically adequate understanding of mystery, but also – and in the same move, and often non-intentionally – reduced 'the space, time and material available for the laity to actively exercise imagination'. At stake is both times 'the control and attenuation of presence'.

'What kind of longing is hidden in the rites I participate in?' asks Toine van den Hoogen, professor of fundamental theology at K.U.Nijmegen (The Netherlands), in *Untitled: On Denoting Sacramental Presence*. To answer this question, it is necessary, he continues, to change our linguistic programme (which forms the framework of the processes of denoting linguistic signs). Tertullian's explorations of *sacramentum* and Augustine's theology of the confessions show a strong linguistic programme: signs and reality are linked together in an equivalent and analoguous way: in it 'words are signs of a reality that is present in these signs'. In these strong programmes signifier and signification manifest an economy of salvation which is directed upwards: human beings transcend their condition towards God. In the christology of Schoonenberg, on the other hand, which is the product of a hermeneutical approach, the direction is inverted, while the linguistic programme has changed. The signifier now is 'the history of Gods becoming God-for-us' (Jesus denoting God's kenosis), the signification 'the becoming a person' of human beings who are 'nonexistant'. In a similar way, van den Hoogen then reinterprets sacramental presence as the becoming manifest of 'Gods wisdom in the mundane realities of an everyday world'. This involves a weak linguistic programme, in which language is conceived as a labyrinth, a network, referring to its own immanence.

Faculty of Theology   Lieven BOEVE
Katholieke Universiteit Leuven
Sint-Michielsstraat 6
B-3000 Leuven

MAIN PAPERS

POSTMODERNITY AND THE WITHDRAWAL
OF THE DIVINE

A Challenge for Theology

In this article I try to give a general description of the postmodern condition, hereby focusing on the collapse of the grand stories. In order to grasp what this means, a short sketch of modernity will be given, and the way in which political theology and liberation theologies have reacted to it. Then follows a philosophical examination of the deconstruction of onto-theology as has been carried out by Heidegger and Derrida. Ontotheology and its metaphysics of presence gives way to an awareness of the withdrawal of Being (*Sein*) in the moment of its manifestation (Heidegger), and to a presence that has always already been lost while it still continues to send disturbing signals in favour of a decentering release of differences (Derrida). Following this, a sociological approach to postmodernity reveals that underneath the postmoderns' levity, the spectre of a dual society looms, especially when attention is paid to the phenomenon of globalisation which has suddenly become coextensive with postmodern glitter[1]. It is in this context that the question is raised about the future of religion in a climate where the discontents of postmodernity are felt. While most sociologists predict a resurgence of fundamentalist groups, I have rather opted for exploring the perspectives of a sacramentality of life, for believers who do not want to confine their religiosity to sacred places and rituals. The contention of this article is that sacramental experience remains truncated to the extent that theological reflection and Church institutions busy themselves only with strictly religious themes (life is a gift from the God of love), without having these come to bear on the social context of a postmodern dual society. The article therefore concludes by placing the question of justice on the agenda once again.

---

1. For this topic see G. DE SCHRIJVER, *Paradigm Shift in Third-World Theologies of Liberation*, in ID. (ed.), *Liberation Theologies on Shifting Grounds* (BETL, 135), Leuven, Leuven University Press & Peeters, 1998, pp. 36-71.

I. FROM MODERNITY TO POSTMODERNITY

1. *Modernity's Expulsion of the Divine and Transformation of the Sacred*

In theological circles, modernity has been mostly associated with humankind's emancipation from a divinely ordained order, which is replaced now with new universal principles of order. Starting from the 17th century, European intellectuals asserted that human society can be fabricated, i.e. human behaviour can be channelled into patterns of rational conduct and social engineering will succeed in creating a new 'enlightened' humanity. Centred around the modern state, powerful institutions provide the basic structures for identity building, such as schooling, legislation, and police forces. Fuelled by nascent capitalism, modern times embark on a journey of industrialisation and continuous technological progress. Instead of other-worldly concerns (punishment or reward in an after-life), this-worldly utopias come to the fore promising maximum happiness to as many people as possible. The 'good life' becomes attainable within one's life span 'before death'.

This new ideal of humanity has regularly led to tensions between church and state, which had now become two separate powers. In some countries, waves of anticlericalism arose, of which Voltaire's *écrasons l'infâme* is symptomatic. With missionary zeal, enlightened philosophers fought the parochial mentality not only of agrarian, feudal society, but also of the clergy, whom they deem responsible for the people's continued backwardness: "*Les philosophes* named the clergy, old wives, and folk proverbs as the teachers responsible for the lamentable state of popular habits"[2]. Enlightenment culture came to resent dogmatic beliefs and devotional practices, decried now as superstitions contrary to the scientific mind.

Did the disdain of premodern beliefs necessarily lead to an eclipse of religion? Looked at from a distance, some will say: 'no' or 'not entirely'. For western civilisation had been so imbued with Christian values that a core of it continued to inspire the new secular institutions built upon the ruins of the old regime. These institutions even appropriated a 'sacred' aura which was tacitly borrowed from religion. In a retrospective view, one must indeed acknowledge that some type of Hegelian dialectics had been at work, in which higher phases of development come into existence by negating and taking up the lower ones into a higher synthesis, but always in such a way that the phase which

2. Z. BAUMAN, *Intimations of Postmodernity*, London, Routledge, 1992, p. 9.

had been overcome continues to have an effect on the higher synthesis. *Aufhebung* or 'sublation' has in Hegel's system a double meaning. It means the cancelling of a state of affairs, but also its hidden persistence. With respect to the sacred that has been annulled by the secular state, some authors have aptly made use of what in German is called *'Säkularisate'*, i.e. secular remainders of sacred symbols. To note some examples: modern jurisprudence is a secular remainder of divine justice; the work-ethos of the industrialised world is a successor to, and continuation of, monastic asceticism; the communist dream of a classless society is a *Säkularisat*, a secular remainder, of all saints' blissful existence in the heavenly city[3]. In short, to the extent that modern secular institutions and movements take the needs and interests of the citizens to heart, they acquire an aura of inviolability, reminiscent of the aura of sacred glory that had rested on religious institutions and organisations. When they stand in need of legitimisation, the secular will even set out to underline this sacred aura. Yet can this appeal to reminiscences of old really be trusted?

2. *Denouncing Lust for Power – for God's Sake*

Institutions wrapped in borrowed sacred glory easily turn into the demonic. They may abuse their authority in a totalitarian way and still legitimate their lust for power by referring to their quasi-divine respectability. Modern states, even when clothed with sacred glory, still remain modern states, bent on self-maintenance, expansion, and growth – at the expense, if necessary, of weaker segments within and outside their confines. The coercive methods used by the modern state can be cruel; but they are always justified by the state's noble mission of enhancing the prosperity of the nation, or at least of those who are its most meritorious citizens in terms of wealth, productivity or social status. In order to defend these citizens' free initiatives and their vested interests in the market, wars must be waged or scapegoats selected. In Nazi-Germany, this led to the ruthless extermination of the Jews, "sanctified" with the slogan "God with us" (*Gott mit uns*). The holocaust had been carefully prepared. Nothing was left to fortuity. And the efficient bureaucracy, discipline, and calculation involved in it make it quite clear that the *Shoah* is a 'characteristically modern phenomenon', the triumph of rational efficiency in getting rid of the unwanted[4]. In the meantime,

---

3. See H. BLUMENBERG, *Säkularisierung und Selbstbehauptung*, Frankfurt, Suhrkamp, 1974, pp. 106-113.

4. Z. BAUMAN, *Modernity and the Holocaust*, New York, Cornell University Press, 1989, p. XIII.

ceremonial pomp to cheer the leader and his invincible army had blinded
the common German to the atrocities; so much so that in the post-war
period most citizens said "sorry, but we didn't know anything about it"
(*wir haben doch davon nichts gewusst*)[5]; "all of this has been kept a
secret from us".

The holocaust has been the sinister eye opener for theologians like
Metz, Sölle and Moltmann to engage in a political theology that sides
with the victims of history. Christian awareness, they said, forbids one
to become oblivious of the mass extermination that took place before
the eyes of the nation, with nobody protesting against it. Henceforth,
Christians must be determined not to forget their past complicity, and
to forgo future cowardice by injecting a moral sensitivity into the deal-
ings of politics. The political theologians take seriously their prophetic
task to keep alive the memory of the victimised. For them, the secular
world is an arena wherein believers must act in a responsible way, in
the name of God. Instead of regarding human autonomy and responsibility as a threat to God's majesty, they realised that within a world
come of age "God has no other hands than our own" to intervene in his
work of creation[6]. This persuasion brought them to denounce open and
covert abuse of power in politics. They wanted to put their finger on
the precise spots where the modern ideal of social engineering had
gone astray, derailments which – as their analyses show – flow from
the cunning of 'instrumental rationality'. Rational planning on the
highest levels of politics and economics usually reckons with partial
losses and set-backs for which the lower strata of society must bear the
hardships.

It is at this juncture that Latin American liberation theologies join the
chorus of protest voices. These theologies have made themselves the
mouthpiece of the poor masses, which stand on the periphery of the economic World System and are exploited by that system. Making use of
Marxist social analysis, theologians like Gutiérrez and Boff have pointed
out that the expansion of capitalism rests on the search for cheap labour
and lowpriced resources all over the globe. In this light, they link the
increase of the wealth in the centres of decision – North America and
Western Europe – to the aggravation of poverty in the Two-Thirds
World. As Gutiérrez says: "The dynamics of the capitalist economy
lead to the establishment of a centre and a periphery; simultaneously

    5. D. SÖLLE, *Gegenwind. Erinnerungen*, Hamburg, Hoffmann und Campe, 1995,
p. 35.
    6. *Ibid.*, p. 62: "Ich spürte deutlich, dass Gott, wie Teresa von Avila wohl gesagt hat,
'keine anderen Hände hat als unsere', um etwas zu tun".

generating progress and growing wealth for the few and social imbalances, political tensions, and poverty for the many"[7]. This observation raises the question of God's justice as superior to humanly conceived justice. The poor are encouraged not to put up with their situation of dire poverty, nor to regard it as a destiny pre-ordained by God. For God, or at least the God of the Bible, has a 'preferential option for the poor', as can be read in the Magnificat: "He has satisfied the hungry with good things, and has sent the rich empty away" (Luke 1,51-53). While the poor easily understand that their predicament is not willed by God, liberation theologians complete this insight by showing that their misery has structural roots: Today poverty is 'man made', and must therefore be combated. As Ellacuría says: "Oppression is not the necessary product of the natural laws that govern the world. Oppression is the product of human history, and thus a sin and wickedness repudiated by God. Oppression is the denial of the Covenant; it banalises the confession that Jesus Christ became our brother"[8].

Modernity came up with the idea that human society is 'fabricated'. Liberation theologians look at the same phenomenon, but from the standpoint of the victims on the underside of history. They make it clear that oppression is 'man-made' and sinful, and want to bring an end to this state of affairs. They do this through their own commitment and by raising the poor masses to the awareness that they are able to change their situation, provided they stick together and close ranks. Only this way can a (likewise 'man-made') civilisation of human solidarity arise. The wretched of the earth are able to believe in the 'God of life' and to express this belief in their commitment to a commonly shared social project. However, the fact that they conjoin their belief in God with the success of a mass movement – the base communities – makes it seem that their enterprise has a modern ring to it: they believe in the grand story of a liberation from below.

3. *Postmodernity. The End of the Grand Stories*

By the end of the 1970s, Jean-François Lyotard initiated the idea that we are moving towards a period in which the grand stories have lost their appeal and credibility[9]. By 'grand stories' he meant the social

7. G. GUTIÉRREZ, *A Theology of Liberation*, New York, Orbis Books, 1988, p. 51

8. I. ELLACURIA, *La iglesia de los pobres sacramento histórico de liberación*, in *Studios Centroamericános*, 1977, p. 715.

9. J.-F. LYOTARD, *La condition postmoderne. Rapport sur le savoir*, Paris, Minuit, 1979.

ideals or blue prints proposed by ideologues to give form and shape to a given society. He is particularly afraid that if a preprogrammed set of ideas is used to steer the course of events, the immediate result will be a reign of terror. Not only is Fascism such a preconceived program, but so is Marxism. Indeed, both have had their holocausts: Auschwitz and the German extermination camps for Jews on the one hand, and the Soviet gulag archipelago of forced labour camps on the other. In both cases one is confronted with the logic of modernity, for modernity is intolerant of those who are either unwilling or unfit to enter the system. The deviant voice must be assimilated by force or annihilated. Moreover, Lyotard seems to suggest, the 'microbe' of the logic of modernity is virulently present where social activists – be it on the right or on the left, but mostly on the left – try to impose their vision of a better world. Violence and bloodshed will be lurking around the corner soon, whether in the form of class struggle or boycotts of all kinds.

Lyotard, himself a disillusioned Marxist, has certainly contributed to throwing doubt on the Leftist movements from below. For a long time, however, he did not really impress the Latin American liberation theologians. They had rather to cope with the warnings issued by the Vatican in 1984 about the danger of class struggle and the use of violence as a continuous temptation. Nonetheless, the liberationists were exposed to the postmodern setting after the fall of the Berlin Wall. This event inaugurated the end of the cold war, and that of grand ideologies. The future generations all over the world, it is prognosticated, will gradually become averse to all-encompassing ideologies. Fragmented life strategies, in specialised reflection or self-help groups, will replace the enthusiasm for the device 'proletariat of the whole world unite'. Below I shall attempt to give a description of the ensuing personality structure of postmodern intellectuals (and average people). Before broaching this, however, I would like to tell something about the collapse of metaphysics – the philosophical counterpart of the sociological dictum that grand stories have lost their credibility. I will treat this collapse in such a way that the impact on religion becomes apparent.

II. FROM HEIDEGGER TO DERRIDA

1. Heidegger and the Collapse of Metaphysics

The attack on false or deceptive foundations – or more technically, the rejection of ontotheology – goes back to Heidegger. He showed that in the course of western philosophy the divine or the absolute had been conceived of as the corner stone in the immense cathedral of all that is, the supreme reality in the chain of beings. Ever since Aristotle (or was it already Plato?) this supreme reality has been defined by perfect or pure self-knowledge. The highest God is immediately present to the thoughts of His mind, just as these are present to Him in His act of contemplation[10]. Moreover, the deity's self-presence constitutes the foundation and the model of growth and development in the world. To reach self-transparency and full presence to oneself becomes the grand ideal of philosophers and contemplative monks alike. Translucency towards their inner core and towards the ultimate ground of Being makes them participate in the deity's bliss of self-possession. This is, in broad strokes, the basic pattern handed down from antiquity: the awareness, namely, that a mirror relationship exists between the deity's self-possession and the human person's awakening to self-identity; in order for our understanding to be firm, it must rest on the solid rock of God's self-transparency.

Modernity inherits this pattern and gives it a typical twist. This becomes evident in Descartes who postulated the necessity of God's existence only after his methodological doubt. The deity's immutable self-sameness and transparency must guarantee the permanence and continuity of the Ego, of the Ego which says of itself (and to itself): '*cogito ergo sum*'. 'I think therefore I am', whereby the act of thinking presupposes and discloses our desire for self-possession. What is new to this approach? God's veracity is, first of all, needed to fortify the human mind's awareness of presence to itself. But, secondly, that God is also postulated to warrant the successful conquest of the human mind. The founded is never without the foundation. The mind's wager is never without the deity's backing: this is the Archimedean point from which to start organising our world[11]. Looked at this claim from a more critical standpoint, one might say that the working of the human intellect always projects above itself a superstructure which must square the certainties one already has with a still greater evidence. In modernity, God or "the absolute" becomes the codeword for a solemn affirmation of the victorious unfolding of a human logic that cannot be halted by the slightest remainders of doubt.

Heidegger and his postmodern adepts feel they have to debunk this metaphysics, since it leads to the absolute rule of instrumental reason

---

10. See ARISTOTLE, *Metaphysics* XII, vii, 1072b 22-31.

11. W. KERN & C. LINK, *Autonomie und Geschöpflichkeit*, in F. BÖCKLE (ed.), *Christlicher Glaube in moderner Gesellschaft*, 18, Freiburg, Herder, 1982, pp. 112-113; 138-139. For Heidegger's analysis of Descartes, see M. HEIDEGGER, *Sein und Zeit*, Tübingen, Niemeyer, 1953, pp. 89-101; ID., *Die Zeit des Weltbildes*, in ID., *Holzwege*, Frankfurt, Klostermann, 1963 (first edition 1950), pp. 87-104.

and technology steered exclusively by science. These authors want to retrieve what the metaphysics of conquest have relegated to oblivion: our rootedness in the earth with all the poetic wealth it involves (Heidegger), and our homelessness in a totally regimented world (Derrida). In view of this retrieval two major obstacles must be removed: the priority of permanence over becoming; and the tyranny of 'sameness' at the expense of difference and alterity. Recuperation of what is suppressed in both domains will put an end to the conceptual empire of total (self-)presence.

Descartes' starting point in the Ego (or Kant's transcendental subject for that matter) can be dissolved when temporality is taken seriously: "When we think time radically, the original self or the perduring subject disappears and in its place we find an elusive trace – a mark of presence that is always absent or a sign of an absence that is never present". The metaphysics of presence "is bound up with an understanding of time in which the essential ecstasy is the (ever repeated) 'punctual present...' But as Husserl suggests, the *hic et nunc* is fugitive – disappearing in the very act of appearing"[12]. The *hic et nunc* of time is only a trace of a present that is slipping away, a trace of what is already bending back to disappearance. This "now", as trace of a present that is always on the brink of disappearing, 'dissolves' the self-presence of consciousness to itself.

This dissolution comes to the fore in Heidegger's notion of *Sein zum Tode* ('being unto death'): His analysis of 'existence and time' (*Sein und Zeit*) shows that we are thrown into our being-in-the-world, into a fluidity of time which we try to halt, but whose erring flow is more potent than our will to mastery. Temporality bereft of a clear teleology, that is to say of modernity's schemes of progress and development, plunges one into a sphere of anxiety, from which only a poetics of awe and wonder may save us. From the basis of disenchantment we are invited to reflect again on the abyss that separates Being and beings (*das Sein und die Seienden*). This leads Heidegger to develop Being (*Sein*) as an unfathomable reserve of gracious possibilities. But we are also to see that these possibilities, because they erupt from an original chaos of indeterminacy, will always surpass the historical capability of the entities (*die Seienden*) in the world, that is to say of the human beings and of the things they have (and have made) at their disposal. In other words, the abysmal difference between 'Being and beings' smashes the modern illusion that our world would be makeable/fabricated. Such a slogan is

---

12. M. TAYLOR, *Deconstructing Theology*, New York, Crossroad, 1982, p. 95.

ungrounded, given the fact that the Abyss of Being (*Abgrund des Seins*) is itself beyond calculation.

This, in turn, makes Heidegger meditate on a poetic presence that borders on the uncanny. Commenting on Parmenides' *estin gar einai* 'Being is there, it is given' (in German: *Es gibt das Sein*), he explains that the presence of the 'Ground' of all that is has not yet been fully grasped when one defines it as a factual 'being there', a given in its matter of factness. On a deeper level one must say that this presence 'is giving itself' in an act of communication. "Es gibt das Sein" is poetically evoked as a gracious 'presencing', as an act of self-giving (*Es gibt sich*), but always so that the mysterious instance of giving (*Es*) withdraws into sacred anonymity in the very moment it opens up the eventful space – the result of the gift – within which beings acquire their destiny and numinous quality: "Being enters the domain of destiny in that it (Being!) gives itself. But this means, reflected upon from the standpoint of destiny: Being gives and withholds itself in the same gesture"[13].

This basic insight leads, then, to the awareness of the reciprocity of 'Being and the receptive mind'. This is the way Heidegger interprets a next dictum of Parmenides: '*to gar auto noein esti kai einai*' (*Das Selbe nämlich ist Vernehmen – Denken – sowohl als auch Sein*), which he explains as: "Receptive thought and Being pertain to the same, belong together on this basis"[14]. This statement inaugurates a task still to be accomplished, for if human beings are to live up to their destiny, they must make efforts, through an ecstatic way of existence (*ek-sistieren*), to shield the truth of Being from profanation. The human being is the 'shepherd of Being' (*der Hirt des Seins*)[15]. A basic condition for carrying out this shepherding is that one realises one's place within the fourfold (*das Geviert*). For the theatre where the shepherding is enacted is the oscillating plane formed by a twofold polarity, the polarity of earth and sky and the polarity of the mortals and the divinities. This scene implies that Being that one must shield from profanation is neither God (in heavens) nor the Ground of the world. Being that shines forth from and through the things in the *Geviert* is rather

---

13. M. HEIDEGGER, *Über den Humanismus*, Frankfurt, Klostermann, 1968 (first edition 1949), p. 23: "Zum Geschick kommt das Sein, indem Es, das Sein, sich gibt. Das aber sagt, geschickhaft gedacht: Es gibt sich und versagt sich zumal".

14. M. HEIDEGGER, *Identität und Differenz*, Pfullingen, Neske, 1957, p. 14: "Denken und Sein gehören in das Selbe und aus diesem Selben zusammen".

15. M. HEIDEGGER, *Über den Humanismus* (n. 13), p. 19: "denn diesem (dem Geschick) gemäss hat er (der Mensch) als der Ek-sistierende die Wahrheit des Seins zu hüten. Der Mensch ist der Hirt des Seins".

in a tautological fashion 'itself', a fluid of highest simplicity or a chaotic Openness which escapes phenomenological description. When in his *Letter on Humanism* Heidegger raises the question "what Being is", he insists on answering it with a necessary tautology: "What is Being"? Beings is just Itself "(*Es ist Es selbst*)"[16]. It is 'itself' in its anonymous epiphany (*Lichtung*) and withdrawal, and is as such that which is closest to the human being's poetical and ecstatic existence. While the anonymous abyss of Being manifests itself in beings (in rocks, animals, works of art, machines, angels and gods), it is at bottom nearer to us than all these mediating 'things'. For through all these mediations Being as such remains 'itself', just as the sacredness of its *Ereignis* remains itself. Nonetheless it is true that Being and reflective thought belong together[17]. For it is precisely in virtue of the manifestation *and* withdrawal of Being that reflective thought in its various forms can happen. Being's withdrawal into its anonymous *Es Selbst* renders possible – grants, and gives way to – the diversity of appearing.

2. *Derrida: Postmodern Dance of Difference and Differentiation*

Whereas Heidegger still endeavoured to keep united the diversity of things and their togetherness within the realm of Being, Derrida resolutely opts for the right of difference or as he prefers to write it, 'différance.'[18] He wants to go beyond Heidegger in positing a notion of difference which is prior to the ontological difference of 'Being and beings' which Heidegger had professed. He does so with the help of structuralism, and its claim that structure precedes the event and is in that sense more fundamental. For the late Heidegger the event or *Ereignis* was crucial to elicit the awareness of one's belonging to the sacred realm of Being with its ambivalent promise of grace and destiny. But, according

16. *Ibid.*, p. 19: "Doch das Sein – was ist das Sein? Es ist Es selbst. Dies zu erfahren und zu sagen, muss das künftige Denken lernen. Das "Sein" – das ist nicht Gott und nicht ein Weltgrund. Das Sein ist weiter denn alles Seiende und ist gleichwohl dem Menschen näher als jedes Seiende, sei dies ein Fels, ein Tier, ein Kunstwerk, eine Machine, sei es ein Engel oder Gott. Das Sein ist das Nächste. Doch die Nähe bleibt dem Menschen am weitesten".

17. E. Brito points here to a tension in Heidegger's thought. This thought oscillates between a phenomenological approach and an aphanology which ends up with a 'resonance of silence' (*Gelaut der Stille*). See E. BRITO, *Heidegger et l'hymne du sacré* (BETL, 141), Leuven, Leuven University Press & Peeters, 1999, p. 732.

18. J. DERRIDA, *Différance*, in *Bulletin de la Société Française de philosophie*, LXII, No 3, July-September 1968, pp. 73-101 (distance from Heidegger specified at pp. 75 ff.); reprinted in *Marges de la philosophie*, Paris, Minuit, 1972, pp. 3-29 (Heidegger discussion at pp. 34-39).

to Derrida, this focus on *Ereignis* still obeys the logic of phonocentrism (the eventful speechact conjures up a presence), thus suppressing the more necessary process of writing and rewriting[19]. Only a structuralist approach to writing does justice to the hiddennesss of an archi-writing of which only traces can be reconstructed in a continual, differential process of *écriture*. With this emphasis on the text, Derrida partially leaves behind the Greek neo-paganism of Heidegger to embrace the Jewish heritage of Cabala. As we will see, this allows him to be more attentive to real historical facts (or mishaps), whereas Heidegger ends finally in resignation before the dark turns of destiny.

Heidegger had used the fluidity of temporal sequences as a springboard to refute the modern metaphysics of conquest. Derrida does the same, but in a more radical way. He deconstructs the notion of enduring self-presence (typical of the transcendental subject), by pointing to a still deeper continual *deferral* ('*différance*') of such presence. With that différance in view, any attempt at holding on to full presence is decried as a megalomania meant to suppress one's mortality[20]. Our awareness of presence is, in fact, always already shot through with bullets of absence. To explain this, Derrida has recourse to the platonic notion of *khoora*[21], that is to say, to some indeterminate, chaotic condition which was already there before the Demiurge set out to impress order upon it. According to his reading of the *Timaeus, khoora* is not just welcoming ordering patterns or ideas, but rather receives them in order to confuse their intelligible imprint. *Khoora* is a place of 'negativity' meant to keep us within the confines of ambivalence.

In *How to Avoid Speaking? Denials (Comment ne pas parler?)*, a critical essay on negative theology and Heidegger's relation to it, he makes it clear that for him the negativity of *khoora* is not a threshold allowing the transition towards a higher form of communication with the Sacred. He surmises that such a threshold of transition is, in fact, to be found in negative theology. For there the negation, radical as it may be, is seen as preparing the way for beholding the supereminent disclosure

---

19. E. BRITO, *Heidegger et l'hymne du sacré* (n. 17), 346-350. Brito remarks that compared to Heidegger's neutral *Es* (in *Es gibt*) Derrida's approach aims at the conceptualisation of a still more neutral structure: 'la différance derridienne... neutralise le Neutre lui-même, le neutralise au second degré, et ainsi l'accomplit' (*Ibid.*, p. 346).

20. See also J. LACAN, *The Four Fundamental Concepts of Psychoanalysis*, New York, Norton, 1981, pp. 58-59, as quoted in M. TAYLOR, *Alterity*, Chicago, The University of Chicago Press, 1987, p. 92.

21. *Khoora* is in Plato's *Timaeus* the name for a pre-existent chaotic matter upon which the imprint of a geometrical form (*idea, eidos*) is to be imposed. This then is the beginning of order.

of God's self-communication from beyond the limits of common under-standing. When Dionysus the Areopagite, says for example that God is not Being (or when modern commentators inscribe the name of Being under a cross), this does not at all mean that the mystic comes in touch with God as nothingness. The refusal to predicate Being to God rather aims at purifying the notion of its mundane or contaminated connota-tions, so as to prepare oneself to be transported with joy in the encounter with God's 'luminous darkness'. The mystics are, in other words, drawn from a non-purified to a purified state, thus crossing a threshold which brings them to higher awareness. Crossing this threshold is often painful, for one has to abandon one's usual ways of thinking and living. Nonetheless the adventure is worthwhile. Pseudo-Dionysius knows, as it were "in advance," that with God's help, this final leap will be possible. The 'certitude' is expressed in the prayers (the "encomium") he addresses to the One-on-the-other-side, whom he believes will draw him over the threshold.

To make his own position clear, Derrida speaks of a threshold which can never be crossed, For him the *khoora* is a 'medium', a 'place' or a 'limen' which discourages any mystical ascent or dialectical 'crossing over'. It acts rather as a stumble block which makes our clear concepts fall into pieces. What we deemed to be fulfilment turns out to be a mix-ture of fulfilment and absence. Ambivalence and ambiguity become the hallmark, signs of our basic finitude. Our neat logic of 'either/or' dis-solves into its opposite 'neither/nor' (as distinct from 'and/and'). The 'neither/nor' makes Hegelian dialectics pointless: it is impossible to reach a higher synthesis through negations. It also makes us question the enterprise of Heidegger, who still thought that abandoning the tendency to gain a hold on things would draw us into the Abyss of 'Being', preg-nant with bliss. Not even Heidegger was always immune to the siren-song of ontotheology.

Contrasting *khoora* with Heidegger's *'Es gibt Sein'* (Being is there, and it is there as giving), Derrida points out that *khoora* cannot be con-ceived of as 'giving something'. Applied to *khoora*, *'es gibt'* can only mean that *khoora* 'is there', although in a mode of 'being there' that can never be located in space and time, since, strictly speaking, *khoora* is before time and history. Moreover, what certainly cannot be said is that *khoora* 'gives' something (the second meaning of *es gibt*). *Khoora* is not instrumental in bringing about order; it does not contribute to making human history meaningful; it gives no promise; it does not aim at elevating human beings into semi-Gods; it does not lure them into activating poetic powers which turn them into 'shepherds of

Being'[22]. *Khoora*'s negativity only interrupts the magic circle that mega-lomaniacs weave around themselves; it demolishes the mirror palace of stable self-presence, without any prospect of final recovery.

The only activity *khoora* is engaged in is the issuing of admonitions of erasure. Its disenchanting labour consists in sending signals from an immemorial past. These signals find their way into our 'writing', Derrida's term for stabilised, elaborated reflection. They insert themselves into our treatises and written accounts, in the form of subversive traces or cracks that enfeeble the solid constructions we try to build on the shifting sands of fugitive impressions and fragmentary insights. From time *immemorial khoora,* as an indeterminate place of spacing, time and again unsettles, without us invoking its name. In our conscious life we have no natural desire to listen to its voice. But the terrifying effects of it reach us through uncanny stimuli and disturbing traces which, as it were, erupt from a traumatic wound that haunts us. It is worth noting that Derrida is not alone in referring to an immemorial past. Other authors, too, with the intention of subverting modernity's reach for the future, plunge into the same tunnel of anteriority. Lacan designates this anteriority as 'the "real" that is *always* missing, *forever* lacking. It is not "here" (*da*) in the first place, but always already "gone" (*fort*). As such, the "real" is something like a "non-original origin." Having never been present, this origin cannot be re-presented', that is to say can never be captured in clear knowledge[23]. The real thing can only be imagined in phantasms... Levinas describes such irreducible anteriority as the "unrepresentable before", Blanchot as the "dreadfully ancient". This time before – this "non-original origin" – 'is' like a "primal scene"[24] which has gone underground, and from there invades our consciousness[25].

---

22. J. DERRIDA, *How To Avoid Speaking? Denials*, in ID., *Languages of the Unsayable*, New York, Columbia University, 1989, pp. 35-37: "The Khoora is a place, or rather a non-place... It must have been 'there' as the 'there' itself beyond time or in any case beyond becoming... Radically nonhuman and atheological, one cannot not even say that it *gives* place or that *there is* the khoora. The *es gibt,* thus translated, too vividly announces or recalls the dispensation of God, of man, or even that of the Being of which certain texts by Heidegger speak (*es gibt Sein*). Khoora is not even *that* (*ça*), the *es* or *id* of giving, before all subjectivity. It does not give place as one would give something, whatever it may be; it neither creates nor produces anything, not even an event insofar as it takes place. It gives no order and gives no promise. It is radically ahistorical, because nothing happens through it and nothing happens to it".

23. Heidegger links 'representation' to the modern scientific habit of reducing things to 'represented things', that is to say: to objects to be scrutinised with the help of the subject's intellectual tools. See M. HEIDEGGER, *Die Zeit des Weltbildes* (n. 11), p.84.

24. M. TAYLOR, *Alterity* (n. 20), p.93.

25. Derrida, too, points out that "one glimpses *khoora* only in an 'oneiric manner" (J. DERRIDA, *How to Avoid Speaking? Denials* (n. 22), p. 33).

This brings us to the heart of spacing, and difference. One would be tempted to call *khoora* the matrix of diversity and conclude that 'in the beginning' there was a 'source' of heterogeneity and differential relations. This statement is neither correct nor incorrect (the neither/nor comes to bear). For one cannot tell much about how *khoora* exactly functions as source, except that it emits stimuli with negative effects, and that these hold out the prospect of a dance of differences. Difference is given an opportunity whenever persons and institutions allow themselves to be unsettled in their closed existence. At that moment of disturbance an openness is created towards recognising the other as other, in the I-Thou relations but also where we act as public persons (the generalised 'Third'). Whenever persons and institutions react to *khoora*'s unsettling signals, a world of proliferating plurality emerges. The happy result of *khoora*'s negative admonitions is the spinning forth of ever changing webs of asymmetrical relations – up to the point of creating an endless dispersal. One ought to recall that *khoora* does not *give* us anything; not even a yearning for ultimate harmony[26].

The dispersing effect of *khoora* is also expressed in Derrida's notion of '*différance*', the 'future'-oriented counterpart of *khoora*[27]. While *khoora* is the primal region of spacing, '*différance*' or *deferral* denotes temporalisation and an incessant shifting of relations in the flux of time. *Différance* tells us that any affirmation of total presence must be deferred again and again, if we are to do justice to the many (often unasked for) tumultuous actors that insist on populating the scene of presence[28]. *Différance* reminds us that 'each element appearing on the scene of presence is related to something other than itself, and that in this way 'it keeps within itself the trace of past elements, and allows itself to be vitiated by the mark of its relation to future elements'[29]. Because of its appearance in traces and marks '*différance*' is,

---

26. I would like to draw attention to the subtle difference between Plotinus and Derrida. In Plotinus' henology the 'One' can only communicate to the lower ranks of being what It does *not* possess (See E. GILSON, *L'être et l'essence*, Paris, Vrin, 1948, p. 42). This means that the One cannot give birth to oneness but only to plurality (according to gradations). Yet, and this is the difference with Derrida, because the One *gives something* from Its own superabundance, all the entities in the world yearn for returning to the One. Derrida has foreclosed this yearning by stating from the outset that *khoora does not give anything*. For certain commonalities between Heidegger and Plotinus, see E. BRITO, *Heidegger et l'hymne du sacré* (n. 17), pp. 340-342.

27. This 'future'-orientation does not include any clear finality.

28. This gives a clearer picture of what is meant by 'presence shot through with bullets of absence'.

29. J. DERRIDA, *Margins of Philosophy*, Chicago, The University of Chicago Press, 1982, p. 28.

in fact, pre-linguistic[30]; it rather shows up in a dream-world of symbols, and 'increasingly dislocates itself in a chain of deferring and deferring substitutions'[31]. In other words, pre-linguistic *'différance'* lets itself be felt in the many occurrences where the 'different' comes to disturb and unsettle our ingrained habits of holding on to 'sameness' *'Différance'* is the ally of the 'different' which it shields from being absorbed into symmetrical relations. It makes possible the vibrating dance of erring differentiations, thus fostering a dissemination of plurality.

The ethical implications of such a 'decentred' picture of the world' will be examined in more detail below. Before taking that up, I would first like to give a brief account of what empirical studies tell us about postmodernity. For practical reasons I limit myself to Zygmunt Bauman.

III. A Sociological Approach to Postmodernity.

1. *Postmodern Levity*

The Polish-British sociologist Zygmunt Bauman is a recognised authority in the study of postmodernity. In his work *'Postmodernity and Its Discontents'*[32], he tries to extend Freud's probing into the discontents of modern civilisation (*Das Unbehagen in der Kultur*) to postmodern culture. Like Freud he posits that the gains of a civilisation also entail losses. Modernity's mindset of law and order offered security, but not necessarily happiness; postmodernity's free-wheeling lifestyle entails happiness but not necessarily security. In this but also in previous works, Bauman evokes the younger generation's espousal of the dance of differences, without much care for modernity's centralising pull. Against the grain of Derrida's worries, the youth, as he sees it, *is* already freed from the yoke of the 'same'. They wholeheartedly take delight in the consumer society's pick-and-choose mentality. Yet, from within their excess of free choice new discontents arise, which Bauman brings in connection with globalisation[33]. The free market gone global confronts the yuppie or me-generation with problems they will have to cope with. In order to grasp the quintessence of the postmodern Bauman offers a whole range of tentative approaches, from which I select a few ones.

---

30. *Ibid.*, p. 28: "'Older' than Being itself, such a *différance* has no name in our language".

31. *Ibid.*, p. 26.

32. Z. BAUMAN, *Postmodernity and its Discontents*, Oxford – Cambridge, Polity Press, 1997. I will also make use of Z. BAUMAN, *Life in Fragments. Essays in Postmodern Morality*, Oxford – Cambridge, Blackwell, 1995.

33. See also Z. BAUMAN, *Globalization. The Human Consequences*, Cambridge, Polity Press, 1998.

First the postmodern personality. Modern persons were trained to
become 'soldiers' and 'producers'. They were intent on defending the
nation state with its clear regulations of law and order, and determined
to work for the increase of a gross national product meant to be distrib-
uted among the population (*bonum commune*). In this way, they
believed, the nation state could slowly develop into a welfare state, an
aim approached in postwar Western Europe. Within this grand perspective everyone was proud of upholding discipline, enduring hardships,
and keeping their bodies fit for labour[34]. Identity-building posed no
problem in a milieu where a reciprocity existed between the goals set by
government and industries and the citizens' personal aspirations.

Meanwhile the appearance of the body, as symbol of the postmodern
person, has drastically changed. The youth is no longer interested in a
muscular body disciplined for manual work; they rather prefer a slim
body, kept healthy through diet and trimmed for looking attractive. Postmodern people are, in body and mind, 'pleasure seekers', and 'sensation
gatherers', not 'soldiers'[35]; they are in the first instance not 'producers',
but 'consumers', giving in to the spell of an ever-changing panorama of
attractive commodities. Along with the versatility of fashion, their personalities have become free-wheeling, instead of durable and well-con-
structed. As Bauman puts it: 'The hub of postmodern life strategy is not
identity building, but the avoidance of being fixed'[36]. All relationship is
but a relationship 'with no strings attached to it and with no obligations
earned'[37] so it can be terminated at will 'by either partner at any particular point'[38]. In parallel with this state of affairs, postmodern industries,
too, avoid long term obligations. They close down their factories in
Europe whenever the qualified labour force is cheaper in developing
countries, and move out, thus making the workers feel that have no right
to stable jobs. Against these mechanisms of redundancy and exclusion,
the nation states are impotent, bereft as they are of the means to keep the
free circulation of capital within their borders.

Postmodern philosophies also try to articulate the above characteristics, while usually turning a blind eye to the hard facts of economy and
marketing. Couched in philosophical jargon, their message sounds as
follows: postmodern persons have successfully freed themselves form

---

34. Even the 'reserve army' of provisionally unemployed did their best to prove that,
if hired, they, too, would contribute to the growth of the nation.
35. Z. BAUMAN, *Postmodernity and Its Discontents* (n. 32), pp. 146 and 179.
36. Z. BAUMAN, *Life in Fragments* (n. 32), p. 89.
37. Z. BAUMAN, *Postmodernity and Its Discontents* (n. 32), p. 88.
38. Z. BAUMAN, *Life in Fragments* (n. 32), p. 89.

the centralising pull of fixed norms and structures. They dare to defy the rule of 'sameness' and join the dance of delightful dispersal, thus enjoying the 'unbearable lightness of existence'. Attentive to differences, and playfully erring in a labyrinth of ever changing signs, they celebrate their escape from the totalising grip of full presence. At the cognitive level, they realise that there will always be hesitance between affirmation and negation – that each clear answer is pregnant with a myriad of unresolved questions. To forget this would again pave the way for a systematic thinking that crushes the 'otherness' of the 'other'. So it is better, they think, to opt for the fascination of ambivalence and undecidability, as this comes to the fore in the ironising 'neither'/'nor'. They do this from the awareness that the rich undercurrent of life, if censured by clear-cut definitions, will at any rate spill over its definitional boundaries to unleash an avalanche of erring images – the real home for artists to live in. Postmodern people no longer feel the need to construct stable pillars for bridges across the shifting sands of fleeting events. This is the picture one gets, for example, from Mark Taylor's early work *Erring. A Postmodern A/Theology* [39], a theological reading of Derrida.

Bauman, now, would certainly welcome some elements of the above picture[40], but on the whole he rejects some generalisations behind it. For as a sociologist he knows that different groups in society understand postmodernity's overall atmosphere quite differently. The distinction he draws between tourists (elites) and vagabonds (outcasts) may illustrate this.

Bauman first used the symbol of tourist or stroller to contrast it with that of the pilgrim fathers who embarked on a specific journey. In order to attain their goal the latter were willing to leave behind comfort and continue their march with gratification deferred until later. Pilgrims live up to the hardships of Protestant work ethics. Tourists, on the contrary, are postmodern pleasure-seekers. Their strolling is not rectilinear but rather a meandering through series of episodes with neither a past nor consequences[41]. Here one is to do with the 'man of leisure', the consumer who in search of ever new sensations wanders from shopping mall to shopping mall, and from one exotic place to another. Tourists

39. M. TAYLOR, *Erring. A Postmodern A/Theology*, Chicago, The University of Chicago Press, 1984.

40. See, e.g., Z. BAUMAN, *Postmodernity and Its Discontents* (n. 32), p. 167, where he also distrusts clear-cut definitions.

41. Z. BAUMAN, *Life in Fragments* (n. 32), p. 92: "Psychically, strolling means rehearsing human reality as a series of episodes – that is, as events without a past and with no consequences".

leave their home because they hope to find elsewhere what their homely routine cannot deliver[42]. They become nomads of a special kind, feeling at home in virtual reality, and behaving as strangers in a world whose hard reality shatters their fancy of virtual images. Nomadic erring has an artistic ring about it.

2. Existential Insecurity an Opportunity for Religion? Life in a Dual Society

At a certain moment Bauman tells us that it is grossly misleading 'to apply the term "nomads" indiscriminately to all contemporaries of the postmodern era'. To do so, would gloss over profound differences[43], that is to say the differences between tourist and vagabond. Indeed, vagabonds 'are travellers refused the right to turn into tourists'. They are the undesired immigrants and refugees who have no guarantee of a permanent stay, always pushed to look for a safer place[44]. At bottom, vagabonds also are implicit consumers; they would like to embrace the lifestyle of tourist, but they cannot, and this is their frustration. While tourists are the heroes of postmodernity, vagabonds are its victims: 'The tourists stay or move at their hearts' desire. They abandon the site when new untried opportunities beckon elsewhere. The vagabonds, however, know that they won't stay for long, however strongly they wish to, since nowhere they stop are they welcome: 'If the tourists move because they find the world irresistibly *attractive*, the vagabonds move because they find the world unbearably *inhospitable*'[45]. At his juncture one ought to acknowledge that the postmodern ideal of decentredness – its dwindling moving away from the centre – reveals an intrinsic antagonism. Its highly praised heterogeneity is basically Janus-faced.

This brings us to the heart of the matter, to a problematic which cannot be captured by postmodern philosophising alone. The contemporaries of the postmodern area live, in fact, in a dual society with a split that haunts them. The irruption of vagabonds on the scene of the pleasure-seekers makes these latter people realise the fragility of their own situation, for the slightest mishap will turn them, too, into unwanted vagrants. This frightening perspective confronts them with existential insecurity, in spite of their enjoyment of the good things of life. The

---

42. Z. BAUMAN, *Postmodernity and Its Discontents* (n. 32), p. 91.
43. Z. BAUMAN, *Globalization. The Human Consequences* (n. 33), p. 87.
44. *Ibid.*, p. 93: "Vagabonds are travelers refused the right to turn into tourists. They are allowed neither to stay put (there is no site guaranteeing permanence, the end to undesirable mobility) nor search for a better place to be".
45. Z. BAUMAN, *Postmodernity and Its Discontents* (n. 32), p. 92.

difficulties postmodern people have in taking decisions relates exactly to this. They are never sure that what they have decided on – in view of courting, financial planning or job security – will not turn against themselves. Every move on the chessboard is full of dangers. So they constantly worry about 'missed opportunities' or opportunities they think have failed to seize[46]. Life remains enigmatic: one does not even know whether one's undecidable situation is a curse or a blessing. To get rid of anxieties many postmodern men and women have recourse to counselling, to rescue their vacillating psyche. At the public level this need for security is reflected in the many prisons and refugee asylums which are needed to keep unwanted vagrants and bandits secluded. To guarantee their citizens' peace of mind postmodern societies become police-states. In most Western countries, more money is spent on police protection and prisons than on welfare benefits[47].

The crucial question to be asked in this context is: do the discontents of postmodernity pave the way for a new religiosity? Will existential insecurity prompt people to return to religion? Some theologians will say yes, intimating that the absence of meaning will serve as a springboard for the disenchanted to gradually come to appraise life as gratuitous gift and donation. The time is ripe, they say, to once again honour God as the giver of life, the only antidote enabling people to come to grips with the meaninglessness that erupts from underneath the surface of postmodern glamour[48]. Others, and Bauman is among them, are not that sure that a straightforward return of the Sacred will take place. For them, a recovery of the Sacred can occur only when the insufficiencies that individuals experience are seen as part of the contingency of the human species, and not – as is the case now – in painful contrast with the (not yet vanished) idea of the omnipotence of the human species[49]. Only if the weakness of the species as such is recognised, can premodern religiosity flourish again; but this position has no firm premises today. Postmodern thinking moves, after all, within the orbit of the consequences of modernity[50].

---

46. *Ibid.*, p. 178: "Postmodern men and women, whether by their own preference or by necessity, are *choosers*. And the art of choosing is mostly about avoiding one danger: that of *missing an opportunity*".

47. *Ibid.*, p. 204: "As the expenditures on collective and individual welfare and social wages are cut, the costs of police, prisons, security services, armed guards, and house/office/car protection grow unstoppably". See also Z. BAUMAN, *Globalization. The Human Consequences* (n. 33), pp. 116-122.

48. See e.g. J. MILBANK, *Postmodern Critical Augustinianism. A Short Summa in Forty Two Responses to Unasked Questions*, in *Modern Theology* 7 (1991) 225-237.

49. Z. BAUMAN, *Postmodernity and Its Discontents* (n. 32), p. 183.

50. Even when postmodern philosophers speak up for a deferral of total presence, this deferral is still caught up in modernity's global movement of autonomous self-assertion.

3. Neo-orthodox Revivals. A Postmodern Phenomenon

As a substitute for religion, it is said, some will try to obtain psychi-cal peak experiences to exorcise life's insecurities. New Age, then, would be the answer. Others, it is also asserted, will rather join 'postu-lated' communities, as is the case with neo-orthodox groups (*inté-grisme*), religious sects, and fundamentalist revivals often with a tribal ring about them. A great deal of literature has been spent on the various group formations aimed at retrieving 'the basics.' Alongside the benefi-cial effects this communitarian mushrooming may have – a re-apprecia-tion of religious ceremonies of old, a certain austerity of lifestyle, etc. – they also have certain shortcomings, as will become evident below.

Can we regard such 'back to the basics'-formations as a return to pre-modernity? Unanimity is growing among specialists that fundamentalism, as a broad category, is a postmodern phenomenon, because it feeds on postmodern insecurities. It is an attempt to get rid of 'freedom of choice', for under the dictates of the consumer market postmodern persons must necessarily chose, and they are never sure whether they have made a good choice, and not instead missed a vital opportunity. Membership in a fun-damentalist group would seem to exonerate them from this heavy burden. For now they will have guides – in continuity with therapists – who are going to tell them what they must do in matters of religious practice and ritualisation of their lives. The new communities give them back a sense of firm anchorage, although in most cases this involves 'postulated' rather than 'organic' communities: for the only thing which cements members together is their dissatisfaction with the uncertainties of the postmodern setting. This setting, as has already been suggested, cannot be separated from the phenomenon of economic globalisation, that is to say from the increasing influence of a consumer market, on one hand, and a dismantling of the public services of the nation state, on the other.

Bauman is correct when he says that candidates for sects and also tribal groups are to be found first and foremost among the flawed con-sumers, among those who feel they have become "unfulfilled producers, or people cheated at the division of surplus value"[51]. This picture recalls the proletariat described by Marx, but with this difference: today's new poor are, to their own frustration, lured into the mimetic mechanism of consumerism[52]. This shift in perspective makes Bauman say that 'fundamentalism is a radical remedy against the bane of postmodern,

---

51. *Ibid.*, p. 183.
52. For the link between mimesis and consumption, see M. SHAPIRO, *Reading the Postmodern Polity*, Minneapolis, University of Minnesota Press, 1992, p. 58.

market-led, consumer society – *and* its risk-contaminated freedom.' But, he adds, the remedy consists in 'healing the infection by amputating the infected organ – by abolishing freedom as such, in as far as there is no freedom free of risks'[53]. It is evident that in these circumstances no real force of resistance is to be expected, as this was the case with radical labour movements and Christian liberation groups. If the new poor are to join 'religious revivals' (charismatics, neo-orthodox 'integralists'), their faith input will be rather confined to the therapeutic needs of the group. And this focus on the inner circle obviously occurs at the expense of a serious social practice, and at the expense also of a substantial basic option that gives a solid orientation to one's life. The abdication of freedom in the hands of gurus and sect leaders hardly results in a durable commitment to societal needs. 'Fundamentalists' (to use this broad category once again) have a keen eye for postmodernity's discontents; but they hardly offer viable solutions with an overall social impact.

IV. SACRAMENTALITY OF LIFE

Today serious attempts are made to retrieve sacramental life, but the methods used are highly 'speculative', espousing the abstractness of postmodern anti-metaphysics. Jean-Luc Marion, for example, engages in a radical deconstruction of closed circularities of thinking, from the vantage point of God. God and God alone draws us unto Himself from the other side of every human endeavour to come into contact with Him. Even a religious phenomenology which tries to describe the religious object in its purity, it is said, can hardly avoid the pitfall of establishing a symmetric relation between the 'knower' and the 'known'. It tends to reduce the divine to an 'object' of our desire, an idol made in our image[54], whereas God's icon is the *logos incarnate*, who as the genuine image of God – living up to His volition – has the power to illuminate our hearts and minds. This means that only those who are drawn into a radical receptivity to God's donation find themselves in a right relation to God. They live in conformity with God's icon whose penetrating light overrules every human – or cosmos – centred intellectual endeavour to situate oneself before the Sacred.

Marion's 'reversed' phenomenology makes him issue warnings against each and every horizontal search for wholeness from within the

---

53. Z. BAUMAN, *Postmodernity and Its Discontents* (n. 32), p. 184.

54. J.-L. MARION, *God Without Being*, Chicago, the University of Chicago Press, 1991, p. 10: "The idol depends on the gaze that it satisfies; since if the gaze did not desire to satisfy itself in the idol, the idol would have no dignity for it".

tissue of the world. He decries them as humanism, as 'idolatry', a way of capturing God's ineffable character (*ipseitas Dei*) in this-worldly schemes of expectancy. One is to do with a theological deconstruction that measures itself against the asymmetries of postmodern deconstructionists. His thesis that life on earth, if recognised as such, is a gift from God aims at overcoming Derrida's thesis that *khoora* does not give us anything, except the disturbing awareness that life is full of ambiguities and differences we have to cope with. It also aims at going beyond Heidegger's anonymous act of giving (*Es gibt das Sein*), to replace it with the recognition of the One who charges himself with the act of bestowing the gift. For as long as there is only the anonymous act of opening an eventful space of beauty and destiny, carried out by a withdrawing Being (*Sein*) without a recognisable face, one cannot properly speak of an act of giving in which the character of the Giver appears, the God of love[55]. In short, against Heidegger's neopagan cosmic religiosity, and against Derrida's nomadic erring understood as a cabalistic praise of the 'absent One', Marion wants to intimate that God, the creator of the universe, is Love, and as such empowers us with an ecstatic love towards the Giver.

I must confess that I have mixed feelings about Marion's enterprise. On the one hand I appreciate the rigor of his speculative thinking, and also his maturation over the years. Indeed, in his early work *L'idole et la distance* and, too a lesser degree, in *Dieu sans l'Être*, one could still have the impression that he 'rectified' Heideggerian and Derridian phenomenology with the help of a theological phenomenology[56]: the ultimate light that makes things visible shines forth from the splendour of revelation. God's self-manifestation in the created realm stems from beyond Being (and from beyond our reflection on it). But in his later works he seems to exceed, by framing his initial insights in a method which stretches them in a new and original way, the very possibilities of philosophical phenomenology[57]. There he develops a philosophical approach of gift and donation which prepares the reader for experiencing the superabundance of God's love. So, I'm certainly delighted with

55. E. BRITO, *Heidegger et l'hymne du sacré* (n. 17), p. 736: "Le donner qui œuvre dans le *Es gibt* Heideggerien n'admet pas une instance première qui prendrait sur elle d'opérer le don d'une donation", with reference to J.-L. MARION, *L'idole et la distance*, Paris, Grasset, 1977, pp. 294 ff.

56. *Ibid.*, pp. 261, 718.

57. See J.-L. MARION, *Étant donné. Essai d'une phénoménologie de la donation*, Paris, PUF, 1997; and J.-L. MARION, *Metaphysics and Phenomenology: A Summary for Theologians*, in G. WARD, *The Postmodern God. A Theological Reader*, Oxford, Blackwell, 1997, pp. 279-296.

many of his insights. But on the other hand I'm nonetheless hesitant about some aspects of Marion's approach. My reservations, I repeat, relate not so much to certain possible flaws in his speculative reasoning (on the contrary I admire his refinement). They rather flow from questions I have about their practical use, specially for people struggling with the postmodern context of globalisation.

True, speculative insights also have an impact on our lives. I find it particularly useful, for example, that Marion, and also John Milbank for that matter (whom I can only mention in passing), present, as an alternative to secular nihilism, a theological nihilism which, its own way, deconstructs closed circularities of thinking[58]. This theological nihilism – or should one call it 'negative theology'? – introduces us, indeed, into the royal road to mysticism: in order to perceive God's presence in the world one must discard overly narrow human conceptions of God. Emptiness and receptivity are prerequisites for the awakening of a contemplative gaze. And this gaze makes us see – even in the absence of meaning – the shining through of divine light in cultic objects and rituals, as well as in symbolic enactments of the believing community. And these experiences find their prolongation in every day activities.

Yet, and here I come to my critical remarks, what I observe is that most of the literature about sacraments and sacramentality which follow the above line of thought tend to content themselves with musing on intra-ecclesial topics, related to sacred places and sacred times. But I see hardly any development of a mystical or sacramental vision that envisions one's place within the contemporary social context. If allusions to this context occur, they are immediately framed in clichés that exalt the beauty of 'Christian love', and the flourishing of virtues of charity and reconciliation in the Christian community. This vocabulary, however, obscures social antagonisms, rather than laying them bare. It also easily lends itself to be filled with anecdotes and narratives taken from the inner circle of neo-orthodox and charismatic groups. But, again, there is not much sense of a contemplative gaze which tries to come to grips with societal problems. Nor does mystical 'emptiness' serve as a receptacle for harbouring the agonies of today's world. In short, sacramentality is rediscovered, but mainly within the confines of church life. And its social impact is minimal, so that one may speak of a truncated sacramentality.

---

58. I borrow the term 'secular nihilism' from J. MILBANK, *Theology and Social Theory. Beyond Secular Reason*, Oxford, Blackwell, 1990, p. 5; and contrast it with 'theological nihilism'.

It is here that Christians can learn something from ethically committed persons in civil society. In *Postmodernity and Its Discontents* Bauman appeals to the moral feelings of those who take to heart the scandal of a dual society. He points out that people in democratic systems, as a majority, vote for measures that enhance their own security – such as reinforced police control, seclusion of unwanted immigrants, and cuts in the latter's welfare programs. But, he adds, these measures go against the grain of what solidarity means: that is 'the recognition of other peoples' misery as one's own responsibility, and the alleviation and eventually the removal of misery as one's own task'[59]. As I see it, this concern prepares the way for lifting the 'truncation' I just mentioned. For as long as we put up with the defence mechanisms that accelerate the growth of a divided society – 'exclusion and brutalisation of potentially "problematic" strata' of the population[60] – God's light is hindered from shining forth from the very core of life in society. It is obscured in a twofold way: through the desperation of wandering have-nots, and the excess of possibilities of free-wheeling tourists. As long as this split remains there as an open wound, the presence of God – and of life as a gift, for that matter – shows only its disfigured appearance. I can scarcely imagine an abundance of sacramental presence in a world at large, in which on one hand excessive glamour neutralises God's light, and dire misery, on the other hand, cries out for mercy. I believe that Dorothee Sölle is correct when she says that the dark night of mysticism is today intensified by the painful awareness of human-produced afflictions[61]. Can a God beyond ontotheology be insensitive to those whom the system excludes?

V. CONCLUSION: THE QUESTION OF JUSTICE

I realise that these considerations about God's presence and absence adopt a much more horizontal approach to things than Marion's vertical approach. But it is precisely a preoccupation with this horizontal plane that allows one to perceive antagonisms in history which are easily glossed over in meta-reflections (I avoid the term metaphysics) on how the finite relates to the infinite. Such an overall view may assist people in discovering one's mystical 'spark of the soul', but at the same time it also threatens to make them lose sight of historically situated forms of

---

59. Z. BAUMAN, *Postmodernity and Its Discontents* (n. 32), p. 63. See also *ibid.*, p. 204: "The road of the free requires, as it were, the freedom of all".
60. *Ibid.*, p. 62.
61. D. SÖLLE, *Mystik und Widerstand. Du stilles Geschrei*, Hamburg, Hoffmann und Campe Verlag, 1997, p. 16.

class antagonism and discrimination – forms which also come to bear on the manner in which one celebrates the breakthrough of God's light and luminous darkness. What I'm suggesting is a 'praxis of liberation' inspired by a non-truncated sacramentality of life, knowing that such a praxis is not an easy enterprise after the collapse of the Grand Stories.

Perhaps one should have a closer look at certain postmodern strategies which philosophers offer, and which all deal with taking asymmetrical relations seriously. I think of Levinas' considerations on justice, at the level of the 'generalised Third', that is, at the level of macro-ethics and politics. There he suggests that the irruption of the naked face of the other (of various others respectively) should make us critically examine the appropriateness of general laws which make abstraction of the otherness of the other. Are they 'just' laws, resting on a momentary consensus or on a consensus deemed binding in the past? And is that the reason why they must be respected? Or must one rather regard them as 'unjust', in as far as they are only provisional approximations to a type of regulation that in the long run is expected to do justice to groups of people now condemned by the law? To question the adequacy of laws and to request their reform appears to be an act of anarchy in the name of a deeper moral sense of equity[62]. I also think of Derrida's treatment of the same topic, in which he brings up the aporias entangling a judge who feels bound to abide by the law. For law and individual act violently upon each other: they tend to suppress each other. Hence the basic aporia one has to face; on one hand, the symmetrical rule of the law cannot do justice to the asymmetry of the persons, whereas this asymmetry must, on the other, be kept in limits through a law which is not just to everybody (and – to aggravate the aporia: can this anomaly in turn be tolerated?)[63].

Postmodern activists will thus never have real peace of mind when venturing to speak up for the rights of excluded groups and against laws which condemn them. Transgression of the general rule becomes, in a sense, inevitable. But not without raising the question of whether one is not (and to what degree?) doing violence to a system of laws that cannot simply be annulled but which rather must be pushed to engage in a search for more appropriate regulations beyond earlier rules of consensus. Or to

62. See Bauman's rendering of Levinas' development in the 1980s, Z. BAUMAN, *Postmodernity and its Discontents* (n. 32), pp. 46-57.

63. See M. Taylor's rendering of Derrida's essay *Force of Law. The Mystical Foundation of Authority. Deconstruction and the Possibility of Justice* (*Cardozo Law Review*, 11, nos 5-6; July-August 1990, pp. 919-1045), in M. TAYLOR, *Nots*, Chicago, University of Chicago Press, 1993, pp. 72-94.

put it differently: the 'anarchic' transgressors must realise that there are limits to actions which, however, they cannot afford *not* to undertake. Postmodern ambivalence thus becomes part and parcel of 'liberationists' who try to live up to admonitions flowing from their nearness to a fulfilling but also disquieting God.

However, if God is experienced this way – as the fulfilling source which also unsettles – then it would seem as if Marion and Derrida are not as far apart as one might at first sight suppose. To recognise (with Marion) that life is a gift from God does not dispense one from making use of disturbing strategies (Derrida) on behalf of the excluded. Sacramental contact with an asymmetrical God prompts one to take seriously asymmetrical relations in society and to act accordingly, in solidarity with the dispossessed[64]. Our voice of protest, on the horizontal plane, echoes the protest, on a vertical plane, of a God who refuses to be captured in flat symmetrical relations. The God-question ought to be lived and answered in the practice. The aim of such a practice can consist in making the excluded feel that what they are going through is neither merely the result of a dispensation of destiny (Heidegger), nor a consequence of their allegedly restricted capability of rewriting the proliferation of an unfathomable archi-writing (Derrida). Perhaps the attempt to explain to them that God is love and that life is a gift/donation from God – enabling the receivers to engage in an exchange of love (Marion) – must take the detour of patiently creating opportunities for the excluded to experience what a non-debasing exchange in real life means. Those who have not experienced gratuity in real life can hardly be expected to understand the meaning of divine gratuity expounded in learned discourses.

Faculty of Theology   Georges DE SCHRIJVER s.j.
Katholieke Universiteit Leuven
Sint-Michielsstraat 6
B-3000 Leuven

---

64. This is also the method of E. DUSSEL, *Etica de la liberación en la edad de la globalización y la exclusión*, Madrid, editorial Trotta, 1998; see, pp. 118-120.

POSTMODERNITY AND SACRAMENTALITY

Two Challenges to Speaking about God

The Western world is living through today a time that is only comprehensible as being inserted in the major development of a process, a process that is not, properly speaking, sudden, but has been going on a long time and that appears today in the form of a crisis of models, paradigms, and values. The impact is very strong on those who are living through it and especially on the generations who have already experienced another state of affairs and who find their certainties and all their most fundamental supports threatened. All these factors raise to emphasise a crisis of global dimensions, which seems to make the history of the world go backwards and even to turn on the hinges that supported it and guaranteed its identity[1].

Our work claims to analyse more specifically *one* of the aspects of this crisis of modernity, namely, its impact on the manner of living out religion, on the contours of the profile of religious identity, on the ways followed by the so-called religious experience at the heart of the present historical moment. To this end we will start by outlining a short description of what constitutes the so-called crisis of modernity, conscious, however, of the fact that ours, like any attempt to describe the matter, will necessarily be limited and partial, by the fact, not only by the diversity of points of view and possible angles for analysis, but even more of the diversification of the tendencies of the authors themselves who have been occupied with it during the last few years.

1. For the base of what we say about modernity as a globalising and enveloping phenomenon, see, among others, J. BAUDRILLARD, *Modernité*, in *Encyclopaedia Universalis* 11 (1980) 139-141; J. MARDONES, *Postmodernidad y cristianismo*, Satander, Sal Terrae, 1988; M. GAUCHET, *Le désenchantement du monde. Une histoire politique de la religion*, Paris, Gallimard, 1985; L. GONZALEZ-CARVAJAL, *Ideas y creencias del hombre actual*, Santander, Sal Terrae, 1991; G. VATTIMO, *La fin de la modernité. Nihilisme et herméneutique dans la culture post-moderne*, Paris, Seuil, 1987. See especially also the excellent text of H.C. DE LIMA VAZ, *Religião e modernidade filosófica*, in *Síntese Nova Fase* 18 (1991), pp. 147-165, tackling the question of modernity in an original way by making modernity be equivalent to the philosophical thought, therefore questioning the situation of the modern "turn around" after the Middle Ages.

Conscious of this limitation, we insist on the first stage which intends to locate our reflection within a framework of more or less understandable contours.

Immediately following, we propose to characterise the question, initially intending to understand and submit to reflection on the phenomenon named (wrongly or rightly) "return of the sacred" or "return of the religious" in secularised society. We will then continue our work with the aid of the data acquired, no longer on religion in general but keeping ourselves to historical Christianity, which is engaged, in this end of a millennium, in the process of finding again its deepest identity and discovering the adequate way of wording it to a world at the same time secularised and pluri-religious.

We stand still finally at the idea and the concept of God subjacent to the crisis of modernity itself and, on the other hand, at the concrete possibility, which presents itself to the person today, of making from the interior of this crisis, the experience of God as Christianity proposes it. It seems us that the question of God is THE religious question par excellence, since it raises the fundamental questions that characterise, since the dawn of humanity – everything that ends up leading to the symbolic, cultural and ritual organisation that we call religion. The question of Transcendence, of the Absolute, of life beyond the tangible and empirical, of the origins of the world, of the radical Meaning of things, in sum, the last and supreme question which has always marked human perplexity while making it repeat: "Where do we come from? Where will we go?", all this is, in fact, to ask for The One which the experience of the faith confesses and announces as God.

The experience of God thus appears as the great way open to the so much hoped for dialogues of Christianity, not only with the modern world, but as well with the other religious traditions[2]. In the same way, it seems to us the privileged way for Christianity to advance always further in search of its own identity and the adequate means to make it known and proclaim it in language understandable to contemporary ears. The final objective of our exposition will be thus to look further into the characteristics of this experience at the heart of Christianity and to make it the subject of our reflection, which will allow us to arrive at

---

2. The question of God shows itself today as the path of possibility for the interreligious dialogue. Cf. the reflections on *theocentrism* which succeeds *christocentrism* in the attempts of Christianity to dialogue with other religions, in some recent works: J. DUPUIS, *Jésus Christ à la rencontre des religions*, Paris, Desclée, 1989; ID., *Les religions commes voies de salut?*, in *Spiritus* 33 (1992) 5-14; M. FITZGERALD, *Panorama du dialogue interreligieux et questions théologiques*, in *Spiritus* 33 (1992) 92-103. See also J. DUPUIS, *Vers une théologie du dialogue interreligieux*, Paris, Cerf, 1997.

some conclusions that we hope can contribute to the contemporary debate.

I. Crisis of Modernity and the Religious Question

Linked to a historical and structural crisis, the idea of modernity appears to be merely the symptom of that crisis, for instead of analysing it, it only expresses it, and only ambiguously, making work very difficult for the analysts and the intellectuals who, grounded in their specialities, endeavour to understand it and to grasp all the twists and turns of its significance[3].

Culturally, modernity was the period of the total secularisation of the arts and sciences; *economically*, it was the period marked by the primacy of productivity, of the exacerbated intensification of human work (the degenerated fruits of which one may see today with the passage from a civilisation of work and progress to a civilisation of consumption, of immediate and rapid obsolescence, and of leisure considered as pleasure without restraint); *politically*, it was the period of the transcendence abstracted from the State, bearing such marks as the institutionalisation of individualism and the private property; chronologically and temporally, it was the period of a new conception of time and of how one lives it: a chronometric, linear and historical time. Modernity thus carries, among its outstanding characteristics, that of no longer thinking of itself mythically, no more conforming to religious parameters (and, concretely, to a religion, Christianity) but to a new vision of the world, which claims to ignore the absolutes, to know and make a place for a new conception of the "kronos", where eternity is replaced by an always "contemporary" and universally "simultaneous" temporality[4].

The idea of progress – understood as capable of carrying more and more of the world forward, conquering it, and placing it at one's disposal by means of science and technology – is the foundation of the ethics of the modern person, the key to the allocation of his time and energies.

---

3. On this subject see what J. BAUDRILLARD says in *Modernité*, in *Encyclopaedia Universalis* 11 (1980) 139-141. He goes so far as to say that modernity "makes crisis a value, a contradictory morale".

4. See on this subject *ibid.*, p. 140. We place the citations in italics. See also what G. VATTIMO says in *La fin de la modernité* (n. 1), p. 9: "Seule la modernité confère une portée ontologique à l'histoire et une signification déterminante à notre situation dans le cours même de cette histoire". See morover the thesis proposed by H.C. DE LIMA VAZ, *Religião e modernidade filosófica* (n. 1), p. 150, "notre modernité est vieille d'au moins vingt-six siècles, ou à tant remonte la lignée des modernités à l'origine de la nôtre", demythologising the attempts which claim to show modernity as a chronologically postmedieval chronological "innovation".

It is especially important to achieve the goals dictated by the desire to progress, to succeed[5]. Instead of an ideology, of a system of practical directives for everyday life, the doctrines of irreversible and unlimited progress installs itself as a profession of faith, a belief and even, at certain moments, an apogee of faith in oneself. Believing themselves to be their own supreme being, disposing of science and technology to penetrate the most remote folds of knowledge and arriving at the most advanced dimensions of human ability, modern people conceive of themselves as privileged parameters, the highest points of reference for establishing what is positive or negative, real or imaginary, good or bad[6].

People thus intoxicated with their dominance over nature will necessarily have, as well in this as in anything else, relationships of domination and possession. It is not only a matter of a representation of human experience within the framework of a given phase of the evolution of science, technology, or productive forces. It is here a question of a phenomenon of organisation in depth, affecting a total way of orienting oneself within reality[7].

Anthropocentric by cultural configuration, modern people end up believing themselves – why deny it? – anthropocentric "in essence". On the way towards the never completed perfectibility of progress, they divorced themselves from nature and from their bonds with the environment, bringing about thereby that which presents itself today as the threat of a catastrophe on a planetary scale. And the imminent and in a sad way real risk of the destruction of the ecosystems is rooted in the bankruptcy of the model and the paradigms which, by ignoring nature, think of human beings as isolated and not as beings which form part of a larger whole[8].

---

5. See what J. MOLTMANN says on this subject in his book *Dios en la creación*, Salamanca, Sígueme, 1985. See also the interesting reflection on modern history that G. VATTIMO makes, *La fin de la modernité* (n. 1), p. 13, in characterising it as the search for a condition of innerworldly perfection which leads to the idea of progress, and in comparing it to the Christian conception of the history of salvation.

6. See on this subject M. GAUCHET, *Le désenchantement du monde* (n. 1), pp. 82-83.

7. Cf. J. MOLTMANN, *Dios en la creación*, especially the description of chapter 1, and moreover A. GARCIA RUBIO, *Unidade na pluralidade*, São Paulo, Paulinas, 1990, especially chapter 14, pp. 440-467. See also, more recently and from a different, more ethicophilosophical perspective, the book of N. MANGABEIRA UNGER, *O encantamento do humano. Ecologia e espiritualidade*, São Paulo, Loyola, 1991. Very recently, another work collects reflections on ecology under a distinctly Christian perspective: A. GARCIA RUBIO et al., *Reflexão cristã sobre o meio ambiente*, São Paulo, Loyola, 1992.

8. See, on the emancipation of man and the road to loneliness, L. GONZALEZ-CARVAJAL, *Ideas y creencias del hombre actual* (n. 1), pp. 87-110. See also P. VALADIER, *La Iglesia en proceso. Catolicismo y sociedad moderna*, Santander, Sal Terre, 1990, pp. 38-39 (ed. *Catolicismo e sociedade moderna*, São Paulo, Loyola, 1990).

The emancipating will of the individual, an integral part of his effort to dominate the world and material things, has proven to be a factor of an unceasingly growing isolation, by excluding him from any alliance, any authentic relationship, not only with material things, but also towards his fellow creatures. The anthropocentric ideology, pushed to its ultimate consequences, brings together the advent of modernity with that of the individual, by giving the individual to itself and by elevating it to the rank of the first and ultimate point of reference.

In so doing, it abandons the human being in loneliness, in isolation from those who should be its equals: other men and women. The poisoned corrupted fruits of modern anthropocentrism are a very clear symptom of this, revealing the distances and divisions within humanity: racism, ethnocentrism, "machismo", which discriminate human beings according to race, ethnicity, and sex.

In wanting to get rid of all that could inhibit its emancipating desire, the human being, to tell the truth, emancipated itself from itself and, in emancipating itself, ends up possessing, in the confusion of its values in crisis, only one thing: its own loneliness. The bankruptcy, painfully felt at the present time by several human groups, of the model or paradigm, of the structures and symbols of reference that would enable them to situate themselves in the world, is to tell the truth, only the experience of their own bankruptcy. Made for the relationships, they do not at all manage to establish the longed for relationships. Emancipated, they are chained to and controlled by the most despotic and terrible of oppressors: themselves, their own egos, which they passionately seek to maintain by accelerating the march towards success and power, while being helped by psychoanalysis, the means conceived and introduced by modernity to cure the wounds of which it is the cause.

All these proceedings have made of reason the great companion of the human person in search of self-understanding, of the assimilation of its personal existential identity, of its place in the world. Modernity, according to a considerably large number of its theorists, is characterised by a process of rationalisation[9].

Pitiless, reason excludes any concurring instance and makes its way compartmentalising the knowledge, and consequently, the *living* of human beings, sectioning off the domains, dividing the topics, schematising and

---

9. Cf., for example, M. WEBER, *Ensayos sobre sociología de la religión*, Vol. I, Madrid, Taurus, 1983. On page 19, in the Introduction, Weber starts reaching the roots of this rationality in Christianity. His thesis, according to us, is debateable, but we prefer to leave it until later. See morevoer on modernity as the era of reason what L. GONZALEZ-CARVAJAL says in *Ideas y creencias del hombre actual* (n. 1), p. 77.

segmenting reality, all in the name of a total comprehension, without restrictions, of the world, where the image of one integrated cosmic unity is broken into a thousand pieces. Its place is taken by a segmented vision, differentiated into subsystems, equipped with its own logic and a plurality of values[10].

Popularly called "the age of reason", modernity made it its goal to go all the way to the bottom of an all-encompassing rationality that claimed to completely explain reality. Nothing is real, nothing true, without the sanction of modernity.

In the face of this exclusion of all explanatory systems not of rational origin, the sacred and the religious are to some extent swept to the periphery of history. Characterised as prescientific and premodern, they see their importance vanishing, indeed their very centrality as the key to the explanation of reality. Unable to prove empirically or show "immediately" their utility, effectiveness, or functionality, they see their bankruptcy prophesied, their death decreed by victorious reason, by science, by the institutions born of modernity.

For humanity, answers must be sought in the *world*, and no longer in the *sacred* or the *transcendent*. This is what modernity – having arrived at the pinnacle of its functional reason – seemed to affirm: the emancipation of humanity from the myths and the gods who have prevented it from fully assuming its autonomy and freedom. This is the triumphal entry of the so-called phenomenon of *secularisation*, which has proceeded, one after the other, in removing the influence of religion from all domains of human life. All the duties fulfilled by society (political, economic, scientific) are "autonomised" with respect to religion, which ceases to inform them, not only with regard to their identity. But even in connection with their religious practice, in accordance with the practices of the Church on the matter, which confers on these duties a "temporal" character which is more and more accentuated [11].

With respect to individuals, modernity makes them pass from a predetermined religious situation, sociologically and culturally acquired by heritage, from being destined to a religious membership fixed in advance in the premodern world, to a plurality which involves the necessity of

10. Cf. J. MARDONES, *Postmodernidad y cristianismo* (n. 1), p. 20.
11. Cf. L. GONZALEZ-CARVAJAL, *Ideas y creencias del hombre actual* (n. 1), the chapter on secularisation, especially the distinction that he makes between *secularisation* and *secularism*, pp. 50-52. Cf. also P. VALADIER, *Société moderne et religion chrétienne. Analyse de philosophie sociale et politique*. And also, in the bibliography at the end of the text, the numerous reflections on the theme, given by M.C. AZEVEDO, a pioneer in the reflection on the theme of modernity and the secularisation in our country.

free choice[12]. In a world no longer completely religious, especially in a Western world once mainly and explicitly Christian, they must make their choices, their options, by taking account of this state of affairs.

It is undeniable that a modern society is one characterised in particular by the changes, radical and deep, which have occurred in its relationships towards itself, its traditions and, consequently, its religion. The term *secularisation* refers to the complex and pluriform phenomenon of the invasion of the rationalisation of the natural and social life, which entails the development of experimental science, the growth of a new relationship – of instrumentalisation, experimentation, effectiveness, calculation – of human reason with reality, in all its domains, including the confrontation with its customs, myths, beliefs, and traditions[13].

One cannot, however, consider the process of secularisation to be linear or inescapable, the primacy of instrumental reason to be homogeneous and free from conflicts. More and more, in the contemporary West, one perceives deep questionings, considerable critiques regarding the ingenuously omnipotent and optimistic pretension of instrumental reason, which often degenerates into the folly of political, economic, and scientific totalitarianism[14].

As it is not, to a great extent, the reason of the philosophers, even those who are devoted to pure science, but almost always the reason of the technicians, this type of reasoning is most appropriately named "instrumental reason", instead of releasing individuals and societies, risks making them instruments, enslaving them by strongly influencing the domain of intersubjective relationships, by eroding the major reference symbols by which human existence held onto its traditional structures[15].

The so-called crisis of modernity thus encloses the questioning of this state of affairs, characteristic of the evolution of the primacy of instrumental reason as the major point of reference for the modern society. Human beings, in approaching the end of the millennium, realise the fact that modernity, having brought numerous positive contributions to the advance of humanity, risks nevertheless banishing, or diluting the values and points of reference which are fundamental for their self-understanding as a human beings, for their identity and their life on earth.

12. Cf. S. BRETON, *La religion s'efface-t-elle de nos sociétés modernes? Libres propos sur Le désenchantement du monde de Marcel Gauchet*, in *Revue de sciences philosophiques et théologiques* 69 (1985) 556-567.

13. Cf. C. LIENKAMP, *New Religious Movements: A Theological Evaluation*, in *Research Project on New Religious Movements – Dossier – Supplement*, Rome, FIUC, 1990, p. 826, citing P. BERGER.

14. Cf. P. VALADIER, *Société moderne et religion chrétienne.*(n. 11), p. 2.

15. *Ibid.*, p. 3.

Among these values are the importance of desire and affectivity, the place which is due indisputably to the poetic and the symbolic in the production of knowledge, the capital relevance of gratuity as constituent of human life. And, as the modern paradigm falls into crisis and is found questioned at its deepest roots, other paradigms, like the one of post-modernity or the phenomenon of New Age, emerge on the horizon and attempt to replace it.

Without discussing the question of the validity of the naming of these allegedly new paradigms, we will restrict ourselves to considering the symptom expressed by the fact of the possibility of their existence[16]. As it appears modernity and its partner, instrumental reason, did not succeed in sealing off the primordial thirst, nor in bringing answers to the ultimate questions of humanity. Moreover, as reason was transmuted into "instrumental reason", it failed to exhaust the emancipatory potential which had broken through so strongly with the turning of so-called "modern times".

The modern paradigm, although on certain fronts full of force and strength, is giving clear signs of, at the very least, partial weakening and crisis. The ideology of progress finds itself questioned in-depth. It is doubtful that the social, political and economic systems which brought their best resources and energies to them, arrived at good port, at least when it comes to providing it with the means of answering the great questions about the meaning of existence and the finality of life, about which human hearts ceaselessly worry. Anthropocentrism is the daily target of the bombardment of the more or less moderate charges made by the various ecological movements, always with the cannon of denouncing and exposing the crimes committed on the planet by science and technology, in the name of development and progress[17].

II. RELIGION IN THE CRISIS OF MODERNITY: 'RETURN', 'DECLINE' OR 'NEW SYNTHESIS'?

There has been said and written much on the apparent reappearance of religious phenomenon, considering it as central in Western society at the end of the millennium. And, in the final analysis, one realises that all clear definitions and identifications leave something to be desired. Some

---

16. *Ibid.*, pp. 3-4; L. GONZALEZ-CARVAJAL, *Ideas y creencias del hombre actual* (n. 1), pp. 77-81, e.a.

17. See, on the question of postmodernity and the postmodern, among others, G. VATTIMO, *La fin de la modernité* (n. 1), pp. 169-171; 181-182; L. GONZALEZ-CARVAJAL, *Ideas y creencias del hombre actual* (n. 1), pp. 183-190; J.M. MARDONES, *Postmodernidad y cristianismo* (n. 1), pp. 59-78; D. HERVIEU-LÉGER, *Vers un nouveau christianisme?*, Paris, Cerf, 1986, p. 358.

speak about the "return of the sacred", of "new religiosity". But one can wonder whether the term "return" is really relevant. Is not that which one perceives as "new" actually very old – in the sense of traditional? Is it not perhaps true that the sacred, the religious, was never completely banished from modern society, but has remained under other names, other images, other forms in other spaces[18]?

The crisis of rationality and the so-called "return of religion" are two sides of the same coin, at a time when Western civilisation does the best it can to give a name to this turning point in its history. It is important, however, in speaking about these realities, to disentangle their distinctions and nuances. The crisis of rationality lived by the contemporary person concerns a particular model of rationality, just as the phrase "return of religion" or "new religiosity" does not mean to say that religion was banished from the horizon of reality. The hegemony of modernity never fully imposes itself on a society nor wins over all its domains. A modern society is, by definition, a society of contrasts and contradictions, which makes it very difficult, even impossible, for one to make hasty or simplistic judgements about it[19].

On the one hand, one can analyse how a society is led astray on the road of the visibility and the palpability of its religious expressions. If the faith of a religious community enters into the process of secularisation when it allows itself to be inscribed into the alternative *ideology* or *Utopia* and docs not understand itself any longer if not in terms of this alternative[20] – and one can say that this has occurred in a large measure during the process of Western modernity, "modern" in a different way than the official one[21]" – then one can still wonder whether does not

---

18. On the question "if there is present today a 'return' of the sacred and the religious", cf. among others, M. FRANÇA MIRANDA, *Volta do sagrado uma avaliação teológica*, in *Perspectiva Teológica* 21 (1989) 71-83; ID., *Ser cristão numa sociedade pluralista*, in *Perspectiva Teológica* 21 (1989), 33-349; L.A. GOMEZ DE SOUSA, *Secularização en declínio e potencialidade transformadora do sagrado*, in *Religião e sociedade* 132 (1986) 2-16; L.A. GOMEZ DE SOUSA, *Secularização e sagrado*, in *Síntese* 13 (1986) 33-49; J. SUDBRACK, *La nueva religiosidad. Un desafío para los cristianos*, Madrid, Paulinas, 1990.

19. Cf. C. LIENKAMP, *New Religious Movements: A Theological Evaluation* (n. 13), pp. 816-817; P. VALADIER, *Société moderne et religion chrétienne* (n. 11), p. 4; M. AZEVEDO, *Igreja, cultura e lelbertação*, in *Entrocamentos e entrechoques, Vivendo a fé num mundo plural*, São paulo, Loyola, 1991, pp. 71-74.

20. P. RICŒUR, *L'herméneutique de la sécularisation. Foi, idéologie, utopie*, in E. CASTELLI (ed.), *Actes d'un colloque organisé par le Centre International d'Études Humanistes et par l'Institut d'Études Philosophiques de Rome*, Paris, Aubier, 1976, p.60.

21. Cf. H.C. DE LIMA VAZ, *Religião e modernidade filosófica*, in M.C. BINGEMER (ed.), *O impacto da modernidade sobre a religião*, São Paulo, Loyola, 1992, pp. 83-107, who calls like this, that which, since the 19th century, is called simply "modernity".

exist in the modern and secularised West beside this "imprisonment" of religion, a contracting, a reducing of the great institutions which support the Western tradition. The vacuum thus formed opens an ever-growing space for the individual search for the religious or para-religious. One result of this is that this "supposedly" religious and spiritual search is often confused with the search for personal and private self-realisation, largely as a consequence a feeling of impotence, and of discouragement about the transformation of society[22].

The question of the situation of religion or of a possible "return" of the sacred is one of the most controversial in the modern world. On one side, assertions multiply themselves which would rather posit a "retirement" or the "invisibility" of religion within the framework of modernity. The arguments are varied. The very attempt to juxtapose them testifies to the enormous variety in their perspectives and origins. From the moment that "saying" and "doing" are separated from each other, belief and its religious expression are no longer possible[23]. The era of the religion as structure is finished, though not religion as culture. Religion has lost its social function though perhaps not its subjective role. The modern rupture of the 16th and 17th centuries is basically a religious one, resulting from an inversion in the hierarchical comprehension of the relationship between the human and the divine. Society has come into being without religion, but at the same time it is a society that was constituted, in its most important orderings, by the "metabolisation" of the religious function[24]. Modern life presents many sides with an autonomous development where religion no longer has any great say[25]. The sacred no longer constructs what it evokes, and the religion has from society – in concomitance with other ideologies and inconsistent legends – the function of collecting, in its *language* but not in its faith, any need, any repressed, badly expressed, almost unthinkable desire[26].

All these expressions aim at rendering an account, in a more or less happy way, of the so-called phenomenon of secularisation, one of most

22. Cf. J.L. SCHLEGEL, *Retour du religieux et christianisme. Quand de vieilles croyances redeviennent nouvelles*, in *Études* 362 (1985) 92.

23. Cf. L. PANIER, *Pour une anthropologie du croire. Aspects de la problématique chez Michel de Certeau*, in C. GEFFRÉ, ed., *Michel de Certeau ou la différence chrétienne*, Paris, Cerf, 1991, pp. 47-48, who goes back to the very words of M. de Certeau.

24. Cf. M. GAUCHET, *Le désenchantement du monde*, Paris, Gallimard, 1985, pp. 231, 234, 236.

25. Cf. L. DUPRÉ, *L'autre dimension. Essai de philosophie de la religion*, Paris, Cerf, 1977, p. 9.

26. Cf. M. DE CERTEAU, *Prendre les risques du présent*, in ID., *La faiblesse de croire*, Paris, Seuil, 1987, pp. 89-90; ID., *Penser le christianisme*, in *ibid.*, pp. 248-249.

fundamental characteristics of modern culture. However, would not understanding a modern society in terms of secularisation be to understand it according to a religious semantics? Would that not be understanding social reality by taking as point of reference its confrontation with the religious phenomenon that formerly constituted the most fundamental visibilisation of the aforementioned reality[27]? And, moreover, does not the secularisation which emerges from the Christian West and becomes the structural element of modern culture present a certain connaturality with the Christian message, at least in some of its principles, much more than it would with other religious cultures whose gestation and cultural evolution are free from any Judeo-Christian influence [28]?

If it is certain that modern society carries in its proposal the possibility of arriving at a construction of reality and of knowledge which would do without, to a great extent, transcendence and belief in God, one cannot deny that within our contemporary society was produced during the last decades a full displacement of the sacred on the route of the return to visible space of human life, contradicting hasty assertions in terms of desacralisation, secularisation, etc. Disappointed by some bad fruits of Western modernity – marked to a great extent by the materialism of consumption – humanity begins looking for new forms of expression for religion, which leaves hanging in the air the possibility of doubting that the "disenchantment" of the world really means the dissipation of the religious[29].

The current crisis seems to clarify more and more that it needs a lot for modernity and atheism to be synonymous. And this crisis makes one wonder whether to be the attempt to remove religion in modernity might not be an attempt to substitute, for the traditional Christian religion, a myth: that of modernity itself, which would shelter, under its rhetoric of emancipation, other "mythical" or "religious" components, such as the worship of freedom, the hope of the intra-history realisation, and the faith in universal solidarity[30].

To speak about the "return" of the sacred, of the "re-entry" of the religious, might not be very suitable. Perhaps instead of "return" or "re-entry" one could note the "permanence" of the religious, either in sacral forms considered "degraded" by modern reason (magic, esotericism, sect, etc), or as a vague adhesion to a fuzzy, anonymous transcendence,

---

27. Cf. P. VALADIER, *La Iglesia en proceso* (n. 8).
28. Cf. On this topic, see AZEVEDO, *Evangelização e cultura secular*, in *Entrocamentos e entrechoques*, São Paulo, Loyola, 1991, p. 85, nn. 6 et 7.
29. Cf. M. MESLIN, *L'expérience humaine du divin*, Paris, Cerf, 1988, pp. 52-53.
30. Cf. J.M. MARDONES, *Postmodernidad y cristianismo* (n. 1), p. 126.

resembling rather an energy, a force which does not even reach the level of deism. The religious that remains takes on unexpected forms which, while overflowing the limits of the historical Churches and their religious institutions which up to that point had always been the majority ones, make themselves not easily comprehensible, especially for those which belong to these Churches and have been formed by them[31]. What we see and live in our days, on the one hand brushes aside and minimises the religious and, on the other hand, can coexist and in fact does coexist with it.

The sacred, a reality over which man sees that he has no power, in spite of his efforts of conquest; that which envelopes him on all sides without his being able to name it or entirely understand it – the religious be it the unnameable that man dares to name, the transcendent – which while being expressed, transcends all forms of religious manifestation and expression – is present, although it is hidden, veiled, in the modern society which claimed to have banished it of the human horizon.

If, on the one side, the increasingly more varied and plural occurrence of the so-called new religious movements can give rise to the perception, in modern society, of a new configuration of religion, which estimate as momentary, superficial, transitory, destined for a rapid disappearance, then on another side, the transcendence, the divine, becomes increasingly more invisible and impalpable as it affirms itself in its identity of transcending[32].

This impalpability of the religious, while characteristic of Jewish monotheism, the cradle of Christianity, also characterises modernity. Modernity could thus be considered, perhaps paradoxically but nevertheless true, as the place of the revelation and the veiling of this Transcendence that the Judeo-Christian tradition has named God. It is at the same time a space of the withdrawal and manifestation of the religious[33].

At the moment when what is veiled or repressed, is brought to light, it is normally shown in the form of less "orthodox" figures, more wild and radical than before. This is what nowadays attends the resurgence of new religious movements, the great power of seduction of sects, as well as new and unsuspected forms of prophecy, magic, and astrology[34].

---

31. Cf. P. VALADIER, *La Iglesia en proceso* (n. 8), p. 4.

32. On this subject, cf. R. OTTO, *Lo Santo. Lo Racional y lo irracional en la idea de Dios*, Madrid, Alianza Editorial, 1980, esp. pp. 14-21.

33. Cf. S. BRETON, *La religion s'efface-t-elle de nos sociétés modernes?* (n. 12), pp. 569-570.

34. M. DE CERTEAU calls this phenomenon *retour du refoulé*. Cf. ID., *La faiblesse de croire* (n. 26), p. 254.

On the other hand, in such a pluri-religious world, this revealing can occur by way of an anarchistic combination of alluring options, where the individual avails himself of the various religious goods put at his disposal as he would do with consumer goods at the supermarket[35]. Places of transition, no longer of durable permanence, religions are sought as objects necessary at precise moments, to meet specific needs in the lives of individuals, while the religious sciences take the form of a knowledge of an unstable, fugitive object, and even as the subject of objectivation, which can be described as observable, empirical phenomenon[36].

Many reasons have been advanced to explain this visibilisation of the religious under new groundings and forms in modern Western society. We enumerate, *inter alia*, the threat of an ecological hecatomb which brings up the imminent possibility of the extinction of Western civilisation and even of the entire planet; the bankruptcy of counterculture, dominant all throughout the 1960s and first years of the 1970s, which claimed to reject the world such as it is, awaking the desire for a change and a withdrawal of the individual into himself, with the consequence of the bankruptcy of the project of social transformation – in all its forms – which collapses and loses its mobilising capacity[37]. The modern critique (Marxist, Freudian, Nietzschean) of modernity, far from nullifying the demand for religion, will have supported its revival, leading contemporary Western society to a very different and disconcerting phenomenon, which hardly agrees with a rationalist theory of progressive and inescapable secularisation. And this event might be perhaps only the beginning of a inevitable process inherent in individualistic societies such as ours[38].

The fact is that the apparently massive incredulity, characteristic of our time, has been crossed by the currents of spiritual concern. And this so-called – whatever the exactitude of the expression – new religiosity or new religious conscience, appears to be the confused result of a mixture of cultures and religions on a planetary scale, named "the enigma of our backward march in history". Religion continues to be, if not an enigma, at least a compelling question for contemporary people. No longer an instrument of legitimation or "social destiny", or a key to the

35. Cf. P. VALADIER, *La Iglesia en proceso* (n. 8), p. 87.

36. Cf. H.C. DE LIMA VAZ, *Religião e modernidade filosófica* (n. 1), p. 106. The phrase "places of transition", which we have mentioned in making allusion to the new religious search is from M. DE CERTEAU, who selected it as the title of one of the essays in his work *La faiblesse de croire* (n. 26), pp. 227-252.

37. Cf. D. HERVIEU-LEGER, *Vers un christianisme nouveau?* (n. 17), pp. 151, 162, 185, 333.

38. Cf. P. VALADIER, *La Iglesia en proceso* (n. 8), pp. 69, 76, 83.

comprehension and organisation of reality, but something radical, not only once freely given but still wished, without which the human being is able only with difficulty to only understand himself. Even the most sour and sceptical of the critics of the phenomenon of the religion recognise that if we (moderns) give up the religious in all senses of the term, it does not abandon us and, however finished its career in terms of effectiveness may be, we might never have ceased confronting it[39].

However far one might carry out the description of religious behaviours and the analysis of their forms, the question of its fundamental "why" remains. This is the limit of any functional analysis: religious discourse is the only base of the action, since it institutes action and imposes standards on it[40]. However incapable it might be of bringing technical solutions to the problems of the present time, religion remains the only authority able to relativise the values in the whole of the reality according to its scale of representation[41].

The forms assumed nowadays by the religious search, which expresses itself in so-called "new movements", have persisted for more than twenty years now in the industrialised Western societies. Serious accusations have been made against them. In the first place, they are accused of being irrational and psychologically dangerous. This charge is based on the diagnoses of psychiatrists attesting that the affiliation of the neophyte is obtained by psychological coercion followed by other processes, including brainwashing. It is also charged that they are not as "new" as they claim, considering that they are making use of disciplinary characteristics and ways of formation whose rigour equalises or exceeds that of the monastic orders of the Middle Ages[42].

On the other hand, their followers testify to having found a reason to live, the expansion of their ego, the escape from the narrowness of a limited daily life and the feeling that they are contributing to the advent of a new era[43]. Those who, moved at the deepest level of their affectivity, seek and join the so-called new religious movements, are not led there by rational motivation. And yet could the search for significance and love – without any doubt an essential component of their experiences – be also open to rejection as not-human?

---

39. Cf. M. GAUCHET, *Le désenchantement du monde* (n. 1), p. 67.
40. Cf. M. MESLIN, *L'expérience humaine du divin* (n. 29), p. 16.
41. Cf. *Ibid.*, p. 16.
42. Cf. G.D. CHRYSSIDES, *Can New Faiths Be Reasonable?*, in *Research Project on New Religious Movements – Dossier*, pp. 9-11. See also, C. LIENKAMP, *New Religious Movements: A Theological Evaluation* (n. 13), p. 834.

III. HISTORICAL CHRISTIANITY AND NEW RELIGIOSITY

Historical Christianity, called to confront itself with the new forms of religious expression, finds there only rare points of agreement. The new movements oppose, to the faith in a God revealed and incarnated in Jesus Christ and currently present through the Spirit in the Church – the original and characteristic core of the Christian faith – the belief in reincarnation and karma, the expectation of a new world era, and the law of the cosmic cycles. According to the members of these movements, the goal of individual existence is spiritual realisation, just as the awakening of a planetary conscience is a fundamental principle of collective existence. The anthropology subjacent to these movements makes the body the place of cosmic integration. This cosmic dimension, radically anti-anthropocentric, would also encompass what in Christianity would be christology and the idea of God. The latter, conceived of as ultimate reality and considered central to any religious system, is far from the idea and the experience of the God of the Judeo-Christian tradition, who is at the same time transcendent and also close, personal, nameable and relational[44].

The qualifier "sects" – nowadays usually attributed without distinction to all non-traditional religious groups – brings out their points of contrast with historical and settled Churches which serve as a point of reference for the comprehension and analysis of the aforesaid groups[45].

In spite of all criticism – relevant or not – addressed to them, the fact is that these new religious movements raise deep and provocative questionings to our modern society. When the protective structures which keep at bay the confrontation with the possibility of emptiness and absurdity fall apart during times of historical and social changes, it is natural for the ultimate question to emerge and be discussed. The loss of significance and identity in modernity-in-crisis leads more and more people to search for the foundations of what they are or aspire to be. And

---

43. Cf. P. PELLETIER, *Dimension socio-affective de l'adhésion aux nouvelles religions*, in *ibid.*, pp. 93, 109. See also what D. HERVIEU-LEGER says on this affective and emotional dimension in the development of new religions movements in *Vers un christianisme nouveau?* (n. 17), pp. 144-145.

44. Cf. J.A. SALIBA, *"Religious" Themes in the New Religious Movements*, in *Research Project on New Religious Movements – Dossier*, p. 149; J. VERNETTE, *Jésus dans la nouvelle religiosité*, in *Ibid.*, 245-247. See also the assessment of F.B. DE AVILA, *As igrejas cristãs históricas e a variedade de expressões religiosas*, in *Síntese. Nova Fase* 18 (1991) 167-189.

45. Cf. typology in P. VALADIER, *La Iglesia en proceso* (n. 8), pp. 77-78.

during this search, they can make the encounter with the new religious groups which everywhere abound increasingly more numerous[46].

Observing them, noting the negation that they bring to the modern theories about the death of God and the end of religion, one can examine other topics no less important and which raise very relevant questions with regard to religion, philosophy, and theology. As, for example, the evidence of the fact that we live in a time when experience, if one cannot affirm that it is stronger than reason, must at least find next to it a place with the same degree of importance.

New religious forms grant absolute priority to direct experience over metaphysical reasoning. They are interested in the person here and now, more than with an eternal future; they are directed towards a harmonious relationship with nature rather than regulating the use of it[47]. Without ignoring the risks of alienation and immobility that they can run, one cannot in some respect be unaware of the great question which they leave in the air and which touches on the heart of modernity, secularised in itself, and the institutional forms of living out faith and religion within the framework of this same modernity. Finally, the new religious movements raise the great question which provokes that unique always necessary discussion: the question of Transcendence, of the ultimate base foundation which is revealed as a radical otherness, which attracts and at the same time frightens the human heart, which constitutes the unique common ground open to the interreligious dialogue and the discernment of the religious facts at the present time.

Posing questions about the significance and the transcendent dimension of existence, in the midst of the current crisis of values and the lack of models, implies, necessarily, turning to the only true religious question: what is it that one can, in an authentic way, call God. Religion is the human expression that seeks to put a face on the transcendent initiative which "seizes" and "possesses" humankind in the course of the meanderings of history and reality. Seized, possessed by this reality which he does not always manage to name, man continues to be seduced by it and to seek from it the answer to the questions which at the same time ravish him, torment him, dazzle him and frighten him[48].

---

46. See on this subject J.B. CHETHIMATTAM, *New Religious Movements and Popular Religiosity*, in *Research project on New Religious Movements – Dossier*, Rome, FIUC, 1990, pp. 617-635.

47. Cf. M. MESLIN, *L'expérience humaine du divin* (n. 29), p. 44; J. COLEMAN, *Les nouveaux mouvements religieux*, in *Concilium* 181 (1983), p. 9.

48. Cf. on this dimension of the encounter with God as an experience of seduction and at the same time of fear, R. OTTO, *Lo Santo*, pp. 22-37: *Mysterium tremendum.* (see also my work, *A sedução do sagrado*, in *Religião e Sociedade* 16 (1992) 82-93.)

IV. A POST-CHRISTIAN, POST-MODERN CHRISTIANITY

The present time is for Christianity, in this context of the crisis in modernity and its more or less immediate consequences, and of change on the world religious scene, a moment of difficulty and richness at the same time, where the new contours of society – in which it finds itself a proposal for community and religious life – oblige it to take up the search for an unceasingly renewed understanding of its identity, place and image.

This search, however, is not free from conflicts. A problematic thing, a source of uneasiness for some, of perplexity according to others, Christian identity today does not seem to facilitate the task of those who try to interpret and understand it[49]. It may be that this "hermeneutic gap", which commits us to penetrate every further whenever the question is about defining what constitutes the core identity of the vital experience of being a Christian, properly belongs to Christianity ever since its historical origins. The paradoxical and indissoluble alliance of the flesh and the spirit, of man and divine, brought into the heart of human reality by Jesus-Christ, the Word Incarnate, leaves to humanity the "impossible" task of expressing in human words the unutterable divine. It is hardly astonishing that the hermeneutic and discursive gap thus inaugurated continues to be the source of perplexity and problem to those who seek to approach it[50].

Western civilisation is today in the presence of a Christianity which image differs from the traditional face with which this same civilisation could have identified itself for a long time. It concerns a Christianity which, in sifting through modernity, did not come out of it unscathed. If, on the one hand, in speaking about modernity one evokes the process of secularisation as one of its central characteristics; and, moreover, if this process could mean, among other things, the "disappearance" or the "veiling" of the religious in all its denominations, including the Christian one, on the other hand, precisely because of its characteristics of incarnation of immersion in reality and the world, Christianity is sometimes presented – rightly so it seems to us – as the only religion preferentially able to seal an alliance with modernity and to survive it, effecting a new synthesis on the basis of the crises themselves that are awaken

---

49. Cf., for example, the recent works of C. PALACIO, *A identidade problemática (sobre o mal-estar cristão)*, in *Perspectiva Teológica* 21 (1989) 151-177; M. DE FRANÇA MIRANDA, *Um homem perplexo. O Cristão na sociedade*, São Paulo, Loyola, 1989; or moreover, of D. HERVIEU-LEGER, *Vers un christianisme nouveau?* (n. 17), Chapitre II.

50. Cf. M. GAUCHET, *Le désenchantement du monde* (n. 1), p. 189, "hermeneutic gap" to express the challenge of the Incarnation.

within it with the advent of modern times. Modernity is the cultural and
social matrix where the totality of the social, human and spiritual relations and creations over the last centuries was formed. And Christianity
inscribes itself there, although contradictorily as a historical fact and a
factor of institutional agency.

While able to make an alliance with modern society and culture,
Christianity is called to nothing less than setting itself up as an authority
critical of this same modernity. By refusing the convenient position of
taking a utopian distance from the crisis where its time and its civilisation find themselves, Christianity, faithful to the dictates of the logic of
Incarnation, is obliged to assume a presence in the world, in social,
political, and cultural reality; a presence both authentic and lucid,
engaged and critical. Not fearing to be situated in society and within
modern culture does not mean being in complicity with its various
defects nor demeaning the courage to denounce the wrongs of the time
or to take up the challenge of symbolising an order of the things different from the non-values and ethical and intellectual imperatives that
form the background of modern Western development, unceasingly conveyed via all the roads available to a technological civilisation[51].

It seems important to us to seek to understand all the implications of
the assertion – undoubtedly problematic for some – that the Christian
project, in addition to maintaining its vitality in the face of modernity,
can also associate with it without losing its identity, without ceasing to
exist. If, on the one hand, Christendom, as a totalising cultural and religious project, is proven anachronistic nowadays, on the other hand, it
cannot be denied that the Christian fact remains alive and visible, for all
that it presents today new perspectives and a different image. Marginalised in social life, it appears rather like an individual private business,
no longer shaping, in the same way or with the same degree as before,
the whole of society and culture. It continues to be present, however, and
to have some say in the space that it occupies at the present time[52].

The fact that Christianity finds itself today in crisis of identity could,
to a great extent, be attributed to a secular practice of perceiving itself as
a grounding principle for the comprehension and interpretation of reality, associated with a very pronounced ecclesiocentrism, which has led
to the idea that Christianity derives only, or at least mainly, from the

---

51. Cf. on this subject what J.M. MARDONES says in *Postmodernidad y cristianismo*
(n. 1), p. 87; D. HERVIEU-LEGER, *Vers un christianisme nouveau?* (n. 17), p. 319.
52. Cf. on this identification of Christianity as a critique of Christianity on modernity,
P. VALADIER, *La Iglesia en proceso* (n. 8), pp. 131, 132, 137; see also J.M. MARDONES,
Postmodernidad y cristianismo (n. 1), p. 122.

ecclesial institution. And this crisis is certainly not without relation to the fact that, in undergoing the impact of the awakening of the modern process that forced the doors of the Church in an enslaving irruption, numerous historians, theologians and other thinkers – Christian and not – wondered, at a certain moment of mid-century, if Christianity might not be dying or ready to shatter[53].

We come to the threshold of the millennium, and it seems that Christianity continues to live, though under features rather different from those it held formerly. Immersed in the crisis of the modern society with which it is associated, it receives a good share of the questionings addressed to this same society, which obliges it to rethink itself as a proposition, as a relation. Starting from the Christian proposal, there emerges a basic ambivalence of which the result is a kind of relationship to the religion which neither constitutes a pure and simple refusal of modernity nor a pure and simple alternative to the values of the modern world[54].

V. NEW QUESTIONS AND NEW SUBJECTS AT THE HEART OF HISTORICAL CHRISTIANITY

As being *anthropocentric*, modern Christianity is questioned by the alternative movements and the ecological interrogation initiated by the apocalyptic threat that weighs on the planet. Even if the central axe of Christian thinking, discourse and acting has, in the postconciliary phase, passed from the ecclesiocentrism mentioned above to a more marked christocentrism, which seeks in the reflection on the person and project of Jesus Christ, the essence of the identification of being Christian, Christianity is no less anthropocentric. Or, better said, this will have emphasised even more strongly its anthropocentric characteristics. It is in the name of growth, of the development and of the full realisation of the man, the centre of the theological and pastoral concerns of the Church, that the most significant Christian movements of the last decades were constituted and assembled[55]. This anthropocentrism is

53. We refer here to the celebrated works produced in Europe in the last decades, in which the titles let mesure something of the content: L.E. MOUNIER, *Feu la chrétienté*, Paris, Seuil, 1950; W.H. VAN DE POL, *O fim do cristianismo convencional*, São Paulo, Herder, 1969; M. DE CERTEAU & J.M. DOMENACH, *Le christianisme éclaté*, Paris, Seuil, 1974; J. DELUMEAU, *Le christianisme va-t-il mourir?*, Paris, Hachette, 1977. See also, even if from a quite different perspective, the book of the American thinker J. NEEDLE-MAN. *Lost Christianity*, San Francisco, Harper & Row, 1985.

54. Cf. D. HERVIEU-LEGER, *Vers un christianisme nouveau?* (n. 17), p. 16.

55. We refer here principally to the movements more centered on the struggle for justice, social and political militantism, etc., and to the currents of theological thought that derive from them. In Latin America, concretely, we note the whole of the ecclesial

based on christology, on Jesus-Christ, Lord of the Church and Redeemer of humankind[56].

Ecology poses itself as a question to a Christianity thus anthropologically constituted, and opens it up to a fuller reflection on the totality of creation, on nature and on aspects of the Christian proposal other than the anthropological one. The repercussion of this question at the heart of the Christianity of today obliges it to enlarge its reflection, even on its own identity, to include more than just the anthropological angle. This new perspective brings important consequences to the understanding of many aspects of the Christian revelation, even to what concerns God, its central object of interest and that which its organisation flows from and to. The experience and vision of God as Creator, not only of humankind but of all that exists, and the implications of the centrality of creation as the act of God that inaugurated history are unceasingly studied in the work of important theologians of the Christian Churches, Catholic or Protestant[57].

Other alternative movements – the *feminist movement, black movements*, and all those that deal with the *indigenous cause and cultures –* address themselves in their turn to the inside of historical Christianity and question the decidedly masculine institutional configuration, conceived and organised according to the model of white, developed, European society. In making one hear other voices and rendering visible other subjects in the life of the Church, these movements raise and bring under attention aspects of Christianity barely touched upon until very recently, or rework, on the basis of their own experiences, certain old and traditional aspects from other angles and from other perspectives[58].

mobilisation set off by the Medellin Episcopal Conference in 1968, and the three axes that fundamentally regulate a good part of the life of the Church after that date: the struggle for justice, the laying out of base communities and a theological thought founded on the reality of the most impoverished.

56. Cf. the encyclical of Pope JOHN PAUL II, *Redemptor hominis*, the first of his pontificate.

57. Cf. the ever more numerous reflections on ecology that populate the world of Christian publications. We underline two: J. MOLTMANN, *Dios en la creación*, Salamanca, Sígueme, 1985; A. GESCHÉ et alii, *Création et salut*, Bruxelles, publications des Facultés Universitaires Saint Louis, 1989. It is equally worth mentioning, in Asian theology of recent times, the global tendancy to underline, in a special way, the element of the cosmos and creation in its reflection. Cf. above all the work of theologians such as S. RAYAN, T. BALASURYIA, M. AMALADOSS, among others. We refer also, in terms of a more Latin American and Brazilian work, to the recent book of A. GARCIA RUBIO, *Unidade na pluralidade*, especially chapter 14. And also to the recent publication of A. GARCIA RUBIO et alii, *Reflexão cristã sobre o meio ambiente*, São Paulo, Loyola, 1992, chapter 1, note 6.

58. It seems impossible to enumerate here all the works published in recent times on the question of women and on racial and ethical questions. We cite some examples that

VI. CHRISTIANITY AND INTERRELIGIOUS DIALOGUE

The other line of questioning addressed to Christianity today concerns ecumenism and the ecclesial dialogue. It is not only about the intra-ecclesial dialogue between the various trends found inside of one Church but even more about an interreligious dialogue in which Christianity and other religions seek together points of reference for a convergence that can lead to a common ground[59]. This includes the lines of questioning addressed to traditional Christian Churches from the great not-Christian religions as well as from new religious movements.

Though they are criticised many times for their morals not strictly conforming to the doctrinal and ethical principles of Judaism and Christianity, the fact is that several of new religious movements have a rather strict moral code, sometimes even more than is the case in the Judeo-Christian frame of reference itself. We could cite, as an example, "Santo Daime", an ecologically based religion, present especially in the north of Brazil, where it is normal that the members cultivate values such as chastity and even virginity and where hierarchical relationships to the authorities of the movement testify to the deference and respect towards the ranks and various stations of the persons of the group[60].

aim more closely at the question of the relationship between modernity and Christianity: J. CONE, *A Black Theology of Liberation*, New York, Pippincott Company, 1970; H. ASS-MANN et al., *Teologia negra – Teologia de la liberación*, Salamanca, Sígueme, 1974; S. BENHABIB & D. CORNELL (ed.), *O feminismo como crítica da modernidade*, Rio de Janeiro, Rosa dos Tempos, 1991; M.C. BINGEMER (ed.), *O mistério de Deus na mulher*, Rio de Janeiro, ab 1990; *O segredo feminino do mistério*, Petrópolis, Vozes, 1991; X. PIKAZA, *La mujer en las grandes religiones*, Bilbao, DDB, 1991.

59. Cf. the ever more numerous works over the last years on this subject. We cite the following: H. KÜNG, *El cristianismo y las grandes religiones*, Madrid, Europa, 1987; A. GESCHÉ, *Le christianisme et les autre religions*, in *Revue théologique de Louvain* 19 (1988) 315-341; J. DUPUIS, *Jésus Christ à la rencontre des religions* (n. 2); *Vers une théologie chrétienne des religions*, Paris, Cerf, 1998 among others. Cf. also F. COUTO TEIXEIRA, *Teologia das religiões. Uma visão panorâmica*, São Paulo, Paulinas, 1995, with a new large bibliography. On the dialogue from pneumatological perspective, see also my: *A pneumatologia como possibilidade de diálogo e missão universais*, in F. COUTO TEIXEIRA (ed.) *Diálogo de pássaros*, São Paulo, Paulinas, 1993, pp. 111-121; *The Holy Spirit as Possibility of Universal Dialogue and Mission*, in L. SWIDLER & P. MOJZES (ed.), *Christian Mission and Interreligious Dialogue* (Religions in Dialogue, 4), Lewiston – Queeston – Lampeter, The Edwin Mellen Press, 1990, 34-41.

60. Cf. the various works on this religious movement published recently. We cite the following: L.E. SOARES, *O Santo Daime no contexto da nova consciência religiosa*, in *Cadernos do ISER* 23 (1990) 265-274; R. ABREU, *A doutrina do Santo Daime*, in *Cadernos do ISER* 23 (1990) 253-274; M. CAMURÇA, *Da alternativa para a sociedade a uma sociedade alternativa*, in *Cadernos Atualidade em Debate I* (1990) 19-36. Cf. on this subject the commentary of J.A. SALIBA, *Religious Themes in the New Religious Movements*, in *Research Project on New Religious Movements – Dossier*, Rome, FIUC, 1990, pp. 156-157.

The figure of Jesus, central to Christianity, also appears in these movements, but from a point of view other than that of the Christian tradition; his death and resurrection are questioned, and consequently so is his divinity[61]. Other figures of Christianity, such as Mary and the saints, are invoked by several of these movements, without however fulfilling there the same role as they do in Catholicism.

In these movements the communitarian dimension is very strong; it is surprising to note that certain new forms of Christian communitarian search (the Charismatic Revival and other groups frequented by Catholics and non-Catholics) are similar to them both in terms of motivation (marked by a strong affectivity) and in the expression of connectedness. It should however be recognised that these groups, criticised for "alienation" by others more aware of and engaged in the historical Churches, show several features similar to those of the so-called new religious movements, while remaining inside the institution of the church, and having, like them, a great capacity for attraction and recruitment.

In the analysis of this whole, the sects constitute a phenomenon apart[62]. Of a rather fundamentalist stamp, they always keep, though in a veiled way, a protesting attitude towards traditional Christianity, especially with regard to the Catholic Church, which is reproached for soiling the purity of the Gospel. At the present time, by accentuating the eschatological principle of a millenarist coupé, as well as the pneumatic-spiritual principle, in opposition to the preponderant role of the dogma in the Church according to their interpretation, the sects enjoy a very marked seductive power and gain contingents of increasingly more people who participate in their rituals in an increasingly intense way.

Even in considering all their ambiguous aspects, one can legitimately wonder if the seduction, increasingly stronger, exerted by the sects even to former members of the historical Christian churches, might not be the equivalent of a serious questioning addressed to these same churches.

---

61. On the manner in which the figure of Jesus is present in the new religiosity, see the book of J. VERNETTE, *Jésus dans la nouvelle religiosité* (n. 44), as well his most recent article, by the same name, in *Research Project on New Religious Movements – Dossier*, Rome, FIUC, 1990, pp. 245-272.

62. We employ here the term "sects" according to the definition of Max Weber, who opposed the concept of "sect" to that of the "church", but in asscribing to it the characteristic that seem to fit better with the mode of organisation of religious groups, in Brazil and in other parts of the world, which are called "sects"; people who believe in Jesus, gather together around the Bible, with ritual that is marked by the affective and emotional, claiming direct inspiration from the Holy Spirit who speaks throug the mouth of the faithful, whoever that might be, without hierarchical rigorism. On the discussion of the concept, see P.F.C. DE ANDRADE, *Sinais dos tempos: Igrejas e seitas no Brasil*, in *Perspectiva Teológica* 23 (1991) 223-240, especially pp. 224-225.

One may wonder if the success of the sects in the diffusion of their proposal and message – with all the ambiguity associated with the methods and means employed – would not have something to say to the historical Christian churches about the coldness of their liturgies, about the bureaucratisation of their institution, about the necessity of reconsidering the affective dimension of the communication of their proposal[63].

Eastern religions and Islam are other religious traditions that present themselves as instances of interpellation and dialogue with regard to Christianity. In the West today, and even inside the Church, it is not uncommon to employ techniques and elements of Eastern religious source with the intent of coming to the aid of the practices of prayer and meditation of the Western Christians. The charm exerted by these traditions, these thousand-year-old schools of meditation and prayer, is at the origin of the rediscovery, by many Christians – old and new – of the contemplative dimension, inherent in all Christian life and apparently relegated to a secondary place because of the value placed on action, on liberating historical engagement, the necessity and urgency of which are underlined.

There is however, inherent in this process of rediscovery, this borrowing of techniques of prayer to aid in the experience of God, the ambiguity and the risk of assuming the worldview and the doctrinal contents of these traditions, which at many points fundamentally diverge from Christianity[64].

Basically, the great challenge, the great scandal, for Christianity in the multi-religious world of today continues to be the faith in Jesus-Christ,

---

63. See on this subject R. BERGERON, *Les sectes et l'Église catholique*, in *Research Project on New Religious Movements – Dossier*, Rome, FIUC, 1990, pp. 599-616. See also my text *A sedução do Sagrado* (n. 48), pp. 82-93. See moreover what J. HORTAL says in his address to the 30ᵗʰ General Assemby of the Episcopal Conference of Brazil (CNBB) (cited in the introduction to this work, Note 3). Although in referring more closely to Brazil, its pertinence is even more ample, in our view. The accusations that he enumerates of the sects against the the Catholic Church, are, among others, the following: the weight of the institution, the quasi-federative structure of the Catholic Church, etc. Also on pages 4-5, he gives some of the principle motivations of those who have abandoned the Catholic Church for the sects: deeper personal relationships, the emotion of the supernatural and the search for the wonderful, immediate solution to alarming problems, and the privatisation of religion.

64. The Congregation for the Doctrine of the Faith draws attention to these risks in the document *Lettre aux évêques de l'Église catholique sur quelques aspects de la méditation chrétienne*, issued in 1990. The difficulty resides mostly in the consequences of brainwashing that could occur from these techniques and in which the consequence could be the bringing of the faithful to turn their back on the horizon of the Incarnation, essential to the attendance upon and understanding of the Christian mystery, and thus to Christian prayer and meditation.

Son of God and Universal Saviour. Recognising and proclaiming the singularity of the event of the Incarnation of the God whom no one has ever seen and yet who is revealed in the historical particularity of Jesus of Nazareth is an inescapable requirement of Christianity. On another side, this is what is more and more contested by other religions, who support the thesis that there are mediations other than that of Jesus for the revelation of God. And the same thing can be found in those currents inside Christianity, which propose to reconsider the unicity of Jesus[65].

However, the interreligious dialogue is not without an offer of hope and prospects to Christianity at the present time, concretely, to the measure that it obliges Christian theology to make theocentrism and the mystical experience or the experience of God the starting point of its discourse, and moreover obliges it to find the balance between the pneumatological way and the Christological way in reflecting and developing the concept, idea and experience of God[66]. In this way of true conversion to the other religious confessions, of sincerity in the joint effort to arrive at approval and dialogue, Christianity realises the immense difficulty, even the impossibility, of giving up that which constitutes the deepest part of its identity: faith in Jesus-Christ, Word of God incarnate in historical time and space, which disrupts, in incarnating itself, the very idea of time and space that had governed human spirit and life. It is this new temporality which Christianity inaugurates and celebrates in history by inventing an "other" time, liturgical time – which is merely the annual repetition of sidereal time by the remembering of the Incarnation and the entire life of Jesus [67].

Christianity, today as always, is called to find in the secularised, postmodern and multi-religious world, a new but faithful way of "saying"

---

65. Cf., for example, such works as the one of P. KNITTER, *No other name? A critical survey of christian attitudes toward the world religions*, Maryknoll, Orbis, 1985. Cf. also the writings of M. AMALADOSS, R. PANNIKAR and others. The matter is also commented upon by J. DUPUIS. *Pour une théologie du dialogue*, in ID., *Jésus Christ à la rencontre des religions* (n. 2), pp. 299-313.

66. In opening up quite a number of perspectives, the document of the Pontifical Council for Interreligious Dialogue, *Diálogo e anúncio* (19th May 1991) constitutes without doubt an important contribution to this process.

67. Cf. the beautiful pages of M. MESLIN on this subject, *L'expérience humaine du divin* (n. 29), pp. 146-147. See also, on the circling that is brought about in time by the Christ event, H. C DE LIMA VAZ, *Religião e modernidade filosófica* (n. 1), p. 105, where he qualifies as anachronistic non-philosophical civilisations, as diachronistic our philosophical civilisation, and as *catachronic* Christianity, since it recuperates and saves the time that is passing by, by referring it to the unrepeatable and unique singularity of Christ, from now on the permanent present, the single "modern" that never passes away.

the God who is at the centre of its identity, of tracing the contours of His profile in a way that can be contemplated by our contemporaries.

VII. The God of Christianity: the Possibility of a Profile?

It would be rather simple to enumerate in a few pages the attributes and the characteristics of the God whom the Christian faith adores by naming him and calling upon him as Father, Son and Holy Spirit. Twenty centuries of Church history and theology would supply an abundance of material of incontestable orthodoxy, allowing us to carry out this task at the level which is possible and of sufficient adequacy. And yet the ineffability of the mystery of God would necessarily lead us to a stopping point, where our poor human language would acknowledge itself to be incapable of describing what happens only in the deepest part of the human being: the experience of this God. This experience is, however, the inevitable way of access to the knowledge of this same God in a way that is not purely theoretical, which would risk not even approaching the true core God's being, existing and acting.

The current situation of Christianity, and thus that of the theme of God, could be to a great extent summarised in the following observation. After the centuries-old conviction that the other religions or religious traditions revolve around Christianity, which was considered to be the centre of world religious phenomenon taken as a whole, it is now time to recognise that the centre around which all the religious traditions revolve, *including* Christianity, is God[68]. The concept of God, or the Transcendent, or Ultimate Reality, is considered basic to all religious systems, considering that it gives a meaning to the world in general and to human life in particular. The authentic religious question thus continues to be – in spite of the whole process of modernity, the crisis of secularisation and other phenomena – precisely that which relates back to that which humans can authentically call God[69].

One of the pretensions of modernity has been to withdraw the question of God from the horizon of humanity. In trying to define it, one says that secularisation is precisely the process, active or passive, of the return to the *saeculum*, that is to say to the profane world, from a reality

---

68. On this matter, see J. Dupuis, *Quelle théologie chrétienne des religions?*, in *Jesus Christ à la rencontre des religions* (n. 2), p. 137. Affirming what he calls a change of paradigm, the author quotes the title of the early work of the English author J. Hick, *Christianity at the Centre* (London, McMillian, 1968) a paradigm which would have occurred since then of an evolution towards a greater interreligious 'inclusivism'.

69. In *Research Project on New Religious Movements – Dossier*, Rome, FIUC, 1990, p. 149; see also J. Vernette, *Jésus dans la nouvelle religiosité* (n. 44), p. 13.

that was closely related to God and religion. Modernity and secularisation may be thus deeply connected, gathering even from this fact a positive evaluation if one considers the secularised civilisation as superior
to those which are not. It concerns the civilisation of rationality, of
emancipation on all levels, where humanity, having left its infancy,
would no longer need a Supreme Being or an Absolute Subject which
would dictate to it the standards of conduct and organisation[70].

The crisis of modernity, far from throwing this process to the ground,
raises its principal banners and proposes to radicalise the cultural and
conceptual "death" of God. Beside the reappearance of the religious,
analysed in the preceding section, atheism has not disappeared from the
Western horizon. And it is no longer a matter of an unspecified atheism
or of a pure and simple non-religiosity. It is actually a matter of a religious indifference which does not concern itself at all with trying hard to
reason out the existence or non-existence of God[71].

Modern times basically recommend the very disappearance of God
and any trace of his existence. There is more: while modern atheism
denied God in order to affirm a human project – the death of God would
be the price to be paid so that autonomy and human freedom might
finally emerge and fully develop – contemporary postmodern atheism
and religious indifference threaten to drive humanism out straightaway,
by questioning the consistency and the existence itself of the foundations
of society and of the globality of the real[72].

Not wanting to inherit anything from the death of God, contemporary
atheism is not the atheism of expropriation and reappropriation from the
believer to the non-believer, from the religious to the secular, from faith in
God to faith in man; in that atheism there remains an attachment to a nos-
talgia and to other "truer" values, to other "more authentic" cultures[73].

Postmodern thought – characterised by "deconstruction" and the relativisation of all the apparently solid conceptual edifice of modernity –

70. Cf. A. VERGOTE, *Religion et sécularisation en Europe occidentale. Tendances et
prospectives*, in *Explorations de l'espace théologique* (BETL, 90), Leuven, Leuven University Press, 1990, p. 551.

71. See on this subject P. POUPARD, *Discours inaugural du Symposium da Costa Rica*,
in *Athéisme et Foi* 27 (1992) 1-11. See also in the same issue, the article by A. CHEUICHE,
La indiferencia religiosa en el contexto de la modernidad, pp. 33-40.

72. Cf. The synthetic and precise description of this supposedly postmodern atheism
given by J.M. MARDONES, *Postmodernidad y cristianismo* (n. 1), pp. 82-86. See also L.
GONZALEZ-CARVAJAL, *Ideas y creencias del hombre actual*, Santander, Sal Terrae, 1991,
principally pp. 153-178; P. VALADIER, *La Iglesia em proceso* (n. 8), p. 33 (éd. *Catolicismo e sociedade moderna*, São Paulo, Loyola, 1991).

73. Cf. G. VATTIMO, *La fin de la modernité* (n. 1), especially p. 29.

also questions any attempt at talking about the unutterable Absolute that Christians and other religions call God; it regards any discourse with pretensions to universalisation and totalisation as reductionist and inadequate and ends up in indifference and disenchantment. And, in so doing, it opens to Christian thought and discourse an apparently new, but in truth very old track, which leads to mystery and to plurality as an admission of the impossibility of thinking and completely talking about Being, whatever its aspect might be.

It follows that, not only reason and reflection, but also the desire and the thirst for the infinite and transcendence are driven back to an aporia that could have the reverse side of offertory, of confidence, of surprise being filled with wander in the face of Mystery. And that could have the effect – again reverse and paradoxical – that the experience and discourse about God could find, by means of these times which would appear at first sight so hostile, an unimagined possibility of fruitfulness[74].

If the objectivity of the world – one fruit of modernity – is the extreme result of the separation from God, a separation that in its turn liberates man and institutes him the subject of knowledge, making him autonomous with regard to divine intelligence and normativity, it is possible to examine the problem from another angle. Namely, the supreme foundation of things – such as God has delivered it and – in employing the language of the faith – revealed it to man, although barely perceptibly, and intimately accessible to the human intellect, albeit only partially[75]. And then God – or Transcendence, according to the conception of modern man – withdraws himself, leaving man prey to his labour and his disputes[76]. Religion and the experience of God would from then on be conceived of as the discourse of man on God with aiming to define his relations with Him and also as a sequence of visions of the world[77].

Today, at the time when we are enduring and painfully experiencing the crisis of modernity or of the advent of postmodernity, it is possible to understand a little better the conception that we have just outlined. Any manner of speaking about God fails and its radical inadequacy is

74. See what J.M. MARDONES intimates on this subject, *Postmodernidad y cristianismo* (n. 1), p. 110. We say "could appear" to make it clear that this is not an affirmation.
75. On this subject, see M. GAUCHET, *Le désenchantement du monde* (n. 1), pp. 56-60.
76. See the commentary on the book by M. GAUCHET given by S. BRETON, *La religion s'efface-t-elle de nos sociétés? Libres propos sur Le désenchantement du monde de Marcel Gauchet*, in *Revue scientifique, philosophique et théologique* 69 (1985) 567.
77. On this subject, see M. MESLIN, *L'expérience humaine du divin* (n. 29), Paris, Cerf, 1988, pp. 33-39. Where the author records the way in which this is done by the principal thinkers of modernity.

reminded of. The radical experience of mystery questions a modern discourse that would claim to clearly trace all things, including the "retirement" and the "death" of God. The relativisation of all cultural premises and the critique of the modern project alert one to the hasty and badly made utilisations that might enclose a discourse on God with pretensions of legitimating all institutionalisations, all systems. And the end of anthropocentric humanism (with its perverse androcentric and ethnocentric derivatives) opens the way for a new indistinct vision, to a new perception – which would turn as a consequence in a new experience – of a divinity, still not clearly perceptible or nameable but which makes it possible to understand, though in a discreetly veiled way, its power to charm and seduce, and which provoke the desire to experience it.

It follows that it would not be relevant to admit as a premise that we live in a time of weakening of the faith in God and of the reflection about him. Although one can certainly not forget that the modern era proclaimed the inevitability of the decline in religions, going as far as supporting the thesis of the death of God, the identification of modernity with atheistic humanism contains an insupportable reduction. Indeed, the project of modernity has generated religious indifference rather than the negation of God precisely. And at the same time the crisis of the aforesaid project has demonstrated that a society, unless it finds its foundation in God, will slowly and inexorably dissolve[78]. The proclamation – correct or not, more or less well founded – of the advent of so-called postmodernity and of the alleged return of the religious allows one to see that it is rather difficult to decree the banishment of God from the human horizon, and that, to the contrary, the search for God continues to stir up the heart of humanity without taking account of the risk incurred by all official or quasi-official discourse on God that certain institutions invoke to find themselves – what has happened at some – irreparably out-of-date[79].

In short, if atheism – understood in modern terms – continues to be a question that is posed when the problem of God is mentioned, it should still be recognised that it is no longer the only one. Perhaps even this atheism should be recognised, if not as contributive, at least as present in modern culture[80]. And the Church inserted in this culture finds itself, by

78. On this subject, see what Cardinal P. POUPARD says in his opening speech for the symposium in Costa Rica, pp. 8-9.
79. On this question, see what P. VALADIER has to say in *La Iglesia en proceso* (n. 8), pp. 44-65.
80. See on this subject what D. HERVIEU-LEGER affirms in *Vers un nouveau christianisme?*, Paris, Cerf, 1986, pp. 303-304, and the critique given by P. VALADIER, *La Iglesia en proceso* (n. 8), pp. 63-74.

this fact, surrounded by pluralism and faced with a new alternative for understanding its identity and the identity of the God whom it proposes to proclaim and serve.

VIII. FROM SEDUCTION TO EXPERIENCE

Karl Rahner, considered – rightly so – as one of the greatest theologians of the twentieth century, affirmed that the Christian of the future (we would add, of the present) will be a *mystic*, that is to say, somebody who has experienced something, or will be nothing at all, even less a Christian[81]. Since time immemorial, and today more than ever, speaking of God, from the perspective of the Christian faith, means speaking about an experience, or, better still, starting from an experience. An experience that, in fact, because it is divine, is profoundly human ever since the moment when, in the fullness of time, the Christian faith proclaims, God Himself was made flesh, was made humanity, the Word Incarnate, in Jesus Christ.

Incarnated, human, and therefore particular, this experience is no less universal or total. It is because of the fact that there is necessarily a relationship, always particular, between the Christian option and its alterity – i.e., with what is not it, not by opposition but by going beyond – that this experience can recognise the God who is the object of its desire and its reason of existence. Recognising oneself as particular and historical means recognising, not only one's existence and limitations, but also that of the other, a sign of the Other that nothing can embrace, the always greater God[82]. Thus, at the same time that the experience of God means seeing nothing, perceiving nothing in particular while participating in a visible and universal "experience-ability", it is still nothing less than seeing, hearing, touching, in a word, experiencing, the God who reveals Himself and who manifests Himself by the most limited concrete: the face, the flesh of the other, and by the historical and social fabric in which this other lives out his incarnated condition and his concrete existence[83].

If it suddenly appeared – rightly or not – that Christianity may have partially lost the possibility of expressing itself by the word, of proclaiming before the world of today, with a loud and understandable voice, the God who is at the heart of its experience, it would be to a

---

81. Cf. K. RAHNER, *Escritos de teología VII*, Madrid, Taurus, 1972, pp. 75-81.
82. Cf. on this subject the beautiful reflection of M. DE CERTEAU, *Penser le christianisme*, in *La faiblesse de croire* (n. 26), pp. 261-262.
83. *Ibid.*, p. 315.

great extent the result of the divorce which was slowly established between the experiences and practices of the faith on the one hand, and on the other hand, of the important and significant human experiences that manage to move and to mobilise what is the most profound of the human being. To the degree that these experiences, structuring and heavy with signification, lose their analogy with the Christian experience in the area of the person, community and the ecclesial field, they cease to be of a realising type and salvific. In short they do not merit being called, strictly speaking, experiences of God[84].

At the present time, religious pluralism and, consequently, the quest for the dialogue between religious traditions, which occupy – and perhaps preoccupy – the traditional Christian Churches, are finding in the experience of God a fertile soil for possibilities of progress. Although one cannot, with regard to the experiences that occur within various religions, quite simply reduce them one to another or identify them the one with the other, it is undeniable that religious and mystical experience can be used as a privileged ground for the theological dialogue, insofar as it returns the human being to fundamental questions of significance: Where do we come from and where we will go? What is the meaning of human existence, with its burden of suffering and death? What is the source of this movement that we share, which brings us into relationship, which carries us out of ourselves into solidarity and communion with the other, and which is THE response to the interpellation by an Absolute of which we are aware and in which we believe[85]? The answer – though mysterious and veiled – to these questions, and the simple fact that it concerns us, signals *the experience of God* as the indispensable criterion for Christianity, not only for advancing in the understanding of its identity, but moreover for going forward toward the *difference* which challenges it and paradoxically renders it increasingly faithful to the core of its fundamental truth.

As a starting point for dialogue in a pluri-religious world, the experience of God also presents nothing less than the possibility, for the human being, of living out the fundamental anthropological dimension

---

84. Cf. on this subject the affirmation of M. DE FRANÇA MIRANDA, *A Igreja Católica diante de pluralismo religioso no Brasil. Avaliação teológica*, pp. 84-85. Moreover, and more explicitly related to Catholicism, we believe that it is possible to extend this to the level of Christian experience in more ecumenical terms: "According to us, the knot of this problem lies in the divorce between the expressions and practices of faith on the one hand part, and, on the other hand, the significant human experiences of our contemporaries. The present crisis in Catholicism is a result, in good part, of this rupture".

85. J. DUPUIS, *Unicité et universalité de Jésus Christ*, in *Jésus Christ à la rencontre des religions* (n. 2), p. 309.

of gratuity. While walking on the road of the experience of God, man notes that The One which his heart desires does not at all surrender to the immediacism of his needs, and even less to the consuming "frenzy" of certain psychological states and emotional conquests. The experience of God, while occurring on the level of desire, can only occur gratuitously, leaving him or her who has felt it in the grip of an always unappeased desire and thus always capable of desiring and, consequently, of experimenting[86].

The Judeo-Christian tradition recognises and assumes the natural presence of the desire in the human being. Scripture does not fail to take into account this human desire deeply rooted in the vehemence of the aspiration for life in its fullness, in which the fundamental element is the establishment of personal relations with God[87]. However this experience does not consist, for Judaism and even less so for Christianity, in a permanent satiety or in the unfinished enjoyment of all desires.

If, on the one hand, it is certain that "only the desire is capable of qualifying the relationship of God with man"[88], on the other hand the relation established by this desire places man before the very "difference" of God: a difference of the desire of the Other, the encounters of which can be made only in renouncing oneself, in conversion, in the examination of one's own desires. It is the only way, in the Christian experience, of opening a space for that God can desire in man and consequently for allowing man to desire only God, by increasingly identifying his desire with the divine desire. It is thus the human being who, in the experience, is *seized* by God, and not the other way around. And his experience, if it is true, entirely escapes his control.

So, if the experience of God occurs on the level of desire – not being able to occur otherwise – it is also necessary to say that it occurs as a *mystery* – a revealed mystery, undoubtedly, the mystery of love which comes close in saving but yet remains a mystery. There is no natural

---

86. Cf. D. BERTRAND, *La théologie négative de Michel de Certeau*, in C. GEFFRÉ (ed.), *Michel de Certeau ou la différence chrétienne* (n. 23), pp. 120-121, in commenting on M. DE CERTEAU on the question of the experience of God. See also A. VERGOTE, *Verticalité et horizontalité dans le langage symbolique sur Dieu*, in *Explorations de l'espace théologique* (BETL, 90), Leuven, Leuven University Press, 1990, pp. 543-548.

87. Cf. the number of biblical texts that express the even corporeal repercussions of human desire: Ps 42; Ps 123, 3; Ps 63, 2; Ps 130, 6; Ps 73, 25-28 and others. Jesus himself speaks to his disciples in terms of desire (cf. lc 12, 49-50; 22, 15). The Bible itself ends with the cry of impatient desire of the Bride who calls out for her Beloved: Maranatha! Come, Lord! (Ap 22, 17.20). Cf. the beautiful commentary of M. MESLIN, *L'expérience humaine du divin* (n. 29), pp. 383-385, on these passages of Scripture.

88. Cf. on this subject what is said by M. MESLIN, *L'expérience humaine du divin* (n. 29), p. 386. See also our text: *A sedução do sagrado* (n. 48) (The seduction of the sacred).

logical transition between the daily experience of life and the experience of God, although the former is the place where the latter occurs. One may speak of an analogical knowledge, on the basis of the fundamental perception that no-thing, no reality, is able to express transcendence. Also, with regard to any human experience of transcendence, the term "mystery" is the more appropriate one for defining the discovery of God as the Absolute who attracts and invites to experience.

On the level of this communication, therefore, silence is more appropriate to the experience of God than speech. Silence, the companion of the experience and the intimate comprehension one gets by experiencing it, enjoying it and finally by realising the insufficiency of words and concepts to express it, by keeping silent in order to really possess it. It is a mystery of death immanent to awareness and human language when it comes to expressing God, or better, to speaking of the experience as a possibility of knowing the Absolute. It is there that one recognises that everything begins *before* humanity and that this one arrives, in one way or another, only "subsequence", too late to be present to the Mystery and to have full contact with it[89].

And yet the Incarnation of the Word in Jesus of Nazareth says to the Christian that, purely by the grace and mercy of God, time itself has received a new significance and this "subsequence" has been redeemed, and thus his religious experience consists in the insoluble union of two seemingly (humanly) irreconcilable poles: the theological fact that God lets himself be experienced while at the same time being Absolute and Father. Defined as love from the very beginning of Christianity, this God reveals himself as a father in the personal and intimate relationship that he maintains with humankind, a relationship whose primary point of reference is loving union maintained with Jesus of Nazareth, in who the Christian faith has recognised the Beloved Son of the God never seen by anyone[90].

The mystery of Incarnation of God in Jesus Christ thus reveals, not only that the divine Absolute is experienced by humankind as fatherhood, but moreover that this experience makes it possible to glimpse a difference and a plurality even in the interior of Gods existence, then experienced as Father, Son and Holy Spirit[91].

The great difficulty of speaking intelligibly today to modern, postmodern, and/or post-Christian ears, about the God of the Christian revelation, perhaps results, not only but mainly, from the fact that, for

89. G. MOREL, *Questions d'homme*, vol. II. *L'Autre*, Paris, Aubier, 1977.
90. Cf. the beautiful text of M. PERINE, *Transcendência e mundo. Aproximação filosófica e visão cristã*, Belo Horizonte, autocop., 1991, pp. 19-10.
91. Cf. M. MESLIN, *L'expérience humaine du divin* (n. 29), pp. 404-405.

some time, historic Christianity attached only little importance to experience and even to a *pedagogy* of the experience of God[92]. Fearing the intimism and the subjectivism engendered by modern individualism, which could lead to alienation, to a disengagement from community and history – which, to a certain extent, had already occurred and still occurs – Christians became pitilessly suspicious with regard to everything that would come from the domain of religious experience and would have appearance – however remote – of being near to the so-called mystical experience. Apparently this would be reserved only for a small half-dozen of privileged people, almost always dedicated to contemplation in a cloister, exposed to the most diverse psychological suspicions concerning their "normalcy" and "mental health".

It appears however that these suspicions have finally begun to be relativised and that the hour has come in which the Christian Churches must deal seriously with the question of the experience of God, lest they fail in their mission at this delicate moment in history. Even the thinkers who agree more with the nihilism subjacent to the modern project arrive finally, albeit with regret, at the conclusion that an atheistic or a-religious society is incapable of bringing to humanity answers or questions other than those that are psychologically despairing and "causing stress". This makes one wonder – while admitting that alienation or illusion is neither a way nor a goal desirable to humans – if despair, depression and madness would be one[93].

On the other hand, to wish, to want (to desire), is always to want something and, in last analysis, it is to wish for happiness. Ethics and moral action express the belief in this possibility of building a happy time and space, in which the human person can arrive at her integral development and fully enjoy her potentialities[94]. All that, in the world, is

92. There is no lack of accusations on this matter, be they from within the Christian world (J. SUDBRACK, *La nueva religiosidad* (n. 18), esp. p. 99), or from outside (e.g. J. NEEDLEMAN, *Cristianismo perdido. Uma viagem de redescoberta*, São Paulo, Martins Fontes, 1987, pp. 102-103: *"... enquanto monges e freiras católicos estão ensinando todos os tipos de coisas, da botânica até os negócios, não são muitos os que estão ensinando as pessoas a orar"*. This is a citation of W. JOHNSTON, in *Christianity in dialogue with zen*, which the auhor accepts entirely. This subject is more extensively treated in our article *A sedução do sagrado* (n. 48).

93. On the deficiency of significance in post-religious society, see what is affirmed by M. Gauchet in the last pages of his book *Le désenchantement du monde*, p. 302, ending with this frightening statement: "Le déclin de la religion se paie en difficulté d'être soi". For another perspective, see the text of D. BOGOMOLETZ, *A ilusão necessária*, in *Caderno Atualidade em Debate I*, pp. 4-18.

94. See on this subject what M. PERINE says, following Kant, in *Transcendência e mundo. Aproximação filosófica e visão cristã*, pp. 7-8.

lack of this plenitude and sign of the absence of this state of affairs, challenges ethics and human action.

The ethical attitude that the Church calls love (agape) neither finds itself at odds with the experience of God nor denies the assertion that this God, revealed by grace, would be an object only of desire, never of necessity. If on the one hand humanity, in the grace of the contemplation and at the deepest level of the experience of God, can feel the proximity of the Ineffable Absolute never seen by anyone, on the other hand, man can perceive a depth – the home of the Him who challenges one by coming from the heart of reality – which he experiences as an authentic manifestation of the divine.

There is more: it is this dialectical movement – of the experience of infinite in finite, of the challenge that comes from the heart of the finite which leads up to the ethical act, that by intervening in the finite and transforming it, touches at the same time the fringe of infinite – that allows man to become aware of this Absolute which lovingly governs life for him, the Same who reveals, in Jesus Christ, his name of Father. In going to the base of his human existence, poor and limited, marked by many conflicts, by injustices and restrictions of all kinds, man becomes aware of a divine origin which withdraws itself from the field of one's experience, or better, from one's awareness, from the knowledge which one might have from this experience [95].

Today, more than ever, the moment of the crisis of modernity forces upon the Christian the duty of rendering to God a worship that necessarily engages him or her in the service of his or her neighbour and in presence and ethical action in the heart of society. The praxis can then be for the Christian a sign of the God of his faith, and yet far more of what he lacks than in what he has in abundance. The insufficiency of means and conditions favourable to the realisation of this praxis testify to the greatness of his referent and of that which confers on him structure and significance. In a world where the fundamental questions are formulated more openly than before, in a world where the thirst for significance and fundamental ethical imperatives is felt in a way more than ever before dramatic, Christianity is called to reflect, in its human acting, the very acting of the divine[96].

And with this intention, the guarantee of universality and globality that allows one to identify, in the human praxis, the imprint of the

95. Cf. A. VERGOTE, *Verticalité et horizontalité dans le langage symbolique sur Dieu* (n. 86), p. 545.

96. Cf. P. VALADIER, *La Iglesia en proceso.* (n. 8), pp. 126-127 (Brasilian edition cited).

divine, paradoxically requires the most insignificant of demonstrations and the apparently most limited of actions: serving the poor. Universality, unless it includes those who are most lowly situated, most maltreated, and neediest in the world, would only be one more ideology. The guarantee of the authenticity of a revelation is found in the capacity that it has, while not being discriminatory, of addressing itself preferentially to the poorest, most forsaken, and most exploited[97].

Just as all domains of human acting, the preferential option for the poor, a fundamental requirement for the knowledge and the proclamation of God of Christianity, is not without ambiguities and risks. Concretely, in Latin America and in Brazil, where this praxis has been one of the watchwords of sectors expressive of the Church, from the episcopate to the laity, these risks are going to be clearly felt in the enormous richness of the ecclesial experience of the last decades.

Continuously accused by many people – and not without some accuracy – of a complicity with some of the most negative aspects of modernity (hegemony of the effectiveness, proud presumption of being part to the secrets of the course of history and of holding its reins, exacerbation of militancy of, feverish activism to the detriment of other aspects of ecclesial life), the practice of the option for the poor nevertheless remains an invaluable corrective measure with regard to the risks inherent in a postmodern "evasionism" that would underline the sensualist and inaugural thought and would give primacy to sensation – in the sense of spontaneous and immediate pleasure – over sentiment[98].

Also not exempt from these risks are the ecological movement, the feminist movement and the others that are bringing new questions and subjects to the field where pride of place was held, until now almost exclusively, by the theology of liberation, from the perspective of a praxis understood mostly in socio-economic-political terms. Thus, the theology of liberation itself, with all that it signifies of advancement and positive points for the Church in the Latin-American continent and even on a world level, is not free of the aforesaid risks, inherent in the modernity of which it is, to some extent, a daughter. So it seems to us that she is equally not exempt from still needing to find a theoretical – that is to say, theological – expression in support of this praxis[99].

This could be due, in part, to the fact that this theoretical adequacy – that is to say, theological adequacy – cannot be realised except in God,

97. Cf. J.M. MARDONES, *Postmodernidade y cristianismo* (n. 1), p. 113.
98. Cf. *ibid.*, p. 115.
99. Cf. on this subject the very pertinent remarks of C. PALACIO in his article *A identidade problemática (a propósito do mal estar cristão)* (n. 49), p. 163.

or better said, in the experience of God, that confers substance and a reason for being on this praxis, lays bare its ideological temptations, and
judges the authenticity of its existence and evangelical radicalism. For
there is the means of minimising the tempting calls which could lead the
praxis to absorb the vices of modernity. We believe that the option for a
praxis with a determined orientation, answering an ethical requirement
which emerges from the very heart of disfigured reality, proceeds from
the experience of God, its primary origin. An experience which will be,
moreover, constantly nourished and critiqued by everything that this
praxis will imply. Thus, the aforementioned experience, if it is truly
authentic – truly of God – will go on purifying human action from the
temptation of pride and power, since it will render ever more manifest
the sovereignty of God in the steering of the course of history.

By acting in grace, by laying down determined objectives while
knowing that the major objective has already been attained by the Incarnation, life and death of Jesus Christ, the Christian will be able to feel
and savour the presence of this God with him disconcerting and always
surprising ways, who constantly makes, at every moment, one feel the
constitutive inadequation of his revelation over against to each and every
political, socio-economic, cultural and even religious scheme or model
that would claim to express it[100].

By being inspired and interpreted in this way, human action will be in
reality the image of the divine action that is at its origin, its primary
source. The non-logical mystery, the mystery of salvation, which has
acted from time immemorial as a liberator and interferes in reality in a
saving way, the God of the Christian faith continues to reveal himself,
today more than ever, as the mystery of love and compassion. His
action, contrary to the canons of effectiveness of modernity, does not
privilege the domains of creation whose fruits, in terms of progress,
transformation, development, are made to be felt in a more palpable and
visible way. He interferes, however, precisely at the place where oppression has made its most predatory work rather than revealing its created
and divine origin. For his habitation, he privileges spaces and the situations where he can only be seen indistinctly and even *sub specie con-
traria*. Thus, beyond and even more than a mystery of compassion, this
mystery inspires the human praxis that desires to experience it and to
testify to its truth and love.

---

100. Cf. on this subject the recent work of the protagonists of liberation theology
themselves, such as J. SOBRINO, *Espiritualidade da libertação. Estrutura e contéudos*
(Col. Telogia da Libertação – Comentários, 10), São Paulo, Loyola, 1991, among others.

IX. Conclusion: Theology – Vulnerability of the Reason

Theology claims, by definition, to be organised speech, reflection and discourse on this God who is the fundamental question, not only of faith but even of human existence itself. However, though it is language, it is in truth meta-language, secondary speech, which comes subsequently, following the experience of God and the praxis in which man can experience the transcendent and the divine in their distinct and immanent manifestations.

At this moment in our life, of the crisis of modernity, of the diversification of a field of religion which becomes more and more complex, theology is in its turn questioned concerning its identity and the very meaning of its existence. If the identity of Christianity is at this time problematic, what about the language of the theology, which claims with extreme boldness to organise the discourse on God using poor, limited, and now somewhat diverted, human reason?

And yet it is perhaps more urgent than ever that theology rediscovers its primordial vocation and its significance, in order to be able to pronounce the word which is proper to it, object to the covetousness, conscious or not, of humanity. More concretely, theology must, here and now, concentrate its attention in a special way on That which is the central object of its content, the frame of its method: God himself. This is the only way that would lead theology to really become what it is and what it is called to be: that is, theological[101].

For, in the full middle of the complexity and pluralism of the contemporary time, Christianity is not called to solidify into a passive attitude over against the critique of modernity and other religious expressions, but, quite the contrary, to experience, to think – respectfully listening and being diligent in research – and to speak about the mystery of God, who continues, today as always, to act in history and in human life[102].

The cultural dimension of theology, as human discourse on God, is necessarily shaped by history; it is nevertheless undeniable that the primary moment for theology – that which supports it and constitutes the very condition of the possibility of its existence – belongs to a primary otherness, which comes before human speech, which comes before even the thinking that precedes this speech. It is here a matter of the divine otherness in itself, which, in its movement of grace in the heart of cre-

---

101. On the centrality of the theme of God in theology, see G. GUTIÉRREZ, *O Deus da vida*, São Paulo, Loyola, 1991.

102. Cf. on this subject what is said by M. FRANÇA MIRANDA, *A Igreja católica diante do pluralismo religioso no Brasil*, in *Estudos* of the CNBB, by the same name, p. 76.

ation, giving itself and surrendering itself freely, causes not only the discovery, filled with wonder and gratefulness, of its existence, source of all meaning, but moreover renders thought and organised discourse regarding it possible. The human being, consequently, cannot think of knowing It such as it is in the plural and diversified fabric of human life[103]. Without this, organised discourse on the inexpressible transcendent would be forbidden him.

Thus, when it comes to true theology, reason has its citizenship, though this citizenship knows itself to be, even wishes to be, auxiliary, secondary, like that of a handmaiden. While daring to look into and reflect on the mystery that graciously reveals itself to it, proud reason, which modernity has set up as a definitive protagonist which has arrived at the height of instrumentality and of claiming to explain everything, will have no other path, then the one of *vulnerability*, which allows itself to be unceasingly demolished and reconstituted by the revelation of the mystery which always exceeds it[104].

Reason will see – only from the moment that it makes itself vulnerable – extending in front of it the territory hitherto impregnable of theological thought and speech, and it will dare to attempt–though seized by a quivering of apprehension–to construct an intelligible discourse. The fact of assuming, from the inside of reality, this paramount requirement may perhaps cost theology the loss of a bit of the prestige it acquired

---

103. Cf. on the grace of the revelation of God what is said by P. VALADIER, *La Iglesia en proceso. Catolicismo y sociedad moderna*, pp. 136-137; M. DE CERTEAU, *La faiblesse de croire* (n. 26), and others. However, all contemporary theology is indebted in large measure to the advances on this fundamental understanding made by K. RAHNER, the first one to elaborate a consistent text in this way, thereby revolutionising systematic theology, notably the theology of grace and trinitarian theology.

104. Cf. on the impossibility of reason accounting for the mystery of God, M. MESLIN, *L'expérience humaine du divin* (n. 29), p. 226, in citing Pascal. See also G. GUTIÉRREZ, *O Deus da vida* (n. 101); J.M. MARDONES, *Postmodernidad y cristianismo* (n. 1), p. 144. Moreover, see our work *Saber, sabor e sabedoria ou a fé em meio ao conflito das racionalidades*, in C. CALIMAN ed. *Fé, política e cultura. Desafios atuais*, São Paulo, Paulinas, 1991, pp. 83-98. See also, more recently, my work on the God of revelation: *O Deus de Jesus Cristo e dos cristãos*, in *Curso de Iniciação Teológica, Curso de Extensão por tutoria à distancia*, ed. Departamento de Teologia e Coordenação Central de Extensão, PUC-Rio, 1998; *Alteridade e vulnerabilidade. Experiência de Deus e pluralismo religioso no moderno em crise*, São Paulo, Loyola, 1993; *Abba: um pai maternal* in G.B. HACKMANN (ed.), *Deus Pai*, Porto Alegre, EDIPUCRS, 1999, pp. 143-196; *A sedução do sagrado*, in C. CALIMAN (ed.), *A sedução do sagrado*, Vozes, Petrópolis, 1998, 2ª ed. pp. 79-115; *A alteridade e seus caminhos*, in M. FABRI DOS ANJOS, (ed.), *Teologia e perspectivas de futuro*, São Paulo, Loyola, 1997, pp. 21-46; *A post-christian and postmodern Christianity. Liberation Theologies, Postmodernity, and the Americas*, London – New York, Routledge, 1997, pp. 83-94; *Abbá: um Pai maternal*, in *Vida Pastoral 40* (1999) 15-24.

through its effort at integration and "aggiornamento" into the bodies of knowledge legitimated by modern reason[105]. That will give to reason, however, the single element essential to the possibility of reflecting and employing a less unsuitable expression of God, who is an always disconcerting and never exhausted mystery, and who takes pleasure in "destroying the intelligence of intelligent" (1 Cor 1:19) and in making them wonder, in disorder and amazement, like the scribes and the Pharisees before Jesus of Nazareth: "From where does this wisdom come to him?" (Mt 3:54).

Thus, by assuming this constituent and foundational vulnerability, theology will fall in step with Him who, throughout his encounter with humanity, never preserved, never clung to his prerogatives, who laid himself bare and who could be encountered in all that is smaller, more humble, and less important according to the criteria of this world (cf. Phil 2:5-11)[106]. Thus, if the experience of God is basically a interrelational experience and one of vulnerability with regard to an Otherness which, from its absolute difference, in revealing itself, does not do so in overwhelming but in serving and in saving, then the discourse on this experience will not have any other choice than the way of encounter with the same vulnerability, in letting itself be unceasingly influenced by the otherness inevitably present in the relationship that is grounded there[107].

Here, it seems to us, is the linch pin of the discourse on God at this moment in the history of humanity and of Christianity itself. Firstly, there is the fact that the relationship with God, since it is intersubjective and personal, questions and destabilises certain experiences which, though deeply human and fulfilling on the psychological level, are not on the level of the experience of real and personal relationship between

105. See the instigent and acute line of questioning formulated by H.C. DE LIMA VAZ, *Religião e modernidade filosófica* (n. 1), which is quoted higher above.

106. Cf. what M. DE CERTEAU says about the mystery of the revelation of God in Christianity, which works "not without us", in *Autorités chrétiennes et structures sociales*, in *La faiblesse de croire* (n. 26), p. 113.

107. On this subject, see what is said by A. VERGOTE in *Verticalité et horizontalité dans le langage symbolique sur Dieu* (n. 86), p. 540: *"L'être soi-même et le devenir autre......c'est le paradoxe de la reaction à Dieu"*. See also on the humble and kenotic mode of God's presence in the world M. FRANÇA MIRANDA en citant F. VARILLON, in *L'humilité de Dieu*, Paris, Centurion, 1978, p. 84: "Il faut un longue expérience, il faut peut-être toute une vie, pour comprendre un peu que, dans l'ordre de l'amour, comme la richesse est pauvreté, la puissance est faiblesse. L'homme s'incline toujours, quand il pense à son Dieu, à sortir de la sphère de l'amour, à imaginer des attributs qui ne seraient pas ceux de l'amour. Il a fallu des siècles pour que le Dieu des armées soit enfin adoré comme le Dieu désarmé". *Salvação cristã na modernidade*, in *Perspectiva Teológica* 23 (1991) 19, n. 9.

subjects, albeit unequal ones. Secondly, there is the observation that this experience profoundly influences the discourse on all things that concern this relationship, which is, in sum, what we interpret here as theology. On the other side, however, this necessarily other, marked and modified dimension of the experience of God and of organised discourse about Him causes theology to be much more exposed and neither able to prove itself as such nor able to constructs its discourse except in a way that is kenotic, and stripped bare[108].

It is necessary however to pay attention to the symbolic, "sacramental" form that this kenosis of theological discourse entails today, which is perhaps different from that of yesterday. If, at the apogee of modernity and secularisation, explicit language on God sought indirect ways of speaking, in the name of respect for plurality and religious liberty, trying the path of dialogue with modern atheism and agnosticism and opting many times for mute testimony where only the gesture counted and where ethics was the sole common denominator driving towards dialogue, today the situation no longer appears the same.

It could be that the major and more demanding part of vulnerability at this moment consists in taking up again the explicit proclamation, in using religious and mystical discourse when speaking about God[109]. Not out of opportunism or in order to make a place for oneself in the field of religion, which has been transformed into a immense supermarket of opportunities where each one can choose for oneself a recipe to one's taste. But rather to make resound, among the plurality of denominations which today invoke the thirst for transcendence and spirituality in which humanity is caught up, a Name which continues to love and call humankind to the permanent dialogue of love and communion[110].

It is this name that Jesus of Nazareth referred to as Father. And it is this name that, by taking root inside the most fundamental psychological necessities of the human being, expresses the most transcendent divine Being – The Wholly Other. To name God as Father, to recognise his paternity and to really express it, is to recognise Him as the foundation and origin of the human being is something outside of him, and to allow

108. M. DE CERTEAU, in *La faiblesse de croire* (n. 26), in *ibid.*, p. 312, points out what this humble form of Christianity might be in the struggles and prayers of the present, by revealing a God who may curiously begin to look like anyone you may meet.

109. On the discretion and, today, the urgency of mystical theology – which flowered in other eras of the history of the Christian tradition – see H.C. DE LIMA VAZ, *Religião e modernidade filosófica* (n. 1), pp. 106-107.

110. On this alternative between veiling and visibility, see what is said in the article of J.P. ROSA, *"Enfouissement" ou "visibilité"? Un débat dans l'Église*, in *Études* 376 (1992) 239-246.

all dimensions of life to freely organise themselves for relationships of true solidarity and fraternity. It is, in sum, to proclaim that divine paternity is not a projection of insecurity, frustration or a human construction, as it has been endlessly repeated in so many critiques of religion, but the Revelation of God as the Father of an Only son, Saviour of humankind[111].

While we do not confuse this experience with the simple search for feelings or emotional compensation which could characterise the appearance of many religious manifestations at the present time, it seems to us that theology finds itself – perhaps more than ever at this moment in history – put on the defensive by the fundamental question of God, the centre of its discourse, and by the manner of talking about Him to its contemporaries. It may be perhaps bold to claim to trace the profile of the Unutterable and Inexpressible God. But, if this same God lets himself be experienced in spirit and truth and even in human flesh assumed and redeemed by the Incarnation of the Word, it will necessarily be possible to talk about this experience. This is what should be, at the present time, the primary occupation of theology, which may be more and more a mystical theology, not only because it is centred on the reflection on what is proper to it, but moreover because it would increasingly take on the form, not of abstracted speculation, but of a testimony of sacramental visibility, of a narration of the interdependent, sympathising and loving relationships of humans with God[112].

Departamento de Teologia   M. C. Luchetti-Bingemer
Centro Loyola de Fé e Cultura
Pontificia Universidade Católica do Rio de Janeiro

111. On the experience of divine paternity, cf. the important text of M. Meslin, *Désir du Père et paternité divine*, in *L'expérience humaine du divin* (n. 29), pp. 297-320. See also my more recent text *Abba: um pai maternal*, (n. 104).
112. This article has been translated by Timothy J. Crutcher.

EXPERIENCE AND CHRISTIAN FAITH

A Response to M.C. Bingemer

1. *Introduction*

It is difficult to highlight particular themes in a paper characterised by such breadth of vision, and such feeling for nuance. The author is clearly intent on doing justice to both the specificity of the Christian tradition, and to modern and postmodern sensibilities. She is fair to all parties to the debate, and I shall attempt to be as fair in focusing on those elements of her lecture which particularly strike me. Of course, my choice of themes is quite personal – a choice dictated by my own research and reflection. I do believe, however, that they relate to the heart of Prof. Bingemer's analysis of the challenges confronting Christians, as they attempt to speak about God in the contemporary context. The themes I have chosen to highlight are the following:

(a)   the appeal to religious experience;
(b)   the specificity of the Christian understanding of God;

2. *The Appeal to Religious Experience*

Prof. Bingemer gives much prominence to the idea of religious experience. She suggests that it provides a way to promote the dialogue between Christianity and both the modern world, and the non-Christian religious traditions. Moreover, it seems to the author to be the privileged route which Christianity ought to take in its quest for its own proper identity and for a language adequate to contemporary men and women.

In appealing to religious experience, especially in reference to interreligious dialogue, Prof. Bingemer inevitably invites comparison with the school of thought which has placed this same theme at the top of its theological agenda, and for the same reason. I am thinking, of course, of the so-called pluralist theology of religions represented above all by John

Hick. Pluralist theology maintains that there is a plurality of independent and more or less equally valid religious traditions[1].

According to Hick, "the most viable defence of religious belief" is the one which is rooted in religious experience[2]. Religious beliefs can be defended as rational because they have an empirical foundation, namely, the religious experience to which men and women of all ages and cultures have testified, and which comes to expression in the world's religious traditions. Of course, Hick recognises that there is no such thing as "pure" religious experience. The concrete religious traditions provide the forum within which religious experience becomes possible, and the categories which allow believers both to express that experience and, most importantly, to identify its source or its ground[3].

For both John Hick and Prof. Bingemer, it seems, religious beliefs are experientially based. And for both authors, too, this fact provides an opening for dialogue among the world's diverse religious traditions. Both authors are also agreed it seems, in maintaining that religious experience involves a movement away from self and towards otherness. According to Hick, religious experience frees us, "at least momentarily, from the burdens of the self-enclosed ego"[4]. According to Prof. Bingemer, religious experience is characterised by an insatiable longing for the Mystery which draws us ever onwards towards itself, and outwards towards others.

These are striking parallels. But there is also a striking difference between Hick and Prof. Bingemer. Prof. Bingemer tends to move easily between speaking of religious experience and speaking of the "experience of God". Indeed, she sometimes seems to use these almost synonymously[5]. Hick, on the other hand, insists that religious experience need

1. For a discussion of the pluralist theology of religions, see T. MERRIGAN, *Religious Knowledge in the Pluralist Theology of Religions*, in *Theological Studies* 58 (1997) 686-707.

2. J. HICK, *The Epistemological Challenge of Religious Pluralism*, in *Faith and Philosophy* 14 (1997) 277-286, at 277.

3. T. MERRIGAN, *The Challenge of the Pluralist Theology of Religions and the Christian Rediscovery of Judaism*, in D. POLLEFEYT (ed.), *Jews and Christians: Rivals or Partners for the Kingdom of God?*, (Louvain Theological and Pastoral Monographs, 23), Leuven – Grand Rapids, Peeters – W.B. Eerdmans, 1997, pp. 95-132.

4. J. HICK, *The Fifth Dimension: An Exploration of the Spiritual Realm*, Oxford, Oneworld, 1999, p. 112.

5. Cf. pp. 67, 68, 92, 99, 100. "Our work claims to analyse more specifically *one* of the aspects of this crisis of modernity, namely, its impact on the manner of living out religion, on the contours of the profile of religious identity, on the ways followed by the so-called religious experience at the heart of the present historical moment" (p. 67); "The experience of God thus appears as the great way open to the so much hoped for dialogues

not be interpreted in a theistic sense. Indeed, as the history of religions makes clear, religious experience is susceptible of both theistic and non-theistic interpretations. Hence, *grosso modo*, the world's religions can be divided into those which regard the source of religious experience as personal and those which regard it as non-personal. In the case of the former, one may speak of God. In the case of the latter, it is more appropriate to speak of the Absolute. Hick avoids both terms and prefers to speak of the source of religious experience as "the Real". Indeed, according to Hick, the only way to do justice to the "varieties of religious experience" is to acknowledge that their ultimate source (the Real) exceeds all human constructs and "cannot be directly experienced by us as it is in itself but only as it appears in terms of our various human thought-forms", that is to say, the forms provided by the theistic and non-theistic religions[6].

And, of course, these forms involve rival and even contradictory truth-claims. So Hick observes that the appeal to religious experience which grounds Christian beliefs can also be heard among non-Christians who adhere to "beliefs that are at least partly, and sometimes quite radically, incompatible with the Christian belief-system"[7]. In other words, according to Hick, religious experience cannot be equated with the experience of God, Christian or otherwise. To put it more bluntly, religious experience, as it comes to expression in the world's religions, does not bring us to the threshold of the personal God of Christianity. On the contrary, if religious experience is taken seriously, then we must be prepared to rise above the limited deity of Christianity and to move towards the absolutely transcendent reality which is beyond any particular name

of Christianity, not only with the modern world, but as well with the other religious traditions" (p. 68); "However, the interreligious dialogue... obliges Christian theology to make theocentrism and the mystical experience or the experience of God the starting point of its discourse,..." (p. 92); "At the present time, religious pluralism and, consequently, the search for the dialogue between religious traditions, which occupy... the traditional Christian Churches, are finding in the experience of God a fertile soil for possibilities of progress" (p. 99); "As a starting point for dialogue in a pluri-religious world, the experience of God also presents nothing less than the possibility, for the human being, of living out the fundamental anthropological dimension of gratuity. While walking on the road of the experience of God, man notes that The One which his heart desires does not at all surrender to the immediacism of his needs..." (p. 100).

6. J. HICK, *The Metaphor of God Incarnate*, London, SCM, 1993, p. 140. See also J. HICK, *An Interpretation of Religion: Human Responses to the Transcendent*, London, Macmillan, 1989, p. 249: "But if the Real in itself is not and cannot be humanly experienced, why postulate such an unknown and unknowable *Ding an sich*? The answer is that the divine noumenon is a necessary postulate of the pluralistic religious life of humanity".

7. J. HICK, *The Epistemological Challenge of Religious Pluralism* (n. 2), p. 277.

or revelation[8]. In this sense, it is a Christian presumption to assert that the only real religious question is the question of what we are to call "God"[9].

In the light of these reflections, my first question to Prof. Bingemer is, therefore, as follows: *Does the appeal to religious experience really bring us very far in the direction of the God of Christianity?* This question returns in the consideration of my second point. Once again, John Hick can serve as a useful contrast to Prof. Bingemer.

3. The Specificity of the Christian Understanding of God

Prof. Bingemer speaks with reverence of the incarnation of God's own son and identifies this as the heart of Christianity. Indeed, she acknowledges that, in the encounter with other religious, Christianity will become aware of the impossibility of renouncing its faith in Jesus Christ, the Word of God incarnated in time and space.

This insistence on the centrality of the doctrine of the incarnation is in striking contrast to John Hick. Indeed, Hick has invested much of his time and energy in debunking this Christian claim. In his opinion, it is at best a metaphor, and at worst the source of centuries of Christian arrogance and even imperialistic aggression. To Hick's mind, belief in the incarnation makes genuine inter-religious dialogue impossible, because the Christian claims to be in possession of a superior truth, a truth personally delivered by God self in the 'person' of God's own Son.

As long as the literal doctrine of the incarnation is maintained, there does not seem to be any real possibility for even a theocentric dialogue, of the type advocated by Prof. Bingemer. After all, if Christ shares the Godhead, then Christ also defines it in some sense. The outcome of the dialogue is already known, at least by the incarnational Christian.

Hick makes allowances for the development of the incarnational claim, but he is convinced that the time has come to abandon any literalist understanding of it. For Hick, Jesus' religious significance consists,

---

8. See J. HICK, *An Inspiration Christology for a Religiously Plural World. Encountering Jesus: A Debate on Christology*, Atlanta, John Knox Press, 1988, pp. 32-33 where Hick explains that "the Real, **an sich**, is not the object of a cult. It is the ultimate reality that we postulate as the ground of the different forms of religious experience and thought insofar as these are more than human projections." See also J. HICK, *The Metaphor of God Incarnate* (n. 6), pp. 140-141; J. HICK, *Interpretation of Religion* (n. 6), pp. 240-249; J. HICK, *The Rainbow of Faiths: Critical Dialogues on Religious Pluralism*, London, SCM, 1995, p. 42-43.

9. See Bingemer, p. 90: "The authentic religious question thus continues to be – in spite of the whole process of modernity, the crisis of secularisation and other phenomena – precisely that which relates back to that which humans can authentically call God".

above all, in his role as exemplar, as model, as a concrete realisation of "one valid way among others of conceptualising and responding to the divine". "Christianity is one among a plurality of authentic responses to the divine reality"[10]. From within Christianity, one can, of course, regard Jesus as "God's agent on earth", as one who "incarnates" "the divine purpose for human life"[11]. In so far as he was "responsive to God's loving presence" and thus reflected the divine love on earth in a "humanly limited way" – albeit "to an eminent degree" – Jesus can be described as incarnating God's love. However, it must be borne in mind that "the 'incarnation' of divine love occurs in all human lives" in so far as these constitute responses to and reflections of the divine love[12].

Hick situates Jesus' contemporary appeal precisely in his "universally relevant religious experience" and his "ethical insights", provided that "these are freed from the mass of ecclesiastical dogmas and practices that have developed over the centuries". For Hick, "all the great religious figures have in their different ways 'incarnated' the ideal of human life lived in response to the divine Reality"[13]. For those of us who follow in their footsteps, "the way to salvation/liberation involves a gradual or sudden conversion to [the] new way of experiencing" the self and the world disclosed by the founder. However, in the case of "ordinary believers, the new mode of experiencing usually occurs only occasionally and is of only moderate intensity"[14].

Religions exist to facilitate the religious experience of reality. They are best understood, in the words of Hick, as "effective contexts of salvation", that is to say, spaces within which human beings can move "from self-centredness to a new orientation centred in the ultimate divine Reality"[15]. The realisation of this goal does not depend on the specifically Christian belief in the incarnation of the Son of God in Jesus of Nazareth, a belief which, as I have indicated, has given rise to much grief.

10. J. HICK, *Metaphor of God Incarnate* (n. 6), pp. 104, 160.
11. *Ibid.*, p. 12.
12. *Ibid.*, pp. 76-77.
13. *Ibid.*, pp. 13, 98.
14. *Ibid.*, p. 154.
15. *Ibid.*, p. 139. See also J. HICK, *Rainbow of Faiths* (n. 8), p.106; J. HICK, *An Interpretation of Religion* (n. 6), pp. 12, 14 where Hick speaks of salvation as "the realization of a limitlessly better possibility of human existence". See also J. HICK, *Interpretation and Reinterpretation in Religion*, in S. COAKLEY & D.A. PAILIN (eds.), *The Making and Remaking of Christian Doctrine: Essays in Honour of Maurice Wiles,*, Oxford, Clarendon, 1993, p. 69: "For we see taking place within each of the great traditions, and taking place to more or less the same extent, the salvific transformation of human life, individually and corporately, from destructive self-centeredness to a new orientation centered in the divine Reality".

My question then is whether the literal doctrine of the incarnation is necessary, either to establish the distinctive identity of Christianity as a religion of love, or to establish Jesus as a unique mediator of salvation.

4. *Conclusion*

I realise that there are no simple answers to the questions I have raised. Moreover, in raising them, I have drawn upon the work of an author whose views I do not always share. However, both the questions, and the views of Hick which I use to highlight those questions, are very much part of the contemporary debate. They are unavoidable. Prof. Bingemer's paper makes very clear that she is well placed to move the debate forward.

Faculty of Theology   Terrence MERRIGAN
Katholieke Universiteit Leuven
Sint-Michielsstraat 6
B-3000 Leuven

INCARNATION OF MEANING AND
THE SENSE FOR SYMBOLS

Phenomenological Remarks on a Theological Debate

"The Word became flesh and dwelt among us" (John 1:14)[1]. Christianity is through and through a religion of incarnation. It is the core of the mystery of Christian faith that God became human at a specific and contingent moment in history. The Son of God took human form in the person of Christ, who is like us in everything but sin. Through his suffering, death, and resurrection He has saved us from evil and given us, already in this our earthly existence, a share in the sanctifying power of divine grace. In Christ, the divine Word has mixed and unified with the concrete reality of our existence. What is separate – the sensible and super-sensible, the profane and the sacred, the temporal and the eternal, the horizontal and the vertical dimensions of time – are made one, but without either element thereby losing its relative autonomy.

In the second chapter of John, verses 13-25, Christ speaks of the temple of his body and identifies it as the dwelling place of his Father in the heavens. Christ is the sacrament of God. His sacramentality permeates his entire life on earth and dominates all of his words and deeds. Through the inspiring power of the Word which he alone bears, both physical elements such as water, bread, wine, oil, saliva, and sand, and physical action such as touching, eating, drinking, and washing are elevated into life-giving symbols and transformed into salvific signs that bind heaven to earth, God to humans.

The union of God and human in the person of Christ finds its high-point in the Last Supper, when Christ identifies bread and wine with his body and blood. Christ himself is not a sign of God's presence in the world. He is at once both God and human. Bread and wine, in contrast, are substituting signs by which he makes himself present, and is always present anew whenever bread and wine are sanctified, broken and drunk

1. I wish to thank Herman De Dijn for critical comments on earlier versions of this paper, and Jeffrey Bloechl for his translation.

in his name. Communion, which comes into being in symbols that He has established, makes it possible for the faithful to share in the fruits of his divine body and so, together with the Church, form the mystical body of Christ. The community of faithful can thus also be called sacrament of Christ.

In the course of history, Christ's words of institution have been the focal point of a remarkable theological debate that peaked dramatically during the period of the Council of Trent, because it accentuated what had already become an unavoidable division between Catholic teaching and the Reformation. The unifying symbol became at the same time an agent of disintegration. Strictly speaking, the theological debate turned around the question of how to understand the *is-relation* in the performative speech act of Christ. That the Eucharistic celebration constitutes the cornerstone of the Christian cult went uncontested. The dispute turned exclusively around an interpretation of the sacramental reality and symbolic efficacy of the Holy Eucharist that was either (too) weak or (too) strong. Is it sufficient to understand the bread and wine as a sign of Christ's body and blood? But if they are nothing more than signs by which Christ only points to His body and blood, then why did he himself not put it that way? Do we take sufficient account of the full range of his words if we conceive of them only as a means to indicate or, later, remember something else? Are they only a particular means by which to again call to mind and imprint on ourselves the memory of a salvific event? Or must we rather affirm and confess that, once consecrated, the bread and wine are more than only signs? How close is the bond between the symbolic sign and the reality signified in it?

This is an extraordinary debate certain to cause astonishment and strike outsiders as ridiculous. It is also simply incomprehensible to the pious believer, and often found misplaced and annoying in the eyes of theologians and shepherds of souls, whose concern for a spiritually fruitful religious posture leads them to seek salvation more readily in the development of a *theologia orans* than in the development of peculiar ontological constructions that threaten to burden the religious heart rather than lighten it.

For divergent reasons, many theologians are of the opinion that it will cost too much to recall a debate that Rome has resolved with two famous dogmas. According to some, this will only put what is already a laborious ecumenical discussion into jeopardy. Emphasis should be placed not on what divides Christians but instead what joins them, and what joins them is a confession of the same faith-content. Theologians, however, who do give these reasons for wishing to bypass this discussion already

defend, if only implicitly, a view of religion in which the religious
impact of a symbolic praxis is rather incidental. Exterior symbols stand
for a content that is not strictly bound to specific externals and that can
be presented and passed on to believers in a more direct manner. The
difficulty with this is that, in fact, one would thus adhere to a view of
religion resisted by the Council Fathers at Trent. According to other theologians, the formulation of both dogmas is hopelessly dated and the
Aristotelian vocabulary they employ can not provide an adequate grasp
of the kernel of a religious sense of symbol. The Tridentine formulation
would promote an incorrect concept of sacrament because a substantial-
ist terminology reifies spiritual meaning.

Sacramentologists wishing to preserve and reactivate the importance
of the sacraments are sometimes equally inclined to leave this debate
aside. They choose to leave the study of the theological issue to historians of dogma who, if they avoid falling into the clutches of scholastic
distinctions, can at most explain what was once discussed and how that
discussion occurred, but can not clarify what was at stake then, and still
less why it remains relevant today for a correct conception of the religious impact of eucharistic symbols.

My own approach will be to follow a detour – and this means without
intervening in the scholastic discussion – through analyses giving new
life to this debate, showing what was at stake in it then, and still is now.
My detour consists of an eidetic analysis of the sense for symbols, or
more specifically for symbolic objects in the non-religious context.
What must be said about this sense points, it seems to me, in the same
direction as the dogmatic, hard kernel defended by the Council Fathers
at Trent, with regard to the Holy Eucharist: *incarnation of meaning*
plays a crucial role in a symbolic attitude (an attitude based on respect
for symbols), and its impact goes unrecognised by what I will call an
intellectualist doctrine of symbol.

My indirect approach to the two Tridentine dogmas is supported by a
double intuition, one of which is anthropological and one of which lies
in the philosophy of religion: a sense for symbols forms the basis of a
religious attitude toward symbols and that attitude constitutes the core of
religion. This statement is consistent with the following: from a theological perspective, the discussion turns around the instituting words of
Christ. But the fact that Catholic teaching and the Reformation have
assigned different scopes to the is-relation in "Hoc est corpus meum"
can not be explained by the difference between their respective chris-
tologies. Regarding the christological dogma, they were tendencies
within Christianity that had been in agreement. What divided them

flowed much more from a different vision of the place and role of symbols in the exercise of faith. There is more than theological argument at work in the dogmas of *praesentia realis* and *transsubstantiatio*.

I will begin by working out my phenomenological analysis of symbols with a focus on a specific class of symbolic objects -namely, relics. Next, I will show how this analysis can throw some light on what came into discussion at Trent. In my concluding remarks, I will show that an attitude which *takes symbols seriously* inevitably comes to swing ambiguously between a literal interpretation that is too strong and a figurative interpretation that is too weak.

I. RELICS AND THE FETISHISTIC ASPECT OF STRONGLY INCARNATED MEANING

In Micheal Polanyi's book *Meaning* – edited with his friend Prosch[2] and published in 1975, shortly before his death – there is a simple distinction made between signs as *indicators* and signs as *symbols*. Polanyi conceives of indicators as vehicles, or transparent references to something else. He calls them "transparent" because they do not attract our attention to themselves. The object of focal interest lies outside the sign. *From* the sign we follow the direction in which the sign points us and we concentrate on what it indicates. The sign itself is of lesser importance because it does not stand at the focus of interest. As indicator of direction, it plays a subsidiary role. *From* the sign, we direct ourselves *to* a point that lies outside of the sign itself. We are led by it like the blind man who follows the indications felt in his hands from the stick he holds out in front of him. "The subsidiary clues are not of intrinsic interest in the transaction. It is the object of focal attention that possesses the intrinsic interest"[3].

Polanyi's examples of symbols are first of all non-linguistic. These include the national flag and a medal or gravestone of someone we admire. In symbols, the *from-to* relation runs differently than it does in indicators. Considered solely as material objects, symbols are without any substantial interest. The flag is an ordinary piece of textile, the medal a piece of gold or bronze, and so forth. But what in itself must be considered ordinary and meaningless, takes on an exceptional weight in and from a symbolic relation. What is of subsidiary importance insofar as it denotes or stands for something else becomes at the same time an

---

2. M. POLANYI & H. PROSCH, *Meaning*, Chicago – London, University of Chicago Press, 1975.

3. *Ibid.*, p. 71.

essential and crucial part of the experience of the symbol, a part that puts its stamp on that experience. The flag and the gravestone are parts of the symbolic process that can not stand on their own, but are nonetheless *essential* parts of what they symbolise. A symbol is not extrinsic to what it symbolises but is itself a part of it. This is something that the symbol has in common with the proper name. A proper name is more than an efficient means of reference[4]. In a certain sense, the name has grown together with the bearer of the name to such a degree that it is a part of him or her. By ruining someone's name we also damage their reputation, and by playing word games with it we also touch the person as such. Symbols function like proper names. Just like someone's name, a flag can also be dishonoured or reviled. To burn the flag is to expose oneself to the wrath of the people. In a symbolic relation, the two terms of the relation are not separate and extrinsic from one another but entangled in one another. This tight relation is a feature equally of obscene words and of everything consecrated and sacral. Obscene words are not merely words that point to something filthy, but are themselves obscene. And a consecrated object is not merely something that stays in relation to something else that is sacred; no, it is itself sacred. What is indicated by the symbol strikes upon the symbol itself, and the force of what it indicates penetrates it. In a symbolic relation the two components of the symbol slide into one another without either of them completely covering the other, and also without the two falling completely together. This mutual entanglement can be described either by saying that the symbol forms a part of what it symbolises, or that it partly contains what it expresses. This latter description is also found in the dogma of the *praesentia realis*: the consecrated host contains (*continet*) the body of Christ.

Whereas in *indication* the object of focal interest lies outside the sign, so that we can leave the sign behind us as soon as we reach its aim, *symbolisation* focuses interest equally on the symbol itself, as bearer of meaning. Whereas the sign as indicator is destroyed when we concentrate explicitly on it, the symbol in fact demands that we focus on it. The symbol is thus not only a point of departure but at the same time an endpoint. We circle around it. In the symbol there occurs an *arrow-loop*, says Polanyi[5], and by this he means that in a symbol the *from-to* relation loops back on itself. The love of country which the flag symbolises is

---

4. A. BURMS, *De navolging van Jacques Derrida*, in S. IJSSELING (ed.), *Jacques Derrida. Een inleiding in zijn denken*, Baarn, Ambo, 1986, pp. 209-211.
    5. M. POLANYI & H. PROSCH, *Meaning* (n. 2), p. 73.

reflected and crystallised – embodied – in the symbol. Our bond with our country reaches an emotional highpoint when we view the flag during ceremonial proceedings. The flag absorbs the horizon of affective associations that we carry with us, and it can move us deeply. A sign brings us somewhere; a symbol, in contrast, can move us[6]. According to Polanyi, indicators are *self-centred*: we integrate that to which the sign calls our attention gradually into our interests, with the result that the sphere of those interests is thus expanded. A symbol that can move us brings about a movement of abandon, a dynamic of *self-giving*. The flag is the concrete embodiment and tangible animation of our love of country.

Symbols are strongly incarnated meanings[7]. The phenomenon of incarnation also plays a striking role in a class of symbols that Polanyi does not mention: relics.

It is well-known that one can become attached to an object belonging to a person who one admires or holds dear. In "My Father's Cigarette Butt as Sacrament", chapter three of *Sacraments of Life. Life of Sacraments*[8], Leonardo Boff recounts how the love and honour he bore his father expressed and concentrated itself in a pious attitude toward a cigarette butt. The insignificant cigarette butt took on unique value for him because it was the remains of the last cigarette his father smoked.

Two dimensions of symbolic action come together in devotion to a relic. On one hand, the relic does have a sign-value, in the wide sense of the word. It is experienced as pointing to something else and radiates an expressive force that touches the imagination. A whole world attached to the loved or honoured person is evoked. On the other hand, the relic is also experienced as unique and irreplaceable; it falls outside the chain of replaceable signs. It falls outside because its force can neither be undone from it nor completely taken over by other signs. Even if one can not see or feel the difference, the *Ersatz*-object still does not have the same value.

Incarnans, that which incarnates meaning – or, in formulated in passive terms, what receives and bears the meaning – and *incarnatum*, that which is incarnated, slide into one another, and their relation is not extrinsic but intimate[9].

---

6. *Ibid.*, p. 71.

7. *Ibid.*, p. 73.

8. L. Boff, *Sacramenteel denken en leven*, Averbode – Apeldoorn, Altiora, 1983, p. 25 ff. E.T.: *Sacraments of Life. Life of the Sacraments*, trans. J. Dewey, Beltsville, MD, The Pastoral Press, 1987, pp. 15 ff.

9. Here I invoke the terminology favoured by my colleague, Rudi Visker.

The surplus value of a relic is not in any way due to itself. What the object is, how it appears, and what it is used for, are all strictly inessential. Its value is due exclusively to its causal connection or relation of contiguity with a dear person. In principle, anything can be elevated to a relic, on the condition that a dear person has briefly touched it or possessed it. The *transformation of values* that the object thus undergoes is therefore dependent on a real, objective connection with a person. One can attach importance to the fact that the object has been touched only if one is acquainted with the sense of symbols. *Without this acquaintance, that being-touched is not meaningful.*

The modification undergone by an object elevated to a relic concerns the meaning of the object and must not be situated on the level of a visible transformation of the chemical substance. Nothing in the primary and secondary attributes is altered. However, while the process of modification concerns only meaning, the object is nonetheless permeated by it through and through. The object is – why not? – transubstantiated. One takes care to hold it apart from other objects. A relic is treated with the greatest possible care, just as the final crumbs of the consecrated host are touched with the greatest devotion and just as the ashes of someone who has passed away are handled with the greatest respect. This devotion to the *incarnans* is an essential part of the *Faktum* of symbolic praxis, and I will call it the fetishistic aspect of symbolic practice.

II. AN INTELLECTUALIST DOCTRINE OF SYMBOLS: SYMBOLS ARE ONLY SIGNS

When I say "intellectualist doctrine of symbols", I mean a theory that fails to properly appreciate the impact of incarnation and passes over the fetishistic approach to symbols that comes with it. It does not conceive of symbols as a distinct class of signs and paints the two, signs and symbols, with the same brush. Just like signs (or what Polanyi calls "indicators"), symbolic objects thus direct a person only to contact with a content. As a means, they must help a person bring the symbolised content before the mind. What matters is that symbols are as clear and efficient as possible in bringing the symbolised before the mind. Just like signs, symbols find their destination in a point outside of themselves. Of chief importance is that the signified arrives well in the mind.

This vision rests on the correct thought that the symbol which evokes nothing is not meaningful. But from this correct thought it does not follow that symbols play only a subsidiary and supporting role. Radicalised to the end, the principles of the intellectualist theory lead to the conclusion that the symbol can by definition be replaced and exchanged: one and the same content can be brought to mind through other channels. Now, this conclusion does not fit with the manner in which a relic functions. The conclusion, in other words, is refuted by the *Faktum* of symbolic praxis – by the way in which people relate to symbols. Were it the case simply that the cup I have inherited from my deceased father and from which I now drink my coffee each morning is significant only because it reminds me of my father, or because it makes me think of something in particular about him (symbols as sign of remembrance), then I should be prepared, without hesitation, to replace that cup with some other mnemonic device. However, I do not do this. For by drinking out of my father's cup every day I kiss my father, and kiss him even when I drink from that cup without actually thinking of him. The cup binds me to my father even when I am not thinking of him, which happens to be the case most of the time. The cup does something for me, in my place. It remembers my father, without me thinking of him. The fact that I do not replace the cup means that it has a value that makes the symbol something more than a replaceable sign. The cup is more than a sign that points to my father; but it is only more than a sign because it is at the same time a sign. This also leads to the following: the cup is important even though as such it does not say anything important about the person who my father was.

We are familiar with the television images of people who are deeply moved by touching and stroking the names engraved on the Vietnam Memorial in Washington, DC. Contact by touching – fingers gliding softly over the letters of those names, kissing a photo of a much-loved child, drinking out of my father's cup, or eating the host at Mass[10] – has a sense of moving contact. And one can not translate the sense of this symbolic contact into the principles of an instrumental doctrine of signs. An intellectualist approach does not only pass by the importance of real contact with a symbolic object (touching the object), but is simply wrong when it asserts that the *incarnans* is nothing more than a useful means to bring something more sharply and clearly to mind[11].

At the same time, however, this mistaken interpretation in fact reveals to us the "peculiar" role that the *incarnans* plays in the *Faktum* of

10. Cf. L. WITTGENSTEIN, *Remarks on Frazer's Golden Bough*, in C.G. LUCKHARDT (ed.), *Wittgenstein. Sources and Perspectives*, London, Thoemmes, 1996, p. 61 ff.

11. For indications of how this sense of the term "incarnation" contributes to reinstating a non-intellectualist theory of religion and ethics, see J. BLOECHL, *Liturgy of the Neighbor. Emmanuel Levinas and the Religion of Responsibility*, Pittsburgh, Duquesne University Press, 2000, Chapter IV.

symbolic praxis. On one hand, it makes a crucial difference in the symbolic attitude whether an object is really touched by someone, or an object is really consecrated. On the other hand, one cannot say what this crucial fact adds to the meaning, or in what sense this enriches the content. This implies two things. *First*: an intellectualist vision of symbols can easily lead the symbolic attitude into embarrassment by asking for justification of respect and devotion for symbols. *Second*: the sense for symbols points in the direction of a sense *sui generis*, because it is impossible to either simply deduce this sense from other interests or reduce it to them, and it also can not be subordinated to other interests. One can not explain precisely *why* symbols are important, *what role* they actually fulfil, or wherein consists their significance.

When one accepts that the incarnation is crucial in the *Faktum* of symbolic praxis, one can ask oneself how to further describe the difference between symbols and non-symbolic signs. So long as one is satisfied with defining this distinction in an exclusively negative manner (e.g., symbolic objects are not only replaceable signs, and they are not only a means to express something), one has no trouble avoiding concepts that shock scientific reason and instrumental thinking. Those who try, in contrast, to carefully describe what it means that a symbol is more than a sign must have recourse to uncommon concepts that run against the current of the sign: symbols are fulfilled and permeated by the reality that is signified in them; they are full of the reality that impresses itself there; they are not only a sign but are themselves partly what they signify; in symbols, meaning and being are contracted; and so on. Such concepts are not in keeping with the nominalistic doctrine of signs on which the intellectualist vision of symbols is based.

An intellectualist vision is thoroughly mistrustful of descriptions such as '*incarnans* and *incarnatum* slide into one another'. It sees them as an expression of a confusion of concepts and lack of capacity to make proper distinctions. A symbolic consciousness would thus be one that is incapable of distinguishing between subjective thought-associations and objective causal relations, or between the psychical mechanisms of association and real relations. What the mind confuses is projected into the object-pole. In taking this view, an intellectualist doctrine of symbol gives a "psychological" explanation of symbols. This view also fits together with the negative assessment of some anthropologists (including, for example, Frazer) concerning the all-embracing symbolic mentality of primitive cultures. According to this view, primitive cultures are still at a "pre-symbolic stage" in the development of the human mind because the primitive mind is not yet capable of making abstraction and making a real distinction between *signifiant* and *signifié*[12]. Pronounced forms of symbolic consciousness in our own culture are then considered as a residue or throw-back to the confused mentality of primitive peoples.

But is it not too easy to merely refer a sense for symbols to a lack of capacity for making distinctions? Symbolic behaviour, whether or not it is all-encompassing as in primitive cultures, is certainly capable of distinguishing between symbols and non-symbolic signs, as well as between different symbols. For some symbols, the incarnation is stronger and more important than it is for others, though there is always some incarnation involved. The impact of that role depends on the rank of the symbol within the symbolic order to which a person is committed.[13] And anyone acquainted with the symbolic practice of his or her culture knows this.

Why not understand the sense for symbols not by referring them to a primitive lack of capacity to make distinctions, but rather from an awareness that they are a separate class of signs? And why not understand that sense in terms of respect for what truly deserves respect?

III. TRENT AND THE FEAR OF AN INTELLECTUALIST EVAPORISATION OF THE WORDS OF INSTITUTION

The foregoing analysis of symbols can shed some light on the theological dispute that took place at the Council of Trent. Both the dogma of *praesentia realis* and the dogma of *transsubstantiatio* attempt to protect the *proper nature* of symbols that make up the core of Christian worship from an intellectualist vision that goes too far in hollowing out the 'incarnatedness' of symbolic meanings and the contraction of *signifiant* and *signifié* that comes with it. The dogmas concern, strictly speaking, only the Holy of Holies, the Eucharist. In the Holy Eucharist, the sacraments all find their origin and fulfilment. The Holy Eucharist is the symbolic event that founds and supports and Christian community, as well as brings it constantly to life again. It is the symbol that binds all

---

12. On this, see A. IACONO, *Le fétichisme. Histoire d'un concept* (Collection Philosophies, 38), Paris, P.U.F., 1992, pp. 116-117.

13. In a primitive culture, not all fetishes are equal embodiment of the god or gods worshipped there – no more so than does everything that the Church consecrates exude the same religious power. A celebration of the Eucharist is more worshipful than is the blessing of a moped. In a primitive culture, one can certainly distinguish between the real presence of the gods in a fetish and their presence in such forms of apparition as dreams and visions. Someone who honors a relic of his father has not lost his sense of these sorts of distinctions. He does not confuse the symbolically mediated presence of his father with the presence of his father in living flesh and blood.

the other symbols together and raises them up to symbols of Christ's real presence. In the Holy Eucharist, the *that* and the *what* of symbols coincide. Both dogmas pronounced at Trent are expressions of the insight that symbols are an *objective fact* of the life of faith. Symbols are not the product of an underdeveloped mentality. What defines humans and distinguishes them from animals is that we are open to symbols and capable of relating ourselves to them in an appropriate manner, which is to say, in a manner conforming to the nature of symbols themselves.

But at the same time – and this complicates an analysis of the two dogmas – both dogmas are in danger of being dragged into a speculative metaphysical discussion that, contrary to its own intention, puts the independent and irreducible character of symbols (and symbolic praxis) under pressure. For the notion of *transsubstantiatio* is embedded in a speculative metaphysics that attempts to found the meaningful character of symbols on an ontological theory, with the result that symbolic practice becomes dependent on the correctness on its ontological assumptions. The truthfulness of these speculative, ontological assumptions must justify the meaningful experience of symbols. It is this that puts the autonomy of symbols under intense pressure. Should the conceptual elaboration of those ontological assumptions prove untenable, nonsensical or absurd, then one must, at least in principle, be prepared to give up the religiously inspired vision of symbols that one had set out to defend. However, the impulse toward grounding them ontologically flows in part from the fear of an intellectualist vision and the psychological explanation that comes with it. But by anchoring symbols in a theory of being, one nonetheless puts their autonomy at risk.

1. *The Dogma of Praesentia Realis*

After long and subtle discussion, the Council Fathers at Trent established the following dogmatic article of faith:

> If anyone denies that the boy and blood, together with the soul and divinity of our Lord Jesus Christ and, therefore, the whole Christ is truly, really, and substantially contained [*contineri*] in the sacrament of the most holy Eucharist, but says that Christ is present in the Sacrament only [*tantummodo*] as a sign [*esse in eo ut in signi*] or figure, or by his power: let them be anathema[14].

---

14. H. DENZINGER, *Enchiridion symbolorum definitionum et declarationum de rebus fidei et morum*, ed. P. HÜNERMANN, Freiburg – Basel – Rome – Wien, Herder, [38]1999, 1651 can. 1: "Si quis negaverit, in sanctissimae Eucharistiae sacramento contineri vere, realiter et substantialiter corpus et sanguinem una cum anima et divinitate Domini nostri Iesu Christi, ac proinde totum Christum; sed dixerit, tantummodo esse in eo ut in signo vel figura aut virtute: anathema sit".

There are two parts to this dogma: what one must confess, and what one must reject. The theological debate over how to interpret of Christ's words of institution[15] does not turn around the question of *"either* sign *or* not sign?"* Discussion concerns rather the necessity of the proposition that sacramental symbols in the Holy Eucharist are *both* signs *and* not purely signs. This dogma from Catholic teaching thus does not in any way deny that eucharistic symbols fall under the general category of signs. The Tridentine dogma attempts, first, to reject theological inter-pretations which say that bread and wine, even if they are consecrated, are still nothing more than an extrinsic sign of Christ's body and blood. A purely nominalistic sign-relation (*esse in eo ut in signo*), whereby *incarnans* and *incarnatum* remain exterior to one another, is according to the Council Fathers too weak and wrong. Secondly, the proposition that the is-relation must be considered as a figurative, poetic way of speaking is also judged by the Council Fathers as a frivolous and incor-rect interpretation. I will return to this.

What this dogma rejects is the sort of theological vision of symbol that reaches its extreme form in Zwingli. Zwingli reduces the eucharistic symbols to memorial signs. They are, he says, meaningful only because they help us to remember a salvific content. Zwingli thus radicalises the intellectualist propositions already at work in Calvinism. With this, he opens the door for what the phenomenologist of religion Gerardus van der Leeuw calls "the fatal pedagogical explanation of the sacrament"[16]. Not only the Council Fathers at Trent, but also Luther was apprehensive at the Zwinglian intellectualist evaporation of the incarnated mystery of faith. To claim that Christ's words of institution must be understood only in an extrinsic sense is, according to Luther, a devilish sacrilege:

> Sie sagen, das Wörtlein 'ist' gelte soviel als das Wort 'bedeutet,' wie Zwingli schreibt, und das Wort 'mein Leib' heisse soviel als das Wort 'ein Zeichen meines Leibes,' wie Oekolampad schreibt. So würde als Christi Wort und Meinung, nach Zwingli's Text folgendermasse: Nehmet hin, esset, das bedeutet meinen Leib, oder nach Oekolampads Text folgender-masse: lauter 'nehmet hin und esset, das ist meines Leibes Zeichen' [...] O wie stinken hier dem Teufel die Hosen[17].

15. Eucharistic symbols are not relics. A relic is an object that forms a part of a greater whole. The conveyance of meaning from person to object runs via the *metonymic axis of language*. In the Eucharist, the power of Christ's instituting words identifies bread and wine with his body and blood. The signifying-relation is established by the word and thus does not come about via contiguity. Meaning is conveyed along the *metaphoric axis of language*. The two processes have in common the incarnation of meaning.

16. G. VAN DER LEEUW, *Sacramentstheologie*, Nijkerk, Callenbach, 1949, p. 247.

17. Cited *ibid*, p. 77. For a more detailed account of the aforementioned reformation-ists with respect to the words of institution and the Roman Catholic dogma of *praesentia*

2. *The Dogma of "Transsubstantiatio"*

It was not so much the dogma of *praesentia realis* but that of *transsubstantiatio* that stirred controversy. The dogma was pronounced as follows:

> If anyone says that the substance of bread and wine remains in the holy sacrament of the Eucharist together with the body and blood of our Lord Jesus Christ, and denies that wonderful and extraordinary change of the whole substance of the bread into Christ's body, and the whole substance of the wine into his blood while only the species of bread and wine remain, a change which the Catholic church has most fittingly called transubstantiation: let them be anathema[18].

It is said of the term *transsubstantiatio* that it is very appropriate. The dogma does not exclude the possibility that other terms may also be capable of rendering the objective aspect of the unique, mysterious event of the Eucharistic celebration. The term is nonetheless well-chosen because it remains more closely connected with the direct speech act of Christ than do terms like *consubstantiatio* and *impanatio*. It is also preferable to terms like "transfiguration", "transformation", and "metamorphosis", which indicate visible and perceptible changes. In the Eucharist, neither the eye nor the mind sees any difference between objects before and after consecration. While the shape and form of the bread and wine remain unchanged after consecration, the relation of the faithful to that bread and wine is radically altered. The term *transsubstantiatio* is, finally, a striking, evocative, suggestive description because it can, to a great measure, meet the impact of incarnation of meaning and the fetishistic dimension that is less evident in a term like *transfinalisation*, which some Leuven theologians once put forward as a possible alternative. After all, once consecrated, even the smallest crumbs of bread and drops of wine are treated with the greatest possible respect. And this respect is still expressed at the moment when consecrated bread and wine are at the verge of losing their form and becoming inedible and undrinkable. When consecrated bread and wine spoil, one does not

---

realis, I refer to my *De mateloosheid van het christendom*, Nijmegen, SUN, 1998, p. 141 ff. In the present context, I wish only to point out that the Reformation, broadly considered, has not denied *praesentia realis* but has indeed chosen to describe its *modus* with less sensualistic and corporeal metaphors.

18. DENZINGER, *Enchiridion symbolorum* (n. 14), 1652, can. 2: "Si quis dixerit, in sacrosancto Eucharistiae sacramento remanere substantiam panis et vini una cum corpore et sanguine Domini nostri Iesu Christi, negaveritque mirabilem illam et singularem conversionem totius substantiae panis in corpus et totius substantiae vini in sanguinem, manentibus dumtaxat speciebus panis et vini, quam quidem conversionem catholica Ecclesia aptissime transsubstantiationem appellat: anathema sit."

dispose of them in the same manner as one disposes of the remains of ordinary food. No, this always takes place with fitting prayers and according to a prescribed ritual.

The term *transsubstantiatio* circulated for some time in the speculative metaphysical discourse of theologians steeped in a scholastic training. In that discourse, the term functions not so much as an evocative and normative description of what constitutes respect for incarnation of meaning, as the indication of a transformation as real and objective as any physical change in nature, but of a transformation which must be situated on a deeper level of being, on a different metaphysical level lying behind and beneath the physical order, and to which only speculative reason has access. From this perspective, *transsubstantiatio* functions as a justifying and explaining ground for the symbolic practice. The correctness or plausibility of a rational doctrine of being thus becomes decisive for the meaningful character of the symbolic attitude. But if *transsubstantiatio* is the object of a speculative science, then the rational constructions of theology would have to unfold in accordance with the demands imposed by scientific reason; this would mean committing itself to a detailed analysis of everything that happens in the process of change. If speculative theology can not prove that that change can be thought in conformity with the basic principles of a rational ontology, and without inner contradiction, then it must at least be able to show – and this without introducing an excess of ad hoc constructions – that it is not absurd to affirm such a change…

Precisely what happens to the invisible substance of bread and wine? How does their substance disappear? Can the substance change without a modification of accidents? Can the *accidentia* exist without a substantial change, after all? According to Aristotle, this is unthinkable. At precisely what moment does the change take place? With the pronunciation of the first word of consecration, at the second word, or after the entire sentence? If, in a particular case, the *Hoc est corpum meum* is not fully pronounced, is the process of *transsubstantiatio* then stuck halfway to completion? If it comes suddenly to completion, then how does that fit together with the fact that an entire series of words must be uttered in sequence? And what about the volume in which those words are pronounced – does that have any influence on the outcome, and so forth?…

Suppose that respect for relics is not fundamentally different than respect for eucharistic symbols: does it not seem absurd to found the veneration of relics in a rational ontology? Yet however strange the ingenious speculative thought-constructions of theology may appear to us, it is nonetheless understandable that theology used its imaginative force and rational capacities in order to explain the objective character of symbols according to a doctrine of being: on one hand, it thus sought to disarm a psychological explanation of symbols; on the other hand it has tried to use the weapons of the intellectualist view to neutralise an intellectualist view of symbols which has defended a weaker conception of symbols such as, let us not forget it, came about in the first place under the pressure of the emerging modern scientific rationality.

By holding up *transsubstantiatio* as an article of faith, the Council Fathers at Trent have changed the function of this term within rational theology. Once taken up in a dogma, the term no longer functions as an invitation for reason to approach it in a scientific manner. The intention was rather to call a halt to strictly scientific curiosity about the mystery of the Eucharist. The dogma therefore has a two-fold aim: on one hand to protect what belongs properly to symbols from a disincarnated intellectualist evaporation, and on the other hand to put and end to one type of reflection on the Eucharist. By fixing the term in a dogma, it was hoped to stimulate theologians to transform their *theologia rationalis* into a *theologia orans*. The fact that this was indeed the concern of the Council Fathers is confirmed, for example, in the following clarification found in the *Catechism of the Council of Trent*:

> Here it is necessary to exhort the faithful, that they do not seek with undue curiosity the manner in which this change can occur: for we can not understand it, and we also do not find examples of it, as little among natural changes as in the creation of all things. What occurs here we know by faith; how it occurs we must not investigate with curiosity [...] It would be best to enter into dispute over it as little as possible; if however Christian love demands it, then the spirit of the faithful are to be armed with this word: 'with God, nothing is impossible' (Luke 1,37)[19].

Transsubstantiatio functions *in* the dogma not only as a technical theoretical concept, but at the same time as a *limit-concept* and a switch-point. *On one hand*, this dogma permits one, at least if supported by the insight that symbols the most deserving of respect are a separate class of signs, to investigate whether this term, better than any other, reproduces something essential of the real difference between strongly incarnated symbols and weakly incarnated signs. *On the other hand*, the dogma attempts at the same time to protect the truth of faith that is anchored in a symbolic praxis by holding it at a distance from the intrusive curiosity of speculative reason. The dogma is a prohibition and it elevates something to the

---

19. *Catechismus van het Concilie van Trente,* Mechelen, Dessain, 1935, p. 291. This citation comes from section 43, which has been given the following title: "The manner in which this change occurs may not be investigated out of curiosity".

level of devotion. In this much, it resembles taboos. As concrete embodiment of what is sacred, a taboo marks a distinction over against a profane, intramundane order. It demands to be respected and honoured, and
it forbids us to touch it without impunity, to look at it without scruple,
and by extension to submit it without hesitation to the advances of reason. Just as words that directly indicate what is taboo (whether holy or
obscene) are themselves taboo, so too is the dogma a direct embodiment
of what is holy in the Christian cult. The dogma is more than a re-word-
ing of a holy truth of faith; it is itself holy because is bears and incarnates that truth. Just as believers, at the moment of the elevation of the
bread and wine, may not look at the body of Christ without prostrating,
so theologians may not approach the dogma without imposing silence on
their understanding and averting their curious gaze. The dogma calls theologians to lay down the weapons of reason and transform their *theologia rationalis* into a *theologia orans* that kneels before the mysterious
truth and remains in prayer before it. This dogma makes up a part of the
symbolum of Christian faith. In this dogma, form and content fall partly
together; the dogma is also itself what it signifies.

I have argued that *what* Trent says comes closer to the *Faktum* of
symbolic praxis than does a vision of symbol coloured by intellectual-
ism. Or, in milder terms, I have argued that *what* Trent says is not incorrect. Still, the Tridentine dogmas themselves can also put what belongs
properly to symbols under pressure, and this according to *another difficulty* than that which usually arises from the intellectualist approach.
The classical reply to Trent argues that its all-too-literal interpretation
leads to a misunderstanding of the symbolicity of symbols, including a
failure to fully appreciate the fact that symbols do have a sign-value,
after all. Of course, this sort of critique gains force and impact only
when acquaintance with symbols weaken. I wonder if there is not in fact
another difficulty bound up with this, and which I would formulate as
follows: it is not *what* Trent says that is problematic, but *that* it has said
it. Or, formulated differently, these dogmas make explicit something
that, even if it is not incorrect, is meaningful only insofar as it remains
to some degree implicit. Trent threatens to make symbols implode by
making explicit something of how they work. It is indeed so that in sym-
bol-sensitive religious devotion, the *incarnans* plays a crucial role. But
however important it is, in a pious attitude one is aimed neither solely
nor directly at the ultra-concrete anchorpoint. In the liturgy, the objects
elevated into symbols are enveloped in uplifting prayers and songs by
which the *incarnans* is surrounded in a veil of mystery. In this way, the

liturgy is the context in which the all-too-obtrusive and emphatic presence of the *incarnans* is veiled and concealed. Well now, *to directly indicate* the material anchor-point for symbolic practice can have a disenchanting effect, and undermine the evocative force of the symbol as symbol. *To directly indicate* the point which sexual desire circles around can undermine erotic experience. Attempts to focus the erotic, and by extension symbols, too directly on incarnatedness can undermine their sense.

By pointing with a strong, well-developed feel for conceptual precision and a dogmatic accuracy at the mysterious event of incarnatedness, the Tridentine formulation risks producing the very result it set out to avoid. Rather than keeping incarnation at a distance necessary for there to be a sense of mystery, it risks putting incarnation too strongly in the foreground. The dogma itself breaks into the universe of symbols that yields their signifying power when their function remains in some measure *implicit*.

In the period of Trent, theology stood before the difficult and paradoxical task of defending with the necessary precision something that can bear the symbolic practice only when it functions obliquely – which is to say only when it not explicated too emphatically.

IV. PROVISIONAL CONCLUSION: TAKING SYMBOLS SERIOUSLY AND FINDING A BALANCE BETWEEN AN OVERLY LITERAL AND OVERLY FIGURATIVE CONCEPTION OF SYMBOLS

A Roman Catholic view of religion that is based on a sacramental faith-relation calls us to take symbols *au sérieux*. Strictly speaking, to take something seriously means to consider it in a modest, respectful way, which is to say: neither to mock it outwardly and openly, nor to deal with it frivolously. To take symbols seriously, to be touched and moved by them, is not necessarily the same thing as understanding them literally. However, it is indeed the case that one can put their seriousness at risk by asserting, boldly and without reservation, that one does not need to take symbols literally. By affirming straightforwardly that the contraction of *incarnans* and *incarnatum* is only a figurative way of speaking, one opens the door to the thought that symbols present us with a content that can be expressed equally and just as well in some other manner.

In order to protect the seriousness of symbols from a superficial hollowing-out, Trent stresses the importance and necessity of a literal interpretation. But at the same time it is also the case that a certain literal conception can bring symbols in danger: namely, the conception which says that what can only be understood from within the symbolic attitude has the same truth-value as the one claimed by the rational ontology of scientific discourse, whose truth-claims do not depend on what people experience as meaningful. This conception thus makes taking symbols seriously depend on the correctness of theoretical, metaphysical insights. Along this line, one fails to appreciate the sense for symbols as an *ordo sui generis*. In order to avoid the undesirable consequences of a literal, quasi-physicalistic interpretation, one will tend to neutralise it by adding an "as if" (for example: Christ is not really present in symbolic signs; it is only "as if" this were so, only a manner of speaking). Too much emphasis on this "as if", however, can give the impression of not taking incarnation seriously.

Whoever takes symbols seriously must find a balance between two extremes to be both accepted and avoided. Each of those extremes, if taken in itself, is either *too strong* or *too weak*, and it is equally impossible to sustain both at once. Anyone asked to explicate and justify what belongs properly to symbols is led to inevitable embarrassment. The moment someone takes up this question, he or she no longer knows quite what to say: neither literal nor figurative, and literal as well as figurative. Symbols are signs that are not purely signs, but without ceasing to be signs.

Institute of Philosophy   Paul MOYAERT
Katholieke Universiteit Leuven
Kardinaal Mercierplein, 2
B-3000 Leuven

RESPONSE TO PAUL MOYAERT

ON THE DOGMA OF REAL PRESENCE

1. I agree completely with Paul Moyaert's thesis (as and if I understand it!): an "intellectualist doctrine of symbol" clearly gets in the way of seeing the eucharistic event for what it is; I am, secondly, very sympathetic to his hostility to a certain kind of "speculative metaphysics" – and here I shall outline, briefly, a strategy practised by post-Wittgensteinian philosophers (Anscombe and Dummett), which seems (again if I understand him!) to achieve roughly the same result as his "eidetic analysis of the sense for symbols;" but I wonder, thirdly, if there is not a respectably Christian "participationist" ontology such as Catherine Pickstock would advocate – which would gloss the theological claims about "life-giving symbols" that "already in this our earthly existence" give "a share in the sanctifying power of divine grace".

Here I may add a sentence from John of Damascus, recapitulating 1 Corinthians 10,16-17 and 11,17-22. The Eucharist "is called 'communion' and truly it is. For through it we both commune with Christ, and share in his body as well as in his deity, and commune and are united with one another. For as we all eat of one loaf we become one body and one blood with Christ and members of one another. This we may be called co-embodiments of Christ, *sussomoi tou christou*"(cf. *de fide orthodoxa* 4:13).

To understand such "co-embodying", do we not develop a participationist ontology?

2. The Eucharist is the cornerstone of normative Christian worship, that is incontestable; the dispute is about the relationship of symbol with reality symbolised. To bypass this dispute altogether, for ecumenical or other reasons, is already accepting a view of religion in which "the religious impact of a symbolic praxis is incidental". Again I entirely agree with Paul Moyaert.

3. Moyaert insists on the impact of symbolic objects in non-religious contexts. Following Michael Polanyi, he insists on the difference between

signs as indicators (e.g. road signs) and signs as symbols (such as national flags – relics – objects inherited from one's deceased parents, and the like).

4. The "intellectualist doctrine of symbols" conceives symbols as indicators, always in principle replaceable – but this philosophical theory is "refuted by the facts of how people deal with such symbols". Picking up the allusion to the later Wittgenstein, let me sketch the Wittgensteinian moves that seem (to me at least!) to have roughly the same upshot as Moyaert's "phenomenological remarks".

For a start: if you ask me to explain/justify e.g. kissing a photograph of a much-loved child recently or long dead (etc.), I do not know what to say. I may concede that this or that symbolic gesture is "silly", "outdated", that I should have "outgrown" it, and so on, and your demand for an explanation/justification may enable me to see that this or that specific practice is "pointless"; but if I find that you need an explanation for every such practice, I have to say, with the later Wittgenstein, that I cannot "find my feet with you" – you belong to an alien culture – at least if I were to take you seriously; but actually, taught by Wittgenstein and others, I see that you have become so entranced by the craving for explanation that you no longer allow yourself to look at the facts – you have succumbed to a general theoretical scepticism fancied to be the mark of sophisticated modern rationality but which is the curse of modern philosophy – a general scepticism that I should confidently expect to be able to undermine – by bringing you back to practices. Even if I may have to give up this or that practice, I do not give up all such practices – I don't have to explain why symbolic practices as such are inescapable, necessary, illuminating, beautiful, revealing, etc. "Don't think but look", as Wittgenstein would have said; that is don't let yourself be overcome by the craving for a theory; just remember the practices without which our life together would not be how it is – if we were to put the remains of the dead out for the garbage men to take away; if we were completely indifferent to photographs of people we love – and suchlike. Hundreds of examples come to mind – in this or that instance it may be a practice, waiting to be reformed or abandoned, and a sceptical question about the point of the practice might be just what is needed to enable us to disengage from that particular symbolic practice – but we do not require rational justifications for all such practices. If you asked me for a justification for treating my parent's ashes as sacred, as if there needed to be an underlying justificatory theory to explain why such behaviour is reasonable, rational, human, etc., I should not know what to say to you.

Obviously, it does not follow from your being "cured" of – laughed out of – the demand for an "intellectualist" justification for symbolic activity that you will reverence (say) the eucharistic elements – much else has to be in place, in your life, as Wittgenstein would of course remind us; but if you really do nothing without grounding it first of all in reason I should have no idea how to relate to you. I have to conclude that you are either deranged (psychotic) or badly confused by "speculative metaphysics"!

I hope that is not too inaccurate a translation of Moyaert's "phenomenological remarks" into "analytical philosophy"!

5. We don't have to go with J.G. Frazer, the great armchair anthropologist of religion who had so much influence on English literature in the first half of this century: "Symbols are not the product of an underdeveloped mentality. What defines humans and distinguishes them from animals is that we are open to symbols and capable of relating ourselves to them in an appropriate manner". Here again I agree with Moyaert completely; and we could linger over Wittgenstein's "Remarks on Frazer's Golden Bough" (which, historically, one may say, inaugurate the transition from earlier to later Wittgenstein – to the Wittgenstein who strives to expose the absurdities of intellectualist conceptions of language).

6. Moving now to sacramental practices: contrary to its own intention, a certain "speculative metaphysical discussion" "puts the independent and irreducible character of symbols and symbolic praxis under pressure". Thus, the sense of awe at the eucharistic consecration that the notion of transubstantiation is intended to focus is tied up with "a speculative metaphysics that attempts to found the meaningful character of symbols on an ontological theory, with the result that symbolic practice becomes dependent on the correctness of its ontological assumptions". The impulse to ground symbolic praxis ontologically – in a theory of being – reveals an intellectualist view of the symbolic; by anchoring symbolic practice in a theory of being we put the autonomy of such practice in jeopardy. Far from securing the validity of the symbolic action we only deprive it of its autonomy. Right, I totally agree.

7. So to neutralise an intellectualist (nominalist) view of symbols – to call a halt – to put an end to one type of theological reflection – Moyaert cites a splendid remark from the Catechism of the Council of Trent – a prohibition, a taboo – not explaining but marking where explanation stops. (Quite Wittgensteinian!)

8. There is a "development of peculiar ontological constructions that threaten to burden the religious heart rather than lighten it": Moyaert's attack on the "speculative metaphysics" which gets between what happens in the eucharistic consecration and what people are inclined to think happens reminds me very much of the protests of G.E.M. Anscombe and Michael Dummett – seeking (as they do) to save a *theologia orans* from a certain tradition of bad neo-scholastic metaphysics (as they think). Anscombe famously opens her paper on transubstantiation by declaring that it is a doctrine that can and should be taught to little children – and she goes on to describe how a small child might be brought into the Eucharist and allowed to develop habits of reverence (etc.) which would be the context in which talk of transubstantiation might one day become necessary. Dummett, in a less celebrated paper, starts from the age-old ecclesial practice of reserving the sacrament. Both Anscombe and Dummett insist on the priority of the practices over any theoretical account; indeed their point is essentially that attempts to ground such practices in "metaphysics" will only distort them out of all recognition and give rise to sterile polemics.

9. If Catherine Pickstock were here, however, she would (I guess) make the same objection to Moyaert's thesis as she did to Anscombe and Dummett as I presented their non-metaphysical treatment of the Eucharist: it is all too pragmatic; we don't have to agree that all metaphysics is an attempt to secure theorising grounding for symbolic practices that need no such grounding and are only occluded by such attempts. Is it not possible to develop a theo-ontology, a Christian ontology? For the risen Christ to be sacramentally in the consecrated bread and wine is for him, in a certain way, to be so; what is to stop us, supposing this to be the case, from bringing out the ontological implications *post factum*? We may well suspect efforts first to construct an ontology on general principles in order subsequently to locate the church's sacramental events in terms of that ontology; it can be very tempting to speak of an already understood "sacramental universe" within which sacraments have their being, or to speak of some generally sacramental character of worldly being which includes the church's specific sacramentality – but suppose we start, instead, with the being of a particular person, the risen Lord Jesus Christ, and continue by saying such things as that he is "really present" as the eucharistic elements – making an ontological claim, certainly – but what counts, surely, is the direction of thought – what one takes as given and what one may then need or wish to interpret. Is not the problem with the bad (supposedly neo-scholastic)

metaphysics that it started from general ideas about the language of substance (etc.) and sought then to fit in the presence of the risen Christ,
whereas we might start with our being *sussomoi tou christou*?

If (as Moyaert suggests at the beginning of his paper) we take the
eucharistic event as symbolic in the sense of making available the eschatological realities – enabling participation in the "sanctifying power of
divine grace" – are we not acknowledging an "incarnation of meaning"
which the anti-intellectualist insistence on the primacy and primitiveness
of symbolic practices such as you find in such post-Wittgensteinians as
Anscombe and Geach certainly allows to appear for what it is – but does
freeing this "incarnation of meaning" from illusory and distorting
attempts to secure it on an ontological foundation necessarily rule out all
post factum contemplation – '*theoria*' – of the ontological implications
of participating, sacramentally, symbolically, in the being of the "sacrament of God"?

University of Oxford   Fergus KERR
Blackfriars
St. Giles
Oxford OX1 3LY
England

THE LANGUAGE OF SACRAMENTAL MEMORIAL

Rupture, Excess and Abundance[1]

This contribution has to do with the language of sacramental celebration, as it relates to the topic of the conference, sacramental presence, and to the issues raised for celebration due to trends that are dubbed postmodern. After some prefatory remarks, it will deal with rupture, excess and abundance as aspects of the language of sacramental memorial to be taken into account in this context. It will conclude with some thoughts on the use of meontology in sacramental theology.

I. Prefatory Remarks

There are three sets of prefatory remarks. The first relate the topic of language to the issue of sacramental presence. The second set indicate in what way the paper enters the debate about the postmodern disruption of modernity. The third explain the sacramental heuristic of language event which is at work in the paper.

1. *Presence*

What is said here about language relates to the issue of sacramental presence as presently discussed in two ways. In the first place, relying on something as traditional as Thomas Aquinas's description of the sacraments as signs, it is evident that sacramental celebration takes place in a moment of tension between past and future. As Aquinas explains, sacraments are simultaneously signs of past, present and future. What is signified of the present can be grasped only in as much as this is given in virtue of both past and future. What is present comes from the past and even as given is already passing into the future. This is true not only of what is given in communion but even of the presence of Christ

---

1. This paper is in some fashion a *repetitio*, since it is based on and in places extracts from the author's book, *Sacrament: The Language of God's Giving,* New York, Crossroad, 1999, but in other places pursues this thought along different avenues.

himself "in truth". What this paper intends to show is how liturgical language expresses this transition and tension, and how it needs to be interrupted and reshaped in order to be faithful to its character of commemoration.

In the second place, theoretical terms used in ecumenical dialogue need to be taken with some caution when they are related to what in fact takes place in celebration. Current ecumenical description has dealt with the relation of Eucharist and sacraments to the Cross of Christ by using such terms as re-presentation, re-enactment and making-present. Though this has been fruitful in bringing about greater understanding between Churches, this vocabulary should not be strained to suggest that excess of presence of which onto-theology stands accused.

2. *Modernity and Postmodernity*

Whenever one speaks of the modern and the postmodern, the exact sense of the prefix *post* is always in question. Thus it is useful at the start to quote what Charles Jencks says in his book, *What is Post-Modernism?*:

> Post-Modernism is not Anti-Modernism; it is neither traditionalism nor the reactionary rejection of its parents. It does not...reject the Enlightenment project; that is, the social emancipation of humanity, increasing freedom and universal rights. Rather, it rejects the totalising arguments with which universal rights are often imposed by an elite on a subservient minority (along with so much else). Modern liberalism fought for the 'universal' rights which the First World now partly enjoys; post-modern liberalism argues that the agenda of multiculturalism, and the rights of minorities should be asserted where they do not diminish the rights of other minorities. In this sense it is the direct heir of its parent and could not have occurred previously. It is quite true that the logic of modern and post-modern liberalism are different, and sometimes in conflict, but that does not make either of them invalid. They are both necessary to the concept of justice in society[2].

As the same author puts it, we do not choose post-modernism in the way in which our forebears chose modernism with its refined projects of rational creation and control, but it chooses us[3]. That is to say, it comes upon us in two ways. First, it emerges from the negative impact of the most appalling events that mark the failures, which are one with the

---

2. C. JENCKS, *What is Post-Modernism?*, London, Academy Editions, Revised Edition, 1996, p. 15. The influence of Martin Heidegger and Jacques Derrida are amply treated in other papers at this conference but are not the preoccupation of this paper which is concerned with liturgical performance.

3. *Ibid.*, p. 15.

excesses, of modernity and give rise to disillusionment with its project. On the other hand, it arrives with a resurgence of creative power that results when the totalising endeavours of the modern project lose hold. While horrendous memories float over us, contradicting the human project and rendering it suspect, there are also creative powers of expression and language that emerge when they are released from subservience to some ideal or ideological controlling power. Thus the postmodern emerges in contradiction to the totalitarian instincts of the modern, not denying its achievements, but seeking to include and diversify, and be open to the creativity of the excluded and the marginal, those who remain other to the dominant. It includes deconstruction in the effort to heed the other, the other meaning and the other person, and to keep signification open.

When the modern entered sacramental theology could be debated. There is a sense in which it came with the effort at a retrieval of the priesthood of all believers after the Second Vatican Council. This meant designing a liturgy that would promote full, active, conscious participation, recognising this as a community action rather than a clerical one. Persons were thus given a role which they did not have when hierarchical ritual codes were taken as the expression of the social order of the Church. On the other hand, however, a more negative side to modernity appeared in the rationalistic and programmatic way in which renewal was too often approached. The reaction in some quarters has been a move to restore an excess of hierarchical ordering and to bring back relics of a romanticised premodern past[4]. In other quarters, in the effort to break free of ideological control there is little sense of tradition in liturgical celebration.

Today, sacramental celebration, with its twin, sacramental theology, is in a phase in which the modern and the postmodern are at odds. The postmodern emerges from its rupture with the modern through two types of suspicion/retrieval that are in turn in conflict with each other. The first is the retrieval of the medieval, as seen largely through Bonaventurian eyes with its neoplatonic idealism. The second, which is pursued here, is the opening to the creative power of language. It shows itself in liturgies of inclusion, in liturgies of the marginal or excluded, in an opening to a diversity of cultural roots, even in face of the pretensions of the Roman Rite. What is common in these efforts is a new sensitivity

---

4. Interesting perspectives on the advent of the modern may be found in L. DUPRÉ, *Passage to Modernity. An Essay in the Hermeneutics of Nature and Grace,* New Haven and London, Yale University Press, 1993, and G. LAFONT, *Histoire de la théologie,* Paris, Éditions du Cerf, 1988.

to language and an effort to retrieve not just a repressed past but a power to speak[5].

Some seem to think that postmodernism indulges in referring sign to sign, without any other referent. When it comes to appropriating a tradition it is more important to see postmodern evaluations as a critique of sedimentation and of imposed order. Thence one may inquire into the ability of this critique to open the way to generate meanings from the texts, and to bring persons and communities into communion across a diversity of intersecting interpretations. What is held off is the design to effect unambiguous uniform meaning in favour of the effort to converse and communicate within the diversity of ways of looking at a common referent and heritage. In considering liturgical traditions, this prompts inquiry into the polysemy of rites, symbols and texts, and into the circumstances and processes of their ongoing interpretation.

3. *Sacrament: A Language Event*

Sacramental theology must inevitably however start with an awareness of the breakdown in the work of tradition or handing on. This shows itself in three ways: (a) Narrative breaks down in face of the repressed and the uncontainable; (b) Order breaks down in face of the exclusions that come to light from the roots of dis-order; (c) Ritual breaks down in face of the claims of the sensual aesthetic of active forces in the world that have not been appropriated into Christian perceptions.

In doing a theology of sacrament that attends to this postmodern breakdown of the tradition of rite and celebration, or in other words to the *lex orandi* as generative process that is at risk, we are helped by what Jencks notes as trends in post-modern expressivity. The three trends which he notes are[6]: (i) from few styles to many genres; (ii) from purist to kaleidoscopic sensibility; (iii) from exclusion to inclusion. To these, he seems to add elsewhere in his work, the effort to be "popular", that is, for the people, while not giving up on being elitist, that is, doing what only a few can do because of their special skills.

The heuristic within which both the breakdown and the emergence of creative expression may be appropriated is that of sacrament as a language-event. This indeed fits within a larger context in which the redemptive act itself is considered as a language-event. Jesus was manifested at his baptism and on the Cross as the Word coming forth from God, and

---

5. This expression is deliberately borrowed from R. CHOPP, *The Power to Speak. Feminism, Language, God*, New York, Crossroad, 1991.
6. C. JENCKS, *What is Postmodernism?* (n. 2), p. 55-61.

those who believed gave testimony to this in their preaching, in their lives and in their writings. The written Word passes on the sayings and teachings of Jesus, and the narratives of his passion and death. In the narratives of the resurrection in the Spirit, there is added the hope of the Second Coming, the assurance of the presence of Christ in his body the Church, and the gift of the Spirit to animate this body, enabling it to keep memory and interpret the truth, in word and in deed. It is in what is proclaimed as the Paschal Event that the redemptive operation of Word and Spirit has its centre, and it is this which is at the heart of sacramental remembrance in the Church.

The perception of sacrament as language-event seems an apt heuristic with which to engage the note of the discontinuous and the disruptive that marks our sensitivity to broken time. It allows us to see God's action in the past and in the present, without having to relate them by an unbroken sequence of events, and without having to look for some causative force outside language usage itself. A ritual or sacramental event relates to an event within time past through the capacities and power of language to carry it forward, and to allow it to enter afresh into lives, however they may have been disrupted and broken. By that same token, the heuristic of language event brings sacramental expression into the realm of the practical. Redescribing reality through remembrance of the Cross, sacrament points to the Christian praxis which goes with such remembrance. On this account, the heuristic of language event could also be called a heuristic of poesis and praxis. It is concerned with the forms and power of language, and at the same time with the paradigms of Christ-like action that are evoked through this language.

II. THE LANGUAGE OF SACRAMENTAL MEMORIAL

Within this perception of sacrament as language-event, a post-modern theology of sacrament is here considered under three headings: (1) Sacrament is by its nature a rupture, in virtue of its character as memorial and as ritual; (2) Sacrament is an excess, in virtue of the power to speak that comes from appropriating the Word as open sign; (3) Sacrament is an abundance of gift-ing, in remembrance of creation, covenant, redemption, mission of Word and Spirit forming the Church as body of Christ in the form of the divine agape.

1. *The Rupture of Sacrament*

Sacrament is a memorial action in which word in its various genres intertextualises with rite in its various genres to create a saying rather than simply a said. One might well start with ritual as being the more elemental expression[7], but let us in fact begin with the process of narrative, narrating, which has been given so much attention in modern theology as counteraction to an excess of reasoned argument.

Four points then are made under this heading. First, account is taken of how the modern story has been ruptured by the advent of the postmodern. Second, it is said that, whatever the peculiarities of this particular disruption, it is in the very nature of narrative to be disrupted if it is to perform its role of establishing identity in the lives of communities and societies. Third, it is shown how this occurs in sacramental narrative, Fourth, this is applied likewise to ritual action. The third and fourth points are those most amply developed.

2. *Narrative and the Postmodern*

The attention to narrative is partly induced by the role played by narrative in biblical revelation, and partly by a more secular awareness that narrative is a primary mode of trying to give a pattern to being in time and passing across time. Narrative offers plot and vision and gives a coherence to reality and to expectations.

However, the postmodern perception is that narrative inevitably breaks down. Looking for the reason for this leads us to see that the telling of tales is in effect a constant dialectic between remaining the same and becoming the other. The dialectic is rendered almost impossible today, socially and culturally, when narrative must struggle with the memories of unspeakable, unassimilable, suffering. Can there be any genuine continuity between a remembered past full of promise and a present that is so vulnerable to evil and suffering? Is meta-narrative possible? Are we not led to rely more on "petits récits" that have less ample scope but narrate how it is possible to live faithfully and with hope of some transcendent force in the time-limited, in the limits of small events that can be encompassed in fewer words? To take a literary analogy, is this not the time for the short-story rather than the epic novel?

3. *Why All Narrative Is Disrupted*

Paul Ricœur notes an aporia in human expression which serves as insight into this transition[8]. He has amply noted the role of narrative in

---

7. This is how I proceed in the book *Sacrament* (n. 1).
8. See P. RICŒUR, *Oneself as Another*, Chicago, University of Chicago Press, 1990.

framing time-consciousness, in expressing life in the transition of time, and in maintaining a sense of identity across time and even across epochs. At the same time, he has also noted that the urge to reconsider the story, even to retell it, comes not from within the story itself but from some ethical imperative that originates outside the story and within the person or community when faced by some event, some need or some challenge for which the standing narrative offers no clear response.

In considering what might be called the narrative of modernity, which is one of progress and development, we can see how this is put into question by the evil that interrupts the placid surface of the story and by the ethical imperative of addressing this evil. Such response however is not found within the story itself and hence it challenges the modern self-consciousness and sense of identity to which it gives rise.

4. *Sacramental Narrative*

The potential of Christian memorial emerges from breakdown and from the readiness to release the power of keeping memorial from subservience to the meta-narrative of modernity. However, if the memorial of Christ is itself presented as meta-narrative[9], it too will be unable to integrate the realities of evil and the ethical challenge which arises from the convergence of the proclamation of the kerygma of love with this evil. After all, it does not take too much reflection to know that the Christian story and memory have in the past allowed complicity with the evil of the times and the victimisation of those who did not fit well into this narrative. Hence as we talk of Gospel and culture, or of liturgy and culture, we may well ask what are the characteristics of Christian narrative or of the narrative of Christ. Is there really a meta-narrative or does one find a number of related but nonetheless differing narratives?

Looking back to the original Christ event as a language event one notes the plurality already present in the beginning, as well as the ways in which it is interrupted by other language forms that prohibit any excess of coherence and do not allow the system to leave the "other" outside the pale of the community's story and values. Furthermore, through history, the passion narrative has taken on many different forms,

---

9. If the story is here recorded as a story of *kenosis* of divine self-emptying, that is not by way of saying that it is a meta-narrative, at least not in the sense that its plot has been set down once and for all in an unchangeable way. What does not change is the reference to the event of Jesus of Nazareth as a divine event and what is always explored is the meaning of this event. If the accent is here on *kenosis*, it is because this is an apt way to remember the forms taken by God's love in a time when in Europe and North America the modern is being crossed out, and on other continents the forms of colonialism.

ecclesiastical and popular. The narrative has been assimilated in multiple alterations into diverse languages, cultures, lives. Communities are one with their origins, yet they are different. There are too many disruptions, eruptions, to allow the pretence of unadulterated sameness. Narratives, memorials, have to alter to pass over the disruption and to assimilate the different.

This is the way of metaphor. It is an open sign, in its efforts to redescribe reality. It is never just repeating if it is a live metaphor. It is always redescribing the realities that come its way, and so must contextualise itself differently, insert itself into freshly woven plots. Whether we think of the metaphor of the Pasch, or that of God's reign, or that of sacrifice and priesthood, or that of the Cross, we cannot but be aware of how these metaphors of the language of revelation have been textualised into different story patterns. They are related to diverse conditions and visions of human existence, so that even as they redescribe reality they themselves are open to di/eferred meaning.

Biblical metaphors occur first of all in the proclamation of God's advent in prophetic and eschatological, even indeed apocalyptic, terms. Thus it is especially with the proclamation of the Kingdom of God, of the Wisdom of the Cross, of the coming judgement. These then interrupt the memorial narrative with new expectation and are woven into its retelling and reconstitution. When taken into it, the narrative as retold is an interruption.

Apart then from the above considerations on the interruption and rupture of narrative, there is the truth that the memorial of Christ and the narrative of his death is always a rupture of time-consciousness and expectation. When Johannes Metz wrote of the memory of Christ's death as a dangerous memory, he included in this image the sense of the "apocalyptic sting" that awaits those to whom this story is proclaimed. In some ways, this is also inherent to Wolfhart Pannenberg's idea of the resurrection of Christ as proleptic of human history. Both authors refer to the fact that when faced with the judgement on human history inherent in the death of Christ, human endeavours and their aims are called into question. The story which a society or a community projects for itself is interrupted, even ruptured, and the future is seen to come not from ourselves but from what is given to the world in Christ. There is no way of thinking about sacramental memorial that does not take this into account, but to do this it is necessary to attend to the role of narrative in keeping memorial.

Not only, however, does the narrative of Christ's death interrupt the human or social narrative, but in the process it is itself interrupted. In other words, over time, within sacramental or religious celebration, the Christ narrative itself breaks down. The breakdown is due to a threefold reality. First, it breaks down in face of events, situations and conditions which in its given form it cannot accommodate. This is verified in what has already been said about facing the catastrophes of the outgoing century in hope and with a living memory of Christ. Second, it breaks down in proclamation and prayer when other forms of discourse interrupt its flow with different perspectives. This happens in the course of sacramental celebration itself, as when eschatological sayings or apocalyptic discourse of their very nature challenge the smooth flow of narrative[10]. It also happens when formal liturgical celebration is dispersed or thrown into disarray by the expressions of popular religion. Instead of being seen as a departure from what is proper or correct, popular religious expressions, as for example on Good Friday or in novenas, need to be considered as ways of expressing faith in a Christ who is closer to the people than the one proclaimed in the texts of an *editio typica*. Thirdly, the Christ story as narrated in liturgy breaks down when faced with new ethical imperatives, that come from the convergence of God's Word and gift with promptings that arise when the Christian community is confronted by the face of the other. One may perhaps act in response to this challenge out of an overflow of love, or the community may engage in actions that meet the question of the face, but this then has to be integrated into story in order to be integrated into a sense of Christian identity, or being one in Christ and in his memorial.

When interrupted in one or other, or even in all of these ways, the Christian community, in diverse time and places, within its sacramental celebrations forges a new telling of the story of Christ's passion and death that responds to the imperatives of rupture. Or if it does not, sacrament is *de facto* replaced as expression of faith by the ritualisations of popular religiosity. Or perhaps by an appeal to other saviours, whether secular or sacred, which the baptised share with the surrounding society.

The narrative of which we have spoken, with all its characteristics and interruptions, is carried over into the blessing prayer of sacramental action. Indeed, it is therein that one sees most clearly how a particular community and culture appropriates the story and its key metaphors. This could be exemplified by seeing how the metaphor of *sacrifice* is differently appropriated to the death of Christ and to the eucharistic

---

10. This kind of interruption can also be caused by ritual action, as is explained later on in this essay, when human vulnerability or experience emerges in face of the memorial narrative within ritual action.

action in prayers such as those of the Roman Canon, the Liturgy of Mark, the Byzantine anaphora of Basil of Caeserea, and the more recently composed eucharistic prayers for use in Kenya and Nigeria. It could also be exemplified in an examination of prayers in different traditions for the blessing of baptismal water which would consider how the baptism of Jesus in the Jordan is related to Christian baptism, or how the imagery of Romans 6,1ff is joined with that of rebirth in John 3 in expressing what happens in this sacrament. In comparing such prayers, one would find both a plurality of prayer forms and a diversified interpretation of the same root metaphor for Christ's death or for the sacramental action, before which claims to meta-narrative would seem feeble..

5. *Ritual*

Narrative and prayer are associated in all sacramental liturgies with ritual action. Rituals are deemed a theurgy, an action of transcendental or divine power. They are actions that order life and order community, that resolve conflict, that reconcile members, that guide through transitions, and that bring healing. They are said to engage with mystery, or in Turner's phrase they introduce into *communitas*, while still respecting and maintaining structures and their socialising power. In all of this, the energy and power of the rite is attributed in a particular way to bodily action.

On the other hand, rituals may be considered as disclosures of human vulnerability and incompleteness. Bodily rites, in their very intensity of rhythm, bring to the surface the modes of being in time and space, together with the tensions inherent to this condition of being human. Rites associated with birth, marriage, adolescence and death, express the enigma and vulnerability of existence. In times of transition, from childhood to adulthood, from single status to marriage, persons are caught in a present that has an ambiguous relation to past and future. Rites associated with seasons underline the debility of human control over the very necessities of life, and dependence on much greater forces which humans cannot even understand. They look for harmony with these forces, but cannot guarantee it without appealing to higher powers for their clemency and bounty. Rites for the assumption of office look to that level of communion in life where there is no differentiation, and in that very act reveal how fragile communion is. Rites of healing touch the forces of evil to which humans constantly feel subject and from which they need release.

When these enigmas, these mysterious encounters with time and with cosmos, are made to surface, myth or saga eases the transition and projects a universe of order, in which human beings have a place. They promise healing, and pretend to a coherent whole. If the myth or saga comes into question, when the body language associated with them continues to be used it creates feelings of dislocated being. In that sense, even within paradigms of wholeness there is a disjunction between given existence and desired existence.

6. *Christian Rites*

Sacramental ritual often assumed many of the qualities of mythical projection, offering the vision of a well ordered universe where all falls under divine providence and plan. Now, however with the dissolution of such certainties, the unique character of the Gospel's response to ritual desire comes newly to surface. It radically demythologises the quest for lasting life and the quest for cosmic order, by asking for identification with Jesus Christ in his self-giving and self-emptying. Accepting the disjunction between being vulnerable and the desire for life without death, all the enigmas of *chaosmos* are handed over to a divine wisdom that is loving but quite often incomprehensible. It is a wisdom located not in the vision of a cosmic order, but at the table of a repeated and constant table-sharing among the weak of the earth. That is where initiation, the passage through conversion and the struggle with the elements of life and death in the chaos of water, leads disciples.

There is a ritual distinctiveness in Christian sacrament that puts the focus on domestic rites, not on festive or cosmic ones, however much these are appropriated or respected. It is this which gives the particular sense of being in time that is proper to the memorial of Christ. There is ritual transfer from sacrifice, rites of passage, cosmic rites, indeed from the whole language of cosmic identity, to the loaf and the cup, to the tub of water, to the jar of oil, shared in daily living. A people has its identity and its relations to things of life and of earth, and to the transitions of time, in these rites in ways that ground any spoken word.

This is an extraordinary transition. Other religions of course have their common meals, regular as well as festive and cultic. The Gospel makes the daily meal, the regular sharing of a community, the centre-piece of its communion with and in the divine, as proclaimed in the Christ Event. All of the aspirations to communion with cosmos, to communion with spirits and deities, that religious ritual brings to expression, are finally located at this table. They are invested in this act of sharing the one loaf and the one cup, with the food and drink of daily toil, daily sustenance, and daily want. This is what is symbolic or metaphoric about Christian sacrament: it makes religious aspiration, all that is customarily located in sacrifices, temples, at altars, in seasonal assemblies, in rites of passage, converge at the common table of weekly gatherings. There is ample room for the recovery of a greater esteem for the body, in the regard for bread and wine, and in the esteem of the hands that sow, harvest, knead, bake and crush, and in the pleasures of bodily sharing, as well as in the distress of bodily want. There is place too for the recovery of new forms of social ordering and relating, when the focus of ritual is truly on the preparation of the table and on sharing at it, where what is remembered is the self-gift of Christ, and what is shared is the body broken and given, the blood poured out in a covenant of grace. Christians belong most truly to time at the common table. It is there that they discover their relation to cosmic time, to the time immemorial of the world's beginnings, and to the "time beyond time" in which they enter the mystery of God.

This is a practical wisdom learned through ritual that bears on love between neighbours, and love between foreigners, and on the care of those who need care. It is a wisdom of trust in a divine providence and presence that touches daily lives. It is all that Jesus taught about the presence of kingdom of God "today." It opens table participants to open to the outflow of the Spirit that touches all flesh and teaches us to say, "Abba, Father," in the quest for daily bread, enough for the day and no more. It is from within this wisdom, gained from this prosaic ritual of shared daily communion, that a community hears and confesses the proclamation of the Cross, with its own renunciation of mythic, religious and philosophical wisdom, as well as its promise of life.

7. *Transgressing the Symbolic Code*

Following the pattern of symbolic codes, Christian sacramental rites adopted the role of establishing Church Order, offering a universal pattern for behaviour within the society of the Church. When Christianity and the civic order were practically coterminous, Christian rites offered patterns of Christian living that were also patterns of living in civic society. Today, in what is sometimes termed a post-Christian age, it is clear that the fulfilment of this role has been ruptured. However, it is here affirmed that the rupture of ritual symbolic codes falls within the very nature of the twist given to rite in the Christian dispensation as it originally emerged.

The focus described above entails entering a new horizon. It means taking the enigma of death and of life, of past and future, into the Cross of Christ, at the table. The rite in which death and life are faced "in their battle" is the daily rite of table-sharing, the rite of putting bread and wine on the table, to be shared as one loaf and one cup. It is from day to day that the Christian faces death and is renewed in the promise of life. It is in what is required to live day by day with others and for others that death is faced, and the constant passing from past to future, with no very tangible hold on the present. Only parabolic wisdom serves in this encounter. There is no great myth or saga to encompass all of reality in an imaged wholeness. The Gospel heard at this table is made up of "petits récits", of unsynchronised stories of passion and death, offering different paths of entry into the one Christ, who bears the face of all suffering, and is without comeliness.

It is in face of this that we can locate the process that is sometimes called *ritualisation* in today's Christian communities. There has always been a measure of this in the history of devotion and liturgy, but today it has reached a high-point of double-coding, especially among groups that seek inclusion rather than exclusion.

8. *Ritualisation*

Under this subheading, we can consider how the process of ritual change in fact occurs. It is not only in African and Asian Churches that the need for cultural change in sacramental celebration is perceived. Within the western world also there are those who believe that ways of accommodating current cultural changes have to be found, and some think that how this is done emerges from celebration itself, rather than being pursued on purely theoretical grounds. As congregations celebrate a sacrament, with authorised books at hand (if not always in hand), a process has come to the fore which can be best understood under the name of *ritualisation*. This means attention to known and traditional rites, along with attention to other ritual forms, and a somewhat free way of accommodating to community situations. There are patterns but they are not rigid. The community knows the traditional, but it tries in its own accommodations to negotiate the meaning of this tradition, to weave it into the lives of the congregants, and to invest the rites with their faith perceptions, social concerns, and cultural forms. There is always some play between the written and the oral, the known ritual actions and the enfleshment of these rituals in actual practice.

A measure of ritualisation takes place at any time, no matter how consolidated the ritual code may seem to be. Congregations always accommodate this to their own situation in life, culture and society. It is the extent and diversity of this phenomenon which marks the life of Churches in these decades. Communities are experimenting more with liturgies, and more consciously diversifying or adding new elements, drawn from a variety of sources, not exclusively from recognised Christian traditions. The ritualisation process is not uniform, nor motivated by the same aspirations. Some resist changes in sacramental ritual, in favour of what they have known, or heard of, from the past, which they find more sacral and more cohesive. Hence, despite the official changes they find ways of ritualisation within their own sense of tradition. For example, exposition of the Blessed Sacrament gains new momentum, or devotion to the saints and to Mary can overshadow Sunday liturgy, as with celebrations in honour of the Divine Mercy on the Sunday after Easter. In other cases, and among rather different kinds of communities, primacy is given to the devotions associated with the enigmatically labelled popular religiosity, to feasts in honour of Our Lady of Guadalupe, Saint John the Baptist, and local patrons. Others find that the *editio typica* of many a sacramental rite retains too much of the hierarchical, of the boldly masculine image of God, and so even within the execution of the newly revised liturgy incorporate more communal rituals, more inclusive language, and more roles for the non-ordained[11]. On some continents, people incorporate rites that they know from cultural religious traditions, such as the veneration of ancestors, forms of communion with the dead, or healing rites.

Much is done by instinct for what is suitable, but it can resist clear articulation of meaning. Catherine Bell has pointed out the difference between the ritual mastery which enables congregations or communities to appropriate the traditions in their own way, and the insight into all that they do and effect in this process. As she says:

> [Ritualization] is a way of acting that sees itself as responding to a place, event, force, problem or tradition. It tends to see itself as the natural or appropriate thing to do in the circumstances. Ritualization *does not see* [emphasis added] how it redefines or generates the circumstances to which it is responding. It does not see how its own actions reorder and reinterpret the circumstances so as to afford the sense of a fit among the main spheres of experience – body, community and cosmos[12].

This paragraph reminds us of the important relations to which community gives shape in Christian liturgy, as in all ritual. Even the naming of God is done within a certain compass, pointing to the body-self, to the community to which one belongs (or from which one distinguishes

---

11. On a variety of practices in feminist liturgies, see M. PROCTER-SMITH & J.R. WALTON (eds.), *Women at Worship. Interpretations of North American Diversity,* Louisville (KY) – Westminster, John Knox Press, 1993.

12. C. BELL, *Ritual Theory, Ritual Practice,* New York – Oxford, Oxford University Press, 1992, p. 109.

oneself), and to the cosmos, earthly and heavenly reality, in which the human community must find its place. In the process of ritual sacramental change, it is helpful to know that these realities are involved all the time, however clearly or less distinctively invoked[13].

In brief, the rupture of meta-narrative and of the hegemony of ritual opens the way to a new discovery of the abundance of language, as the truly open sign, in the interplay of metaphors, allowing speech to the marginal, and in ritual pointing to the location of divine power in the exchange of bread, wine, oil and water, for those who experience the rupture of their existence and of their expectations.

9. Sacramental Excess

The breakdown noted in narrative and ritual opens the way to ritualisation and the explorations of the potential in sacramental tradition. The rupture of sacramental expression is not a "breaking down" but a "breaking up", when it is crossed with the language of the other, or when it is confronted by the face of the others who have been excluded or at best left on the margins of the symbolic code. The sacrament in effect becomes an "open sign." This is what allows us to see sacramental celebration as excess. This can be appreciated only by attending to the *saying*, the signifying, as process, rather than letting the tradition be constituted by the *said* or the signified. As Rebecca Chopp says adroitly, basing her observations on Christian feminist discourse as it is allied to emancipation:

> As the perfectly open sign we may say what Word is, in our best approximation, but also how it sustains the process of speaking. Here the Word is not that which breaks into discourse, or one that governs it, rather it is the full inclusivity of discourse; it creates and restores speech, it both allows symbols to have meaning and pushes against any fixed meaning. The Word/God is the sign of all signs, connected, embodied, open, multivalent, all the things a sign can most perfectly be, but the Word/God is this in the perfection of all perfection and thus, in full openness, creativity and gracefulness creates, sustains, and redeems all words in their ongoing process of signification[14].

Such excess is impossible without emptying. To be open to the unsaid, the word has to be emptied of the said. Indeed, this is the process of the

---

13. Ritualisation is not to be confused with liturgical miming, which is the endeavour to set ideas or ideals to ritual enactment. If people think up a rite, even one using traditional elements such as fire and water, to express ideals which they have in mind, this is miming, not ritualisation.

14. R. CHOPP, *The Power to Speak* (n. 5), pp. 31-32.

incarnation of the Word and indicates the place that the written word has within a sacramental process of oral interchange.

Whenever the written is taken up into a process of oral expression and intersubjective exchange, it is in a sense emptied through a process of hermeneutic and recovery that is allied to the lives of those who *are speaking, saying*. While the written is necessary to the original liberation of word and signifying in order to create a distanciation that allows for appropriation into another community and setting, it risks sedimentation and can be subjected to the policing of "authentic" interpretation. The relation to the cultural, social, religious and ethical situation of the time of formulation has to be considered in order to access not the simply said but the saying. To the extent that this can be caught, the hermeneutic of suspicion intervenes but actually makes possible the hermeneutic of recovery. In scriptural exegesis, the insertion of the Word into tradition, the historical-critical method, and even the method of the analysis of literary form or genre, pinpoint meaning only to release its fuller potential when transmitted into a situation of oral discourse, where it relates to other lives, gives forth the power of fresh speech and opens up to a new saying.

It is in this light that some insight is attained into the mystery of the Word made flesh. In ancient times, Word was spoken but was then taken into a situation of human discourse when in virtue of the Word spoken the Word became flesh, narrating and narrated flesh. While we most readily speak of the self-emptying of Jesus Christ in his being handed over unto death, we should not forget the self-emptying process of being set in writing. All the power of the living Christ is emptied into the written Word, the Word handed on through writing. The process of handing on through oral discourse however never halted but continued in conjunction with the writing down and the transmission of the Word writ into papyrus and codex, and so with its ongoing interpretation and appropriation in living communities. The Word made written is also emptied of its sedimented meaning to be emptied out as open sign into the words, actions, lives of this, that or other community, in this or that time and place.

Sacrament indeed has its own parallel in codified rituals. Christ on the night before he was betrayed, as it is narrated in the Gospel, emptied himself not only into death but into sacrament, a self-emptying by which he could continue to live among his disciples. The ritual was codified in the breaking of the bread, in the celebrations in bread and wine to which were conjoined codified rituals in oil and water, which were also given a beginning in various interpretations of scriptural texts. The Word

became flesh, became writing, became ritual. The process of an emptying which gives rise to new life, to newly inculturated expression continues, for ritual as for writing. It is in the emptying that allows for saying that the excess of sacramental language emerges.

10. *Sacramental Abundance*

To find in this not the excess of words, of signs interplaying inter-
minably with signs, but an excess of divine abundance we can link these
considerations to the metaphors of Cross and Gift, or *cross-ing* and *gift-
ing,* as well as to the true presence of Christ in the eucharistic sacrament,
to which all other sacraments lead, point or lead back.

11. *Sign of the Cross*

Christianity always looks to the Cross of Christ as the act of redemption. However, it must be obvious that in the course of time this has been
diversely interpreted. It is victory over death, it is the passage through
death, it is the price of redemption from the evil that nails Christ to the
Christ, it is the paying the price of satisfaction for sin, it is the assurance
of the forgiveness of sins by divine justice, of divine justification. While
the event as narrated can be spoken of in all these more or less theoretical terms, the experience inherent in the event itself has also fascinated.
Devotion is addressed to the heart of Christ agonising on the Cross, as
he faces the agony, even the terror, of death or as he contemplates sin.
The theologically sophisticated also try in various ways to analyse this
experience. In their different ways, for example, Martin Luther and Hans
Urs von Balthasar see the death of Christ as a drama in which he
encounters the very pains of loss of God. Such speculations are an
endeavour to spell out a meaning that emerges from the willingness to
be annihilated, to be made nothing, in death when it is freely embraced
for others. Others will analyse the death of Jesus more psychologically
as the loss of self, of the loss of the sameness of selfhood that evaporates
in dying. Indeed, postmodern contemplation of death points to the fact
that death is the one event to which the now passive subject cannot testify. Only others can give testimony to it, not oneself, oneself being now
given over to the otherness of the dead.

If Christ now lives in the Church it is by the testimony of others. This
is living testimony because it is the testimony of the Spirit, the Spirit
who in human and ritual speech allows the Cross to be spoken of, to be
rendered living in the vitality which it gives to life and action. Indeed,
because this is so we speak more readily of the testimony given to the

resurrection and already in the Gospel narratives the story of the resurrection is what constitutes the testimony to the power of the death, of the death on the Cross. This however is not an event belonging within time as we know it, though it has its traces in time, but is an event that can be narrated only as an event of faith, as a testimony.

From this point of view, the Cross of Christ is a crossing-out. "It is better for you that I go," Jesus is narrated to have said in face of his impending death. One might say necessary. He could not live on in testimony to the power of God's love except in dying, except in the testimony of others to the power of love born from the Cross, and proclaimed as resurrection and the hope of resurrection. To remember Jesus only as a teacher, or even primarily as a teacher, is to reject the testimony of the Cross. It is to refuse to let him be "crossed out," in order to be raised up and to live now by the testimony of those who speak, act and suffer in the power of the Spirit.

When Paul in his letter to the Corinthians testifies to the power of the Cross it is by way of saying that it can be embraced neither by religious institution nor by philosophical explanation. Or at any rate, it cannot be sedimented in any institutional form, nor in any philosophico-theological discourse. These have their place, but their place is found only in their readiness to be in turn "crossed out"[15].The abundance of life which is offered in Christ is offered in the readiness of those persons and things who testify to him to be crossed out, so that the Word may be abundant in its giving voice and expression to all to whom it is proclaimed and by whom it is received.

12. Sacrament of Gift-ing

Gift-ing is also a transforming and power-giving metaphor by which we can speak of the action of divine *agape* communicated through the missions of the Word and the Spirit as they are allied to the proclamation of the Cross and the testimony to the resurrection, a proclamation and a testimony verified under the conditions of rupture and crossing-out.

The metaphor is in fact suggested by liturgical history. The English word '*economy*' is taken in the sense of exchange, or sharing in what is communal possession. It roughly corresponds to the French '*échange*', the Italian '*scambio*', the Spanish '*intercambio*', or the German '*Wirtschaft*'. If '*economy*' is here preferred to '*exchange*', this is by way

---

15. This thinking is borrowed from the French writer, S. BRETON, *Le Verbe et la Croix,* Paris, Desclée, 1981.

of a play on words which points to an entire order which is built up on an exchange or a sharing in gift. It is an attempt to translate the Greek *'oikonomia'*, or the Latin *'commercium'*[16].

In gift/giving the giving is not reducible to the gift/given, nor is the giver represented (either figuratively or as totally present) in the gift. The problem with humans in giving gifts is that it is hard for them to recognise this distance, and this irreducibility. The giver would like to be fully known and acknowledged in the gift, would like to build a bridge that overcomes distance between the giver and the gifted, the lover and the loved. But both gifted and giver need to recognise in gift/giving the otherness of the other, the fact that the two are not and cannot be the same. When the one to whom the gift is given is given the due of being other, then the gift/giving is a giving in freedom. In turn, the gifted is free when in the enjoyment, the living out of the gift, the distance and otherness of the giver is affirmed. Gifts are spoiled when either the one giving or the one receiving wants to objectify the other person in the exchange, to represent the other person in a way that belies the distance.

Feminist writers have suggested that the problem of turning gifts into barter, and loading them with expectations, is a peculiarly male one. Women, it is contended, are much more free in living out of gift, and in living gift-giving as a free, unencumbered act. Possibly this is because they are so vitally connected with the primordial gift, which is the gift of life, of life to be lived, to be lived in plenitude and generously. Hélène Cixous expresses this pithily in the following paragraph:

> How does she give? What are her dealings with saving or squandering, reserve, life, death? She too gives *for*. She, too, with open hands, gives herself – pleasure, happiness, increased value, enhanced self-image. But she doesn't try to "recover her expenses." She is able not to return to herself, never settling down, pouring out, going everywhere to the other. She does not flee extremes; she is not the being-of-the-end (the goal), but she is how-far-being-reaches[17].

The "impossible" gift, or the "eschatological" gift, or the "womanly" gift, is one that gives the gift of freedom. That is, it opens up possibilities of free action for the recipient, who is impaired neither by the nature of the gift nor by the expectations of the giver, nor by the need to try to

---

16. Some of this is taken from D.N. POWER, *Sacrament: An Economy of Gift,* in *Louvain Studies* 23 (1998) 143-158.

17. H. CIXOUS, *Sorties: Out and Out: Attacks/Ways Out/Forays,* in A.D. SCHRIFT (ed.), *The Logic of the Gift: Toward an Ethic of Generosity,* New York – London, Routledge, 1997, p. 159.

be the same as the other, but acts purely out of an appreciation of the gift in itself and out of what it opens up as possible. Nonetheless, there is a relationship between giver and recipient, some exchange or participation in the gift, for it is the passage from one to another, without loss to the giver, and in a mutual living from the gift. The gift of life may indeed best exemplify this, for all that in the pettiness of our humanity at times it is given with strings attached. When a mother gives birth to a child, she gives it life. When parents care for a child, they open up the gift of life to it. The ideal reception is for the child to value life as the parents do and to live freely from this gift, not out of a sense of indebtedness to the parents. The child's living leads to life's enhancement, and moves it to give to others out of this gift. There is a flow to true gift, that means it is not consumed but passed on and given increase in this very passage.

Some aspects of the analogy can be clarified further[18]. The accent in the analogy of sacrament with gift is on the giving. We are making a comparison with gifts that are in the giving, with a giving that never ceases. The analogy with motherhood serves, once we recognise that this is a constant giving of life, and is not reducible to a biological fact. Another feature of gift that is brought to the fore is that there is no fusion between giver and gifted, that the giving gives rise to participation and mutuality, but never means total identification with one another, and does not require a representation of the giver to the given which obscures the distance between them, or their otherness. The response of the gifted to the giver is one of drawing from the source and finding union, but not one of giving back. A fusion of giver and receiver would mean that gift-giving ceases in the merging of the two into one, in the common and undifferentiated possession of one thing.

Furthermore, gratuitous giving moves toward and into the future. A purely gratuitous gift cannot be a "present". At Christmas people give presents, which have as their purpose to enhance the moment, to spell out good cheer for the hour. Gift giving, as distinct from presents, is such that it is ordered to the future. The best gift will continue to enhance life with its giving, with the expectation that its fullness will be realised only in the future. To give somebody a dividend in stocks, without expecting a return on it oneself, might be an example, even if a necessarily weak one. The value of this continues to increase, in a measure not known at the time when the giving starts.

18. Compare J.-L. MARION, *Prolégomènes à la charité*, Paris, Éditions de la Différence, 1986, pp. 147-181.

Gift giving and gift given can be paralleled with saying and said, where the former is never reducible to the latter. The one giving the gift addresses the one on whom the gift is bestowed, calling forth a response. However, here too the sayer and saying cannot be represented by the said, either figuratively or as though totally present.

These qualities of giving provide an analogy for what is done in the sacraments, with the giving of Word and Spirit, and with the divine address thereby speaking. The gift of life, of forgiveness, of communion with the Word, of the inner grace of the Holy Spirit, are truly a share in God's own life and love, but even in giving God remains unpossessed in the sense that there is no fusion of the divine with the human and that the divine remains mystery. Attempts to categorise God, to represent God through thematising giver and gift, are a block to the giving. Furthermore, the sacramental gift is not a "present", it is not consumed in the present passing moment, nor indeed fully possessable in that moment, but is eschatologically oriented. The gift/giving continues to increase, being at any one moment beyond measure.

If we can use the language of the "exchange of gifts", or in Latin, the *divinum commercium*, this is to underline that what is given is the seed of participation and mutuality. It is a being together, a loving together, a covenantal relation by which both God and people pledge and work for the enhancement of the same gift. It does not mean that the beneficiaries are giving something back to God. When those who celebrate sacraments in faith receive the gift of the life given in Christ, of the divine *agape*, they enter into its flow. The self-giving love of God shows forth in the self-giving love of Christ. The self-giving love of Christ shows forth in his giving of himself for sinners on the Cross, and in the self-giving of the table of his body and blood in the sacrament of the Eucharist. This self-giving love of Christ shows forth further when through the Spirit it is embodied in the Church, which in turn gives that life, pours out that love from within itself, so that others may share in it. Bestowed upon, Christians are in turn bestowers. The communion established through sacramental giving is totally from God and not in any way going back to God, and is a communion with the Father through Christ and the Spirit.

It is to this gift of divine *agape* that the testimony of Christ and Spirit spoken in sacrament witness, and it is this gift that is brought to life anew when the Church brings the Gospel and the sacraments into the lives and cultures of peoples. It is this which sets up the order of divine justice, where human relations, being in the world, the hope for the transcendent, and the naming of God, are vivified by gift and its flow. It is in the bestowal of this gift that humans are given the freedom to love and to live. It is with this gift in their hearts that they enter the drama of redemption, seeking to give witness to God's love in the following of Christ and in the power of the Spirit, so that the world may be transformed. It is through this gift that they break through and enlarge the boundaries and limits of human being in the world.

13. *Presence in Truth*

The distinction between the Eucharist as the sacrament of Christ's presence and as the sacrament of the Church, his Body, arose from early medieval tendencies to contrast presence in sign and presence in truth, with negative consequences for what was affirmed about Christ's own presence. Through the use of analogies for understanding the unique character of sacramental presence, scholastic theology was able to affirm presence in truth of the "whole Christ". These efforts of Thomas Aquinas and others to resolve this issue, both logically and metaphysically, are not the concern of this paper. What is considered here is how the presence of Christ in truth must be related not simply to the sign of the bread and the wine but to the Church, his Body. There is no instant of predication of this presence, whether in use, before use, or after use, which does not refer to the Church, as visible reality. Early eucharistic theology knew nothing of a separation between presence in the body of the Church and presence of the body in the sacrament. Indeed, in his reference to the *habitudo* of the Risen Christ to the Eucharist Thomas Aquinas retained something of this perspective which includes Christ's sacramental presence in the Church in the doctrine of the Resurrection[19]. Furthermore, scholastic theology and the Council of Trent always related the presence of Christ in truth, in substance, and in reality[20], to the sign of the bread and wine and to the words of Jesus. This of itself implies that Christ is present in truth, in and through the offer of his body and blood, by which the Church is one with and in him, and not otherwise.

The point can be pursued further by acknowledging that the resurrection of Christ in the Spirit means the continued historical embodiment of Christ in his Church. At the centre of this is the sacramental embodiment

---

19. *Summa Theologiae* III, Q. 76, art. 6, c., and ad 3m.
20. The three terms, substantially, really and in truth, were never meant to be separated. They are complementary ways of affirming the presence of Christ. The post-Tridentine tendency to isolate "real presence" from the other terms belies its proper intent and context and also runs counter to the priority of the term, "presence in truth".

which lives by reason of the memorial of the Cross, but this is located in specific places and times. There is no way of speaking of the resurrection that does not take the Church into account, just as there is no right way of speaking of Christ's eucharistic presence that does not take the actual, visible, historically eventing and passing, reality of the Church into account. When the presence in truth of the body and blood of Christ is affirmed this has a necessary and sacramental relation to his embodiment in the Church.

When we speak of Christ's presence in truth in the eucharistic sacrament we need to ponder the fact that this means his embodiment through the signs of the bread eaten and the wine consumed in the community that gathers to keep memorial. The ingestion of these elements is the transforming ingestion whereby the bodies of the communicants are transformed. The actions and the bodies thus nourished and joined in meal become the here and now visible manifestation of the Christ whom they embody. The presence of Christ under the signs of bread and wine is not to be isolated from his presence in the Church. Since they are sacraments of the Church by the same token that they are sacraments of Christ, the sacramental presence of Christ in truth is one that appears and is realised in the sacramental transition from past to future, caught up within the historical realities lived by his Body, the Church. By what they ingest, those gathered are in virtue of the sacrament the embodiment of Christ in the mystery of his Cross, Resurrection and Final Coming. The way in which Christ is now truly present in the world is through the gift of his sacrament to those who are his members, so that they are one in him by the Spirit and the living embodiment and testimony of his gift-ing, of this gift-ing which comes about through this sacramental *kenosis*, an emptying which is a fullness of promise and expectation.

III. SACRAMENTAL MEONTOLOGY

Is it for real? The question is naturally raised as to whether it is possible to exploit the turn to language in doing sacramental theology without some recourse to metaphysics. Does either a neoplatonist idealism or an Aristotelian theory of causality necessarily recur? Certainly, they are not to be forgotten or abandoned for they have set boundaries and directions of thought that can still offer service[21]. That they need not dominate the present moment of sacramental reflection and catechesis may be

---

21. I have discussed the meaning and gains of the theory of sacramental causality in the work of Thomas Aquinas, in D.N. POWER, *The Eucharistic Mystery: Revitalizing the Tradition,* New York, Crossroad, 1992, pp. 230-235.

considered by following along the road of Meontology traced by the French philosopher/theologian, Stanislas Breton[22].

Meontology, as practised by Breton, is not a rejection of ontology but it sets its limits and marks the point where poetic and metaphoric language take over in naming the ineffable. Even as they set important limits for sacramental discourse, both the way of eminence of the scholastic tradition and the anthropological turn of contemporary theology say too much of God, whereas it has to be acknowledged more forcefully that nothing of this world can be predicated of God.

In elaborating on the structure of human being, Breton makes ample reference to its relational character, the *esse ad* without which there would be no *esse in se*. Creatures stand in relation to each other, but above all they have their existence in relation to the One and live out their lives in quest of the One. They seek in creativity and freedom, in "writing themselves" from within traditions, to construe and live this relationship but they cannot do so without the apt use of language and the retrieval of images and metaphors used in narrative and other forms of poetic speech and address. The logocentrism of past theologies of creation, grace and sacrament inhibit creative expression because they disbar language in favour of inner concepts.

To express the presence of the divine that is gift-ed in revelation (and this is applicable to sacrament), Breton prefers a retrieval of neoplatonism to neothomism or to transcendental Thomism. In this, more attention is given to God event-ing and gift-ing than to eminent predication. Taking much from the philosophies of Plotinus and Proclus, he leaves behind the image of emanation of lower being from higher, but conceives the relation of the world to God in terms of the gift of life and being from God, and of the desire of the many to seek reintegration with the One who is principle of all that is. Rather than using analogical predications to affirm God's eminence and imminence, Breton prefers the thought that God is nothing of anything which proceeds from the One. The naming of the One, of the ineffable, in prayer and sacrament is metaphorical, with however an ontological vehemence that is to be attributed to the saying, gifting and eventing of the Word and the Spirit in our midst, and which orients those who listen, receive and pray to the reintegration of self into God by the acceptance with gratitude of his gift. Through sacramental celebration and an ethical life that flows from this, this return is made along with those of whom one keeps memory in

---

22. Among his numerous works, for the purposes of this reflection it is enough to cite S. BRETON, *Le Verbe et la Croix* (n. 15).

remembering the irruption of the divine into the world through love. The love of God, through the mystery of *kenosis*, enters even into lives left semantically empty in their own time, that is untold and unexpressed within the prevailing discourse. It enters into lives that defy remembrance because they are non-lived, seemingly pure suffering without even the possibility of creative and free action, and gives them expression. The power of the language in which the memory of the Cross is kept, when it is allowed its power to rupture, its excess and its promise of abundance, is to surrender the quest for the self, personal and inter-subjective, to the God whose traces in history are found in the love of Christ and the power of the Spirit in the midst of human suffering. God is named from within this suffering and through an appropriation of the Name into new situations of human suffering. Through this naming within the memorial of the Cross, God events as love even in the midst of discontinuities, sufferings and ambiguities in which there is no intelligible pattern. Sacrament in its rupture and excess needs no theories of providence, no overarching meaning of history, to find in suffering either God's action or the punishment for human sin or the exercise of the permissive will of God. As creative memorial, it is a simple and clear faith that God events as love in the midst of suffering, not because God causes it or allows it, but because it is there and where it is, God is.

IV. Conclusion

This paper started with some thoughts on the relation of the postmodern to the modern. This led to remarks on the power of language to negotiate a way of being and creatively serve a tradition. From this there came the description of sacrament as a language event. As a language event, it was considered as rupture, as excess and as abundance. The metaphors of Cross and Gift were forwarded as imagings that allow the presence of Christ in his Pasch to emerge as a constant pass-ing into lives opened by sacramental memorial to the future of God's event-ing. Finally it was suggested that the demands of speculative discourse may be met by the discourse of meontology that conjoins rather than replaces the poetic. The ultimacy of this surrender is a contemplation which occurs beyond the language of celebration and sacrament, a movement that language itself facilitates through the expression of doxology.

V. Summary

To get beyond a metaphysics of causality and presence, or theories of the transcendental subject, sacramental theology has to attend to the language of sacramental celebration. This is the key to an understanding and appropriation of what is given through the sacramental economy of the Christian dispensation. Hence, the paper will outline an analysis of the verbal, corporeal and visual elements of sacramental language in its fullness. The plurality of cultural forms is inherent to traditions of sacramental language, so that comparison rather than reduction to a common form is demanded for an appreciation of the modes of divine gift through sacramental memorial. This attention to language shows the sacramental economy to be a rupturing of myth, metaphysics, and the consciousness of self. It invites into a life where the excess and abundance of divine gift is a revelation of the excess and abundance of love, imaged primarily in the self-emptying of Jesus Christ and the pouring out of the Spirit that engages his disciples in this act of self-giving.

Department of Theology   David N. POWER
Caldwell Hall – Room 125
The Catholic University of America
Washington, DC 20064
USA

RESPONSE TO DAVID N. POWER

It is a great pleasure and a privilege to comment on David Power's reflections upon sacrament and sacramental theology as well as on their interrelationship. Over the years I have been learning a great deal on sacramental theology through reading David Power's books and articles and from our conversations at the annual meetings of *Concilium*.

In his paper Power clearly expresses the need to relate Christian thinking on the sacraments, and in this case, especially on the Eucharist, to the changing context from modernity to postmodernity. Rather than getting lost in the intricacies of some postmodernist projects that instrumentalise the postmodern condition in order to disseminate their often highly subjective views on one thing or an other, Power concentrates on the actual insights to which a critical and self-critical reflection on the conditions in which theologians do theology today may lead. Among these insights the rejection of totalising arguments figures most prominently. The condition which we in the West experience as post-modern has sharpened our view on language. Power speaks of a new sensitivity to language and an effort to retrieve not just a repressed past but a power to speak (p. 138). Moreover, he clearly sees the hermeneutical demands which our attention to sacramental expressions raises for us, when he says that in "considering liturgical traditions, this prompts inquiry into the polysemy of rites, symbols and texts, and into the circumstances and processes of their ongoing interpretation" (p. 138).

On the strength of a thus sharpened attention, Power draws attention to the fragility and fragmented nature of any process of tradition, including the liturgical one. He then diagnoses the postmodern breakdown of the tradition of rite and celebration as well as the inevitable breakdown of any narrative in the process of remaining the same and becoming the other. Against this background Power offers the following thesis: "The potential of Christian memorial emerges from breakdown and from the readiness to release the power of keeping memorial from subservience to the meta-narrative of modernity" (p. 141). By approaching sacrament as language-event, Power can now trace the openness of the signification of sacramental performance. The Christian sacraments lead to disruption/rupture in view of their character as memorial and ritual. This rupture in turn leads the Christian community to forge "a new telling of the story of Christ's passion and death that responds to the imperative of rupture. Or if it does not, sacrament is *de facto* replaced as expression of faith by the ritualisations of popular religiosity" (p. 144).

Though not fully enlightening us here as to the exact connection between sacrament as language-event and sacrament as ritual[1], Power proceeds now to consider ritual action and the process of ritualisation. He exemplifies the process of ritualisation by looking at the Eucharist: "it makes religious aspiration, all that is customarily located in sacrifices, temples, at altars, in seasonal assemblies, in rites of passage, converge at the common table of weekly gatherings"(p. 145-146). Ritualisation, he reminds us, does not follow a rigid path, rather there is always "some play between the written and the oral, the known ritual actions and the enfleshment of these rituals in actual practice" (p. 147).

Moreover, rituals expose the vulnerability, incompleteness and tensions of our human existence, they point to the disjunction between given existence and desired existence. In that sense, sacramental rituals include the possibility of rupture and therefore the possibility of opening up new horizons. The cross of Christ crosses out any cosy experience of sharing in the name of Christ.

Power sums up his argument so far in the following words: "the rupture of meta-narrative and of the hegemony of ritual opens the way to a new discovery of abundance of language, as the truly open sign, in the interplay of metaphors, allowing speech to the marginal, and in ritual pointing to the location of divine power in the exchange of bread, wine, oil and water, for those who experience the rupture of their existence and of their expectations" (p. 149).

Finally, Power discusses two further features of sacramental action: excess and abundance before attending to the reality-status of sacramental reflection within the postmodern context.

Excess refers to the openness of sacramental celebration and *abundance* to the Christian experience of crossing and gifting. Rupture and possibility are thus taken up again at another level. The sacramental action in the name of Christ can lead to a new release of freedom. By offering the gift-giving of freedom, a flow of true gifting is set in motion in contrast to a given gift (a present) which cements existing and static connections.

---

1. For more information on Power's view on this connection see his book *Sacrament: The Language of God's Giving*, New York, Crossroad, 1999.

Rupture, excess and abundance are thus dimensions of a sacramental communion that lives from giving without possessing and from transforming without sedimentation. This flow of gifting and transforming requires a corresponding theory of reality. The criterion for such a theory lies in its potential to express the event-ing nature of God's love that manifests itself in sacramental action. In Stanislas Breton's *meontology* Power finds such a suitable theory where "more attention is given to God event-ing and gift-ing than to eminent predication" (p. 158).

I would like to offer six comments on David Power's stimulating paper. I shall concentrate especially on the dialectical relationship between liturgical/sacramental action and the need for further theological reflection.

1. There can be no doubt that Power has succeeded in freeing our appreciation of sacramental action from a narrow ecclesial performance to a creative process. Once again, it would seem, that the ancient insight into '*lex orandi, lex credendi*' comes to its full right. As is commonly known, the ongoing liturgical movement and renewal in many Christian churches as well as the increasing ecumenical activity on the ground level of the churches have changed many a traditional emphasis in sacramental performance. In many Western contexts, for instance, the emphasis on community building seems to have reduced or even replaced other traditional emphases in eucharistic celebrations, such as divine presence, redemptive activity and socio-political and ecological transformation. In my present liturgical and theological context of post-Christian Sweden, this new motivation for and strength behind a ritual action poses the question whether any new event-ing of sacramental action is in, however critical, continuity with the Christian tradition of focussing on the redemptive force of the cross of Christ. In other words, how can a theology of sacramental action challenge a dynamic praxis of sacramental action and vice versa? There is not only good praxis or good symbolic action, there is also bad liturgical praxis (as the Reformers of the 16th century knew only too well). Moreover, there is not only good rupture and bad confirmation to be observed in our liturgical praxis. Hence, the question of criteria for the theological assessment of liturgical praxis needs to be raised.

Though I clearly welcome Power's emphasis on sacramental flow and poetic creativity, what I am asking for is a more dialectical consideration of ongoing sacramental action and critical and self-critical theological theory. Such a dialectical consideration would require a more contextual approach to existing sacramental practices, surely a task that transcends the limits of a single paper. Nevertheless, I wonder if David Power would like to illustrate the potential of a mutually critical relationship between specific sacramental actions and his generalising post-modern theory of sacramental action.

2. With regard to the sacrament of penance I would like to ask in what way the statement 'Your sins are forgiven' could be interpreted meontologically? In what way is this instance of performative action open to new diversities of genres and styles? It would seem to me that some sacramental actions are more open to poetic creativity than others.

3. I wonder whether Power's strong identification of sacramental action as a language event is as creative in all instances as it seems. Does not such an identification also run the risk of reductionism? Christian sacramental actions certainly do contain a strong linguistic side. But they include more: They also include a physical, bodily expression which transcends verbal language and signification. Although any interpretation of sacramental action necessarily involves language and acts of signification, the sacrament's very potential of rupture owes itself to an activity deeper or, if one prefers, larger than language. Contemporary youth, though not only youth, respond particularly well to the non-verbal nature of liturgical action. At a time of much mistrust against words, liturgical action, once again, proves to be a major carrier of Christian faith. Hence, Power's predominantly linguistic heuristic in this paper would seem to be in need of some ammendation[2].

4. Inter-religious encounter opens up new possibilities for transformed liturgical action and sacramental theologies and thus also raises the question of criteria for the assessment of liturgical action and rupture as adequate or inadequate.

Let me give two examples: During a recent visit to Japan I have become aware of the great potential of inter-cultural and inter-religious transformations of sacramental actions in particular and liturgical actions in general. I have enjoyed new physical positions in Christian liturgies and I have witnessed the inclusion of a number of Shinto elements into the celebration of the prayer of the church. However, a tangible absence of Trinitarian presence in some of these liturgies prompted me to ask my Jesuit hosts what role Trinitarian witness plays in Japan. The answer was: virtually none.

2. Again, Power's recent book offers more clarification and discussion of this point. Cf. *ibid.*, pp. 120-148.

More recently, I was involved in a continuing education course for priests in the Church of Sweden to which also a new age shaman was invited. He was asked by the Lutheran bishop to perform the ritual of a drum voyage in the church. In the name of Christian tradition I protested against the performance of a new age ritual in the Christian church. As a hermeneut, I am fully aware that the tradition in whose name I protested is a broken, fragmented and ambiguous tradition with a sad record of exclusion of women and a number of other 'others'. Yet, I felt that this ritual encounter between new age shamanism and Christian liturgical space was wrong in spite of the bishop's insistence on its poetic attraction and creative rupture. Does David Power's sacramental theory affirm or challenge my theological judgement?

5. Christian sacramental action is expected to deepen faith, hope and love in the community that gathers in the name of Jesus Christ. The community's worship is christomorphic and theocentric. It is open to God's eschatological transformation in genuine love, i.e. love that respects God's divinity and the human community's humanity. I agree with David Power's hermeneutics of suspicion when applied to the Christian expressions arising out of the modern project and I assume he wishes to apply that same level of suspicion to the post-modern condition itself, in fact to any context and condition. That a mere belief in the self-authenticating nature of some revolutionary or poetic transformation might lead to new forms of totalisation, Martin Heidegger and other thinkers had to learn the hard way during the length of Hitler's reign and thereafter. That is why I would like to echo very strongly David Power's call for a critical and self-critical hermeneutics of sacramental action especially in our post-modern context.

6. Finally, I wish to express my unease with the tendency of isolating the paschal memory from the larger Christian memory in which the death of Jesus Christ is remembered. For an isolated reference to the death of Christ is not an adequate Christological criterion. Rather the memory of the resurrected crucified opens up the Christian imagination towards a more adequate understanding of and praise for the triune God's transformative presence in our world.

SUMMARY

In this response to David power's paper I attempt first to restate the paper's main argument and then offer six brief comments on the paper's constructive proposals. Although in agreement with the main direction of Power's thesis in favour of a more dynamic and creative understanding of liturgical action in the context of postmodern thinking, I ask for a more explicit discussion of the dialectical relationship between ongoing liturgical praxis on the one hand and critical and self-critical theological assessment on the other. Hence, the question of criteria becomes urgent if we wish to be able to distinguish between adequate and inadequate forms of Christian liturgical praxis.

Faculty of Theology   Werner G. JEANROND
Lund University
Allhelgona kyrkogata 8
S-223 62 Lund
Sweden

THE CHURCH AS THE EROTIC COMMUNITY

*We are discontinuous beings, individuals who perish
in isolation in the midst of an incomprehensible
adventure, but we yearn for lost continuity*[1].

I. THE FRACTURE

There is a rich and complex liturgical interchange prior to the distribution of the eucharistic elements. It is called the fraction. The interchange has disappeared from the modern Catholic mass, though it is retained from the old Sacrum Missal in the Anglican rite. The Priest holds the wafer over the chalice of wine and breaks it into two saying: "We break this bread to share in the Body of Christ." The congregation respond with: "Though we are many we are one body because we all share in one bread." In this contribution I wish to unfold an examination of the church as the erotic community through a reading this interchange. For this small piece of liturgy focuses Christian thinking on the singularities of embodiment *and* participation.

Four aspects of this interchange concern us:

First. Participation follows fragmentation; only on the basis of the broken body of Christ can the distribution of that body be affected. The fracturing here is positive, not negative. The fracture participates in and promotes the greater displacement of Christ's body such that there might be an expansion of the one body as subsequent other bodies come to share in it. Each fragment of the wafer is the whole body of Christ, being offered to and received by each communicant. The interchange here between Priest and congregation affects the eucharistic interchange between Christ and believer. "Affects" does not imply a casual connection such that the first interchange causes the second interchange to be.

---

1. G. BATAILLE, *Eroticism*, trans. M. Dalwood, London, Marion Boyars, 1987, p. 15.

For the first interchange is not outside and isolated from the second, even though the second has not taken place yet. The first interchange between Priest and congregation already participates in the second interchange between Christ and believer. The participation is temporally complex. It might be said to participate in it proleptically insofar as all things find their place in Christ eschatologically. It might be said that the participation issues from that which has been constituted (i.e. individual discipleship and corporate identity) through the practice of previous eucharistic interchanges. But the participation also takes place in and as the present performance. We will return to this temporal present, participation and presence later.

Second. The community of the faithful are established within Christ through the pronominal shifter "we". Here, and for the first time in the eucharistic exchange, both the Priest and the congregation speak as "we". "*We* break this bread" and "*we* are many *we* are one". The repetition of the "we" by the Priest and the "we" by the congregation is not identical. The first "we" is employed collectively by one on behalf of the many; its has the logic of synecdoche. It also bears the sense of instructing, demonstrating or teaching the faithful the meaning of the action. The words institute the fraction as a certain kind of action. Not that they need to announce that "we are involved here in a symbolic act" or that the words form a distinctive interpretation of the act. Rather, word and act are both performative. But because the "we" is synecdocal, it is an ambivalent shifter. For who belongs to and makes up this "we" when only one person announces it? The second "we" is antiphonal and gives the historic and concrete content to the first "we". It is a "we" of affirmation, of faith, the we of "Amen". We are the we. In the iteration "we are many we are one" it is the "we" which turns contradiction into a paradox that remains hidden in the mystery of "sharing". The "we" bears us over the oxymoronic, the ancient problematic of the one and the many. It does so not as rhetoric – signs concealing an absence of content. It does so as performing an acceptance of the Priest's "we". Furthermore, each speaker speaks the "we". There is no atomised individualism here. "We" is the proper human subject, not "I" – "we" as physical and psychological beings, as particularised male and female, sinner and saint, able and disabled, of this race and that, of this social class and that. Each speaking the "we", voices an equivalence – all participate equally. This does not mean that distinctions are erased, for the we is many. But the distinctions are held within the tension of that mysterious paradox of the many being one. Distinctions are affirmed within the "we", for the repetition of the rhythm "we are" is not identical: "we are many we are one". Difference here is made possible by affirming similarity: relations emerge from the logic of analogy. It is an analogy which is enacted, practised. For the participation that enables each to speak as we, rather than a collection of "I's", is performed in a number of different ways. It is performed by the verbal agreement with the Priest's "we" which is coupled with the action of the fracturing. Each affirms a part within that action by the affirmation. It is performed by the stepping forward and kneeling to receive: by participating in the liturgy, a participation that has been going on throughout. It is performed through the reception, the eating, the digestion of the elements. The physiological absorption of the one Body of Christ within the body of the believer, so that the two become one flesh. The interchanges announce a complex corporeality, a transcorporeality, in which participation finds its ultimate figuration in erotic consummation. Becoming one flesh is the mark of participation itself. The recited "we" affirms that the church lives, moves and is nurtured as a particular type of erotic community.

Third. The community, while one, while many, affirms its location in Christ, but by that very sharing in Christ it participates in the displacement of the body of Christ announced in the breaking of the bread. This is a third aspect of the fracture, which is given more explicit expression in the final dismissal following the eucharistic feeding: "Go in peace to love and serve the Lord". To employ a distinction found in Michel de Certeau between place (*lieu*) and space (*espace*), the "we" is not bound by the institutional place it finds itself in, nor the civic place that locates the institutionalised place. The "we" walks and opens up spaces in and beyond the given and material locale. The we participates in a rhythm of gathering and dispersal that shapes its walking, its pilgrimage. The erotic community it forms transgresses all boundaries. It moves out in love and desire and produces a complex space which cannot be defined, cannot be grasped as such, labelled by sociologists, mapped by geographers. It is itself a fractured and fracturing community, internally deconstituting and reconstituting itself.

Fourth. Through the liturgical exchange the actions and pronominal assertions of identity employ, emphatically, a present continuous tense: "we break", "we are", "we are" and "we share". Questions concerning time, representation, and the nature of participation (its relationship to mediation) all announce themselves in the use of this verbal mood. The use of the present tense parallels the verbal mood of the institutional narrative, rehearsed from its first utterance at the Last Supper, it is performed in the present and in every present enactment of the command to "Do this in remembrance of me" enjoins: "This is my body", "This is my blood". The deconstituted we is reconstituted by that making present again, albeit differently now, what was handed down to it in the past and which it passes on into the future. For it is we who break the bread not just the Priest, we who do not touch the wafer. The action is representative of our action in two ways: it stands in for something we cannot each individually do and it describes that very representative act. To the temporal, corporeal and spatial complexity I have outlined in 1-3, a mimetic complexity is added. These complexities are mutually implicated in and constitutive of each other.

It is on the basis of an exploration of the present tense of this liturgical interchange that the erotic nature of the ecclesial community can best be approached. Our contemporary culture idolises the present, the seizure of the present, and that this seizure is a secular eschatology, a mimckery of eternity as the fullness of time. The eroticism of secular living is orientated around the experiencing of the present as such; implicated, that is, in a certain metaphysics of time and corporeality. By examining the nature of presence in the Eucharist we can come to see what is different about the church as an erotic community. The significance of the other three complexities of the fracture liturgy will emerge with respect to examining the theological relationship between the present and presence, time and participation.

What, then, is the relationship between this liturgical use of the present continuous and sacramental "presence"? There are four possible answers to that question. First, that they are the same: the present tense presences because it performs what it utters or, as Marshall McLuhan taught: the medium is the message. Secondly, though present (as in a verbal tense) and presence share an etymological root, we are concerned with two different "language games" or discursive categories, the one grammatical and the other ontological. That is, that just as there remains an unbridgeable gap between words and the world, between what is and the representation of what is, so the present tense names a presencing it cannot institute or be part of it. We could see these first two options in terms of a see-saw between univocity and equivocity. The third option, the postmodern option, is to describe the relationship between present and presence as undecideable, as part of an economy in which a trace of something arrives and is deferred simultaneously: the relationship is a differend, the economy one of *differance* – a Yes, a Promise which is also a Yes, Yes, a Promise of what is not yet. The final option is that there is some analogical relationship between the present tense and presence such that difference nevertheless participates in similitude.

Since neither univocity nor equivocity can form a theological basis for community, the last two options are the more important ones to examine. To some these options may appear to be identical (we can recall Derrida's ambiguous remarks concerning the construction by Levinas of an analogy *sui generis*)[2] and it is exactly here that a postmodern understanding of sacramental presence, and the communities it forms, must define itself. The first two options represent the two forms of linguistic philosophy which have been at the centre of the poststructuralist critique. On the one hand, there are the ontotheological resonances which Derrida baptised as logocentrism, which began to increasingly gain credence following Duns Scotus' *Expositio in metaphysicam* where all transcendentals, particularly existing and willing, can be predicated of God and creation univocally. On the other, there is the correspondence theory of signification which establishes the dualism between mind and world and the problem of how words hook up to what is out there which began to establish itself with nominalism. But before examining the *theological* implications of these two options a more fundamental issue arises with respect to them. Heidegger pointed to it first, though not in this way: being has a history. What I mean by this is that the present and presence do not come to us as transparent, transhistorical concepts. They come to us bearing all the accretions of prior usage and transformation. This will be very important for what I wish to argue. For I will suggest that the current talk about the present and presence, whether in the Enlightenment longing for immediate knowledge which grounds the empiricisms and positivisms of the natural sciences (and sets up the correspondence theory of language) or in the postmodern critiques of logocentrism and insistence upon the *graphe,* are operating with very modern, and untheological, construals of these terms. In other words, the disappearance of the body and the creation of imaginary and virtual communities is predicated upon an understanding of a relationship between time and desire which must be theologically challenged if a new analogical world-view is to be constructed.

This can be put more succinctly with three examples. The first is Aquinas on the what the Church will later term the real presence: "in

2. J. DERRIDA, '*At this Very Moment in this Work Here I Am*', trans. S. Critchley, in R. BERNASCONI & S. CRITCHLEY (eds.), *Re-reading Levinas*, London, Althone Press, 1991, pp. 44-45.

this sacrament he is present to be nourishment"[3]. Later he emphasises: "Christ is... really present"[4]. The second is Calvin, also writing about the flesh and blood of Christ in the eucharistic rite: "we may confidently consider them as truly exhibited to us, as if Christ himself were presented to our eyes, and touched by our hands"[5]. The third is Slavjo Zizek with respect to those worries he has about cyberspace: "What brings about the 'loss of reality' in cyberspace is not its emptiness (the fact that it is lacking with respect to the fullness of the real presence) but, on the contrary, its very excessive fullness (the potential abolition of the dimension of symbolic virtuality)"[6]. What I am suggesting is that the use of the term present/presence in these three citations is implicated, for each, in distinctive historical, linguistic, social and metaphysical matrices. The words bears only a distant family resemblance to each other. If this is so then the postmodern deconstruction of present/presence, as Zizek performs it in his own Lacanian way, need bear little relation to the traditional understanding of presence or grace whereby the salvific life of Christ is shed abroad through the Church. The latter, in fact, may be used to critique the former: deconstructing the deconstructive economy itself – and redeeming the endless semiosis of sense by establishing an analogical order. That, *in nuce*, will be the argument of this contribution.

So taking these three examples, let me first sketch a genealogy of presence. Then we will see the implications of this genealogy with respect to the fracture liturgy and sacramental communion. Finally, we will see how the fourth aspect of that liturgy concerned with the present and presence has to be understood, can only be understood, with respect to the other three characteristics of the liturgical performance. Together these characteristics will enable me to define the operation of desire, the formation of persons-in-communion and the analogical nature in the Christian church.

II. THE BIRTH OF PRESENCE

1. *Augustine/Aquinas*

It has to be emphasised that other than the employment of the copula "is", early accounts of the Eucharist do not use the language of

---

3. T. AQUINAS, *Summa Theologiae: The Sacraments* [Vol.58], trans. D. Bourke, London, Blackfriars – Eyre & Spottiswoode, 1975, IIIa.q.76,1.

4. T. AQUINAS, *Summa Theologiae*, IIIa.q.76, 8.

5. J. CALVIN, *Institutes of the Christian Religion* [vol.1&2], trans. J. Allen, Philadelphia, Presbyterian Board of Christian Education, 1936, p. 643.

6. S. ŽIŽEK, *How to Give a Body a Deadlock*, in J.F. MACCANNELL & L. ZAKARIN (eds.), *Thinking Bodies*, Stanford, Stanford University Press, 1994, p. 155.

presence. The New Testament accounts simply employ *estin*, and this is repeated in Ignatius of Antioch's statement in his *Letter to the Smyrneans* that "the Eucharist is the flesh of our Saviour, Jesus Christ" and in Justin Martyr's statement in his *Apologia* that that "which nourishes our flesh and blood by assimilation is both the flesh and blood of that Jesus who was made flesh". The question, then, arises whence did the language of presence emerge, and more particularly when did the adjective of "real" preface the use of presence? For what is added to, what is being suggested by, the addition of that "real"? What I will argue is that the employment of "presence", and most particularly the term "real presence", is not metaphysically innocent and places us on the road to Derrida's notion of logocentrism and Lacuna's negative construe of that as the Real. The secular fixation upon the present has been partly produced from within the changing traditions of Christian theology.

Throughout mediaeval accounts of sacramental presence we are concerned with the nature of analogy. It is the collapse of analogy and the movement towards univocity, the transparency of "clear and distinct" ideas, that can be traced in the difference between Aquinas and Calvin's notions of "presence". As the analogical world collapses so the notion of "participation" changes – as we will see. From out of the earliest discussions of what I have called the ontological scandal of that "is" – the "*est*" in *hoc est corpus meus* – the language of appearance comes to be employed. The *Mystagogical Catechesis* gives us an instance of this: "we consume these with perfect certainty that they are the body and blood of Christ, since under the appearance of bread the body is given, and the blood under the appearance of wine". But the language of appearances is not to be identified with the language of presence, even more "real presence". Appearance is *species*, that is a mode of existing. Appearance is not divorced from the true; appearance is a participation in the true. Augustine emphasises this: "This sacrament... doesn't present you with the body of Christ in such a way as to divide it from you. This, as the apostle reminds us, was foretold in holy scripture: They shall be two in one flesh"[7]. We become what we eat. This is important, for the distinction between visible and invisible according to this logic does not constitute a dualism: the visible, when read theologically, manifests the watermark of its creator. The visible and corporeal is always suspended, and incomplete. Things cannot fully realise themselves in the

---

7. AUGUSTINE, *Sermons* III/6 and III/7, trans. E. Hill, New Rochelle, New City Press, 1993, 228b.

present for Augustine. For having created, God maintains and sustains that creation throughout what we have seen Gregory of Nyssa term its *scopos*. The creaturely realm is always subject to time.

When we come to Aquinas, the key exponent of the Eucharist, all this should be borne in mind. For despite the ubiquitous use of the words present/presence/real presence by translator's, Aquinas does not employ that language in his account of sacramental realism. That he knows of the Latin *praesens* and *praesentia* is manifest. He uses the former in his discussion of time – the present (*praesens*) is a temporal location and God is omnipresent[8]; he uses the latter with reference to Christ's bodily presence (*sua praesentia corporali*) in history. But he goes on to refute those who consider "the presence of Christ's body (*praesentia corporis Christi*) as if it were present in a way that is natural for a body to be present (*prout est praesens per modum corporis*)"[9]. The language of *praesens* and *praesentia* only have reference to temporal and historical corporeality and have to be understood analogically[10]. And there is a studied avoidance of using such language with respect to Christ's giving of Himself in the Eucharist. So when we have statements like "whenever this sacrament is celebrated he is present in an invisible way under sacramental appearances", the Latin is actually *"Invisibiliter tamen sub speciebus hujus sacramenti est ubicumque hoc sacramentum perficitur"*[11]. There is no mention of "presence" and the language of appearance is, again, the language of *species*. Aquinas will talk about how "the very body of Christ exists [*verum corpus Christi... existat*]" in the sacrament, and he will talk about how Christ is really there [*vere esse*][12]. But throughout the whole of Quaestio 76 of the *Summa theologiae* – under a subtitle given by the editors of the translation "Real Presence" – despite the repeated use of the term "presence" by translators, the Latin *praesens* and/or *praesentia* is never used by Aquinas.

Two questions emerge at this point. Why does Aquinas avoid using the term and when did the term start getting used as a description of what Roman Catholics believe concerning the Eucharist? I suggest the fundamental reason why Aquinas does not engage in a discourse concerning *praesens/praesentia* is because the celebrated theologian who

8. T. AQUINAS, *Summa Theologiae*, I.q.8 a.3.

9. T. AQUINAS, *Summa Theologiae*, IIIa.q.75.2.

10. "Medieval theology in most of its varieties viewed with intense suspicion any doctrine that took God's presence in the world too litterally" A. FUNKENSTEIN, *Theology and the Scientific Imagination,* Princeton, Princeton University Press, 1986, p. 25.

11. T. AQUINAS, *Summa Theologiae,* IIIa.q.75.2.

12. T. AQUINAS, *Summa Theologiae,* IIIa.q.75.2.

had already done so, namely Augustine, had concluded that "As for the present, it takes not up any space"[13]. The Latin is even more resonant when we recall Augustine's concern with the nothing or *nihil* out of which God creates all things, and that all things are good insofar as they have being and evil insofar as they lack being: "*praesens autem nullum habet spatium*". Augustine is thought to have been the first theologian to give theological consideration to the present as such, articulating a concept of the eternal as that which is complete all at once in the present without past or future (presence as divine omnipresence)[14]. This returns us to the discussion of "appearances" and the relation of what is visible to the invisible: "Nothing passes away in the eternal but is present as a whole. No time, however, is present as a whole [*sed totum esse praesens; nullum uero tempus esse praesens*]"[15].

Aquinas' understanding of time is indebted to Augustine's. For both, the temporal participates in and is made possible by the eternal. That is why Augustine goes on to elaborate, in that famous discussion of time, that in the soul (which participates in the eternity of God): "The present time of past things is our memory; the present time of present things is our sight; the present time of future things is our expectation"[16]. In creation, the present does not exist outside of the future and the past; time is a certain stretching (*distentionem*) of the mind as it moves within the mind of the Trinitarian God. To have a pure present, to have a discourse on presence, would be to reify something which has no existence in and of itself in the creaturely, for Augustine[17]. Similarly, for Aquinas, the sacrament while visibly present to the senses, celebrates the *anamnesis* of Christ's words in the Upper Room and looks forward to the beatific celebration to come. Its nature, then, as Aquinas states, is a *viaticum*. It is not the mechanism for some arbitrary deliverance of the now as grace. Neither is it a magical commodity, enchanting the material. It is not an object at all in the stasis of some objectively real, the stasis of "the present time of present things". The present *qua* present is the glorification of the visible as self-revealing, as in possession of their own being, as self-validating. This is a fundamental axiom for empiricisms and

13. AUGUSTINE, *Confessions*, trans. H. Chadwick, Oxford, Oxford University Press, 1991, XI.15.

14. R.J. TESKE, *The Paradoxes of Time in Saint Augustine*, Milwaukee, Marquette University Press, 1996, p. 22.

15. AUGUSTINE, *Confessiones*, XI.11, 13.

16. AUGUSTINE, *Confessiones*, XI.20.

17. This may partly explain why Anselm's ontological proof was ignored in the mediaeval period but picked up avidly from the seventeenth century onwards.

positivisms. Such a view of material existence is implicated in the meta-physics of light. For Augustine and Aquinas, created beings have no access to the purification of the present as such. To enter the daylight forever constitute beatification. Only God as omnipresent views things in the eternal present. The language of *praesens/praesentia* is, therefore, I suggest, the language of idolatry (reifying that which cannot be plucked out of time and fully present to itself) for Aquinas. Hence, when it is employed – to describe Christ's visible and historically specific body and condemn those who cannot "envisage a spiritual, non-visible" body – it is drawing attention to the way Christ is not present in the Eucharist as *praesens* would suggest and, therefore, sacramental pres-ence cannot employ the language of *praesentia*. We will examine this further with Calvin, for both Aquinas and Calvin have Augustine as their explicit source at this very point. Access to things present in themselves is only available to God who knows all things and sees all things as they are eternally. Pretence to immediate access is illusory and evidence of a darkened understanding.

We touch here on a question which is central to understanding anal-ogy and the way the word "presence" or "the present" functions ana-logically. It is a question concerning the relationship between the Trinity and creation. We will examine this more fully towards the end of this contribution. For the moment let me suggest that we might understand Aquinas' reluctance to equate the presence of the historical body of Jesus Christ with the presence of Christ in the Eucharist, in terms of God as Father not being present in the way God as Son is present and the presence of God as Son differing from the presence of God as Spirit. Karl Barth articulates something of these differences when he describes the triunity of the Godhead in terms of "modes of being".

So when then did "real presence" become current within Roman Catholic belief? The term does not appear in the Fourth Lateran Coun-cil's definition of transubstantiation in 1215. The reference does cer-tainly appear in the decrees of the Council of Trent, which, on October 11th 1551 opened its thirteenth session on *de eucharista* with the follow-ing discussion: "On the Real Presence of our Lord Jesus Christ" and the English now does accurately translate the Latin, for the words are "*de reali praesentia*". Furthermore, the contents of that first chapter pro-nounces that: "our Lord Jesus Christ, true God and true man, is truly [*vere*], really [*realiter*] and substantially contained [*contineri*] in the August sacrament of the Holy Eucharist under the appearance [*sub species*] of those sensible things [*rerum sensibilium*]" He is "sacramen-tally present [*sacramentaliter praesens*]" to us. Now what is remarkable here is not only the employment of *praesens/praesentia* but also the adjective real [*realis/realiter*]. The word is often used to translate Aquinas' treatment of the Eucharist, but is not found in Aquinas, who will use *vere*. It was a newly coined word in Late Mediaeval Latin. *Realiter* is found earlier, and used consistently by Aquinas as a synonym for *vere,* but *realitas* as thing [*res*], or fundament [*fundus*] is only found in the discourse of jurisprudence in the early twelfth century. The earliest theological use of *realitas* and *realis* is in the work of Duns Scotus and William of Ockham. In Ockham's various treatises on the Eucharist both *realis* and *praesens* are used, but not (as far as I have been able to ascertain) ever together. In a way that remarkably anticipates the language of the Council of Trent, in *De Corpore Christi* Ockham will writes about Christ being "truly and really available [*vere et realiter continetur*]" in the bread and the wine[20]. The dictionary of mediaeval Latin notes concerning the earliest use of *realis* that "The precise sense is uncertain". In other words, the language of the real was not available to either Augustine or Aquinas. In fact, its direct relation to "thing" [*res, reipsa, reapse* and *revera*], to the opacity and self-manifestation of an object, would only amplify the discussion and refusal of the language of *praesens/praesentia*. For it reaffirms an idolatry of the visible, a reification, a commodification quite at odds with the understanding of the creation and the sacrament in Augustine and Aquinas. Significantly, it is Scotus and Ockham who also initiate, as part of their discussions on the intuitive cognition of objects in the world, investigations into presence. *Praesens/praesentialiter* in Ockham, comes to refer to the definite location of things, to a certain rigorous spatialising, and to a specific and isolatable temporality, the now, the instant, the immediate. Ockham registers a shift towards the modern obsession of the seizing the present; a shift also towards space as location.

It is in following the Scotist and Ockhamist trajectories of scholastic thinking that we first discover the coming together of "the real" and "presence". Commenting on the *Sentences* of Lombard in the early

18. Augustine's teaching on Christ in the eucharist is fragmentary, hence both Aquinas and Calvin can cite him as an authority in markedly different ways.

19. For Ockham's conception of the eucharistic, which drew upon him much criticism, see G.N. BUESCHER, *The Eucharistic Teaching of William of Ockham,* Washington, The Catholic University of America Press, 1950; E. STUMP, *Theology and Physics in 'De sacramento altaris': Ockham's Theory of Indivisibles,* in N. KRETZMANN (ed.), *Infinity and Continuity in Ancient and Mediaeval Thought,* Ithaca, Cornell University Press, 1982, pp. 207-230.

20. Quoted in G.N. BUESCHER, *The Eucharistic Teaching,* p. 9; see also W. OF OCKHAM, *De Sacramento Altaris,* ed. T. Bruce Birch, Burlington, The Lutheran Literary Board, 1930, p. 166.

fifteenth century, the French bishop, Jean de Ripa, employs the terms *realis/realiter* with respect to distinctions in God. This is traditional, but Ripa develops a natural theology in which the distinction of personal properties in the divine essence "*sit recessus a summa redemptitate reali*"[21]. As Francis Ruello commentates upon this passage: "*la distinction formelle entre l'essence divine et les propriétés personelles peut-on inférer que leur identité reélle soit moindre que si l'on faisait abstraction de cette distinction*"[22]. There are degrees of reality and God is the ultimately real, He is "*immensus causaliter*"[23] – a univocity of Being relates one to the other. When Ripa then turns to the discourse of presence although Ruello observes that there is a difference between "*la présence divine et la présence de la créature*"[24], it is a difference of degree. Among created things God "*est praesens hiis quos per internam sanctificationem gratificat*"[25]. It is in this sacramental and univocal universe that the words *realiter* and *praesens* come together for the first time. Ripa writes: "*Deus est realiter praesens infinito vacuo imaginario extra celum*"[26].

One more link in the story can be made by examining the exposition of the Mass written by the fifteenth century Ockhamist Gabriel Biel. Biel's role in the transmission of the heritage of mediaeval scholasticism to the early Reformers gathered around Luther is now well documented[27]. Significantly, the influence of Biel's theology on the Council of Trent had already been noted[28]. He might almost be quoting Ockham, when he writes: "*corpus Christi vere et realiter contineri in sacramento*"[29]. But whereas Ripa discusses God's "real presence" in creation, Biel specifically speaks about a doctrine of the Eucharist: "*corpus Christi realiter sit praesens per divinum beneplacitum*"[30]. Again, like Ockham, Biel will emphasise the way this presence punctuates the temporal with the eternal now. *Praesens* is concerned with time, the *nunc*,

21. J. DE RIPA, *Conclusiones*, ed. A. Combes, Paris,Vrin, 1957, p. 207.

22. F. RUELLO, *Theologie naturelle de Jean de Ripa*, Paris, Beauchesne, 1992, p. 690.

23. J. DE RIPA, *Conclusiones*, p. 224.

24. F. RUELLO, *Theologie naturelle de Jean de Ripa*, p. 734.

25. J. DE RIPA, *Conclusiones*, p. 223.

26. J. DE RIPA, *Conclusiones*, p. 222.

27. J.L. FARTHING, *Thomas Aquinas and Gabriel Biel: Interpretations of St. Thomas Aquinas in German Nominalism in the Eve of the Reformation*, Durham, Duke University Press, 1988.

28. C. FECKES, *Gabriel Biel, der erste grosse Dogmatiker der Universität Tübingen in seiner wissenschaftlichen Bedeutung*, in *Theologische Quartalschrift* 108 (1927), pp. 55 and 75.

29. G. BIEL, *Canonis Missae Expositio*, Lectio XLVIII, Heiko A. OBERMAN & W.J. COURTNEY (eds.), Wiesbaden, Franz Steiner Verlag, 1965, p. 236.

30. G. BIEL, *Canonis Missae Expositio*, p. 232.

the *instans*, such that the eucharistic conversion is "*non successive sed instantance*"[31]. The present is now a commodity to be abstracted, a property to be grasped.

The first English employment of the term "real presence" is in the 1552 Book of Common Prayer where there is a direct refutation of the Council of Trent's doctrine of transubstantiation with regard to kneeling to receive the Eucharist: "It is not meant thereby, that any adoration is done... unto any real or essential Presence there being of Christ's natural flesh and blood". Calvin does not employ the terms *realitas* or *realis* – only *vere*/*vrai*. The use of the word "*realis*" may well be at odds with the general sense of the Council of Trent's doctrine of the Eucharist. For the language of appearance [*species*] remains, and *species* and *praesens* sit uneasily alongside each other unless the appearance is a veil behind which the presence hovers – which is the Calvinist understanding of the Eucharist quite manifestly attacked in the seventh session of the Council of Trent, in canons 7 and 8 and repeated in canon 8 of session thirteen. A change or transformation occurs in the elements such that a sacrifice takes place (cf. session XXII) for "in it [the Eucharist] the same God is present [*Deum praesentem in eo adesse*]" (XIII.5). Possibly the Council is adopting the theology of Ripa and the point is being made that only God can be present and/or real, for while all else appears only God is true Being (Ripa's *summa redemptitate reali*). But since the metaphysics of the Eucharist are downplayed – in favour of a pragmatics of liturgical execution – this is not explained and still runs contrary to Augustine and Aquinas' avoidance of the *praesens*/*praesentia* language. The nature of Christ's being with us in the Eucharist has nothing to do with either reality or presence in the way these words came to be understood from the early fifteenth century onwards.

2. *Calvin*

The reification, and the literalisation, of presence affects understandings of corporeality and community, and orientates desire towards that which is available now. A sense of a haunting, an ectoplasmic aura behind or beyond the material will lead to an emphasis on "spirituality" at the expense of the body – and eventually the emphasis upon solitary religious experience as the authentic mark of sanctity. The opacification of the natural prepares the metaphysical ground for the secular, demystified world-view (and later the scientific world-view and the capitalist cult of worldly goods). It prepares the ground also for the adoption of

---

31. G. BIEL, *Canonis Missae Expositio*, p. 243 and 247.

eucharistic language and liturgical *accoutrement* by State rulers for State ceremony[32]. We are entering the society of the spectacle. Two key phenomena make manifest this new metaphysical trajectory such that the language of *praesens/praesentia* comes to be employed in order to describe the Eucharist in early modernity. The first is the increasing attention to the visible display of power and charisma by the ecclesial institution, noted by both Henri de Lubac (1949: 281-88) and Michel de Certeau. Certeau observes: "This Eucharistic 'body' was the 'sacrament' of the institution, the visible instituting of what the institution was meant to become"[33]. He interprets this change as a crisis concerning the illegibility of creation which followed Ockhamist nominalism. Space is too short to follow his argument here. But the increasing emphasis upon the visible – which Augustine relates specifically with the presence of the present – led to the multiplication of fraternities of Corpus Christi, particularly in Italy in the early sixteenth century. Andre Duval notes: "*l'affaissement progressif du sens du symbolisme sacramental au profit d'un gout excessif de l'efficacité – la disproportion entre une dévotion envahissante à la Présence réelle et une mésestime pratique de la communion – l'obscurcissement, au sein*"[34]. Following du Lubac and Certeau, he finds in the late Middles Ages "*la ruine du mystère eucharistique*"[35].

But the most determinative producer of the discourse of presence and the present, is the fierce discussions among the various Protestantisms in which the Eucharist becomes central for defining new ecclesial identities. Let us begin at the very heart of the matter for Calvin, Book IV of his *Institutes of the Christian Religion*, chapter XVII and section 9 where he details his view on the sacramental elements (bread and wine), sacramental presence and participation. Significantly, Calvin defines his own doctrine of the Eucharist in contrast to all the other leading accounts and by rejecting all the interpretations of scripture which vouchsafed these accounts in favour of what his own inquiry "into his [Christ's] genuine meaning [*de genuino sensu / le sens vrai et naturel*]"[36] – which presumably is that interpretation put forward

32. L. MARIN, *Food for Thought*, trans. M. Hjort, Baltimore, John Hopkins University Press, 1989.

33. M. DE CERTEAU, *The Mystic Fable*, trans. M.B. Smith, Chicago, University of Chicago Press, 1992, p. 83.

34. A. DUVAL, *Des Sacraments au Concile de Trente*, Paris, Les Éditions du Cerf, 1985, p. 57.

35. A. DUVAL, *Des Sacraments au Concile de Trente*, p. 57.

36. J. CALVIN, *Institutes of the Christian Religion*, vol. 1 & 2, trans. J. Allen, Philadelphia, Presbyterian Board of Christian Education, 1936, p. 668 [1021/372].

(asserted) by Calvin himself. We will use the English translation, but I wish examine the Latin text of 1559 (the last text Calvin revised) and the French translation of it which Calvin prepared. By consulting the Latin text it will be more evident how his Latin differs from Aquinas' (and therefore his understanding of the sacramental economy) and by consulting, when necessary, the French text we can gain some insight into how Calvin is using certain Latin terms, terms which he frequently shares with Aquinas. One passage is key:

> the breaking of the bread is symbolical [*symbolum esse / le signe extérieur de la substance spirituelle*] and not the substance itself [*non rem ipsam*]; yet, this being admitted, from the exhibition of the symbol we may justly infer the exhibition of the substance [*verum hoc posito, a symboli tamen exhibitione rem ipsam exhiberi, rite colligemus / toutefois nous pourrons inférer de ce que le signe nous est baillé, que la substance nous est aussi livrée en sa vérité*]; for unless any one would call God a deceiver, he can never presume to affirm that he sets before us an empty sign [*inane symbolum / un signe vain et vide*]. Therefore, if, by the breaking of the bread, the Lord truly represents the participation of his body [*corporis sui participationem vere repraesentat / représente au vrai la participation*], it might not be doubted that he truly presents and communicates it [*quin vere praestet atque exhibeat / qu'il ne la baille en meme temps*]. And it must always be the rule with believers, whenever they see the signs [*symbola*] instituted by the Lord, to assure and persuade themselves [*certo cogitant ac sibi persuadeant*]. For to what end would the Lord deliver into our hands the symbol of his body except to assure us of a real participation of it [*verum eius participatione*]. If it be true that the visible sign is given to us [*praeberi nobis signum visible*] to seal the donation of the invisible substance [*invisiblis rei donationem*] we ought to entertain a confident assurance that in receiving the symbol [*symbolo*] of his body, we at the same time receive the body itself [37].

Calvin does not use the term "real presence" to describe either his own teaching on the Eucharist or the Roman doctrine. Neither, does he use the word "real [*realis*]", but consistently uses the term *vere/la vérité/la vrai*. He also consistently uses, to define his own position, the verbs to represent [*repraesentare*] and to be present [*praesentare*], although in the passage above we have *praestare* and he will also use *exhibere*. What is evident in this central passage is a series of dislocations (and the word in deliberately chosen for the new spatial order Calvin evidences). The first dislocation is between sign (Calvin uses *symbolum* and *signum* interchangeably, as my polytext shows) and thing (translated substance but in Latin *rei*, not Aquinas' *substantia*). The French maps this onto a second dislocation – between the exteriority of the sign and the spiritual,

---

37. J. CALVIN, *Institutes*, p. 651 [1009-10/357-8].

inner, materiality of the signified. The third dislocation is concomitant with both of these – that between representation (*repraesentat*) and presentation (*praestet* here which translates more accurately as to be ready at hand, to be available, to be waiting there, but on other occasions *praesens*). Finally, there is the fourth dislocation between the visible sign and the invisible thing.

Ironically Calvin will defend his teaching with respect to a distinction Augustine draws between the sign [*signum*] and the signified [*res*]. But he fails to appreciate the Neo-platonic logic that relates *signum* to *res* for Augustine, the dialectical relation between symbol and reality. Christ's body defines bread, Christ's blood defines wine, for Augustine. Aquinas, who also appeals to Augustine on exactly this matter, understands the participation of the sign in the signified. Aquinas and Calvin appeal explicitly to an instance when Augustine does employ the language of presence. It is in his commentary on the Book of John, in his exegesis of Jesus' statement to his disciples that the poor you have always with you, but me you do not always have with you[39]. Augustine explains that this statement does not contradict the final statement to his disciples that he will be with them always because, in the first saying he is speaking about his present body [*praesentia corporis sui*], the body available to sight for the forty days after his death. This body is no longer with us [*non est hic*], for Christ sits at the right hand of God. Nevertheless his presence remains [*hic est*] for his glorified presence is not withdrawn [*non enim recessit praesentia majestatis*]. The way to interpret the Scriptural crux, then, is to draw a distinction between the present body [*praesentiam carnis*] and what is always with us, the presence of Christ's glory [*praesentiam majestatis*]. The Church had the carnal body for a matter of days; it retains the presence of Christ by faith [*modo fide tenet, oculis non videt*].

It is significant that, for Calvin, this passage, which never once speaks of the sacraments, when he quotes in it section 22 of chapter XVII of *Institutes*, provides him with Augustine's understanding of the

---

38. As the commentator to the modern French edition of the *Institutes* points out: "Calvin emploie a plusieurs reprises le mot substance – dans ce chapitre, mais il ne lui donne pas le sens philosophique ou théologique. La substance est pour lui synonyme de présence – vivifiante." J. CALVIN, *Institution de la religion Chrétienne. Livre 4*, Geneva, Labor et Fides, 1958, p. 349. Missing also in Calvin, and related to the avoidance of *substantia* is an account of appearance *species*. In its place is a language of "corporal signs / corporealis signis" (J. CALVIN, *Institutes*, p. 652 [1010]); "earthly signs", "carnal presence / carnalem... praesentiam" (J. CALVIN, *Institutes*, p. 656 [1012]); figuration and of exhibition [*exhibitione/bailler*].

39. AUGUSTINE, *In Johannis evangelium tractatus*, 50,13.

Eucharist. Augustine authorises Calvin's discourse concerning presence, and the dualism between carnal and spiritual presence which Calvin's teaching about the Eucharist centres upon. Aquinas, on the other hand, does not either read this passage back into an account of transubstantiation, nor make the distinction between the present body and the presence of Christ's glory. The difference between Aquinas and Calvin here relates to their doctrines of creation. Dualisms, for Calvin, deepen the opacification of the natural opening a space between the subjective believer and the objective fact – bread, wine. He is obsessed with spatial determinants throughout his account of the Eucharist. The body of Christ is in heaven, He descends to us, spanning the distance through his Spirit. We are below and every object, whether divine or creaturely, has its own proper location. In the space between the subject and the object, observation, calculation, measurement and evaluation enter. In a move that predates the founding dualism of Descartes *Meditations*, Calvin also anticipates the theological scepticism that waits in the metaphysical wings of such a dualism: "for unless any one would call God a deceiver, he can never presume to affirm that he sets before us an empty sign [*inane symbolum* / *un signe vain et vide*]." Modern secular thinking is founded upon this ability to doubt.

The significance of accepting the possibility of "an empty sign" – elsewhere described as "a vain or ineffectual sign [*inani aut vacu signo*]"[41] – cannot be underestimated. It points to a nominalist metaphysics, but also to a curious tension in Calvin's description of the eucharistic communication. For elsewhere he insists on a form of analogy which suggests a univocity of being: "We conclude, that our souls are fed by the flesh and blood of Christ, just as our corporeal life is preserved and sustained by bread and wine. For otherwise there would be no suitableness in the analogy of the sign [*Neque enim aliter quadraret analogia signi* / *Car autrement la similitude du signe ne conviendrait point*]"[42]. The Latin verb *quadrare* and the French verb *conviendre* are frequently employed to define the nature of the analogy pertaining between Christ's body and the eucharistic elements: "There would be no consistency in the signification, if the external sign were not a living image of the truth which is represented by it [*Nec vero significatio aliter*

---

40. Compare Augustine's understanding of space and materiality as he views the body of Christ as an extendible body: "He didn't depart from heaven, when he came down to us from there; nor did he depart from us, when he ascended to heaven again. I mean, he was still there while he was here" (AUGUSTINE, *Sermons III/7*, 263a).

41. J. CALVIN, *Institutes*, p. 651 [1010].

42. J. CALVIN, *Institutes*, p. 650 [1009/357].

quadraret, nisi veritas quae illic figuratur, vivam effigiem haberet in externo signo]"[43]. But these formulations structure a mode of analogical reasoning (by proportion) which, in the eighteenth century, became the basis for not only a natural theology, but inductive, *a posteriori* proofs for the existence of God. An ontotheology surfaces here. For the formulation seeks to demonstrate a mathematical relationship:

$$A = A1 \qquad \text{or} \qquad \text{Christ} = \text{soul}$$
$$B \quad B1 \qquad\qquad\qquad \text{bread} \quad \text{body}$$

Christ is to the soul what bread is to the body, despite the dualism (indicated by the bar) separating Christ from external sign and the spiritual from the carnal. The Latin *quadrare* implies as much. So that, on the one hand, participation and communication are possible only the basis of a univocity A=A1 ("Christ truly becomes one with us") and B=B1 (he "refreshes us by the eating of his flesh and the drinking of his blood"). While, on the other, an equivocal relationship holds between A and B ("the breaking of the bread is symbolical and not the substance [*rem*] itself [*le signe extérieur de la substance spirituelle*]" as between A1 and B1 ("the Holy Spirit transcends all our senses"). Calvin's position – which again demonstrates the collapse of analogical reasoning such as Thomas understood it – illustrates a tension Amos Funkenstein traces back to the Scholastics of the late Middle Ages, in which the "movement towards a minimal construction of God's presence competed with a counter-movement that sought a maximal construction in an ever more literal sense"[45].

This tension in Calvin also relates to the tensions between equivocation and univocity, transcendence and immanence. The collapse of analogy opens an aporetic space that the dualisms of modernity, establishing the instrumentality of reasoning, attempt to span. Dualistic thinking substitutes for mediation. It cannot itself mediate, but it establishes a logic that gives a definition to one thing (the objective, the natural, the public)

43. J. CALVIN, *Institutes*, p. 656 [1013].

44. One notes here Calvin's discussion on the relationship of words to things: "things ordained by God borrow the names of those things of which they always bear a definite and not misleading signification, and have the reality joined with them. So great, therefore, is their similarity and closeness that transition from one to the other is easy". (section 21, new translation). The Latin does suggest more hesitancy with regard to the correspondence between word and thing, the tokens standing in for things absent *fallacem significationem semper gerunt* [always bear a distorted signification]. Nevertheless he will speak, both in Latin and in French, of an affinity [*propter affinitatem/l'affinité*] between the object signifed and the sign. See J. CALVIN, *Institutes*, p. 665 [1019/370].

45. A. FUNKENSTEIN, *Theology and the Scientific Imagination*, Princeton, Princeton University Press, 1986, p. 61.

only with respect to its diametrical opposite (the subjective, the cultural, the private). Calvin's analogical reasoning is not analogical at all (where analogy defines the mediation between similarity and difference, univocity and equivocity). This tension manifests itself in Calvin's formula of the participation *of* Christ rather than the participation *in* Christ and the description of the deliverance of Christ into our hands – presumably for either betraying (as in the first such deliverance) or embracing.

This instrumentality of reasoning issues, at times, in logical demonstrations (for all Calvin's insistence upon the sublime and infinite heights of the divine and the limitations of human thinking) against other interpretations of the Eucharist. We must not dream, he warns, of a such a presence of Christ [*praesentia Christi*] as the ingenuity of the Romanists has invented, because it is irrational "that Christ annihilates the substance (*rem*) of bread and conceals himself under its form"[46]. And yet he admits that the descent of Christ "to become nourishment to us" will not "accord with human reason"[47]. A certain form of reasoning counts here, while another form does not. A politics of the rational is evident, where appeal is being made to fixed and stable identities. In French, Christ's genuine meaning [*de genuino sensu*] is *le sens vrai et naturel*, "true and natural"[48]. What makes this reasoning possible is the presupposition of being able to define the nature of a thing (bread) by the human senses: "What is the nature of a body? Has it not its proper and certain dimensions? Is it not contained in some particular place, and capable of being felt and seen?"[49] Things fully present themselves as themselves in definite locations and with definable dimensions. They are identical to themselves and in correspondence with [*propter affinitatem*] the names "invented by men, which are rather emblems of things absent than tokens of things present [*imagines sunt rerum absentium potius quam notae praesentium*]"[50]. Therefore, to take this thing [bread/wine]as a symbol of, as a sign of, rather than simply its own self-authenticating presence, becomes a subjective act of consciousness judgement-making. The "seeing" has to be transformed by a "persuading" and the entertainment of "a confident assurance". Christ offers himself, but our faith receives; the Spirit makes the offering effective, but our faith makes the reception of that effectivity possible. Calvin does not proceed in detail here, but a psychology and phenomenology of reception lies waiting

46. J. CALVIN, *Institutes*, p. 654-655.
47. J. CALVIN, *Institutes*, p. 670.
48. J. CALVIN, *Institutes*, p. 668 [1021/372].
49. J. CALVIN, *Institutes*, p. 671.
50. J. CALVIN, *Institutes*, p. 666 [1020].

for future developments, future examinations of religious experience, and the interiority of self-persuasion and self-assurance sails close to a voluntaristic emphasis in the reception and effectivity of the communication. In turn the subjectivity of judgement is making calls for external legitimation and authentication if the judgement is not to be simply an arbitrary but a true discernment.

But what are the implications of Calvin's discourse for the nature of presence? First, there is a commodification of presence and an investing of it with spiritual value. That which is present is that which is true; it is the authentic as opposed to the simulacrum, the real as opposed to the illusory, the immediate self-manifestation as opposed to the mediated representation. With Calvin there are two forms of this presence: there is the presence of Christ (which invests the eucharistic elements with a certain ectoplasmic aura, for those who have faith) and there is the concrete presence of things felt and seen. But since a common sense, a pragmatic reasoning, governs overall then the way is prepared for the investigation of these things which are in and of themselves and for a new natural science. The discourse of presence is inseparable from reference to things (substance no longer bears the connotations of *substantia* but accords rather to substance as the phrase "chemical substance"). Secondly, and concomitantly, this discourse of things present and subjects as separated observers, calculators and evaluators of this presence, promotes an atomism which is ontological (the world is composed of distinct entities which are themselves composed of smaller entities) and sociological (society is composed of distinct subjects whose judgement about things may or may not coincide). Thirdly, this discourse of

51. Calvin, as is well known, relates eucharistic presence to a trinitarian operation. The Spirit spans the distance between Christ in heaven above and the believer below. Calvin's trinitarianism, which expresses to my mind a modalism, has been well documented, as, indeed, has Calvin's doctrine of the eucharist. I have dealt with neither of them in depth here since my attention has been upon the complexities of body, space, time and representation as Calvin figures them in his understanding of eucharistic presence. See: B. GERRISH, *Grace and Gratitude: The Eucharistic Theology of John Calvin*, Edinburgh, T&T Clark, 1993; P.W. BUTIN, *Revelation, Redemption and Response: Calvin's Trinitarian Understanding of the Divine/Human Relationship*, New York, Oxford University Press, 1995.

52. Calvin himself speaks of how "we may experience [*sentiamus/sentions*] his [Christ's] power in the communication" (J. CALVIN, *Institutes*, p. 652 [1010/359]). It is the analysis of this 'experience' which is followed through in several recent accounts of the eucharist" (see R. SOKOLOWSKI, *Eucharistic Presence: A Study in the Theology of Disclosure*, Washington, The Catholic University of America Press, 1993; J.-L. MARION, *God Without Being: Hors Texte*, trans. T. Carlson, Chicago, University of Chicago Press, 1991 and L.-M. CHAUVET, *Symbol and Sacrament: A Sacramental Reinterpretation of Christian Existence*, Collegeville, The Liturgical Press, 1995.

presence necessitates and produces a discourse of absence. Signs are "invented by men, which are rather emblems of things absent than tokens of things present [*imagines sunt rerum absentium potius quam notae praesentium*]"[54]. Signs can be empty. We have to persuade ourselves that we are not deceived. The discourse of presence and absence is indissociable from the new spatialising in which the distance opened between two points invokes the desire to span, invade, colonise (or, in Calvin's case, to be colonised [by Christ]). This spatialising produces an economy of desire based upon lack, as not-having, not-attaining, not-reaching. The consummation of that desire is the overcoming of that distance, that absence, that lacking, that difference between. Full presence is then the consummation, the teleology of desire. It is the annihilation of difference. Hence Calvin's early foreshadowing of the later concerns with the sublime in his discourse on the infinity of the divine; infinity being the absence of defining boundaries. Full presence borders here on the indifference of utter absence (which is articulated in Spinoza's third knowledge). As Derrida insightfully comments with respect modernity's onto-theology, "As soon as being and present are synonymous, to say nothingness and to say time are the same thing"[55].

Calvin creates a discursive body which both supplements the distance and absence of the longed for presence [of Christ] and yet maintains that distance and absence. It mimics his own doctrine of the Eucharist. It keeps everything where they are while articulating, and by articulating embodying, the desire to be elsewhere. It evidences one more turn in the Eucharist-as-spectacle that de Lubac and Certeau drew attention to. As Simon Oliver, discussing the nature and culture dualism of Calvin's doctrine of the Eucharist emphasises: "for Calvin, what might be termed the natural and the cultural elements of the Eucharistic liturgy… are mere theatre… In truth, for Calvin, the Eucharistic liturgy is a virtual reality"[56]. It leads to an understanding of the "body" – physical, social and ecclesial – as a virtual community. It is important to recognise how the metaphysics of real presence have been produced, and the employment of the phrase *de reali praesentia* by the Council of Trent demonstrates an early *aggiornamento* mentality on behalf of the Catholic church (though

---

53. Coincidence is possible only if God does not deceive, and so, by faith, subjective judgements can concur *in their interpretation* about the true meaning of things. Otherwise coincidence is arbitrary, and contractual in a world of conflicting evaluations.

54. J. CALVIN, *Institutes*, p. 666 [1020].

55. J. DERRIDA, *Margins of Philosophy*, trans. A. Bass, Brighton, The Harvester Press, 1982, p. 51.

56. S. OLIVER, *The Eucharist Before Nature and Culture*, in *Modern Theology* 15 (1999) 331-353, p. 343.

one at odds with the traditional understanding of sacramental presence). Being and the present, presence and present are conflated. It is this real presence, dominating modernity, which postmodernism inveighs against.

3. Žižek

Žižek, is one of a number of poststructuralists who concern themselves with presence while not a believer in "the fullness of real presence" or what Derrida terms variously phonocentrism or logocentricism. Jean-Luc Nancy, Jean-Francois Lyotard, Helene Cixous and Jacques Derrida all have detailed analyses of presence, sometimes with and sometimes without the inverted commas. Žižek views the transparency of things being present to themselves (and the value attached to that transparency), which masks as naturalism, critically. As an exegete of Lacan, what Žižek treats is the dialectic between the imaginary and the symbolic. He can only treat, then, the effects of truth. For the imaginary, which sustains desire, furnishes objects for what it lacks. The symbolic structures knowledge through chains of signifiers but a gap always remains between the explicit texture of such knowledge and the underlying levels of fantasy which support it. Furthermore, because for Lacan what desire desires is desire there is a paradoxical movement between wanting to attain the goal of one's desire and needing to forestall that final consummation. The imaginary and the symbolic must not collapse into each other – which would be the result of such a consummation. For then we would lose our very sense of reality (a reality which is always and only a symbolic virtuality). This is the inherent danger of cyberspace for Žižek. Nevertheless, as Žižek states, "the status of what we have called the 'real presence of the Other' is inherently spectral". The Other, from whom the subject is detached and for whom the subject longs, haunts and organises the dialectic between the imaginary and the symbolic. He calls it "the obscene ethereal *presence* of the Other" which is ultimately related to the third and most foundational of Lacan's psychic structures, the Real. The Real is the void which desire endless circulates. The Other is a little piece of the Real which bears witness to its "presence beyond the symbolic order"[57]. But all attempts to symbolise the Real, into which all meaning and virtuality dissolve, are "so many attempts to avoid the true 'end of history', the paradox of an infinity far more suffocating than any actual confinement"[58]. The massive weight of the Real when it irrupts into the symbolic causes trauma, paralysis.

---

57. S. ŽIŽEK, *The Plague of Fantasies,* London, Verso, 1997, p. 154.
58. *Ibid.*, p. 154.

Now in sketching out Žižek's Lacanian concern for "virtual reality" what I have tried to do is use his own descriptive terms and, in particular, point up the way he employs the language of presence and absence, real presence and the void or emptiness. For although, as I hope is evident, all truth is *mèconnaisance* and we are constantly involved in saving the appearances of things, his analysis is made possible and structured by a dualism. Frequently he marks his employment of words like presence, real presence, sense and reality with inverted commas or by placing them in italics. But however much these words are "under erasure", they are vital to the construction of his own – Lacanian – worldview. Significantly, the negative terms "infinite", "void", "emptiness" are not so marked. For these are Žižek's truth, his negative ontology such that he can speak of the possible effect of cyberspace as: "the phantasic kernel of our being is laid bare in a much more direct way, making us totally vulnerable and helpless"[59].

A metaphysics of presence, which is constructed on the principle of the univocity of being – Being as the *Grund* – and implicated in the onto-theological project where a divine *ens realissimum* completes (and causes) the great chain of being is, then, both necessary and reversed in Žižek. It is necessary as that against which he (and behind him stands Lacan, as behind Derrida stands Heidegger) posits his critique. But his critique is not an overcoming of such a metaphysics. In one sense it is the reaffirmation of the ineradicability of the metaphysical. For his critique reverses the metaphysics by offering a negative ontology, Nothing as a primary substance, an Infinity of differences which renders difference indifferent and this fundamental Indifference as making all things virtual: the Void as the condition for the possibility of.

What is significant is that the similarity between the logical move made here in Žižek to the move made in onto-theology's account of full presence, renders Žižek (and those, like Žižek, who have poststructural critiques of full presence) vulnerable to the same criticisms launched against these metaphysics. Most particularly, Žižek is vulnerable to the criticism that the body, the material world is devalued. In the onto-theological project because what was given ontological priority and value was total presence, the transparency of the thing's self-existence, the self-grounded presentation of its complete meaning, then that which hindered or divided the subject from this "presence" was devalued. Representation, signification were screens or even obstacles to be overcome. That which mediated the presence was epiphenomenal, not

59. *Ibid.*, p.164.

essential. A dualism was established between consciousness and the given which could only be encountered as an object of consciousness. Mediation – through the mind and then the signs which represented the contents of the mind – was always seen as lacking the full presence, even hindering access to the full presence. Signification operated according to an economy founded upon the endless striving for the presence that was longed for and deferred. Empiricism and positivism, in order to examine and exploit the presence of the given, either put aside questions of the mediation of their knowledge – their use of instruments to collect data, their interpretations of that data, the language used throughout the whole process of collection and evaluation – or treated each form of mediation as transparent channels for their knowledge.

In Žižek, what is prior is the negative version of full presence, the Void. That is the Real. What constitutes our knowledge is symbolic and virtual. And the same economy of lack, now a libidinal economy, governs the symbolic and the virtual – albeit with the added complexity that we cannot have what we desire because that would dissolve us and the virtual meaningfulness of our world entirely. The body disappears to give attention to the symptom and the phallus (which is not the penis) as the governor of desire.

I could repeat this analysis and suggest very similar results with respect to Derrida's thinking on *différance* (Derrida) or Jean-Luc Nancy's examination of *corpus* or Jean-Francois Lyotard's accounts of the sublime and the unpresentable. But what I wish to demonstrate by the genealogy of presence we have undertaken is that sacramental presence is not a mode of the metaphysics of presence (and absence). And hence it cannot be approached or understood in terms of this metaphysics or its crossing. We cannot proceed to understand the theological exchange within the Eucharist via phenomenologies either Husserlian[60] or Heideggerian (Marion and Chauvet). Or, more accurately, if we do so proceed, we are framing theological accounts of what it is to be something, what it is to understand creation as governed by Christ and sustained by the Godhead, by metaphysical accounts which have reified and commodified presence and the present. In this reification they have perpetuated various atomisms (ontological, material, social) that open up nihilistic spaces, and function within various dualistic matrices which are ultimately Gnostic. All of which we have seen embryonically there in the early modern (Calvin), and fully developed in the postmodern (Žižek), discourses on presence.

---

60. R. SOKOLOWSKI, *Eucharistic Presence* (n. 52).

III. EUCHARISTIC PRESENCE

Let us return to that question I posed at the beginning. What is the relationship between the present tense and presence? If eucharistic presence is not what is deemed presence in modernity how does it differ? Augustine's understanding of time is essential here: the present is not a distinct entity. There is no isolatable moment, no now that can be calculated and infinitesimally divided. We cannot experience the present as such. In modernity time is an endless series of distinctive nows, nows which because they are valued as such have to be grasped as such in order to get the most out of them. Participation is measured by and a mode of stimulation. To enjoy the instant is to experience the thrill, the buzz of being there. Orgasm, *jouissance* becomes the measure of the moment which devalues eros. Since the now is commodified, and likewise access to the experience of the now, then getting the most out of what is becomes one of the metaphysical bases of consumer greed and one of the rationales for the erotification of consumer culture. And the endless deferment of the consummating now, articulated by so many poststructural thinkers, only fetishises that now even more. In fact the deferment itself can be invested with significance – the prolongation of desire endlessly produces it. Deferment of the now becomes itself part of a libidinal economy, part of the seduction. With poststructuralism, the now, the immediate becomes the unpresentable experience of the sublime, the final ecstasy of oblivion (the end of desiring) that awaits the other-side of the endless chains of signifiers: the immediate beyond the frustrations and laws of mediation. Experiences of this now are revelatory "events" – as Heidegger and more recently Lyotard detail them – or ruptures – as Certeau describes them.

The present is not understood in this way in the tradition's accounts of the Eucharist. The present is not a discrete and isolatable entity, as Augustine reminds us. If it is taken as such it becomes an idol, a pleasuring which is self-aggrandising and, therefore, self-absolving from the community of those who orientate their lives to each other and to God. Such possession of the present would be, for Augustine, a violation of time, a violence with respect to time, that would pitch the one who seizes the day outside the liturgical practice which engages the church. For the Eucharist participates in a temporal plenitude that gathers up and rehearses the past, while drawing upon the futural expectations and significations of the act in the present. In the same way as the Last Supper is both an enactment of the Passover Meal and rehearsal for the sacrifice on Calvary; so the Eucharist is both an enactment of the Last Supper (and therefore a figuring of the Passover), a participation in the atoning sacrifice of Calvary, and a foretaste of the heavenly banquet at the eschatological wedding. In the fracture liturgy, for example, the congregational response is a reiteration of a Pauline formula from his first letter to the Corinthian and an affirmation of a oneness with the those who have gone, those who are and those who are to come. It is in this way that the activity participates in the eternal, for it belongs both to all times and to no one time. Hence the presence cannot be fixed into the present, a present which lies on the other side of representation. The eucharistic activity is implicated in various modes of figuration (of the past and of the future); its understanding of presence is always manifold and excessive to the present and sanctifies the various representations it is necessarily involved in because they are also, simultaneously, various embodiments. There is no space here for the reification, fetishisation, dualisms, atomisms and absences (the lacks, the deferments, the mournings and the arbitrary violences) which characterise modernity's (and postmodernity's) preoccupations with seizing the present as such.

We now have to relate the answer to this question back to those other three inseparable aspects of the fracture liturgy: a participation which disseminates; the constitution of the community of the "we" as many and one; and the transgression by the "we" of the institutional structures in which it foregathers. As we noted these aspects involve various complexities inextricable from the temporal complexity we have so far foregrounded: complexities of corporeality, space and representation.

1. *Participation*

The doctrine of participation, which is a doctrine of the Spirit, cannot be separated from a doctrine of time and a theology (which is also an anthropology) of desire. It is because the present participates in the eternal, in the way I pointed to above, that we who are time-bound, situated in specific temporalities or textualities of time, participate also in the eternal. But our participation is not simply formal, but personal. For the eternal is not the endlessness of the infinite – Hegel's bad infinite as the linear infinite[61]. The infinite is the endless giveness of God in love. We are constituted as those who desire the freedom, goodness and beauty of being loved and loving. Our inclination to crave the other, what Augustine would term our fundamental *appetitus*, is an image of the divine appetite in which the Father craves the Son and the Son the Father, and

---

61. G.W.F. HEGEL, *Elements of the Philosophy of Right*, ed. A.W. WOOD, trans. H.B. Nisbet, Cambridge, Cambridge University Press, 1991.

both the Spirit who maintains the eternal craving open with respect to the world God created out of this excess of loving. We are, then, persons of desire. This is the image of God in whom we were created and we are constituted as persons through the operations of this desire (as Hegel saw). Our desire for God is constituted by God's desire for us such that redemption, which is our being transformed into the image of God, is an economy of desire. Our experience of time is inseparable from our desiring, inseparable also from our longing to understand ourselves.

Desire issues from difference; difference not satisfied in its own differential. There are three modes of difference such that desire is written into the nature of all that is. There is theological difference with respect to the persons of the Trinity. There is ontological difference with respect to the *distema* which separates the uncreated God from creation. There is sexual difference with respect to the webs of attraction that draw us into one another such that one body is mapped onto several others. Difference can only be difference because it stands *in relation to* that which is other: which means that God is not wholly other (*pace* Barth) and Christian otherness cannot be transcendentalised as such (*pace* Levinas and Derrida). The kenosis of incarnation (and its possibility from the foundation of the world in what Balthasar terms God's *Urkenosis*) entails that otherness is always in relation. Difference extolled *as* difference, difference reified perpetuates atomism which can only produce indifference. Difference to be constituted and maintained *as* difference requires an analogical relation. It is that relation which we need to elucidate.

Two distinctions need to be made. First, we have seen already that modernity's subject of desire is implicated in an economy of lack. The lack arises because desire is object or goal orientated. I desire something or to be somewhere. In fact, the object is reified in the desirous look: the look which turns it into that which can feed and pleasure the one who looks. This would be what Augustine, with his understanding of the present for itself as feast the immediate senses, terms *cupiditas*, and Jean-Luc Marion has examined recently in terms of idolatry[63]. It is a craving which lusts. It wants to possess, to put an end to the lack by subsuming that which is other (totally other in this economy). To employ Martin Buber's formula: this desire constitutes the I-It relation. It is in this way that the libidinal economy is indissociable from consumerism, the exchange of "goods" (the word is significant). Now the

---

62. On the relationship of time to desire see E. LEVINAS, *Time and the Other*, trans. R. Cohen, Pittsburgh, Duquesne University Press, 1987.
63. J.-L. MARION, *God Without Being* (n. 52).

Christian economy of desire cannot do without locations for that which it finds desirable, that which is discerns as good, beautiful, and true. The Christian as a subject of desire is attracted by that which is encountered. He or she responds in that attraction, which always has an embodied specificity. Christians desire this and that, him or her. That is why to desire or love God is not a divesting of the world of significance to transcend the world in some pure *apatheia*. Rather to desire or love God is to invest the world with significance, a significance which deepens the mysterious presence of things. And so, in the Christian economy of desire, the object of desire can never be the terminus of desire. The object can never to made an end in itself without betraying the true nature of thing (and the true nature of one's attraction to it). For the participation desire circulates within is far greater than any one location. The economy of desire is one of exceeding the object, exceeding the lack installed by the I-want which object creates. As such, the object of desire takes on a certain density of significance, a rich materiality that cannot be exhausted, cannot be possessed. To employ again an Augustinian distinction, the object desired is to be enjoyed as gifted; rather than simply used, exploited, consumed. Of course, there is, in this enjoyment consumption and use. Enjoyment is not dualistically opposed to use, or lack dualistically opposed to excess. But neither lack nor use governs the operation of desire, such that desire finds its satisfaction in attaining. For what is attained both satisfies and deepens the longing; what is used is both enjoyed and plunges joy into a more sublime wonder. Such that attainment and enjoyment require and produce a certain humility before that which is attractive, a certain surrender to the depth of its divine suggestiveness. There is always one more facet of the thing not revealed, always some mystery pertaining to any object that demonstrates how it exceeds in its significance that which it merely presents to the immediate senses. Objects do not exist in the seizable present; they exist in their contingency in a present that issues from an aorist and issues into an optative tense. Each object is located in a network of relation, invested both with past association and future potential. As Michel Serres puts it, objects are not inert[64]. They are caught up in the motion and the communication of all things through the Spirit of Christ.

Secondly, we have also seen the atomistic communities that issue from economies of desire which define and produce lack: the contractual, the imaginary, and the virtual communities. And I have emphasised how Christian desire this does not operate according to lack, exceeds the

---

64. M. SERRES, *Angels: A Modern Myth*, trans. F. Cowper, Paris, Flammarion, 1993.

I-want lack installs. I desire not because I lack the other, but because the other is closer to me than I am to myself (and makes me aware that what I lack is, in part, myself). It is this logic which we need to elucidate; it is the logic of Paul's statement "My life is hidden with Christ in God." Another way of putting it, is that our bodies occupy a space in Christ's body. Our desire is to understand and be conformed to that which we know we are, and yet also – because we have not the mind of Christ – know what we are not. We are not Christ-like; our redemption is the formation of that Christ- likeness which is ours truly insofar as we occupy this place *en Christo*. The desire is orientated to that which exceeds what we think we know about ourselves and the world we live in. It is not orientated to what is absent, but to what is far too present; and because it is so, demands that we take account of the yearnings it calls forth within us.

These two aspects of desire constitute our participation in the circle of divine Trinitarian love; a love which cannot be limited by our words for it: *agape/eros* or *caritas/amor*. For where desire cannot be solely determined by object or goal, to what extent can we know whether the object or goal of our love (which defines whether it is *caritas* or *cupiditas*) is the object or goal itself or the sheer giftedness of that object in Christ? This is why the operation of love is always also *both and simultaneously* the operation of faith and the operation of hope. Most of the time Christians do not know, Christian believe and hope. Augustine is never consistent in his vocabulary of desire, which has frequently called forth criticism. There is a selfless giving love and there is a proper self-loving *(amor sui* as opposed to *superbia)*. As such we can describe Trinitarian loving as both self-transcending and self-referring to the extent that we can use the language of persons with respect to this mystery. In the same way, our loving as it participates within God's loving is always reaching beyond and forgetting itself, but, in that very activity, loving itself most truly. As with the Prodigal Son, the coming to oneself is also a movement towards the others one has separated oneself from in one's voluptuous greed for the world's "goods".

This twofold loving is the logic of the fracture: both celebrating the intimacy of oneness and taking that celebration out into the world: "we *break* this bread to *share*". In the breaking, the fracturing, the extension beyond a concern with one's own wholeness, is a sharing that will constitute our own true wholeness. Put in another way, the labour of love and formation of self in love, requires the redemption of self in the formation of others. Hegel saw this. The one is also the many. This leads us directly to the constitution of that "we".

2. *The Pluralised Body*

At the opening of his own theological anthropology, Karl Barth wrote that the internal covenantal basis in creation issues from the truth that "Man is no longer single but a couple" (Barth:, III.1, 308). The ego does not exist in and for itself – the goal of self-sufficiency taught by the Stoics, which has become both the fundamental axiom of modern epistemologies and liberal ethics, and Nietzsche's heroic *Übermensch*, is the utter denial and destruction of selfhood as it is theologically understood. As such social atomism is sinfulness. Hegel again: "To be evil means in an abstract sense to isolate myself"[65]. The privatisation of the self constitutes a turning back of creation to the chaos, the nothing from which God called it forth. It is the ultimate denial of creator and creation, and therefore the analogical world-view. The cult of celebrity, the production of personalities, the exaltation of the customised, the designer labelled – are not simply trading in illusions, trafficking in simulacra, they promote that which is evil. For they deprive this world's goods of their goodness; they negate and corrode the orders of creation. Utterly opposed to this atomism – which Augustine would see as founded upon fear, the fear of losing, of dispossession – is the I as We, the identity of the One as the Many. This is not the negation of selfhood or proper self-love. Levinas, critically developing Buber's I and Thou formula into I-as-hostage-to-Thou, as responsible for, responsive to, accusative in the face of the other (*autre* as well as *autrui*) puts the I always under erasure. As accusative – "Here I am" – it is infinitely accused. The I is continually martyred, continually exiled from itself towards the totally other. But this is the otherside of liberalism's optimism in moral autonomy; the critical reaction to the philosophy of humanism with its belief that all things can be resolved through dialogue. As such this reactive ethics works within and perpetuates the same logic (which is what we discovered with respect to postmodernism critique of presence). It does not announce an alternative logic of relations. For it demands a certain violence, even though it is the opposing violence of liberalism's autonomy. If humanism's self is ripped from social dependence, asserting its own rights and freedoms (and the exercise of its rights as the exercise of its freedoms), contracting out its own obligations to do that which authenticates itself as independent and sole author of its own destiny, then Levinas' denial of that simply asserts the priority of *ipseity* and

---

65. G.W.F. HEGEL, *Lectures on the Philosophy of Religion Together with a Work on the Proofs of the Existence of God*, vol. III, trans. E.B. Speirs & J. Burdon Sanderson, London, Routledge and Kegan Paul, 1962, p. 53.

illeity, the accusative and being accused for the other, which calls for a violence towards the self in its sub-jection to the absolutely other. The absolute authority of the I is exchanged for the absolute authority of the other: the same logic holds for both positions. And being infinitely responsible, abstractly responsible, as Hegel understood, is without content. I freeze before the endless possibilities for putting that responsibility into action, knowing that by being responsible here, for this, I am not able to responsible there, with respect to that. Ethical action, as such, becomes arbitrary because its universalism overrides the particularity of where I am and the bodies I am *more* responsible for because of where I am.

The logic of the eucharistic relation in which the one is the many, the I as the We, refuses both the liberal ethicaland the reactive ethical accounts of personhood. The love of the neighbour is correlative to the love of oneself. The desire for the neighbour's good is correlative to the desire for the personal good. And God is the true correlative of both desire and the good. The I is utterly singular. Called forth to be and to become in a specific time, the narratives of that I are its own (though no one I can grasp anything but a minuscule number of them), and a specific social context. The person is called forth to be and to become as a specific embodiment, a specific physiology, a specific genotype of a specific set of genotypes – given to the world in this locale. But the I is utterly dependent, what Schleiermacher rightly understood as absolutely dependent[66]. The I does not belong to itself. Hence either the subjection of other to one's will or the assertion of independence are both violences again the divine order, both are expressions of the *libido dominandi*. Just as the present cannot exist in and of itself, but only in relation to memory and expectation, so the I is never the pronoun of an active continuous verb. In being utterly dependent it is always the pronoun of a deponent verb: moving between the self-assertive activity of modernity's ego and the passivity more passive than the passive tense of Levinas' reaction to that egoity. The I is born *in relation to* and that is intrinsic to its being made *in the image of*, for God is also always and only in relation to. The I is given to the We for its own redemption (and perfection). Just as the I is given to the distended-present for time's redemption (and perfection); woven into the textualities and specificities of time as part of

66. For Augustine's account of this state see *De Genesi ad litteram*, trans. J. Hammond Taylor, New York, Newman Press, VIII.vi.12.

67. See Michael Gillespie for an account of assertion and the will with respect to Descartes' *cogito*, in M.A. GILLESPIE, *Nihilism Before Nietzsche*, Chicago, University of Chicago Press, 1996.

the We which celebrates it's oneness in Christ as it also disperses, to expand the nature of the "We-ness".

As one body mapped onto the sacramental and ecclesial body, located in and as the body of Christ, this "expansion" is not concomitant with colonialism. Christian imperialism belongs to the perpetration of violence. The expansion is only possible because, in creation, the space was opened *en Christo* – and all other space is simulacra or, to use a distinction made by Certeau, space (*espace*) becomes rationalised as place (*lieu*). The eucharistic We is a pluralized and pluralizing body that overspills defined places, opening up another space. It is at this point that, in our examination of the We, that we must discuss the way the fracturing and sending out of that We, transgresses institutional bodies that assist in defining, but can never confine, the body of Christ.

3. *The Body of Christ and the Institutional Churches*

Institutions produce what, after Certeau, we can term "rational utopias". This is a place produced by the closed system, what Certeau will describe as "a bubble of panoptic and classifying power, a module of imprisonment that makes possible production of an order"[68]. It is the space of the voyeur, the observer, for whom only what is seen is what is valued, and what is seen is valued by locating it in a certain specified place, with its specified identity. We observed this construal of space operating in Calvin's understanding of both the eucharist and triniarian operations. Descartes clarifies the notion of such space as the extension of what is – a body filled with other bodies which constitutes and produces its extension. Space is isomorphic here with place in such a notion, insofar as space is made up of the sum of all places. Each place is composed, in turn, of discreet objects whose predicates (and therefore identities) can be detailed, calculated. What we observe in this new mathematical analysis of time, space and materiality is the overthrow of the analogical world in favour of the digital. Analyses of space now attend to atemporal structures and the calculation of this sum of all places and its properties.

There are certain presuppositions that such space requires for its rational examination. I will point to three which Certeau himself elucidates and a fourth as examined by Certeau's contemporary Henri Lefebvre. First, that all that is is visible; that there is nothing hidden, occult or mysterious. All things exist insofar as their properties are perceptible

---

68. M. DE CERTEAU, *The Practice of Everyday Life*, trans. S. Randall, Berkeley, University of California Press, 1984, p. 111.

and an account can be made of them; as such, all things are inert. Again
we revisit a non-mythical form of realised eschatology that returns us to
our analysis of the present as fully present above. Secondly, and concomitant with this reification and immediacy of the thing, as Lefebvre
tells us: "The illusion of transparency goes hand in hand with a view of
space as innocent, as free of traps or secret places"[69]. Spatiality, like the
materiality which composes it, is viewed in terms of light and intelligibility. Thirdly, and concomitant with the importance given to the eye in
assumptions one and two, the one who sees is an autonomous unit, a
consciousness, a *cogito*, who in thinking makes/passes judgement.
Fourthly, that this space (now termed the world) is external to and independent of that judging *cogito* (or the mind), such that the mind acts
within it not upon it and, primarily, is passively responsive to what is out
there. Spatiality, here, is mapped in accordance with the dualism of
object/subject – extendible to other dualisms such as body/soul, pub-
lic/private, external/internal. As Lebefvre writes, "the modernist trio,
triad or trinity [is] readability-visibility-intelligibility"[70].

The Churches as institutions produce such a spatiality; as all institutions do. This is not in itself a bad thing. It is a necessary thing. Only as
institutions can they offer places for the organisation of a different kind
of space, a liturgical space. In this liturgical space, activities are performed within a sacred world-view, and what is done is not an end in
itself (a labour, the expenditure of a calculable energy for a definite purpose), but a creative act, expressing, being, a gift to what is other and
divine. Liturgical activity opens up spatial possibilities, spatial complexities. Space, while not separating itself from and dualistically opposing,
place is no longer co-extensive with it; it is excessive to location. In fact,
as Certeau states: "space [here] is a practised place"[71], and this place
escapes all rationalist topologies.

Certeau examines the constitution of this second form of space in
terms of textuality. Here spatial complexities is implicated in representa-
tional complexity. Practises are series of gestures involved in complex
exchanges of signs. He calls this the "space of operations", and to
describe its economics he employs various terms like tactics, delin-
quency, wandering, and transgression. He examines this space of operations in two ways, each of which radically critiques those four suppositions for the rational, utopic space: the visibility and coherence of all

69. H. LEFEBVRE, *The Production of Space*, trans. D. Nicholson-Smith, Oxford,
Blackwell, 1991, p. 28.
70. H. LEFEBVRE, *The Production of Space,* p. 96.
71. M. DE CERTEAU, *The Practice of Everyday Life*, p. 117.

that is; the unity of the subject; the objective facticity of the world. By looking at the practices of everyday, urban existence, he sketches an archaeology of spatial operations. By reading the writings of ethnographers and mystics, the paintings of Bosch, the accounts of demonic possession, he sketches a genealogy in which the space of an itinerary becomes the geographer's map – a genealogy, then, of spatial colonisation. A dialectic is established between rational and transgressional spacing, giving rise to a hybrid or hetero-spatiality.

Certeau wishes to invest this complex form of spatiality, evident in texts taken from the early dawn of modernity, with a contemporary significance and relevance. He wishes to advocate a relearning of this living in which "Places are exceeded, passed, lost behind"[73], this walking within the contemporary city, which eludes the institutions of meaning. Like the monks Daniel and Piteroum, in the stories which open *The Mystic Fable*, this seems to be Certeau's theological task: "to trace, in the symbolic institutions, an otherness already known to the crowd and that they are always 'forgetting'"[74]. Having elucidated the nature of this hetero-spacing – which makes all of us mystics for Certeau, if, as he enjoins, to be a mystic is to be unable to stop walking – we can then access another spiritual spacing, a eucharistic spacing which operates as the possibility for space *as such*.

This is line of analysis developing out of Certeau and, to some extent, against the grain of his thinking. For the world as fully present to itself – the realised eschatology of the rational utopia – is broken up by Certeau's profound analysis of loss, mourning and desire. With respect to our analysis of the Churches – the proclaimed oneness of the body of Christ in which we share is fragmented into various institutional organisations. The "One may no longer be found," as Certeau writes, in the opening pages of *The Mystic Fable*, but the kenotic desire which follows from this nevertheless "is obviously a part of the long history of that *One*"[75]. But the question then emerges, what makes possible this absence which provokes desire and peregrinage? What space, place, body (they are all related) is presupposed in order that there can be practices of everyday life at all? There is an "elsewhere", there is another

72. His younger contemporary, Louis Marin, will term this "spatial play" in his analyses of utopias. Marin's concern with "utopics" bears a close relation to Certeau's concerns with "mystics", as the cross-referencing in the work of both authors bears out. See L. MARIN, *Utopics: Spatial Play*, trans. R.A. Vollrath, New Jersey, Macmillan, 1984.

73. M. DE CERTEAU, *The Mystic Fable*, trans. M.B. Smith, Chicago, University of Chicago Press, p. 299.

74. *Ibid.*, p. 43.

75. *Ibid.*, p. 1-2.

country which "remains our own, but we are separated from it"[76]. It is the manner in which Certeau alludes to that elsewhere – which circumscribes the nature of that other place – that is significant for our present analysis. We will discover there the final spiritual space and recognise it as none other than the eucharistic site.

All the stories of each I, that produce each sense of persons with respect to the We, organise spaces – self-consciously so in the internal geographies of St. Teresa's *Interior Castle* or St. John of the Cross' *Ascent of Mount Carmel*. What Certeau describes is the way in which the organisation of these spaces opens alternative spaces in historical systems of fact. They do so in two distinctive and deviant ways. Deviant, that is, in relation to the four suppositions of the "rational utopia". First, the We practises a manner of speaking from elsewhere – thus deconstructing the autonomy of the I and the priority of its judgements. Persons are produced, just as the soul is formed, disciplined or perfected, through welcoming and following the voice of the other. In various activities (liturgical acts of confession and acts of prayer which invest the everyday acts of writing oneself onto the social body with theological significance), these subjects reveal themselves as partly spoken from elsewhere. The "I" becomes a shifter in a "topography of pronouns", becomes a "siteless site"[77]. So judgements are not made easily, for the truth of what is seen has to be given to the subject, not simply read off from what is. Secondly, these activities make visible a spatiality – akin to the mansions, rooms and gates of Teresa's internalised Crusader castle – which is invisible: thus subverting modernity's idolisation of presence as appearance. In this way the Word takes on a body; that which calls becomes enfleshed in the practices of living and the narratives of each one's itinerary. An alternative spacing is established in relation to a specific historical and cultural context. Certeau situates the work of Teresa and John of the Cross within a social context that had impoverished their aristocratic positions; within a church which was more concerned with the visibility of its powers than its spiritual truth; within a symbolic system "which disintegrates at the end of the Middle Ages"[79].

But it is exactly at this point that we need to proceed more carefully with Certeau. What he terms his heterological spacing announces an

---

76. *Ibid.*, p. 2.

77. M. DE CERTEAU, *Mystic Speech*, in ID., *Heterologies: Discourse on the Other*, trans. B. Massumi, Minneapolis, University of Minnesota Press, 1986, p. 90.

78. For a further examination of space in St. Teresa's work see S.H. HUGHES, *A Woman's Soul is Her Castle: Place and Space in St. Teresa's Interior Castle*, in *Literature and Theology* 11 (1997) 376-384.

79. M. DE CERTEAU, *The Mystic Fable*, p. 91.

aporetics, but what is this produced and productive alterity which forever stands in/as the penumbra? Ricœur, at the conclusion of *Oneself as
Another* maps out the problem (in a discussion of alterity in Levinas): is
this other another person, or my ancestors for whom there is no representation and to whom I am so profoundly indebted, or God or an empty
space[80]. Certeau himself asks: "Is this space divine or Nietzschean?"[81].

The first spacing, Certeau's "rational utopia" perceived the world
univocally: things were as they were named, and there was no reminder
or mystery about what he elsewhere calls "the positivities of history"[82].
This is the world of institutional bodies like churches, bodies we pass in
and out of. The eucharist, we recall, collects to disperse within such
institutional bodies. The alternative spacing announces that the We as
the interdependence and interrelationship of so many self-narratives, so
many self-practices open up the rational place to produce a social space,
an aporia within organised places. But Certeau goes on to suggest –
though he does not develop his thinking here and therefore leaves himself open to the charge of nihilism – that the eucharist, the sacramental
space offers a notion of body beyond the institutional and social which
analogically relates the two. Conscious of Henri du Lubac's work
L'eucharistie, he writes that before the thirteenth century there was that
linear spatiality in which the Church as Eucharist, God's Word in the
world, produced "the 'liturgical' combination of a visible community or
people (*laos*) and a secret action (*ergon*) or mystery"[83]. The hidden, the
spiritual, the mystical was both other and yet part of the world. An analogical relationship pertained. The community participated in this alterity, and, as such, the practices of this community were all liturgical.
Certeau writes: "The fact is, the linear series extending from the apos-
tolic origins (H) to the present Church (C) is sustained in its entirety by
the sacrament (S), conceived as a unique and everywhere instituting
operation (the mystery), linking the *kairos* to its progressive manifestation. Distinct time (H and C) are united by the same invisible 'action'.
This is the paradigm of 'the tradition'"[84].

We can examine this another way. Complicit with the production of
any spatiality is the production of a body. In the sacramental world-
view, physical bodies, social bodies, ecclesial bodies, heavenly bodies,

---

80. P. Ricœur, *Oneself as Another*, trans. K. Blamey, Chicago, University of Chicago
Press, p. 355.
81. M. de Certeau, *The Mystic Fable*, p. 175.
82. *Ibid.*, p. 105.
83. *Ibid.*, p. 83.
84. *Ibid.*, p. 83.

textual bodies, and the body of Christ all cohere palimsestically. They do this because each of these bodies has permeable boundaries, fluid boundaries. As Certeau writes about the mediaeval copyist, distinguishing him from the Renaissance translator (who was also printer and typesetter): "the copyist transformed his body into the spoken word of the other; he imitated and incarnated the text into a liturgy of reproduction. Simultaneously, he gave his body to the verb ('verbum caro factum est') and made the verb into his own body ('hoc est corpus meum') in a process of assimilation that eliminated differences, to make way for the sacrament of the copy"[85].

Certeau concludes that the continuity of that tradition came to an end with the thirteenth century. But, first, Certeau's conclusion may be wrong. We may, with the collapse of belief in rationally organised spaces, be opening a space in which the tradition can once more be heard. That which brought about the changes from the thirteenth century onwards, is now being challenged; modernity is closing and new concepts of time, space and materiality are emerging. Secondly, this conclusion would not invalidate Certeau's observations with respect to the possibility of employing them to develop a theological account of the way the one body of the We, made up as it is of so many singular bodies, each, according to its desire, extended into and operating within various social and political bodies, produces a space which is an excessive to those institutional ecclesial places. The Church is the body of Christ, but "sustained in its entirety by the sacrament (S), conceived as a unique and everywhere instituting operation (the mystery), linking the kairos to its progressive manifestation" it cannot be fixed, God cannot be housed. That would be the greatest commodification of them all, the danger of which is evident in the "reali praesentia" of the Council of Trent. The institutional churches are necessary, but they are not ends in themselves; they are constantly transgressed by a community of desire, an erotic community, a spiritual activity. Within these places, organised by them, desire for God and God's desire for us opens a liturgical space which distends over all the other bodies which participate in and produce it. The body of Christ desiring its consummation opens itself to what is outside the institutional church; offers itself to perform in fields of activity far from chancels and the cloisters. In doing this certain risks are taken and certain fears can emerge within those who represent the institution. As Mary Douglas has noted with respect to the permeable boundaries of the body: "Why should bodily margins be thought to be specifically

85. Ibid., p. 119.

invested with power and danger"[86]. But permeability being the nature of Christian embodiment[87] then the institutions of the body of Christ are serving a purpose much greater than their own survival. This is where the tensions arise. The structure institutions offer is simultaneously constraining and enabling. In this lies their potential for alienation, on the one hand, and reification, on the other[88]. Alienating *and* reified, the institution of the Church becomes mausoleum, drawing its power to attract more from the heritage industry and urban tourism. The body of Christ lives on, beyond its precincts: each member of the eucharistic We writing God's name elsewhere in the world – redeeming it through desire. It is the erotics of that redemption that we must go on to sketch.

Religions and Theology   Graham WARD
Faculty of Arts
University of Manchester
Manchester M13 9PL
England

86. M. DOUGLAS, *Purity and Danger: An Analysis of Concepts of Pollution and Taboo*, London, Routledge and Kegan Paul, 1966, p. 121.

87. Embodiment as such if Butler is to be believed. See J. BUTLER, *Gender Trouble: Feminism and the Subversion of Identity*, London, Routledge, 1990, pp. 79-141.

88. A. GIDDENS, *The Constitution of Society: Outline of a Theory of Structuration*, Cambridge, Polity Press, 1984, pp. 24-26.

89. The problem for institutions is that they acquire a logic (and inertia) of their own such that although they might begin by serving the needs of the society which establish them, their impulse towards development and the expansion of their influence can bring about a overturning of priorities so that, as Cornelius Castoriadis recognised, society is then viewed as serving them (C. CASTORIADIS, *The Imaginary Institution of Society*, trans. K. Blamey, Cambridge, Polity Press, 1997, p. 110). This is particularly difficult for the Church when it begins to view itself as an institution akin to other economic institutions – encouraging line-management strategies, employment transparencies, feasibility studies, development plans – that it might compete more effectively in the market-place of leisure activities.

RESPONSE TO GRAHAM WARD

Graham Ward argues that the deconstruction of presence, as performed by Jacques Derrida and others, does not necessarily impinge on the presence of Christ in the eucharist. He further argues that a proper understanding of sacramental presence 'may be used to critique... the postmodern deconstruction of present/presence' and so may be seen as 'deconstructing the deconstructive economy itself'. These arguments cut their figures against the ground of 'radical orthodoxy', and since this ground affects why the arguments are launched and how they are prosecuted it needs to be examined, although of course there can be no question of a detailed inspection of its claims in a short response to such a rich and suggestive paper. Still less can there be a nuanced analysis of where Ward stands in respect to John Milbank and others, although it must be noted that 'radical orthodoxy', if it is more than a publisher's brand name, is far from homogeneous[1]. In his article on postmodernity in Jean-Yves Lacoste's *Dictionnaire critique de théologie*, Milbank groups Ward and me together in a little school of two. Now, several years after that article was written, Ward seems closer to Milbank than I am, although this is to say neither that Ward and Milbank are always in agreement nor that I and Milbank are always in disagreement[2].

I would like to begin by noting how Ward construes deconstruction and how he positions himself in relation to it. To begin with, he takes deconstruction in a broader and looser sense than I do, freely associating it not only with Derrida but also with Lacan, Žižek and others. To my mind, this brings together birds that are not of a feather, and I will therefore leave aside both French Freud and Slovenian Lacan. Ward rightly sees that deconstruction undoes all claims to the immediacy of the present moment and to the fullness of present being. That is, deconstruction seeks to show that the subject is not present to itself or to another and

---

1. See J. MILBANK, G. WARD & C. PICKSTOCK (eds.), *Radical Orthodoxy: A New Theology*, London, Routledge, 1998.
2. For more detail, see the preface to the new edition of my 1989 study, *The Trespass of the Sign: Deconstruction, Theology and Philosophy*, New York, Fordham University Press, 2000.

therefore needs to be refigured, while also attempting to recast our ontic understanding of a being's temporal status as present and our ontological grasp of being as presence. I use the verbs 'refigure' and 'recast' because, despite what Ward says, deconstruction is not a critique. Among other things, it involves a resetting of critique as we inherit the notion from Kant and others. This is not to say that there is no Kantian moment in Derrida's writings. There is: the broader the text box in which we place philosophy, the more clearly can we see the lines of filiation that join Derrida to Kant. But this is not to time to speak of how Derrida negotiates the critical philosophy.

Whatever else it is, deconstruction involves a thorough and patient tracing of a concept, polarity or motif through history. A motif in Plato, for instance, will be seen over time to have been taken into complex networks, incorporated in contexts that change its sense and function. These contexts are studied, as are the ways in which they are influenced by what is inscribed within them. Not only does deconstruction give us a better idea of the history of our ideas and images but also it enables us to think them otherwise. We see that they can be re-inscribed in unfamiliar or unexpected contexts where inevitably they will respond to the pressure of other ideas and images. Here is an example. Writing his first letter to the Corinthians, Paul quotes Isa 29,14 ('I will destroy the wisdom of the wise') and thereby establishes an attitude to secular learning and even philosophy that has had a tense history in Christianity. The idea is taken up by Luther when, in the 'Heidelberg Disputation', he writes of the Cross destroying human works, and how one must pass from a *theologia gloriae* to a *theologia crucis*. It is more radically reset when Heidegger takes Luther's phrase *per crucem destruuntur opera* as an inspiration for his notion of *Destruktion*, which in turn guides Derrida in his choice of the word *déconstruction*[3]. So deconstruction can be shown to have a theological past. More interestingly, deconstruction can have diverse Christian futures when re-inscribed in theology[4]. At the

3. See M. LUTHER, *Heidelberg Disputation* (1518) in *Luther's Works*, 55 vols, gen. ed. H.T. LEHMANN, Philadelphia, Muhlenberg Press, 1958-86, vol. 31: *Career of the Reformer* I, ed. H.J. GRIMM. John van Buren offers an illuminating account of Heidegger's investment in Luther's appropriation of 1 Cor 1,19 in his *The Young Heidegger: Rumor of the Hidden King*, Bloomington, Indiana Univesity Press, 1994, pp. 160-65.

4. This has been observed in sacramental theology. David N. Power, for one, observes that deconstruction 'has implications for theology and its reading of tradition with definite consequences for the church's eucharistic confession and celebration of faith', *The Eucharistic Mystery: Revitalising the Tradition,* Dublin, Gill and Macmillan, 1992, p. 10. Louis-Marie Chauvet, for another, seeks to rethink the sacraments after a thorough deconstruction of the onto-theological account of sacrament. See his *Symbol and Sacrament:*

very least, deconstruction enjoins us to read theology very closely, to note what is bypassed, overlooked or ignored, and to be aware of the possible systematic implications of exclusions. 'Theology makes good bedside reading', says Geoffrey Hill in *Tenebrae*[5]. I agree: it does. The trouble is that people frequently fall into dogmatic slumbers when reading or writing it.

Unlike other representatives of 'radical orthodoxy', Graham Ward is by no means simply opposed to deconstruction. John Milbank approaches it with all the weight of his learning, which he proposes to drop on it as quickly as possible. He knows it is nihilism because, after all, for him almost everything is[6]. Yet because he is so intent on making a polemic point, Milbank does not read sufficiently slowly to recognise that, even in his own terms, deconstruction is not a nihilism. It is an affirmation of the Other, and of the asymmetry of all relations with the Other. Catherine Pickstock approaches it with the firm conviction that, because its conclusions are unpalatable to her, its arguments must be invalid. Using a new form of the *argumentum ad baculum*, she beats Derrida's arguments into shapes she detests and then exclaims how detestable they are[7]. Graham Ward, though, does nothing of the sort. He carefully traces a history of the word 'presence' as it is used in sacramental theology, clears Augustine and Thomas of all suspicion, and then stares accusingly at counter-reformation and early protestant theology. The presence that is open to deconstruction, what we Catholics call 'real presence', was invented at Trent; and this fact, we are assured, should not prevent us talking of the presence of Christ in the eucharist.

I do not know if this is true; I would need to check some late medieval theology before agreeing with him[8]. By and large, though, I suspect that he is right; and I applaud his careful tracing of the transformation of 'true presence' to 'real presence' and what happened to it

---

A Sacramental Reinterpretation of Christian Existence, trans. P. Madigan and M. Beaumont, Collegeville, MI, The Liturgical Press, 1995, Part I.

5. G. HILL, *An Apology for the Revival of Christian Architecture in England*, in ID., *Collected Poems,* Harmondsworth, Penguin, 1985, p. 161.

6. On Milbank's understanding modernity is generally characterised by a tendency toward nihilism. See his *Theology and Social Theory: Beyond Secular Reason*, Oxford, Basil Blackwell, 1991. In this regard, see also M.A. GILLESPIE, *Nihilism Before Nietzsche,* Chicago, Chicago University Press, 1995, Ch. 1.

7. See Catherine Pickstock's discussion of Derrida in her *After Writing: On the Liturgical Consummation of Philosophy,* Oxford, Basil Blackwell, 1997.

8. Consulting David Power after the conference I find that the expression 'real presence' is used before the Council of Trent. See his discussion of 'Backgrounds to Trent: Late Medieval Theology of the Mass' in *The Sacrifice We Offer: The Tridentine Dogma and Its Reinterpretation,* Edinburgh, T & T. Clark, 1987, pp. 41-49.

when it entered what Ted Hughes memorably called the 'iron arteries of Calvin'[9]. This attention to history and philology is consonant with deconstruction. It was Heidegger who taught us to walk in fear of 'the metaphysics of presence', which he understood to have two main historical strata: *Anwesenheit* and *Vorhandenheit*. Yet as Levinas has pointed out, Heidegger had no complaint to make against *Anwesen* or coming into presence; and it was Levinas's view that a complaint should have been made in the name of ethics[10]. One can imagine a deconstruction close to Levinas that eschews all talk of presence, and a deconstruction allied to Heidegger that entertains a coming into presence. As an example of the latter, one might cite Jean-Luc Nancy who, as Ward reminds us, evokes 'the birth to presence'[11]. It would take some time to clarify precisely what this 'presence' is, but in outline it is plain that deconstruction need not eliminate all senses of the word 'presence' from its lexicon. Its practice is to rehabilitate the vocabulary of metaphysics, not to strike its words from the dictionary.

For Ward, eucharistic presence 'lies on the other side of representation'; it cannot be fetishised as a commodity. Indeed, it escapes all reification because it looks back to a complex past in the Last Supper and the Passover while also looking forward to the Banquet of Heaven. One must be reminded of Husserl's phenomenology of time in which the present is construed as retention and protention, and equally inevitably one recalls Derrida's reading of this account of the present moment in *Speech and Phenomena*[12]. Rather than rehearse Derrida's argument, which is well known, I would like to note two tendencies in Ward's style of argument, which he shares with his radical orthodox colleagues. The first turns on the judgement that the notion of presence open to deconstruction is 'modern, and untheological'. Now since Heidegger discerned *Anwesenheit* as far back as Plato, modernity is given a quite staggering historical scope. We are used to hearing John Milbank tell us that the rot set into western philosophy and theology with Duns Scotus, but now it seems that corrosion has been around for a lot longer. In addition

---

9. T. HUGHES, *The Warriers of the North*, in ID., *Wodwo*, London, Faber and Faber, 1967, p. 159.

10. Levinas makes the point in his interview with Richard Kearney. See Kearney's *Dialogues with Contemporary Continental Thinkers: The Phenomenological Heritage*, Manchester, Manchester University Press, 1984, p. 56.

11. See the title essay of J.-L. NANCY, *The Birth to Presence*, trans. B. Holmes *et al.*, Stanford, Stanford University Press, 1993.

12. See J. DERRIDA, *Speech and Phenomena: And Other Essays on Husserl's Theory of Signs*, trans. D.B. Allison and N. Garver, Evanston, Northwestern University Press, 1973, ch. 5.

to this, I wonder why one should associate 'modern' so readily with 'untheological', especially since Ward is perhaps the most finely attuned of all the radical orthodox group to the world about us. One finds this logic of 'either-or' all too often in radical orthodoxy, and it frequently goes in tandem with a severe reduction of modernity to nihilism. If nihilism is the devaluation of the highest values, as Nietzsche said it was, then nihilism will be found wherever there is an ascription of the highest value or the highest ground. Nihilism would therefore not be restricted to modernity; it would be found in both the ancients and the moderns. Theology would seek to combat nihilism, of course, although in doing so it would frequently have to diagnose a nihilism at work within itself. Rather than having recourse to a logic of 'either-or', one might do better to make more use of a logic of 'both-and'. I might add that because deconstruction is radically at odds with nihilism, as I pointed out a moment ago, it might be worth further and deeper reflection by the radical orthodox group. The second tendency in Ward's style of argument which he shares with his radical orthodox colleagues is a disinclination to assess an argument on its own terms before introducing a cultural vocabulary to judge its effects. Ward maintains that Derrida, in deconstructing the punctual now, ends up fetishising it because it is shown to be caught up in endless deferral. I'm tempted to respond by saying that 'sticks and stones may break my bones, but names will never hurt me'. What would damage Derrida's account of temporalising is a demonstration that a crucial step in the argument is invalid. A psychoanalytic description of an argument's effects may be very interesting but it can never be coercive when it comes to accepting or rejecting an argument.

According to Ward's account, then, the eucharist overflows the punctual moment because it is caught up in a network that precedes and succeeds it. Put this barely, and in terms of his general account of temporalising, one might well wonder how the eucharist differs from any other act performed by someone aware of the grand narrative of Christianity. It is indeed a 'grand narrative' for Ward, I might add, for we are told throughout that there is '*the* tradition' and '*the* eucharist', and presumably the trick is to retrieve this tradition. Of course when we read Ward closely we see that what is to be regained is not *the* tradition, if there is such a thing, but rather *a* tradition whose contours are neo-platonic and Augustinian. In fact, those who appeal to tradition might well wonder that no attempt is made by Ward to link presence and transubstantiation, and are likely to find the appeal to 'participation in the atoning sacrifice of Calvary' philosophically vague and theologically dubious.

Before agreeing with Ward, we would need to know the scope, strength and status of this participation. We would need to know whether we should distinguish between participation and belonging. This is important in specifying a relation with Jesus. After all, a Christian will be disposed to say that he or she *belongs* to Christ, and does not merely *participate* in a sacrifice. There is a world of difference between participating in a eucharist conceived as a memorial service for a nice chap who was badly treated by the Romans and considered as God changing bread and wine into the body and blood of Jesus. The latter understanding has the power to interrupt our lives absolutely; it is God's invitation to abandon the tyranny of the ego, to affirm that love is stronger than death, and to live in community with him as well as with others, which means to testify to the divine love in affirmation and protest, in seeking justice for the oppressed. The rhetoric of participation has its place, to be sure. I have always liked Charles Simic's image of 'A feeling granted everyone | Of living in two worlds | One of which is unsayable', which certainly answers to a theology of participation[13]. But theologically I would also wish to keep in play the imperative that Rilke drew from a statue of Apollo and that Christians draw from Jesus, 'You must change your life'[14]. I do not find the doctrine of participation, as Ward presents it, to speak sufficiently astringently of the surprise of God and the astonishment that the story of Jesus produces. No doubt about it, we desire God; in Ward's terms, the Church is an erotic community. I would add to this that we are a community only insofar as we remain open to *agape*, which requires us to be turning perpetually towards the gospel and the figure of Jesus drawn there. We may participate in the Church but eschatologically we belong in the Kingdom, and that is why Christians call forth the judgement of Christ endlessly upon the Church and ourselves.

As always when reading Graham Ward, I am impressed by his learning, his care, and his willingness to engage openly with positions that are at variance with his own. As a writer of hymns, I admire his affirmation of the liturgy and the detail with which he attends to it. And I am thankful that his writing on the liturgy is not consumed by a wholly negative thesis as one finds in Catherine Pickstock. (Reading *After Writing*, I am reminded of I.A. Richards who once told his tutor at Cambridge that he

---

13. C. SIMIC, *Independent Testimony*, in ID., *Weather Forecast for Utopia and Vicinity: Poems 1967-1982*, Barrytown, NY, Station Hill Press, 1983, p. 41.
14. R.M. RILKE, *Torso of an Archaic Apollo*, in ID., *Selected Poems*, trans. C.F. MacIntyre, Los Angeles, University of California Press, 1940, p. 93.

thought that history ought not to have happened[15].) In the end, my differences with Ward turn not so much over deconstruction but over christology and exegesis. I would like a more solid presence of Jesus in his christology, by which I mean I would like to find there something less attractive and more challenging, someone who had and has a body, and I would like to find this christology a little more often in attentive readings of scripture. The Jesus of radical orthodoxy is allied to poetry, theory and eroticism. He would not be recognised by Nestorians, although I suspect that the Monophysites would find him intriguing: one does not necessarily get closer to God by pushing one's christology ever upward. Without simply denying all that radical orthodoxy says of the messiah, I would like also to see the Jesus who deals with what Hegel called 'the prose of the world', the Roman Empire, or, in our own terms, daily oppression and misery. An erotic community seems rather thin in the light of a community forever open to *agape*, and I suspect that only reflection on God's love as an induction into mystery, an awareness of how it disturbs the immanence of our lives, will help us to fight oppression and misery, even when they stem from ourselves.

Centre for Comparative Literature   Kevin HART
and Cultural Studies
P.O. Box 11A
Monash University
Victoria 3800
Australia

---

15. See J.P. RUSSO, *I.A. Richards: His Life and Work,* Baltimore, Johns Hopkins University Press, 1989, p. 35.

PRÉSENCE ET AFFECTION

I

Parmi les concepts à peindre sur tous les blasons de la modernité, ceux du *fait* et de l'*objet* sont en bonne place. Le problème de la connaissance n'est pas moderne, et l'existence de disciplines de connaissance ne l'est pas plus. C'est le propre des temps dits modernes, en revanche, d'avoir constitué des réalités prêtes, de par cette constitution, à s'intégrer dans ces processus de connaissance, ou plutôt d'acquisition du savoir, que nous voyons toujours à l'œuvre sous le nom de *sciences*. Le fait et l'objet n'ont d'autres caractères qu'épistémiques, que certaines sciences manifestent mieux que d'autres. Chez le fondateur de la science moderne (on pourrait aussi bien parler de science tout court), Bacon, les faits et objets physiques ont la propriété de pouvoir être interrogés et soumis à la question comme on interroge un témoin en justice. L'objet historique, pour être témoin crédible, doit répondre à un critère énoncé tardivement, chez Troeltsch, mais implicitement présent dès les débuts de l'histoire critique: pour faire acte de candidature à l'inclusion dans la classe des faits historiques, il faut entrer en rapport d'analogie avec ce qui a déjà reçu la dignité de fait. L'objet physique, de par son éminente *disponibilité,* se prête nécessairement à la quantification, à l'expérimentation, à la manipulation, et de telle manière que celles-ci doivent se dire sur un mode intersubjectivement certain: l'objet n'est pas mon mais *notre* objet. Et à l'univers des objets physiques, passés, présents et à venir, la pensée moderne accole un univers des objets métaphysiques, Dieu, dieux, anges et démons, et d'autres, soumis eux aussi à une constitution qui se manifeste dans leur «représentabilité», *Vorstellbarkeit,* reçue comme critère de l'être.

Cela étant admis, une conséquence saute au yeux, la disqualification épistémique de l'affect. Goût, émotion, impression, rien de cela ne peut s'acquitter de tâches cognitives lorsque la connaissance se donne le visage du savoir objectif. L'objet, de par sa constitution, se donne à une perception qui ne sent pas, ou, si l'on veut, se donne à la perception sans se donner à l'affection. La réduction est donc fort claire. Tout un lien entre homme et monde, le lien affectif, se voit mis entre parenthèses ou tranché. Des questions disparaissent alors, et on voit apparaître de façon correspondante tout un ensemble de réalités sous caution, non objectives, non factuelles, les valeurs, dont on pensera tantôt qu'elles n'existent que dans nos goûts et nos préférences, tantôt qu'elles habitent une région du réel autre que le domaine des objets et des faits. Ces rappels, pour mémoire.

II

Épistémiquement hors jeu, l'affect ne disparaîtra évidemment pas, mais il se donnera son visage moderne. Les théories et pratiques qui se battront pour lui sont nombreuses: théories et pratiques littéraires, théories et pratiques du rapport à la «nature», des théories religieuses aussi, auxquelles je restreindrai ici mon intérêt; faisons donc mémoire, dès l'abord, du piétisme, de Schleiermacher, du traité de Edwards sur les *Affections religieuses*. Les Temps modernes, constituant l'objet, le déterminent entre autres par la possibilité d'une soumission à l'expérience. Or sitôt que la raison aura formé son concept de l'expérience, la théologie se trouvera vite embarrassée de vivre aux crochets d'un Dieu dont nul n'a jamais pensé le soumettre à quelque expérience que ce soit. Avec Dieu, toute interaction est impensable, sauf dans certaines hyperboles mystiques. La raison objectivante est tout à fait capable d'avoir son Dieu, un Objet métaphysique suprême qu'elle constitue comme elle constitue les objets physiques, ou du moins de manière analogue – aussi bien faut-il avouer que la raison objectivante est un autre nom de ce que Heidegger nomme «métaphysique», cette figure de la pensée, du pensable et du pensé qui tient sa cohérence (onto-théo-logique) d'un Étant suprême. Mais le Dieu de l'ontothéologie n'est guère un Dieu qu'on puisse louer et fêter, pas plus qu'on puisse le faire entrer dans une logique de l'expérience baconienne. Et pour pallier cela, le christianisme classique (en son centre comme en ses marges) cherchera multiplement à produire un concept de l'expérience, lié à la vie religieuse des croyants, qui permette à celle-ci de répondre en son ordre aux exigences de preuve qui habitent l'esprit du temps. L'exigence de connaissance *expérientielle* – à défaut de connaissance expérimentale! – produira donc un concept tard nommé, celui d' «expérience religieuse». Et lorsque l'expérience religieuse cherche à trouver ses raisons, puis à les argumenter, ces raisons sont centralement celles de l'affect. Dans le piétisme, où le désir d'un Dieu sensible au cœur risque toujours de mettre en danger le contenu confessé, propositionnel, de la foi chrétienne, l'émotion religieuse tend à remplir la fonction de la *preuve*. Dans les *Discours* de Schleiermacher, il l'occupe massivement: c'est en soumettant l'incroyant à une pédagogie de l'émotion que l'auteur le conduit à une certaine reconnaissance des réalités religieuses. Et plus tard, le même Schleiermacher organisera son exposé systématique des doctrines chrétiennes de telle manière que les théories théologiques traditionnelles n'y sont maintenues que dans une mesure, celle où elles peuvent être reçues par une conscience qui raisonne en termes de *Gefühl,* et maintenues dans les limites que leur assigne le *Gefühl.*

De même que la raison moderne constitue l'objet, de même l'affectivité, en son régime moderne, exerce elle aussi des procédures de constitution. Cela n'est pas merveille. Une fois admis que l'affect est pouvoir d'expérience, de manière privilégiée, l'accent se porte sur une aptitude à l'expérience. Le Dieu pâti par l'affect est en fait un Dieu visé, et un Dieu mesuré par angle et portée de visée. Schleiermacher, dans sa dogmatique, est exemple pur d'un penseur dont le Dieu est construit dans le moindre détail pour être senti. La constitution de l'objet physique trouve sa jumelle dans la réduction qui fait de Dieu un objet pour le sentir. En ce qu'elle a de spécifiquement moderne, la connaissance expérientielle de Dieu est paradoxalement un cas de la connaissance objective.

III

C'est à Heidegger qu'il appartint de procéder à la critique la plus brutale de l'objectivation – mais, pour brutale qu'elle soit, elle ne laisse pas d'être forte. Elle joue déjà les premiers rôles dans *Etre et temps,* qui, entre autres, réhabilite l'affect et lui concède un pouvoir cognitif assez grand pour que ce soit une expérience affective, celle de l'angoisse, qui constitue le plus exact révélateur du fait du monde. C'est toutefois à deux autres textes que je ferai appel, plus tardifs: les conférences de Brême, de 1949; et la conférence sur *La chose,* de 1950.

Le propos bien connu de Heidegger, dans le texte de 1950, est de rendre possible ce qu'il nomme un «pas en arrière», et ce pas en arrière doit permettre à l'homme, à celui qui se définit par son pouvoir de mourir, au «mortel» donc, de *veiller* sur les choses. Mais qu'est-ce qu'une chose? La question est posée à une d'entre elles, à une cruche, et elle lui est posée pour en récuser toute interprétation objective. Traitée comme un objet, la cruche est le produit d'une activité artisanale, faite en terre sur le tour du potier, «vide» maintenant mais capable de «contenir» un liquide. Un contenant, fait pour un contenu, et que l'on peut bien sûr représenter, comme tout étant. A ces platitudes, Heidegger objecte un petit travail de description. Laisser apparaître la cruche comme chose, ce sera d'abord la remplir de vin ou d'eau, et apercevoir dans la cruche ce qui nous donne la boisson qui apaise notre soif. Ce sera, plus encore, apercevoir dans ce don la manifestation du ciel fécondant et de la terre fécondée: boisson donnée comme témoin des noces du ciel et de la terre. Ce sera, plus encore, laisser apparaître ceux aussi, les divins, à qui cette boisson peut être donnée à titre de libation. Ce sera donc laisser déployer tout le jeu cosmique – terre et ciel, divins et mortels – du «quadriparti», du *Geviert*. En donnant, la chose ainsi *rassemble* et permet que s'attarde à proximité des autres chacun des quatre qui font l'ordre du tout.

La cruche, le banc, le sentier, la charrue, mais aussi l'arbre, l'étang, le torrent et la montagne, mais aussi, chacun à leur manière, le héron et le chevreuil, le cheval et le taureau, à leur manière aussi le miroir et le bracelet, le livre et l'image, la couronne et la croix – tous ces noms sont noms de choses, et toutes choses, à ceux qui acceptent leurs «conditions» (acceptent d'être des *Be-Dingten,* en laissant derrière eux cette «prétention à l'inconditionné» dont on se doute qu'elle est un trait distinctif de ce que Heidegger nomme la métaphysique, et dont nous admettrons au moins qu'elle est un trait distinctif de la métaphysique moderne), apportent la *proximité* des réalités les plus riches ou des significations les plus graves. L'objet était autochthone dans l'univers de la science, la pensée en quête des choses reconduit au monde de la vie et de la mort. Et elle y reconduit en assignant une mission: parce que les choses sont rares, et que les mortels eux aussi sont rares, comparés à la masse des hommes qui se satisfont d'exister sur le mode du *Lebewesen,* de l'être vivant, il faut veiller sur les choses: les épargner, les préserver des dangers de l'objectivation.

Or, c'est aussi un concept heideggerien que je viens d'utiliser en nommant le *danger*. Il intervient dans la troisième des conférences de Brême, à laquelle il fournit son titre, après une conférence consacrée à la chose et une autre consacrée à l'essence de la technique, le *Gestell* («accaparement»). Du *Gestell,* Heidegger nous dit qu'il laisse les choses sans protection[1]. Mais si un point est bien certain, c'est que la technique, dans l'interprétation heideggerienne, est un âge dans l'histoire de l'être. Le *Gestell* donc ne nomme pas une entreprise humaine mais une époque, celle où l'être se livre à l'accaparement. Et c'est alors qu'est nommé le danger, *Gefahr*. Nom de l'être, le danger est l'être se mettant lui-même

---

1. M. HEIDEGGER, *Bremer und Freiburger Vorträge*, in ID., *Gesamtausgabe 79: 3. Abt. Unveröffentliche Abhandlungen, Vorträge, Gedachtes,* Frankfurt a. Main, Klostermann, 1994, p. 47.

en péril, se soumettant lui-même à des embûches qui viennent de lui, l'être lui-même répondant de l'oubli de l'être. Et le danger, dès lors, d'être défini comme l'essence du *Gestell*.

Pourquoi donc des objets, puisque nous pouvons vivre au milieu des choses? La réponse, que Heidegger ne formule pas plus dans les conférences de Brême qu'il n'y formule expressément ma question, est que les choses sont comme telles en danger, et que nous n'y pouvons rien. Si objet et objectivation il y a, ce n'est pas parce que nous nous tromperions sur les choses, ou parce que nos ancêtres se seraient trompés: c'est que ce qui se joue et se montre dans la chose a aussi l'inquiétant pouvoir de se dérober et de se laisser oublier. Retenons la mise en garde, mais sans oublier l'injonction de veiller sur les choses, une veille par quoi on peut aussi entendre, pourquoi pas, une vigilance proprement philosophique.

IV

Pour le dire en un langage plus sobre, le «pas en arrière» heideggerien a pour principal résultat de nous rendre à un monde (c'est improprement qu'on parle d'un «monde de la science», d'ailleurs, celle-ci n'a qu'un univers) dans lequel la fonction du spectateur a été abolie. On a souvent relevé, généralement pour lui en faire grief, que la théorie de l'œuvre d'art proposée par Heidegger est tout sauf une «esthétique». Ce qui s'y dit, ou passe, s'y passe sans que nul ne soit là pour le voir et percevoir. Non seulement les jugements de valeur y sont absents («beau» apparaît deux fois seulement dans le traité *De l'origine de l'œuvre d'art,* et ce sont deux ajouts au texte primitif), mais encore ils y sont impossibles: personne pour les formuler. Mais est-ce faiblesse des textes? Ce n'est vraiment pas certain, et on y verra plutôt un moyen d'éviter une vieille aporie. Mettant entre parenthèses le spectateur, Heidegger nous propose d'accéder aux choses telles qu'elles sont, et telles qu'elles sont choses, abstraction faite de toute intentionnalité et de toute mesure subjective – abstraction faite de toute *représentation*. Les œuvres sont des choses. Et aux choses, il revient d'apparaître telles quelles, dans toute la richesse de ce qu'elles nouent ou symbolisent – et non pas d'être visées par une conscience et d'apparaître dans les horizons de cette conscience.

Ainsi en va-t-il de toute chose, et du monde dans lequel il y a des choses. Ce monde – *le* monde – n'est rien que nous pourrions viser et représenter, les choses ne sont rien que nous puissions viser et représenter, pour la claire raison que rien ne se montre en fait sans nous inclure dans ce qui se montre. Pas de conscience ni de phénomènes pour se donner à elles. Au contraire, une participation de l'homme, en sa qualité de mortel, au grand jeu de rassemblement, de présence, de proximité, de distance, qui se joue autour de la chose. Prendre connaissance des choses, c'est d'abord les penser. C'est ensuite assurément rendre présence à l'homme au milieu d'elles. Mais cette présence de l'homme au milieu des choses, quelle est-elle? Les textes nous le disent: connaître le chemin, c'est marcher sur lui; connaître la cruche, ce sera s'en servir pour verser la boisson donnée à l'hôte. Toute doctrine de la perception est donc barrée au profit d'une théorie de l'apparition et de la participation (de l'être-à-côté-des-choses) que Heidegger ne développe pas et se contente d'appliquer, ou peut-être de produire chemin faisant pendant un travail de description.

Ce travail de description utilise des mots, et de préférence les mots les plus hauts, des mots qui rendent un son religieux. Les choses de la terre appellent – si la description heideggerienne est correcte – une description qui convoque un sacré, des êtres divins, et même un Dieu. Les choses, à l'évidence, ont du poids, poids d'être et de signification. Non seulement elles exigent qu'on veille sur elles, en raison du perpétuel «danger» qui peut les ravaler au rang d'objets, mais à l'évidence elles sont respectées et aimées du philosophe, et décrites de telle manière qu'elles ne peuvent apparaître en leur plénitude révélante si le mortel qui les rencontre ne les respecte et ne les aime lui-même.

V

Décidons donc de tenir (enfin…) le langage de la *présence* pour nommer un événement (ce mot, faute de mieux, d'autres nous parleraient de don) qui n'advient certes pas sans nous, mais qui n'advient pas du tout face à nous. Alors que le domaine de l'objet ne connaît que de l'être-ici-ou-là et des distances mesurées, le monde qui se déploie à l'horizon des choses abrite le proche, le lointain, la présence, l'absence, des phénomènes dont il saute aux yeux qu'ils n'ont pas de signification objective. Qu'en est-il parmi eux du phénomène de la présence? Heidegger a contribué à lui donner ailleurs mauvaise réputation en conférant comme trait distinctif à ce qu'il appelle la «métaphysique» l'équation de l'*on* et du *paron,* de l'étant et de l'étant-présent. Mais dans les textes qui nous intéressent, rien de ce sens métaphysique, pas le moindre lapsus conceptuel qui laisserait peser des menaces ontothéologiques. La présence n'y veut pas dire que la chose ou ce qu'elle convoque est là, sous la main, dans le présent pendant lequel je contribue à ce qu'elle serve comme chose. La présence, inséparable de l'absence, dit plutôt le jeu, un jeu auquel participent aussi les phénomènes du voilement et du dévoilement, de la proximité et du retrait, et d'autres encore, le jeu selon lequel ce qu'il y a de plus réel se donne dans la durée d'une histoire, dans la séquence d'époques qui ne nous offrent jamais la totalité du plus réel, dans la durée d'une histoire où le plus réel se donne toujours en sa vérité, mais jamais dans l'*ephapax* d'une omnidonation définitive. Présence, c'est cet avènement qui a lieu lorsque le Grec conduit une procession vers le temple, lorsque l'homme donne à boire à son hôte, lorsque le paysan parcourt un chemin de campagne. L'ontologie, qui est une discipline constituée à l'âge de l'objet, ne rencontre sur son chemin que des étants, tout étant lui confie les mêmes secrets de l'être, jamais l'étant ne lui fait défaut; et dire que l'étant détient ontologiquement la présence serait proposer un mot inutile, qui ne nomme rien. Heidegger, qui persiste à faire de la phénoménologie même dans ses œuvres tardives, sait que le même n'est jamais pareil, et que ce qu'il appelle *Sein,* ou *Seyn,* a son histoire propre, qui a place pour des éclaircies et des obscurcissements, et dans laquelle surtout l'être n'est jamais disponible comme pour l'ontologie il est disponible en tout étant. Le discours de la présence, dès lors, sera toujours lié à celui du don, toujours lié à une économie. Et parce que l'être n'est pas une hypostase, n'a pas de subsistance hypostatique, parce qu'il est toujours l'être donné aux étants – que ces étants soient les divins, les mortels ou les cruches –, toutes les transcendances qui abondent chez Heidegger ne supposent pas d'au-delà. C'est toujours ici, dans et autour de cette chose, que l'être fait acte de présence. Et toujours, cet acte est acte dans lequel je suis pris: pour que présence il y ait, il faut que soient pris dans son jeu, car c'est aussi leur jeu, les étants qui composent le quadriparti.

VI

Entrons un peu plus encore dans notre sujet. Un axiome théologique en provenance de Maria-Laach dit qu' «un mystère est quelque chose que l'on fait», et ces quelques mots peuvent nous donner à penser. Le concept de présence a ses lettres de créances théologiques, notamment donc dans la théologie des sacrements (des «mystères»), presque exclusivement dans la théorie de l'eucharistie. Sur les liens que les concepts eucharistiques ont pu entretenir avec la métaphysique, au sens heideggerien, il serait inutile de s'étendre. Sur le concept de présence (celui, d'ailleurs, des concepts eucharistiques qui a connu le passé le plus troublé), il peut être utile de le faire. Une raison à un intérêt: le risque, jamais évité de manière définitive, que le concept de présence eucharistique

suscite quelque chose comme une esthétique de l'eucharistie, une interprétation du regard que les hommes posent sur une chose dont ils croient
qu'elle est présence divine. Or, la présence est comme telle en acte de
don, mais dans la dramatique propre à ce don, dans sa liturgie, l'homme
est toujours pris et jamais spectateur. Il est banal (Maria-Laach, encore)
de dire que la théologie de l'eucharistie doit être une théologie de la
liturgie eucharistique, mais la banalité ici est bonne à prendre. Présence,
en termes eucharistiques, dans la liturgie et surgissant de la liturgie; présence qui se donne dans l'acte – le nôtre – où elle nous rassemble. Qu'il
y ait à voir, certes, et à entendre, et à sentir, et à toucher: c'est l'évidence. Mais rien de cela n'est objet (ni ne doit être mis en danger d'être
traité comme objet). La liturgie se célèbre avec des choses, rien de
moins que des choses: pain et vin, coupes, table sainte et images saintes,
d'autres encore. Elle se célèbre avec des mortels qui veulent y recevoir
un *pharmakon athanasias*. Mais rien de tout cela, pour la communauté
en acte de liturgie, ne possède la qualité du disponible et de l'objective-
ment perceptible. Tout cela est dit *saint,* en un sens biblique que Schelling avait su retrouver, saint comme séparé: ôté de toute perception quo-
tidienne comme de tout usage quotidien, là pour manifester et donner ce
qui ne se donne ni ne se manifeste ailleurs.

C'est donc pour dire, par mode de suggestion, que le don de présence
passe par tous les célébrants et co-célébrants de la liturgie, et aussi bien
par toutes les choses qui occupent l'espace liturgique. Un temps viendra
pour la contemplation. Mais le temps de la liturgie est celui d'un spectacle sans spectateur. (Et tous conviendront que Dieu lui-même n'en est
pas, surtout pas, spectateur!)

VII

La liturgie n'est pas seule à se réclamer d'une dispensation de présence. De Dieu, comme Seigneur de l'univers, on affirme communément
qu'il est présent en tout lieu de sa création: par exemple «par mode de
cause première». A une thèse sur l'univers, on pourrait joindre une thèse
sur le monde de la vie: nulle théologie en bonne santé n'a jamais dit que
Dieu n'était pas à portée de voix chaque fois qu'un homme lui adressait
la parole ou criait vers lui. Et à cette seconde thèse, on peut en joindre
une troisième, que j'accepte totalement: en tout lieu où l'homme veut
faire face à Dieu, les gestes de la liturgie (de l'*esse coram Deo*) peuvent
être posés, et comment ne pas dire que cela est aussi événement de présence? Dès lors, que penser que nous pourrions restreindre au champ
des liturgies sacramentelles? Qu'est-ce que le don eucharistique, en tant

qu'il est présence, nous dévoile qui ailleurs resterait celé? Entre plusieurs réponses: peut-être le débordement de la métaphysique par la théologie.

La proposition qu'adresse une théologie de la présence sacramentelle, celle d'honorer comme étant *là* présent celui qui n'est nul part absent, est assurément étrange, et il faut souhaiter qu'elle rende toujours ce son étrange. Omniprésence divine, autorisation perpétuelle de poser les gestes de l'*esse coram,* tout cela nous tient le langage – satisfaisant? pas pour tous, je le crains – de l'universel et de la loi, du fait sur lequel on ne peut que buter. Présence sacramentelle, dans les limites d'une action liturgique, dans les limites du lieu où sont conservés les *sancta,* voilà qui nous tient le langage d'une particularité irréductible: le langage d'une présence dont nous pouvons fêter l'avent si nous le voulons, mais aussi le langage d'une fête de laquelle nous pouvons nous absenter. Qu'un don de présence advienne là, de fait, là et pas ailleurs, l'affirmation avait de quoi troubler une conscience chrétienne imbibée d'*epistemè* moderne. Mais est-il certain que le concept d'omniprésence divine ne s'est pas chargé d'assez d'alluvions ontothéologiques pour ne pas mériter une confiance extrême? Est-il certain, d'autre part, que ce concept soit nécessairement porteur de bonnes nouvelles? Au Dieu omniprésent, Sartre objectait, avec véhémence charmante, qu'il existait en fait sur le mode du tiers importun, du présent qui impose sa présence. L'objection a sa part de vérité. Et lorsque cette *particula veri* est reconnue, alors l'idée d'un don qui advient ici et non pas là, en un temps et non en un autre, peut apparaître comme salvatrice de nos libertés: comme respectueuse de l'homme qui peut désirer, ou ne pas désirer, être lui-même présent à l'événement du don.

VIII

Les propos que je viens de tenir tendent vers une affirmation, celle du caractère peu moderne de la praxis liturgique chrétienne. Les Temps modernes, pour nommer l'un de leurs plus grands théoriciens, sont ceux de l'*ontologia generalis* suarezienne: ceux où tout étant nous manifeste le plus important, et où, s'il est d'autres particularités que certains possèdent mais que tous ne possèdent pas, celles-ci finissent leur carrière dans une *ontologia specialis* où l'on rencontre, pêle mêle, Dieu, les hommes, les anges et les chats, étant bien entendu (Gilson le dit parfaitement[2]) que

---

2. Voir par exemple le charmant passage autobiographique publié dans E. GILSON & J.-J. COURTINE (eds.), *Constantes philosophiques de l'être,* Paris, Vrin, 1983, 145-147.

le moindre silex révèle tout ce qu'il y a à révéler sur l'être. Les Temps modernes, en tant qu'ils étaient chrétiens, étaient (avec droite consé-quence) ceux d'une aptitude universelle à l'expérience de Dieu, que ce Dieu soit celui de la raison ou celui de l'affect. On nous dit ces temps finis (Guardini l'a dit le premier), et tout ce qui les a tissés ne mérite pas d'être pleuré. Mais si nous voyons se clore l'âge du Dieu dont la raison peut se saisir partout où elle se pense jusqu'à son fondement, et du Dieu auquel l'affect peut se donner accès expérientiel partout où il se laisse émouvoir par une nature interprétée comme trace de Dieu, alors ce peut être une bonne nouvelle que celle d'une donation de présence liée à la particularité de certains lieux et de certains temps.

Qu'on ne m'accuse pas d'ignorance crasse et, pire encore, de générali-sation débridée. Ce que je viens de dire, l'âge classique le savait encore, disons qu'il ne l'avait pas encore oublié: ainsi Descartes déci-dant un pèlerinage à Lorette[3]. Reste que la pérégrination n'est pas atti-tude moderne. La théologie protestante ne l'aime pas, l'*Aufklärung* l'aime presque moins encore. Et Hegel, qui n'a pas tué tout *Aufklärer* en lui, aura son morceau de bravoure à propos des croisades, entreprises théologiquement insensées consistant à reprendre possession d'un tom-beau vide, déserté par celui qui, fort de l'Esprit reçu du Père, vit désor-mais en tout lieu[4]. Mais le pèlerin (dont l'expérience, par ailleurs, est distincte de la *xeniteia* dont je me suis occupé en d'autres temps[5]) n'a-t-il que des naïvetés à dire? Je ne crois pas. En plus de sa participation aux pérégrinations inconfortables et pénitentielles du moine *xenos,* sa pratique dit tout bas, en effet, ce que je dis ici plus haut. Présence, «expérience» de Dieu, tout cela lui apparaît d'abord comme donné dans la fragmentation des lieux et des temps. Tout lieu et tout temps peuvent certes devenir le *kairos* de la conversion. Mais à une dimension univer-sellement kairologique du temps chrétien (qu'il n'est question pour per-sonne de nier), le pèlerin superpose une quête immergée dans le particu-lier. Plus qu'un homme du livre, du livre qui met les Écritures chrétiennes à la disposition de tous et leur permet de dicter leur propre rythme et de trouver leurs propres préférences, il est l'homme des hasards d'un lectionnaire, du hasard des messes votives lues en ce sanctuaire ou

---

3. Cf. DESCARTES, *Oeuvres,* AT X, 217,25-218,2. Voir aussi BAILLET, *Vie de M. Des-cartes,* I, 120. Descartes voyage en Italie de l'automne 1623 à mai 1625. Nous n'avons pas la preuve matérielle qu'il soit allé à Lorette. Mais rien ne permet de penser le contraire. (Je dois cette note à V. Carraud.)

4. Voir le commentaire d'A. CHAPELLE, *Hegel et la religion. 1. La problématique,* Paris, Éditions universitaires, 1964, 48-50.

5. Voir mon *Expérience et Absolu,* Paris, PUF, 1994, §§11ss.

en cet autre. Plus qu'un homme de la règle qu'on se fixe, il est l'homme de ce qui se donne ici et non pas là, de ce qui se prie ici et non pas là, de l'événement de présence auquel il participe ici et non pas là. On m'accordera que tout cela n'est pas moderne, même si, derechef, rien de cela n'est vraiment mort sous le règne de ce que nous appelons la modernité.

IX

Qu'on m'en fasse le crédit, mes remarques ne plaident pas en faveur de l'établissement de cartes du sacré, indiquant à chacun les chemins à suivre, au sens le plus littéral du mot, pour parvenir à l'expérience qu'il cherche. Le but serait de procéder à l'exact contraire, démolir tous les concepts (démolir les pratiques n'est pas mon métier, Dieu soit loué) qui tendent à faire de la vie liturgique une école de l' «expérience religieuse». Mais pour ce faire, des précisions doivent venir. Elles concernent la fonction que doit jouer le recours à Heidegger proposé plus haut par mode d'esquisse.

Ce dont il est question dans la conférence de 1950, et aussi dans *Bâtir habiter penser,* lu en 1951, n'est pas vraiment mystérieux, et achève la longue tentative de pensée païenne (appelons un chat un chat) que Heidegger a faite depuis l'époque des *Beiträge* (1936), de *Besinnung* (1938-1939) et d'autres textes encore inédits, une tentative dont des échos sont nettement audibles dans les commentaires de Hölderlin. Il s'agit là, pour faire bref mais sans fausser les perspectives, d'inscrire les *realia* du paganisme dans un monde réinterprété. Le monde, dans *Etre et temps,* est l'horizon d'une existence athée. Le monde, dans les textes qui nous préoccupent aujourd'hui, n'est pas descriptible sans que du sacré intervienne dans la description, et ce sacré n'est vraiment rien que l'interprète de l'expérience chrétienne, plus précisément de l'expérience liturgique chrétienne, puisse accueillir avec des grognements amicaux. L'expérience liturgique est sans lieu dans le monde décrit en 1927. Telle que je la comprends, elle l'est tout autant dans le monde décrit plus tard.

Reste, et ce n'est vraiment pas peu, que la liturgie a besoin d'une pensée de la chose, et que ce n'est pas se tromper sur la nature du don eucharistique que de dire du Dieu présent qu'il y est présent comme chose, certainement pas comme objet mais incontestablement comme chose. Tenir liturgiquement le langage de la chose, ce serait conceptualiser ce que la théologie contemporaine (et pas elle seule!) a souvent fait sans avoir toujours lu Heidegger, à savoir décrire la liturgie eucharistique comme débordement de sens et comme lieu de la totalité. Un coup d'oeil aux ecclésiologies eucharistiques, par exemple, nous fournirait le témoignage de discours pour lesquels rien n'est absent de la célébration eucharistique, à laquelle participent l'Église en totalité, les anges, les saints, les morts qui frappent encore à la porte du Royaume. Un coup d'oeil à un livret de Guardini toujours bien vivant, *Les signes sacrés,* nous convaincrait de la réelle pertinence théologique des propos heideggeriens[6]. L'économie eucharistique de présence convoque des choses, et ces choses y interviennent comme choses: non pas comme des objets, toujours enfermés dans les limites de leur représentabilité, mais comme des choses, comme des réalités qui se lient et nous lient à d'autres réalités, comme des réalités qui font œuvre de rassemblement. Il y a des choses chrétiennes (la croix), il y a des choses qui se prêtent à utilisation chrétienne (le pain, la cruche, le cierge, l'encens), il y a des choses qui ne se prêtent pas à utilisation chrétienne (la charrue, le taureau). Il y a sans doute, vis-à-vis des choses, un travail chrétien de transsignification, accompli ou à accomplir. En tout cas, pas de liturgie sans choses, et pas de dispensation de présence qui ne passe par l'investissement de certaines choses.

Toute rationalité théologique s'effondrerait bien sûr si nous omettions de voir qu'il n'y a pas, liturgiquement, simple présence *des* choses, mais embrigadement des choses (et de nous-mêmes avec) dans le jeu de la présence. Les choses ne sont rien de moins que des choses. Et lorsque certaines choses nous apparaissent, telles quelles, considérable peut être leur pouvoir d'évocation liturgique: ainsi, par exemple, la mention du pain et du vin à la fin de ce poème de Trakl, *ein Winterabend,* dont Heidegger, on n'en sera pas surpris, efface tout accent chrétien dans le commentaire qu'il en propose[7]. Les choses, toutefois, ne sont pas plus que des choses. Leur besogne liturgique est d'être offertes, et d'être saisies. Et si les choses se mêlent de n'être que présentes telles quelles, alors la liturgie s'abîme dans une célébration de l'immanent.

X

Ayant dit que la liturgie n'est pas une école de l'expérience religieuse, et ayant sous-entendu que le contenu des expériences dites religieuses est aussi souvent païen que chrétien, il me faut ajouter que la théorie du sacrement, entendu comme événement de présence, est aussi une théorie

---

6. R. GUARDINI, *Von heiligen Zeichen,* Munich, 1922, constamment rééd.
7. M. HEIDEGGER, *Unterwegs zur Sprache,* in ID., *Gesamtausgabe 12: 1. Abt. Veröffentlichte Schriften. 1910-1976,* Frankfurt a. Main, Klostermann, 1985, 31-78.

du langage liturgique, à entendre lui aussi comme chose que saisit la présence. Condamné par les hasards de son histoire à une double marginalisation de l'eucharistie, marginalisation de sa célébration et marginalisation de son traitement théorique, le protestantisme n'est pas absent de notre débat, et ce pour le caractère profondément événementiel que ses intuitions natives confèrent à la Parole, telle que distincte de la lettre des Écritures. «Événement de parole», *Wortereignis, Sprachgeschehen*, Ebeling et Fuchs ont fourni de remarquables descriptions conceptuelles du procès liturgique dans lequel les mots prennent vie et deviennent, en effet, les mots de Dieu. Sur des analyses où nous apercevrions souvent une théologie eucharistique qui ne se connaît pas pleinement, il n'y a pas à s'étendre, car nous ne ferions que nous répéter. Mais sur les mots qui accueillent et louent la présence, nous pouvons nous arrêter un peu. Je profiterai de cet arrêt pour nommer, enfin, la *vérité*. Les choses signifient ou symbolisent, elles nous émeuvent, elles rameutent les mots les plus hauts et les souvenirs les plus vénérables, etc., mais parlent-elles, ou bien les faisons-nous parler? Les choses certainement nous parlent, ou font œuvre de signification, dans l'acte où nous les laissons être, ou faisons être, ce qu'elles sont: laisser être le chemin dans l'acte où nous le parcourons, laisser être la charrue dans l'acte où nous la poussons, laisser être la cruche dans l'acte où nous versons à boire, laisser être la croix dans l'acte où nous la vénérons, etc. Et en offrant l'hospitalité aux choses, la liturgie se propose nécessairement d'en user de telle sorte qu'elles puissent y manifester leur sens théologique (et d'ailleurs y bénéficier souvent d'une donation de sens théologique). Voir donc les choses en leur vérité, ce n'est pas peu. Mais il y a plus dans la liturgie: voir le langage aussi en toute sa vérité.

Par vérité, j'entends ici deux concepts, qui me semblent liturgiquement liés: d'une part celui d'opinion droite, d'autre part celui d'un langage poussé à la limite de lui-même. La vérité, en son usage liturgique, est d'abord cette *veritas redarguens* dont parle Augustin, la vérité comme réfutation de l'erreur: c'est d'abord au petit paquet d'axiomes contenus dans le symbole de la foi, et c'est ensuite à la foi eucharistique dont se réclame la communauté qui fête cette liturgie, que se décide à quoi, au juste, nous avons affaire ici ou là. Mais la vérité dont vit la liturgie, c'est aussi, toujours d'Augustin, la *veritas lucens*, brillant de la seule gloire intelligible des mots vrais, certes, mais brillant aussi de la gloire sensible que lui prêtent nos métaphores ou nos cantilations[8]. Aucune version de

8. Voir les commentaires de R. BRAGUE, *«La vérité vous rendra libre»*, dans *Com(F)* 10 (1985) 5-6, 9-25.

l'ontologie des transcendantaux ne m'a jamais semblé recevable, et je n'ai aucune envie de caresser l'idée d'une convertibilité du vrai et du beau. Il y a en revanche, et pour le coup c'est un réquisit liturgique, le devoir, en ce cas, d'honorer le vrai (lequel reste certes vrai dans tous les langages utilisés pour le dire, de l'anglais de Cranmer au *pidgin English* et à la pénible prose de certains missels aujourd'hui en usage) par la splendeur des mots. Le philosophe n'a pas besoin que le vrai soit bellement dit, car c'est en se rendant à ses raisons que nous honorons le vrai (et ce qui vaut du philosophe vaut du théologien académique). Mais lorsqu'ils entrent en liturgie, ni le philosophe ni le théologien académique ne le font ès qualités. Ils le font en tant que croyants. A la liturgie, ils participent comme êtres de chair autant que d'esprit. Et à l'intérieur de l'espace liturgique, les exigences de la chair doivent être honorées: noces du vrai et du beau en un langage qui soit simultanément la plus juste et la plus glorieuse louange. La théologie spirituelle nous dit que c'est tout un art que d'accueillir le don de présence. Le premier rudiment de cet art est sans doute de cultiver un art de la parole liturgique, comme parole vraie-et-belle, comme parole proférée dans les avant-derniers temps et qui veut porter leur marque.

XI

Cette dernière phrase est lourde, intentionnellement, d'une objection. Nous accueillons un mystère de présence. Mais nous l'accueillons dans le monde. Toutes les subversions sont possibles, et franchement nécessaires, à celui qui veut l'existence liturgique: subversions symboliques de l'être-dans-le-monde, distance par rapport à tous les prestiges numineux de la «terre», tout ce dont je parlais dans d'autres recherches[9]. Mais ces subversions ne sont pas institutrices d'un «nouvel être». Elles tentent une manière d'être, et elles le tentent fragilement. Nous ouvrons le non-lieu liturgique, à la force de notre foi, et nous consentons par avance à la non-expérience nocturne dans laquelle nous nous contenterons de savoir qu'un est là en qui nous croyons et auquel nous nous voulons disponibles. Et c'est fort bien. Mais reste, intacte ici et maintenant de toute transfiguration, l'emprise que le monde exerce sur nous de notre naissance à notre mort. Restent ce corps souvent fatigué et cette conscience souvent lasse, cette affectivité qui vit de sa vie mondaine, sur laquelle nous n'avons que peu de prises, restent tous les rappels de la non-réalisation des réalités définitives, restent nos paroles inélégantes et

---

9. J.-Y. LACOSTE, *Expérience et Absolu* (n. 5), §§8-37, 53-73.

nos musiques de pacotille, reste toute la distance à laquelle, même pris dans un jeu de présence, nous demeurons par rapport aux liturgies célestes. La liturgie dit la vérité, et la présence s'y donne vraiment. Mais la liturgie – la nôtre – est affaire historiale, et la présence est donnée dans l'histoire. Et pour cette raison, un dernier concept doit être cité à comparaître, celui de parousie.

Entre deux synonymes apparents (aucune différence sémantique entre le *par-on* grec et le *prae-ens* latin), différencier s'impose à nous pour raisons limpides. On raconte du bibliste C.H. Dodd qu'il aurait acquis l'intuition de sa théorie de l'eschatologie réalisée en participant à une liturgie orientale[10]. Or si un théorème théologique n'a pas besoin de longue démonstration, c'est bien que là où il y a *sacrement,* là le défini-tif n'est pas réalisé (et parler de *mystère* n'y changerait rien). L'expé-rience liturgique est certes celle d'un Dieu qui a «tout dit»[11]. Elle est certes celle d'un Dieu qui ne donne pas quelque grâce créée en souvenir de son passage parmi les hommes, mais qui se donne lui-même. Mais tout cela advient dans monde et histoire. Et dans monde et histoire, la liturgie ne mime l'eschaton, et l'on ne s'associe aux chœurs angéliques, que pour confesser (très vite et sans effort aucun…) que l'on vit les avant-derniers temps, et dans l'espérance d'une parousie. Parler de parousie avoue ainsi que l'élément de la présence *n*'est *que* celui de la présence. Présence assurément, et sans réticence. Mais présence en sa modalité préeschatologique. Présence certes qui nous fournit un certain avant-goût des biens à venir, présence donnée à une chair qui la reçoit parfois en exultant par avance de sa propre résurrection – mais présence seulement. Nos formulaires liturgiques disent vrai lorsqu'ils nous affir-ment qu'«en cette existence de chaque jour que nous recevons de ta grâce, la vie éternelle est déjà commencée», mieux, que «in hoc corpore constituti non solum pietatis tuae cotidianos experimur effectus, sed aeternitatis etiam pignora iam tenemus»[12]. Des gages que l'on «tient», *tenemus,* et c'est bien ce que nous maintenons en parlant de présence. Mais ceux qui ont «reçu les prémices de l'Esprit, qui a ressuscité Jésus d'entre les morts», ceux-ci espèrent encore «que s'accomplisse en [eux] le mystère de Pâques»: «paschale mysterium speramus nobis esse per-petuum»[13]. Entre l'accompli – dans la Pâque de Jésus – et l'inaccompli – celui d'une existence croyante qui se vit ici à l'ombre de la mort –,

---

10. Je tiens cela de Pierre-Marie Gy.
11. Cf. R. BRAGUE, in *Diogène* n° 170 (1995) 49-74.
12. *Missale Romanum,* ed. 1970, praefatio VI de dominicis 'per annum'.
13. *Ibid.*

entre l'ordre de la présence et de la parousie: cet écart porte, et *incontestablement,* le sens de toutes nos liturgies.

XII

Mes derniers mots n'étaient pas ceux d'une péroraison. Après avoir énoncé un incontestable, il me reste à honorer une question encore, celle qu'annonce mon titre: et je ne prétends plus rien dire que de contestable. Y a-t-il, donc, une tonalité affective propre à l'accueil de la présence sacramentelle? Y a-t-il une situation liturgique de l'affect, et qui soit une situation de connaissance? Ces questions une fois entendues, une première réponse consiste à leur répondre que la condition schématiquement pure de l'expérience liturgique est une condition nocturne, au sens sanjuaniste de l'adjectif, et qu'il suffit, pour que liturgie il y ait, que la présence soit «acceptée»[14], confessée. Le don n'a pas à se légitimer en se donnant à sentir; il se suffit à être donné et reconnu comme tel. C'est une bonne réponse, et que j'ai fournie moi-même[15]. Mais offre-t-elle plus qu'un premier mot? Une fois en effet liquidées les – toujours inquiétantes – demandes de jouissance présente, plus ou moins toutes suspectes d'être des demandes de vérification, nous n'en avons pas fini avec l'affect, pour mille bonnes raisons, dont le fait trivial que la liturgie nous engage corps et âme, parole et conscience, intention et affection, entiers, vivants, sentants. Les piétismes demandent un Dieu sensible au cœur, et il est aisé (mais non dénué de pertinence) de leur répondre que l'affect est une *fabrica idolorum* aussi redoutable, et plus peut-être, que la raison (à laquelle Calvin applique la formule). Suis-je affecté par un autre ou m'affecté-je moi-même? Et si c'est par un autre, qui est vraiment cet autre? Ainsi peut se construire un long débat, toujours préoccupé de contenus d'expérience dont on demande qui en répond, s'inquiétant toujours des signatures, signature divine ou signature humaine, qui marqueraient soit le passage de Dieu, soit la méprise de l'homme qui ne sent en fait que son propre désir. Mais, dans les termes de ce débat, comment ne pas percevoir une grande naïveté théorique?

Les questions toutefois cessent d'être folles, et un tantinet perverses aussi, lorsque toute logique de la preuve est mise hors jeu et qu'on note en exergue de toute interprétation qui se veut viable que le lieu expérientiel propre à la liturgie est un entre-deux, l'entre-deux de l'historial

---

14. Sur le concept d'«acceptation», voir L.J. COHEN, *An Essay on Belief and Acceptance,* Oxford, Clarendon, 1992.

15. L.J. COHEN, *An Essay on Belief and Acceptance,* §55.

et de l'eschatologique. Cet entre-deux ne serait-il pas aussi, et de
manière positive, la condition liturgique du sentir? L'expérience liturgique est forte d'un savoir et confesse une présence, mais ce savoir lui-
même est pris dans une logique plus large que celle du langage vrai. De
cette logique plus large, disons qu'elle est de *connaissance,* en donnant
au terme à la fois les harmoniques charnelles qu'il possède dans le texte
biblique et le poids conceptuel de la connaissance par familiarité, *knowledge by acquaintance,* dont Russell parle dans un essai célèbre[16] (qu'il
ne soit pas question de restreindre la connaissance «par accointance»
comme Russell la restreint, cela va sans dire). Et puisque c'est en
contexte liturgique et sacramentaire que nous parlons ici de connaissance, autant ne pas oublier alors que ce contexte est celui d'une initiation. Liturgie, ainsi, comme initiation à la connaissance de Dieu, enten-
due comme familiarisation globale de l'homme? Si nous les recevions,
les termes de l'interrogation promettraient de conduire plus loin que
toute enquête sur le Dieu de l'affection seule, ou de l'affection pure.
Dans le jeu liturgique, l'homme mime et attend, ensemble, le face-à-face
eschatologique. En une même dispensation de présence, Dieu se donne à
lui comme prochain et comme lointain. Peut-être alors l'équilibre liturgique fondamental de l'affect serait-il de sentir l'un et l'autre, et d'être
ouvert, disposé, à l'un et à l'autre, à la proximité dont on (pré)jouit
comme au lointain qui creuse le désir. Dans l'affect, montre Heidegger
(dans *Etre et temps),* l'homme se trouve lui-même *(sich befinden,
Befindlichkeit)* en trouvant sa condition, celle de l'être-dans-le-monde.
Pourrions-nous aussi nous trouver nous-mêmes, dans le déroulement de
l'expérience liturgique, tels que nous savons alors que nous sommes, en
présence de Dieu dans le temps de l'histoire? Selon Heidegger, une
expérience affective, celle de l'angoisse, joue («existentialement») le
rôle de révélateur privilégié de ce que nous sommes dans le monde. J'ai
déjà tenté de montrer qu'il nous est possible dans le monde de prendre
assez de distance par rapport au monde pour y faire mémoire de notre
création, et que cette prise de distance a sa coloration affective, l'*aise*[17].
Pour jouer le rôle d'affect liturgique fondamental, j'ai ma candidate, la
paix. Se propose-t-elle vraiment pour révéler ce que nous sommes et ce
que nous faisons face à un Absolu qui nous réconcilie avec lui? A défaut

---

16. B. RUSSELL, *Knowledge by Acquaintance and Knowledge by Description*, in ID.,
Mysticism and Logic and Other Essays, London, 1918, pp. 209-232. La connaissance
«par accointance» se rencontre déjà chez W. James, qui la distingue de la «connaissance
sur», *knowledge about.*
17. «*En marge du monde et de la terre: l'aise*», in J.-Y. LACOSTE, *Le monde et
l'absence d'œuvre,* Paris, PUF, 2000, 5-22.

de fournir des réponses, qui devraient être détaillées, nous pouvons peut-être indiquer dans quelle direction les chercher.

XIII

D'une situation liturgique de l'affect, il faudrait dire d'abord ce qu'elle n'est pas; et ce qu'on ne peut dire qu'elle est sans se perdre *ipso facto* dans une phénoménologie des états affectifs qui nous les donneraient tous en vrac, la douleur ressentie à la lecture de la Passion, la componction éveillée par le souvenir de mes péchés, etc. – ce qu'elle ne peut être, c'est tout bonnement une expérience pourvue d'un objet déterminé. Sentir comme rien sentir? L'importance jouée par l'angoisse, dans la topique heideggerienne du dévoilement, tient à ce qu'elle n'a pas d'objet. J'ai peur de ceci ou cela, mais je ne m'angoisse de rien, je ne m'angoisse pas non plus de toutes les choses possibles ou réelles, l'angoisse est angoisse du tout, en bloc, et plus précisément de l'être, comme tel, dont elle révèle qu'il n'est pas sans la menace perpétuelle du néant. Et c'est ainsi, parce qu'elle met l'étant en jeu en sa totalité, que l'angoisse me révèle le «fait» du monde: l'être-dans-le-monde comme finitude.

Un sentir qui ne sente rien, mais qui nous découvre à nous-mêmes comme disponibles à une présence capable de peser sur notre affectibilité, la paix n'en fournirait-elle pas le cas remarquable? Etre en paix, en première analyse, ce n'est certes pas manquer de relations pacifiées, toutes distinguables. C'est d'abord être en paix avec: avec tel ou tel prochain, ou avec tel ou tel groupe, ou avec Dieu, ou avec moi-même. Mais lorsque la théologie spirituelle veut parler de paix – *quies, hèsukhia,* un concept latin et un concept grec dont il n'est pas certain qu'ils se recoupent totalement, mais dont il est bien certain qu'ils bénéficient d'un haut niveau d'élaboration –, alors la paix est bien cette situation affective («cordiale») de la conscience à laquelle aucun contenu n'appartient, cette situation néanmoins dans laquelle se décide le destin de tout ce qui peut affecter l'homme pacifié. L'expérience n'est donc pas celle d'une mise hors jeu de la vie du cœur, mais celle de ce que nous pouvons nommer une disposition. En sa réalité affective, la paix devrait nous apparaître comme la tonalité fondamentale d'une vie *réconciliée* – comme l'index d'un salut destiné aussi à la sphère affective de notre être et réalisé aussi dans cette sphère. Mais l'important n'est pas ce qui nous apparaît, c'est ce qui apparaît à l'homme qui fait l'expérience de la paix: et ce qui lui apparaît n'est ni plus ni moins que soi-même comme existant sur un mode qu'il faut nommer d'un mot fort, l'alliance. Se sentir soi-même comme étant en paix, c'est connaître, pour autant que l'affect connaisse, que l'on existe sur le mode de l'être-en-alliance. Et l'alliance, si j'en crois mes auteurs, est le présupposé de toute existence d'homme qui puisse se vivre, de manière non aporétique, sur le mode de l'être-devant-Dieu, de la «relation *coram*» de Ebeling.

A celui qui *est* en paix, je ne crois pas qu'aucun texte spirituel interdise de toujours ressentir cette paix. Atteinte au terme d'une lutte ascétique contre les passions, la paix dit certes le pouvoir de ne pas être troublé. Mais trouble et émotion ne sont pas synonymes, et le cœur paisible ne perd pas quiétude ou hésychie lorsqu'il se réjouit de ceci ou cela, compatit avec telle ou telle souffrance, d'autres expériences encore – mais qui toutes, c'est la pointe de ma proposition, peuvent se vivre en paix.

XIV

Ce que j'ai dit ne suffit pas et n'est pas dit pour suffire: reste à rejoindre le faisceau de questions soulevées par une présence donnée ici ou là, mais non partout, dans une histoire qui nous interdit d'en jouir perpétuellement. Celui dont la théorie sacramentaire nous dit qu'il a des temps et des lieux pour sa présence, celui-ci, outre le fait qu'il est présent, se présente-t-il à la conscience (affective) d'une manière qui nous permettrait, par exemple, de décrire une expérience eucharistique stable, offerte à tous? Je ne le crois pas. A en croire l'historien qui en savait plus que les autres, Betz, la tonalité affective des assemblées eucharistiques (leur «ambiance») a connu une significative modification aux environs du IV$^{e:}$ à un temps où le mystère était d'abord célébré dans la joie succéda un temps où il fut célébré d'abord dans la crainte de Dieu[18]. Rien n'indique que ces deux *Stimmungen* épuisent toute réponse affective possible au mystère de la présence qui advient et demeure. Peut-être l'assemblée eucharistique est-elle de nouveau plus joyeuse qu'emplie de crainte de Dieu. Peut-être de nouvelles attitudes liturgiques pointent-elles. Mais peu importe; et d'un foisonnement de réponses affectives, je voudrais retenir seulement leur banale licéité, le simple fait que la présence est pour l'affect. Que le don de présence soit pour la conscience affective (autant qu'il est pour la prise de parole confessante, bien sûr), si je ne me suis pas trop trompé, cela ne veut pas dire qu'il y a des temps, des lieux et des choses où nous devons attendre qu'il nous soit donné à sentir indubitablement, d'un sentir qui ne se trompe pas sur la

18. J. BETZ, *Eucharistie 1. In der Schrift und Patristik*, HDG IV.4.a, Freiburg, Herder, 1979, p. 56.

réalité de ce qu'il sent, une pression divine sur notre cœur. Cela veut dire, tout au contraire, qu'il y a des temps, etc., où l'Absolu existe pour nous sur le mode d'un don de présence, et que devant ce don s'ouvre l'espace d'une réponse affective, ou plutôt donc de réponses affectives. Sur leur statut responsorial, soyons donc clair: elles ne prouvent pas le don, elles prouvent que nous reconnaissons le don.

Pré-moderne, critique ironique des Temps modernes ou témoin de leur disparition, le pèlerin dont je parlais plus haut mérite d'avoir le dernier mot. Omniprésence divine, transfiguration christique de tout le réel, ces concepts pèsent de peu de poids pour celui qui accepte de marcher un peu afin que lui soit conférée, en même temps que certaines autres grâces, la grâce de la présence de son Sauveur. Une présence qui advient, un avent dont le croyant désire être témoin, un avent qui appelle la réponse du cœur autant que celle de la raison, une présence donnée comme une chose sur laquelle il faut veiller pour éviter qu'on ne la traite comme un objet métaphysique un peu rare: que dit le pèlerin, au fond, sinon que cette présence mérite ses détours[19]?

Institut Catholique de Paris   Jean-Yves LACOSTE
21 rue d'Assas
75270 Paris
France

19. Le texte qu'on vient de lire est une version remaniée de la conférence lue au colloque de Louvain. Les remaniements s'imposaient – le texte primitif contenait de pures et simples erreurs, et je tiens à remercier vivement Ignace Verhack d'avoir attiré mon attention sur elles. Il retrouvera ce que je lui dois.

RESPONSE TO JEAN-YVES LACOSTE

Nous présentons ci-dessous la réponse du Prof I. Verhack après la lecture orale par Mr. Lacoste du texte que celui-ci avait préparé pour le congrès. Certaines des remarques qui suivent ont été assimilées par Mr. Lacoste dans la version finale de son texte.

Je voudrais remercier Mr. Lacoste pour ce beau texte qui nous aura frappé par son raffinement et par sa profondeur philosophique aussi bien que théologique. Le texte est composé de 14 petits tableaux qui, chaque fois, forment une petite unité en soi et qui, ensemble, tracent un parcours qui nous fait réfléchir d'une part au sujet de la place de l'affectivité dans l'accueil de la présence sacramentelle et d'autre part au sujet du concept élargi de 'chose' (≠ objet) impliqué selon lui dans une compréhension de la liturgie eucharistique.

C'est un parcours qui, certes, ne nous livre pas tous ses secrets après une seule et simple lecture, mais qui invite à être lu et relu. C'est pourquoi que je voudrais honorer ce texte en relevant quelque points saillants qui ont retenu mon attention et qui, ici et là, suscitent également des questions comme point de départ d'une réflexion ultérieure.

Vous nous avez tracé un parcours qui, partant de la disqualification épistémique de l'affect au nom du savoir objectif, nous ramène finalement à l'affect pour autant qu'il puisse être compris comme réponse affective au don de la présence sacramentelle. Ce statut responsorial de l'affect ne prouve pas le don, dites-vous, mais prouve que nous reconnaissons le don. Ainsi, vous faites une distinction entre une présence pour l'affect (le don de présence pour l'affect) et le fait de se présenter à l'affect, ce qui ressort du piétisme, c'est-à-dire l'attente d'un sentir indubitable qui ne se trompe pas sur la réalité de ce qu'il sent. C'est ainsi que vous vous démarquez de l'idée moderne d'*expérience religieuse* ou le désir d'un Dieu sensible au cœur (présence pour l'affect). Pour revaloriser l'affect au sein de la condition liturgique, vous vous référez d'abord à la *Befindlichkeit* de Heidegger, dans laquelle l'homme *trouve* révélée sa condition d'être-dans-le-monde. Mais ce que vous cherchez en fait, c'est la *Befindlichkeit* liturgique, qui correspondrait à l'initiation à la présence de Dieu dans le temps de l'histoire. Y a-t-il, pour la seconde *Befindlichkeit*, un lien nécessaire et constitutif avec la première? Je m'explique. Comment concevoir ce que vous appelez *la paix*? Est-ce l'état d'âme de celui qui a été touché par la présence divine – tout comme Heidegger dit de la *Befindlichkeit* qu'elle est constituée par le fait, pour le Dasein, d'être touché (*angegaṅgen*) par l'être et par les étants (la dimension de passivité pathique qui précède toute préoccupation – *Sorge*)? En d'autres termes, s'agit-il d'une grâce, d'un don? Ou s'agit-il du fruit de l'apaisement de l'angoisse à la suite du travail fait par ce que vous appelez les subversions symboliques de l'être-dans-le-monde qui sont nécessaires pour *ouvrir le non-lieu liturgique*? S'il s'agit d'une grâce, d'un don, je ne vois pas très bien comment vous pouvez soutenir votre thèse que le don de présence ne se présenterait pas à l'affect, mais seulement pour l'affect. Quel est donc, selon vous, le lien entre la paix comme tonalité fondamentale d'une vie réconciliée et ce que vous entendez par le statut responsorial de l'affect, que vous semblez relier à une présence donnée ici ou là, c'est-à-dire à l'intérieur de la célébration liturgique?

En marge de cette première question:

J'éprouve quelque difficulté à saisir la portée exacte de votre idée de *non-lieu liturgique*. Certes, ce qui y est célébré est une réalité eschatologique qui dépasse les limites de l'espace et du temps. Les choses saintes ne relèvent pas non plus de l'ordre du «prendre soin» (*Besorgen*) heideggerien, ce qui supposerait d'ailleurs leur insertion dans le réseau du monde des finalités de la *Bedeutsamkeit*. Cependant, comment concilier l'idée d'une présence avec celle d'un non-lieu. Une présence, même si elle n'est pas totale (elle n'est pas sans absence et sans voilement) suppose toujours l'ici de la «chose» liturgique, présence célébrée de façon contingente, comme vous dites, à des temps particuliers et en des lieux particuliers où la communauté liturgique se réunit pour se laisser rassembler autour d'une présence «qui se donne dans l'acte – le nôtre – où elle nous rassemble», «là pour manifester et donner ce qui ne se donne ni ne se manifeste ailleurs». N'est-ce pas postuler après tout un lieu liturgique?

Au centre de votre parcours se trouvent vos considérations heideggériennes au sujet de la chose, en opposition avec l'objet épistémique du savoir constitutif moderne. A l'opposé de l'objet qui se trouve en notre pouvoir, puisqu'il est le produit de nos propres constitutions, la chose rassemble. Nous sommes nous-mêmes pris dans ce rassemblement. La chose rassemble en laissant déployer tout le jeu – terre et ciel, divins et mortels – du 'quadriparti' (*das Geviert*). La pensée en quête de la chose, dites-vous, reconduit au monde de la vie et de la mort. Ce jeu dans lequel la chose se montre et rassemble, est laissé à notre vigilance proprement philosophique.

A ce moment, vous introduisez la notion heideggérienne de présence, non pas dans le sens métaphysique de présence intégrale disponible, mais de présence de l'être dans le jeu historial de dévoilement et de voilement. Cette présence est le fruit d'un don (le don de soi et de l'être) qui n'est jamais total.

Vous passez ensuite au jeu de langage théologique pour évoquer la notion théologico-sacramentelle de présence – pour revenir deux fois à Heidegger; deux reprises dont le sens m'est partiellement échappé.

La première fois, vour revenez à la notion de facticité pour penser le caractère contingent de la célébration liturgique. Chez Heidegger, pour autant que je me rappelle, la facticité désigne ce à quoi nous sommes accculés sans pouvoir nous en déprendre; ce qui a emprise sur nous; ce de quoi nous ne répondons pas. A première vue, je ne vois pas très bien comment cette notion de facticité pourrait servir de base pour penser le caractère «étrange» d'une théologie de la présence sacramentelle. Est-ce que le caractère contingent de la présence sacramentelle (avec la possibilité de la fêter mais aussi de s'absenter) peut vraiment être pensé au moyen de la catégorie heideggérienne de facticité qui connote toujours l'idée d'être jeté et d'une déréliction irréparable. Comment alors relier cette facticité à un don?

Vour revenez une seconde fois à Heidegger afin de pouvoir démolir tous les concepts qui tendent à faire de la vie liturgique une école de l'expérience religieuse. Vous préparez le terrain par un recours à la pensée heideggérienne de la 'chose' qui rassemble: un événement qui n'advient pas sans nous, quoiqu'elle n'advient face à nous (l'homme est toujours pris «dans» l'Eucharistie, il n'y est point un spectateur). Dans la liturgie, dites-vous, Dieu est présent comme chose. L'économie eucharistique de présence convoque les choses comme des choses[1], c'est-à-dire, comme des réalités qui se lient et nous lient à d'autres réalités, comme des réalités qui font œuvre de rassemblement. Quel est ici le rapport exact entre le don de l'être qui se joue dans la chose comme œuvre de rassemblement et le don de la présence divine dans la chose eucharistique? Rompre le pain pourrait avoir une signification sacrée au sens heideggérien, mais cette façon de rassembler la fertilité de la terre et le travail des mortels qui habitent cette terre, ne nous livre pas la signification théologique des choses. Vous évoquez une double présence,

---

1. La croix, le pain, la cruche, le cierge, l'encens.

celle de l'être dans la chose et celle de Dieu dans la chose. Comment elles s'y articulent? Comment s'y opère la transsignification? Si c'est exact qu'il faut démolir la réduction de la liturgie à une école de «l'expérience religieuse» dans le sens intimiste du terme, a-t-on tout dit quand on conclût que l'œuvre de la liturgie se définit comme une convocation des choses pour être offertes à la présence divine. La liturgie eucharistique ne prend pas fin au moment de l'offrande. Son sens n'est pas accompli en offrant l'hospitalité aux choses.

Institute of Philosophy   Ignace VERHACK
Katholieke Universiteit Leuven
Kardinaal Mercierplein 2
B-3000 Leuven

THE BROKEN BREAD AS THEOLOGICAL FIGURE
OF EUCHARISTIC PRESENCE

To try to think, as the present colloquium invites us, eucharistic presence in the actual context of "post-modernity", I have chosen to focus my reflection to the rite of the breaking of the bread. Before beginning with this, I believe it to be important to say a few words about this post-modernity. I leave aside the question of whether this expression is really adequate for labelling the present age. I will suffice with noting, in the footsteps of J. Baudrillard, that:

> modernity is neither a sociological concept, nor a political concept, nor properly speaking a historical concept. It is a characteristic way of civilisation, which opposes itself to the way of tradition, i.e. to all other anterior or traditional cultures (...) Since it is not a concept of analysis, there are no laws of modernity, there are only features of modernity. Neither is there a theory, but a logic of modernity, and an ideology[1].

There is no question here of extending the "features" that characterise this modernity. It is, however, indispensable to explicate a few, for the theological discourse which we will hold on the eucharistic presence of Christ is necessarily marked by these.

These features are henceforth well known from the numerous writings of the sociologists. There is no doubt that one can characterise actual (post-)modernity in a global way, as does J. Baudrillard, by the way in which it valorises newness. In difference from traditional cultures, modernity is "the tradition of the new", capable of making "of the crisis a value". This valorisation of the new, which culminates in "it is good, for it is new", is only the counterpart of what the same Baudrillard calls the absence of the referent, or a philosopher like J. Derrida, the dissemination of sense, heir, in the wake of Galileo, Darwin and Freud, of the loss of centre. Let us be a little more precise. That philosophical thinking concerning the dissemination of the sense in the pure intra-textual "process of signifying" could ever see the light of day, is possible only because – following the Heideggerian thesis of the link between

---

1. J. BAUDRILLARD, *Modernité*, in *Enc. Univ.* XV (1997) 552.

Being and Time – we have arrived at an age of the "historical deployment of the question of Being" which permits it. To be clear, this does
not mean that this thinking should necessarily be dominating in contemporary philosophical schools, but that all are marked in some way by
that which marks it, and which one can call – in a sense to which we will
have to come back to – the end of the metaphysical way of questioning,
for this is in the atmosphere of the time and even constitutes one of the
major symptoms of this time. And one of the characteristics of this
"post-modern" age resides precisely in the effacement or at least the
withdrawal of the real referents to the benefice of the "formal game of
change" (Baudrillard).

This withdrawal can be verified at all levels, and well underneath the
actual virtual images, which are precisely the paradigmatic expression of
the absence of the real referent. So, to limit ourselves to these few examples, commercial transactions are made by a pure game of writing and
anyone can buy anything from anybody by means of a bank card,
through Internet for example; or otherwise, the Norman "farmhouse"
about which the Parisian is dreaming for his holidays has almost nothing
to do, if not for a few ancient walls, with the real farm where the Norman farmer formerly slaved away during all of his existence; as for the
feast, we speak about it all the more as it is more remote from the "real"
traditional feast... Modernity accords, therefore, a great deal of importance to that which J. Baudrillard calls 'imitation, in *L'échange symbolique et la mort*: imitation of ancient habitat, imitation of direct and
"healthy" contact with nature, imitation of feast, imitation of culture,
etc. The importance is not the real "substance" of these referents, but
the game of representation that they permit, a game which is in the end
only one of a pure system of signs where the referent is nothing other
than the code itself. "The medium is the message". This famous formula
of Mac Luhan can be applied not only to media, not only to the system
of the kind formerly analysed by Roland Barthes, but to the whole of the
productions of post-modernity. Moreover, is the thinking of the "dissemination of sense" anything else than the radical philosophical version of this sociological judgement? In a broader perspective, is what we
have called the end of the metaphysical way of questioning not the
expression par excellence of a society which has ceased its foundation in
"God" or in the "Tradition", and which has constantly to endeavour to
make of democratic debate the key to its survival?

This brief analysis reminds us that the ongoing cultural changes are
profound, so very profound that they are spoken about, correctly it seems,
as a "mutation". This mutation touches at the very heart of "subjects",

insofar as it affects the symbolic matrix itself where norms and values are generated. This clearly raises a serious question for theology, if it is true that theology, as discourse of *fides quaerens intellectum*, has as its task to express the mystery of the God revealed in Jesus Christ with new freshness in the cultural categories of a time. With regard to the subject which has our attention, the question posed by this mutation is of particular importance. We indeed perceive immediately that the confession of the presence of Christ in the eucharist clashes head-on with what we consider to be one of the major symptoms of actual modernity: the dissolution of properly objective or "substantial" referents. Indeed, to recapture the problematic of St. Thomas, the eucharist has this uniquely with regard to all the other sacraments that where these latter realise themselves *in suscipiente*, and so happen only *in ordine ad aliud*, namely relatively to the receiving subject, only the first realises itself *in ipsa materia* and *absolute*, so even before its being used by the subject, for it "contains Christ himself" (III, q. 73, a.1, ad 3) – the reason for which it is called frequently "the sacrament par excellence" or even, in an antonomasia, "*the* sacrament", the "*holy*" sacrament. Hence nothing more "objective" than the aforementioned "real presence", and nothing, in consequence, which clashes more directly with contemporary culture. All of this, to be sure, is not new in itself: if one recalls the feats of thinking of which the great scholastics of the 13th century had to give proof with regard to eucharistic presence, which Thomas Aquinas declared "more miraculous than creation"[2], if one recalls the kind of agnosticism which the great Pascal professed in front of this mystery which he confessed as "the most strange and the most obscure secret" of the hidden God[3], one indeed realises that Christian reflection has not waited for our time to perceive in this one of the major challenges launched at believing reason. What is new, on the contrary, is the fact that this mystery clashes not only with reason "in general terms", as in preceding ages, but with the cultural shape of this reason.

I. The Triple Determination of Truth [4]

How then to think theologically this mystery in actual modernity? My proposition will be the following: what is at stake is to cross that which

---

2. *Summa Theol.* III, q.75, a.8, ad 3.
3. PASCAL, *Oeuvres*, Paris, ed. Brunschvicg, 1914, pp. 88-89.
4. This paragraph takes its inspiration from a conference of Joseph CAILLOT entitled *Les dogmes entre histoire et vérité*, published in *Vérité et histoire en théologie*, Paris, Inst. Cath. de Paris, Dec. 1996, pp. 93-113.

indicates the function "meta" of metaphysics with what Paul Ricœur calls the hermeneutic graft of phenomenology. If one wanted to represent this proposition visually, one would make a triangle of which the three points would represent the "meta" of metaphysics, phenomenology and hermeneutics, and of which the surface would represent the range of truth, which can today be enounced only according to the triple determination which we just mentioned. Let us be precise: the phenomenological and hermeneutic determinations of the truth clearly do not simply add themselves to the metaphysical determination; they come to affect this latter profoundly. Let us explain.

1. We can no longer think the eucharistic mystery in the wake of metaphysical theology or classical onto-theology. Yet this does not mean that the metaphysical register of the determination of truth would have nothing to say to us anymore and should be thrown into the dustbin of history. I have learned, especially from Heidegger, that "metaphysics" as a profile of philosophical thinking inherited from Athens is not a mistake which one might erase with one stroke of the pen "as one gets rid of an opinion", but the slope on which Western thinking has inexorably been carried along from the moment when it has forgotten the ontical-ontological difference of being and Being, and that the famous "surpassing" of metaphysics in no way means the rejection of it. On the contrary, it requires that, ruminating for a long time on the tradition of thinking which bears this name, one meditates this on which it founds itself unknowingly, and which is the thinking of "stable foundations", of the *ousia*, of full presence. To surpass metaphysics by "deconstructing" it, is to be brought to clear that which Stanislas Breton has called "the 'meta' function", a term to be understood in the sense of the "metaphor", i.e. of what is only heard well on the condition of being "brought beyond" the term, a "beyond" which the great thinkers have minted as a critical exponent with regard to their discourse under the approximative mode of a Greek *oion* or of a Latin *quodammodo*. This "beyond" has a double range. On one hand, it reminds us that the force of metaphysics is to always have resisted the reduction – be it subjectivist or intra-textual – of truth. The real, in other words, is always greater than our discourses and concepts and imposes itself on them in what should then be called "objectivity". On the other hand, and as a consequence, it permits the interconnection of the whole of humanity under the "objective" instance of truth into a universal community.

Yet this objectivity and universality of the truth can no longer be held without the principle itself taking into account the concrete mediations in which it arrives and gives itself. Being itself deploys itself temporally (*Sein und Zeit*) or, to say this in a simpler way, the truth never comes up in an other way than through historical mediations. As M. de Certeau wrote in this sense: "each affirmation remains internal to a language". And these mediations, according to the term of P. Ricœur, are "long". They are long for a double reason: being numerous (linguistic, historical, psychological, sociological…), they require immense work; being likewise dense, they resist a too easy dissolution and oppose in this way the desire of touching the "Thing" immediately, inhabiting anybody, a desire which, precisely in its metaphysical version, has taken the form of forcing the real to fit into the schemes of reason, or of this most relentless enemy of thinking which is called "the rage of knowing".

The patient passage via mediations has opened up the way firstly to phenomenology, and after that to hermeneutics. The first vitally preserves the souvenir of the "meta" function, because it starts from the thought that truth arises by transcendental donation. But it inscribes this function immediately in the thickness of the concrete things. Because of the intentionality of conscience, the human being is indeed inside him/herself only while being always already on the outside, over there, near the object. As a consequence, the truth gives itself to him/her only in the mediation of the "world" in its most humble contingencies. To recall here certain meditations of Heidegger, everything from a simple pitcher or a bridge to a Greek temple or a painting of Van Gogh, offers itself to the manifestation of truth, i.e. to its deployment in view of an "accomplishment" which is never complete. And this deployment is effectuated in the heart itself of a *chiaroscuro*, of a "clearing" (Heidegger) which is never the pure light of Greek *theoria*. Phenomenology thus struggles with the world's opacity. But it struggles with that opacity with the assurance of being able to epiphanise the true which is always in excess, an excess which prevents the thinker from being able to "control" the real. Phenomenology thus has to deal with the "long mediations", the ones of the thing as it happens.

Hermeneutics also has to deal with long mediations, but this time the ones of the text. We know how much the most recent work of Ricœur has paid attention to this matter, as if for him the "hermeneutic graft of phenomenology" was relieved by an "analytical" graft (in the sense of analytical philosophy of language) of hermeneutics. In his debates with structuralism, especially in *Conflict of Interpretations*, the author has particularly retained the necessity of going through the text so that it gives itself in its structured positivity: "a new hermeneutical era is opened by the success of structural analysis; explanation is from now on the obligatory road of comprehension"[5]. A text carries far more than the intention of its author; largely overflowing this, one finds there indeed not only the personal particularities of the author, (one's "style" and, more profoundly, the history of one's own unconscious desire), but also, in a coded way, one's whole "world" of tradition, culture, socials interests, etc. The same thing happens on the side of the reader (or the listener): one reads the text starting from one's own "world", so from a place which is not neutral. As such, two "worlds" confront each other in all reading of texts, the reason for which precisely "another possible world" is opened up for the reader. This is the very bottom of hermeneutics according to Ricœur:

> To understand oneself, is to understand oneself in front of the text and receive from it the conditions of a oneself [soi] other than the me [moi] which comes to the reading [6].

All writing or all reading is in this way "situated". At the time of St. Augustine, the Bible was not read with the same cultural glasses as during Middle Ages, or at the end of our 20th century. To take an example which is directly linked with the present proposal, no theology of the eucharist was discovered in the story of Emmaüs, or at least not in an immediate way[7].

2. In this context, it is evident that we can no longer think theologically the presence of Christ in the eucharist starting only from the point of view of metaphysical substance. To be sure, the function "meta" – which is like a priority at stake in this domain of thinking – probably expresses something very important, and which we will have to remember. But this metaphysical determination of eucharistic truth can only hold if the aforementioned function "meta" which it bears is thought from the point of view of the two other determinations of which we have just been reminded. The hermeneutical determination has to make clear the cultural particularity of the discourses hold on the eucharistic mystery, that is to make it clear not only from the point of view of aim and argumentation, but also – and maybe even above all – from the point of view of the theological style of writing of the time and the cultural "world" of which the text is bearer. Between, for example, the "metaphorical" writing of the Fathers (cf., for example, the famous "*be*

---

5. P. RICŒUR, *Du texte à l'action. Essais d'herméneutique II*, Paris, Seuil, 1986, p. 123.

6. *Ibid.*, p. 31.

7. Cf. P. PRETOT, *Les yeux ouverts des pèlerins d'Emmaüs*, in *La maison-Dieu* 195 (1993) 7-48.   .

what you see" of Augustine with regard to the eucharistic body), the demonstrative writing of the great systematic syntheses of the Scholastics and the narrative writing of the actual theologians, there are major fundamental differences which have to do with the form itself. The task of hermeneutics is precisely – in going through the texts in the positivity of their historical and cultural alterity – to let appear that the same eucharistic mystery has not been expressed, thought, or lived in the same way according to the times and places. It is evidently not a question of effectuating such a task in this modest contribution. It is nonetheless in this spirit that we will start by looking at the scholastic discourses concerning "real presence".

After having so evaluated the distance which separates us from classical discourse on this matter, we will be driven to try to express the mystery at stake in a new way. We will do so from a phenomenological point of view, gradually focussing our attention on the rite of the breaking of the bread. We would like to bring to the fore that of which such a rite is bearer, and to try and think the mystery of the eucharistic presence of Christ starting from there.

II. THE SCOLASTIC AND TRIDENTINE DOCTRINE OF TRANSUBSTANTIATION: HERMENEUTICAL APPROACH

1. *"Substantia"*

To begin, let us recall some ideas – however well-known – concerning the concept of "transubstantiation". The first is that this concept intends to hold the objectivity of the sacramental presence of Christ in the bread and the wine, affirmed by the Church in the liturgy (especially in the *"corpus Christi"* of communion) while at the same time rejecting the reification of this objectivity. Indeed, from the historical point of view, this concept (used from the beginning of the 12th century by Alger of Liege) has developed in reaction to the ultra-realism of the 11th and of the beginning of the 12th century, where the body of Christ was supposed to adhere in such an immediate way to the species of the bread that a miracle of God was needed (a second one, after the one of the transformation of the bread and wine into the body and blood of Christ) to maintain the veil which hid it. The presupposition was that "normally" one should have seen it – a vision moreover that did not fail in being verified at the time: eucharistic miracles were abounding then[8]!

---

8. Cf. E. DUMOUTET, *Corpus Domini. Aux sources de la piété eucharistique médiévale*, Paris, Beauchesne, 1942. – In addition, let us remember that the theory of Isidore of

Such an immediacy logically resulted in affirmations of a "sensualist" type, according to which Christ is broken by the hands of the priest and grinded by the teeth of the faithful. One understands, without therefore approving it, the reaction of Berenger of Tours, this is to say for what reason, for the first time in history, one came to deny the *veritas* of the presence of Christ in the Eucharist. Neither should it should be surprising that the profession of faith of 1059 officially imposed on this same Berenger could not avoid affirmations close to ultra-realism. The time was clearly short of conceptual tools which were sufficiently refined to respond in an adequate way to the difficulty: how to affirm, in the wake of the liturgical praxis of the Church, the reality of the presence of Christ without erasing the mediation of the *sacramentum* of the bread and the wine? The Aristotelian couple 'substance'/'accident' was for this matter of the greatest help.

It is against such "sensualism", which we have just evoked, that the great scholastic of the 13th century used the Aristotelian concept of *substance*. This *hypokeimenon* – translated literally in Latin by *sub-iectum* (which will become four centuries later the Cartesian "subject") or by *sub-stantia* – points, as known, to the ultimate reality behind the things, that which su(b/p)ports them in unity. It is neither a "this" nor a "that" (extension, colour, taste, etc.), which are "accidents"; even spatial localisation does not belong to it: a substance is only localised by means of its accidents. It is thus nothing that affects our senses (seeing, touching, tasting...). It is pure "potency" to be "actuated" in accidents, and it exists only individuated in them: "Subiectum comparatur ad accidens sicut potentia ad actum; subiectum enim secundum accidens est aliquo modo in actu" (I, q.3, a6). The concept of "substance" is thus a concept of intelligibility of the beings. To say it in the most simple way one can imagine, it enables us to understand why the table or the tree, even if my gaze perceives only the multiplicity of accidents of these, can precisely be called "table" or "tree", i.e. why it can be comprehended as forming a unity, a unity which is of another order than the multiple accidents that I perceive. Thus, through the concept of transubstantiation, i.e. of *conversio totius substantiae*, the scholastics exorcise all spatial representations (especially) because Christ is present on the level of substance, and not of accidents. So the eucharistic body can be neither divided, nor

Seville, who links the term *sacramentum* to *sacrum secretum* was at that time in vogue; it was not until 12th century that the link of Augustine (*sacrum signum*) came to the fore. For the latter, the *sacramentum* is in the first place a sign that reveals, for Isidore on the contrary, it is a veil (*tegumentum*) that hides. This theory could only but reinforce the cultural representations relative to "eucharistic miracles" of that time.

multiplied, neither transported, nor enclosed; only the sacramental sign (accident) can be. What is localised, is the sign, i.e. Christ-in-the-sacrament, hence *in specie aliena*, and not the risen Christ as such *in specie propria*. And the species are not a veil which hides him, for, as glorious, he is invisible. On the contrary, Thomas writes, they are there "so that it might be in them that one sees the body of Christ" (so *in specie aliena*), "and not in his proper aspect" (III, q.75, a.6).

This problematic of Aristotelian substance had the great advantage – on the speculative level – to allow the eucharistic *esse* of Christ to be thought in all of its realism without being victim, as in the anterior problematic, of a representation of immediacy which overran the mediation of the *sacramentum* so directly that it in a way crushed it. On the level of the theology of liturgy, moreover, it went against all representation of Christ, from the rites of Mass, as humiliated in making himself bread, as slave in obeying to the word of the priest, as shattered at the moment of the breaking of the bread, as enclosed in the prison of the tabernacle, as affected by the sacrilegious soul who receives him, etc.; all this was indeed rejected. From this point of view the question – as famous in the time of scholastic thinking as is seems futile today – *quid sumit mus?* is extremely significant [9]. Finally, on the pastoral level, the theology of transubstantiation allowed Christians to understand why the fact of receiving two hosts or only a half at the time of communion procures neither an advantage nor a disadvantage on the spiritual level! A hymn like *Lauda Sion* – thanks to St. Thomas Aquinas – was precisely in charge of explaining and inculcating this to everybody [10].

2. *Aporias*

Such a theory was nevertheless confronted with at least two aporias. The first concerns the concept of "transubstantiation" itself, to the degree that it signifies *conversio totius substantiae*. The scholastics did not fail to perceive an internal contradiction in this expression. For who says "conversion" says passage or transformation from one substance to another, and this rejects all idea of annihilation of the first substance or of substitution of the second to the first: the bread "becomes" (*ginetai, fit)* the body of Christ; it is not annihilated. Yet, according to the physics

9. For a quick survey of the principal theological positions on this subject, see A.M. ROGUET, tome II du traité de l'eucharistie de S. Thomas dans la collection *Revue des jeunes*, Paris – Tournai – Rome, Desclée 1967, pp. 339-340 and cf. P.M. GY, *La liturgie dans l'histoire,* Paris, Cerf, 1990, pp. 258-259.

10. Concerning this passage, one can ask oneself, whatever the beauty of this hymn may be, whether we are not dealing here with a didactic derivative of liturgy.

of the time, there exists no conversion of a *complete* substance into an other: when fire transforms the wood in ashes – to take an image used by Thomas with regard to this – there always remains something of the wood. Are we not therefore dealing with a "creation", for only this latter consists of the apparition of a total newness? Not any more, for creation, understood in strict sense, is conceived of only *ex nihilo*. Thus one finds oneself obliged to cross two contradictory concepts on this point. Even more important is the second aporia, even if well-known: how can accidents subsist without their *sub-stantia*, their *sub-iectum*, their subject of inhesion? Here, Thomas consciously wrings the neck of Aristotelianism. He exhausts himself then in a way to show that the first of the accidents, namely the quantity, can be given by God as substitute for the substance of the bread to the accidents which then persist.

3. *Hermeneutic*

The discourse of Thomas is a typically scholastic one. To be sure, differences exist, on this matter as a number of others, between him and his predecessors or his contemporary scholastics (Bonaventure, for example)[11]. But all are part of the same theological model, a model itself to be understood from the "world" of the time. Let us recall in this regard that this was a time is of clarification and precision. Sustained by a full demography, a prosperous economy, an urbanism coming alive again, flourishing schools of theology, all demonstrate a basic optimism with regard to the capacities of reason with which God endowed humans. The new *scolares*, socially in solidarity with the citizens and their desire of emancipation, and intellectually open to the disputes of the grammaticians and logicians of Chartres or Laon, generate that which "was the project of this (12th) century: faith being elaborated into science"[12], thanks in particular to the refined technique of the *quaestio*. The "symbolic mentality" (id.) of the Roman age remains certainly abiding, but it little by little becomes mastered and ordered. Systematic theological constructions are elaborated then with the same boldness and the same concern for clarity as the gothic cathedrals (E. Panofsky). It is under the effect of this undoubtedly new cultural imperative that for the first time, the need is born, unknown unto then, for precision, for example, the "specific difference" and the number of the sacraments properly speaking.

11. Cf. P.M. GY, *La relation au Christ dans l'eucharistie selon S. Bonaventure et S. Thomas d'Aquin,* dans *La liturgie dans l'histoire* (n. 9), pp. 247-283.
12. M.D. CHENU, *La théologie au XII° siècle*, Paris, Vrin, 1956, p. 329.

A new theological writing thus appears, opposed to the "ancient" monastic theology, which was in fact only "a piece of the divine office" (Chenu). It could even constitute itself only by breaking out of the too heavy pressure of liturgy, to the risk of loosing, as this will happen at the end of the Middle Ages, its living link to the latter and of drifting in such a way towards mere speculation. To be sure, when Thomas Aquinas comments on the Scriptures, he remains close to the *lectio divina* and the liturgy; he does not, however, fear to play with the metaphors and add his part to typology so prized in former times by the Fathers. On the contrary, in his systematic works, his discourse appears as entirely conceived and guided as a formal logic, as a *scientia*.

The discourse of scholasticism clearly requires to be understood hermeneutically starting from this particular cultural world. The focus of the whole reflection on *substantia* must be understood as the way, for the time, to think the mystery of eucharistic presence in new terms, and to think it in its radicality but in short-cutting the serious impasses of the anterior theology (the one, for example, of Petrus Damianus or of Lanfranc), i.e. reifying representation of the mystery. We must see in this kind of contraction of the time on the *substantia* the expression of what I have called before a cultural imperative: the new class of *magistri* could clearly no longer live without elaborating in this domain, as in others, a new discourse. In this sense, to write means to live. Yet it remains nonetheless that this discourse cannot be reduced to the particularity of its cultural location. Moreover, the fact that this type of discourse was dogmatically adopted – even if revised at the council of Trent in function of the couple "substance/species" to avoid the Church having to link itself officially to a particular philosophical system – is of course important in this respect. In the end, hermeneutically understood, the scholastic-tridentine discourse of the conversion of the substance of the bread and the wine into the body and the blood of Christ interpellates today's theologian on at least two levels: on the one hand, in that it expresses the radicality of what the Church believes on this matter; on the other, in that it gives one to think with regard to the links between theology and liturgy.

Radicality

Indeed, the investigated discourse signifies the transformation of the ultimate reality of the bread and the wine, then expressed by the term of substance; but expressed, we are reminded, at the price of a kind of philosophical monstrosity: accidents which subsist without their substance. The term "monstrosity" which I have just used is deliberately

borrowed from the famous analysis which P. Ricœur has made of original sin in *Le conflit des interprétations*[13]. He shows there indeed how
this concept is "desperate" because it "monstrously combines" will and
nature, putting some of the voluntary (the "sin") into the unvoluntary (a
state acquired by nature)[14]. But he does not fail in saluting to the mas-
terly Augustinian enterprise on this point: Augustine has attempted with
a remarkable boldness if not to solve the aporia of the origin of evil, at
least to face it and to think it in such a way that it is attributed neither to
an *Anankè* or an exterior *Fatum*, even if the latter might adopt the face
of God, nor inversely to the sole responsibility of humans. In so doing,
he has somehow rejoined the double intentionality of the metaphorical
language at work in the Adamic myth of Genesis: to clear God of all
responsibility regarding the origin of evil without thereby attributing this
evil to the sole will of humans, for the serpent was already there; at the
same time, to give account in this way for the contradiction which the
human being feels in his/her experience of evil-doing: contradiction
between the necessary imputation of this evil to its author, which
engages his/her ethical responsibility, and the feeling that all the same
this evil was not simply wanted, but that it is the effect of a kind of law
which overflows everybody so as to make one cry out sometimes: "It is
stronger than myself!" (cf. Rom. 7). After all, the Augustinian concept
or rather "pseudo-concept" of "original sin" is "full of a dark analogical richness"[15]. It is not sure that its inventor [16] has known or has been
able to recognise the part of obscurity which the clarity of his concept
held back. To avoid making this tumble to the side of knowledge and
thus to fall back in a "quasi-Gnostic" attitude, he should have recon-
ducted it towards the symbolic images of the Adamic myth from where
he had drawn it. Yet one can only salute the gesture of thought which he
has attempted. There are aporias or mysteries which one must have the
courage to think, even if one knows in advance that they defy all
answers. The origin of evil belongs to such questions which hold for
themselves, for the path they make the thinker go, and not for the knowledge to which they would be assumed to lead.

Would the same not count, *mutatis mutandis*, in the case of the concept
– also philosophically untenable – of transubstantiation? The Council of

---

13. P. Ricœur, *Le péché originel. Étude de signification*, in Id., *Le conflit des interprétations*, Paris, Seuil, 1969, pp. 265-282.

14. *Ibid.*, p. 281.

15. *Ibid.*, p. 277.

16. Remember that Augustine is the inventor not only of the expression but also the
content, which was recognised as essential by the Church from the Council of Carthage
in 418.

Trent has, moreover, been prudent in this respect, and declares that this
concept suits "aptissime" the expression of the faith of the Church. The
superlative must not deceive: it signifies all as well that, in consequence,
other conceptualisations are theoretically possible, on condition of
respecting the radicality of what is at stake in the prefix "trans-" and
which Thomas has thought with Aristotelian concepts. As a consequence, a correct hermeneutical reading leads us to think that it is theologically possible, on this condition, to formulate the mystery of the
eucharistic presence in an other way. The "trans-" (as the "meta-" of
the Greek Fathers: *metaballô; metaruthmizô, etc)* has a warning function indicating – like the light of a lamp flashing on and off – the direction one should not loose sight of.

Link to Liturgical Celebration

The second interpellation concerns the link between theological discourse and the *liturgical celebration*. If Thomas Aquinas has displayed
such efforts to critically approach the eucharistic mystery, it is for the
purpose of giving an account of the language act pronounced at communion: "Le corps du Christ – Amen", itself echo of the "ceci est mon
corps" of the institution narrative. This means that, even for this type of
theology, the liturgy remains a major place of reference. Still, one
clearly has to recognise that scholasticism has not made of this a properly theological locus: was it not constituted – as I formerly recalled –
by taking its distance with regard to liturgy? The language act "*the body
of Christ*" is thus not taken properly speaking as a liturgical text, but as
a theological statement. The ritual context in which it takes place is not
taken into consideration as having a pertinence with regard to the theological significance of the statement. The semantics, in other words, is
judged totally independent from the pragmatics. At the same time, nothing comes to loosen the atmosphere of intellectual reflection in some
way: the concept is hardened to its maximum, without any flaw, without
in any way referring to the liturgical "text" (words, gestures, materials,
etc.) in which it is born and where it could have found the suppleness of
the metaphors. In saying this, I do not intend to disqualify the concept as
such, but to recall that, as in the problematic of original sin developed by
Ricœur, the concept – as indispensable as it may be – must be taken for
a moment of theological reflection and be referred to the ritual symbols
where it has place to avoid freezing into pseudo-knowledge.

I spoke previously about "ritual context". In fact, rituality is far more
than a simple "con-text" accompanying the liturgical text. It is constitutive of the textuality itself of this text, because the latter (the expression

"the body of Christ", as it happens) does not exist to be read "flatly" in an office as a dogmatic text, but to be set at work in the celebration. The enounced is here inseparable from its ritual enunciation (address to the communicant, tune of voice, gesture, posture...). Rituality thus genuinely constitutes the "pre-text" of the text, the page in a way on which the text is written. From the hermeneutical point of view, this means that if truth, in a general way, can not be unbound from the textual mediation in which it happens (cf. the famous "explaining more to understand better" of Ricœur) then the particular truth concerning eucharistic presence can not be enounced outside the very textuality of the evoked liturgical enounced. It is precisely towards this act that we will turn in a moment; not however before having evoked what seems to constitutes the major limit of the scholastic problematic of transubstantiation.

4. *Major Limit*

This passage through the symbolic praxis of the celebration is all the more important when it is opposed to the major limit of the scholastic problematic: the forgetting of the relation. Let us explain ourselves. The heresy of Berengarius had created a real traumatism in the Church in the 11th century. To avoid all risk of relapse in this direction, they started emphasising the link between the eucharistic body of Christ and his historical and glorious body so strongly that they came to the point of loosening the link between this same eucharistic body and the ecclesial body of Christ, a link which had, to the contrary, been strongly highlighted in former times by the Fathers (because the Church was then considered to be the "*veritas*" of the "eucharistic mystical body"). The loosening even takes the appearance, according to de Lubac, of a "*lethal caesura*"[17]. In difference from the body of Christ really present in the bread/wine (*res significata et contenta,* was the 12th century term), the ecclesial body is hence only the *res significata et non contenta* (P. Lombardus). Thus, "the ultimate reality of the sacrament", i.e. the unity of the ecclesial body, "which was previously the thing and the truth par excellence of it, is expelled from the sacrament itself". To be sure, the great scholastics do not forget that the ecclesial body remains the finality of the sacrament. The simple fact that the expression *corpus mysticum* has passed, by the end of the 12th century, from the eucharist (body in "mystery") to the Church is significant in this respect. Moreover, according to the general doctrine of the great scholastics, is not the

---

17. H. DE LUBAC, *Corpus mysticum. L'Église et l'eucharistie au Moyen Age*, Paris, Aubier, 1944.

unity of the Church, by the link of charity, the ultimate *res* of the eucharist? Yet the ecclesial body of Christ no longer belongs to the "intrinsic symbolism" of the eucharist. As a consequence, "from now on it will be possible for one not to mention (this ecclesial body) without doing harm to the integrity of the sacrament"[18].

From this one understands that the connection to the Church is practically forgotten as soon as reflection is concentrated on the analysis of the presence itself and its *quomodo*. This is isolated then as a thing in itself, and is being thought in the sole register of "substance". In this way, the "ad-" implied by the notion itself of presence (*ad-esse*) is put in parentheses to the profit of the sole substantial *esse*. Moreover, does this *ad*, as expression of a relation, not belong, just like the notion of *praesentia*[19], to the accidents? Anyway, even if the expression of *praesentia corporalis* is well admitted by the scholastics, the vocabulary of "presence" was far less familiar then than today and did not have the force given to it since by the rise of subjectivity and by phenomenology. The lexicon then accustomed with regard to the eucharist was that of *esse*, even of *existere*.

The same happens at the Council of Trent. This certainly finds back the patristic vein, in its "Doctrine on the most holy eucharist" (1551), reminding that the eucharist "is the symbol (symbolum) of this unique 'Body' of which Christ is 'the head'" (ch. 2), or once more that it is the *signum unitatis*, the *vinculum caritatis*, the *symbolum concordiae* (ch. 8). But these Augustinian expressions come only in the final stage of a doctrine of which the essential has been expressed before and rather as an appeal to the unity of divided Christians than as a theological expression of the eucharistic presence of the Lord. In any case the Augustinian symbolism, which had for such a long time radiated the theology of the eucharist, had to a large extent lost its force[20]. Indeed, in the tridentine texts this symbolism hardly matches the weight with regard to the four *contineri*, the three *esse* or *vere esse* which have for their subject "the body and the blood of Christ", and also to the three *existere* which have Christ for their subject, which are found in chapters 1, 3 and 4 and the canons 1, 3 and 4; for all the attention is centred on the affirmation of the real presence, from which follow firstly, in ch. 5, the veneration due to the Blessed Sacrament (even if it is said there that Christ

---

18. *Ibid.*, pp. 280-283.

19. P.M. GY, *La relation au Christ dans l'eucharistie selon S. Bonaventure et S. Thomas d'Aquin* (n. 9), p. 242: "Cette notion [de praesentia corporalis] gêne S. Thomas, parce qu'elle lui paraît liée à une localisation", donc aux accidents.

20. Cf. A. DUVAL, *Des sacrements au concile de Trente*, Paris, Cerf, 1985, pp. 55-56.

has instituted the eucharist as nourishment), next, in chapters 6 to 8, communion. The anti-protestant aim of Trent certainly has something to do with this insistence, but as important as this is, the cyclical element does not explain everything: it is, more profoundly, the "archaeology" itself of the knowledge and the theological "epistèmè" which explain this concentration. Moreover, if it is true that the council remained "up to the end prisoner" of the "dualist problematic" separating the "sacrament" (real presence) (1551) from the "sacrifice" ("propitiatory" effectiveness of Mass) (1563)[21], it was difficult for it to think the eucharistic presence of Christ as "being-for", because this "being-for" is the expression of the "sacrificial" gift which he made of his life; and it was difficult for it to simultaneously think the eucharist in its intrinsic report to the Church...

III. The Breaking of the Bread:
A Phenomenological Approach

Whereas the metaphysical theology of St. Thomas moved the liturgical action and hence the relation to the *ecclesia* apart from reflection on the substantial presence of Christ in the eucharist, does the phenomenological approach to the contrary inscribe itself in this field straightaway. I specify that if I have chosen this rite rather than, for example, the one of the elevation, it is for two quite simple reasons: the first is that the elevation is born precisely in connection to the theology of transubstantiation, and meant, at least indirectly, to reinforce the latter; the second is that, from the point of view of the history of liturgy, the rite of the breaking of the bread appears, both by its antiquity and by its symbolism (cf. e.g. 1 Cor 10,16), as a sacramental rite of the first order, which is not at all the case for the elevation.

1. *The Being-for (adesse) Is Constitutive of Sacramental Being (esse)*

a. The rite of the breaking of the bread takes place at a certain moment of the eucharistic celebration. This moment must be taken into consideration. For one could imagine that it opens the latter as it opened the Jewish supper and that it continues from this fact to indicate, by incorporating the whole of the eucharistic liturgy, as is seen with the *klasis tou artou* of the Lukan corpus. Or otherwise, it could be executed during the narration of the institution at the time of the words "he broke it", a

---

21. *Ibid.*, p. 72.

possibility which would confirm the theology of the priest acting *in persona Christi*. It has never been like that in any of the great liturgical families, but there is ample space for thinking that the temptation of it has had to be strong, for one sees certain manuscripts of the Middle Ages prescribing to the priest at that moment to "feign" the fraction/breaking (*fingat frangere* or something of the kind)[22], and that, in any case the priest at that time was imitating Christ taking the bread in his hands and lifting the eyes to heaven before pronouncing the "this is my body". The execution of the breaking at that moment would moreover have been in coherence with the theology of St. Thomas, for the latter goes as far as to declare that at the moment where he pronounces the *verba Christi*, the priest acts no longer *in persona ecclesiae* but only *in persona Christi*[23]. As such, Thomas gives maximum emphasis to the link of the priest to Christ; he interprets it – if one picks up the categories of the semiotics of C.S. Peirce – as a relation of "image" (the picture in comparison to the real) and as a consequence not only as a relation of "diagram" (the geography card in comparison to the area) or as a relation of "indication" (the weathercock in comparison to the wind)[24]. Despite everything, Thomas does not even seem to envisage the hypothesis of the breaking in the narration of the institution. To say this in terms that were not those of the Middle Ages, "memorial" is not at all "mime", and if it is true that the narration of the institution is central in the eucharistic prayer, this is because – as is well-known – the four technical verbs which indicate there the actions of Jesus at the Last Supper structure the whole of the liturgy of the eucharist, from the presentation of the gifts ("he took the bread") through communion ("and gave it to them"), passing through the eucharistic prayer ("said the blessing") and the breaking of the bread ("broke it"). In this logic, the last could evidently take place only after the eucharistic prayer.

22. See R. POTHIER, *La fraction du pain,* Paris, Mémoire de l'Institut Supérieur de Liturgie, 1990.

23. ST III, q. 82, a. 7, ad 3. Cf. B.D. MARLIANGEAS, *Clés pour une théologie des ministères: in persona Christi, in persona Ecclesiae,* Paris, Beauchesne, 1978, pp. 118-122.

24. In fact, the categories of "image" and of "diagramme" are regrouped by PEIRCE in the one of "icon". In good Catholic theology, the link between the representant (priest) and the represented (Christ) does not need to be thought of under the mode of the "image". The "diagramme" and even the "sign" suffice. To the contrary, the relation of "symbol" (in the sense of Peirce, i.e. the link between an object and the completely arbitrary linguistic sign, which represents it) seems insufficient. One presumes the interest of these perspectives to "release" Catholic theology on this subject, notably in the question of the representation of Christ by a woman. Cf. L.-M. CHAUVET, *La fonction du prêtre dans le récit de l'institution à la lumière de la linguistique,* in *Revue de l'Institut Catholique de Paris* 56 (Oct.-Dec. 1995) 41-61.

b. The theological intelligence of the eucharistic presence of Christ from a Christian perspective is necessarily affected by the fact that the rite of the breaking is situated just before communion, so towards the end of Mass. It appears thus as the fruit of a dynamics of celebration, the principal elements of which I would like to quickly recall.

First, if we look at *the whole of the celebration*, we observe that this dynamics moves from the constitution of the assembly as Church ("The Lord be with you": Christ who comes into presence in the eucharist is thus the one presiding the assembly; he doesn't come from nowhere), going through the table of the Word ("Let us proclaim the Word of God": Christ who comes into presence in the eucharist is thus the one speaking to his Church in the Scriptures), to the table of the eucharist ("This is my body which is given up for you"). This shows us already that eucharistic presence can only be understood as the crystallisation of the Word in visible form: *sacramentum est quasi visibile verbum* (Augustine).

Let us now concentrate our attention on the *eucharistic prayer*. Two principal traits need to be highlighted. First trait: eucharistic presence comes up at the heart of a prayer of which the movement goes from the memory of the past in thanksgiving to the memory of the future in eschatological supplication. In this perspective – as C. Perrot has highlighted formerly in an article which became famous – eucharistic presence can only be understood starting from a "double distance between the yesterday of Golgotha and the future of Parousia". Its relation to the Parousia prohibits it from be reduced to a simple historical evocation of the cross which would assimilate the Christian meal to Greek funerary rites; its relation to the past of Golgotha prohibits it from remaining in the register of pure Jewish expectation; and the gap between the two crosses its very truth of presence with the mark of absence, which prohibits conceiving it as a "full" presence, in the Gnostic way[25]. This reminds us that, from the point of view of ancient tradition, of which liturgy continues to let us hear the echo, the category of "memory" is far more important than the one of "presence", and that, from the properly Christian point of view, the second asks to be understood starting from the first.

Second trait: this presence cannot be dissociated from the epiclesis. This latter – at least in its achieved form which it has acquired since the

25. C. PERROT, *L'anamnèse neo-testamentaire*, in *Revue de l'Institut Catholique de Paris*, April (1982) 21-37.

end of the 4th century, notably in the Antiochean tradition – has a theological structure which is the following: that the Spirit sanctifies the bread and the wine to make it into the body and the blood of Christ, *in order that* those who will participate in it through communion be assembled (by the same Spirit) in "one single body". When, as in the eucharistic prayers of Vatican II, this epiclesis is double (before and after the institution narrative) it splits that which the unique epiclesis of the Antiochean tradition expresses in a single prayer[26]. This link with the epiclesis reminds us not only that the sacramental "body" of Christ is a "spiritual body", hence not representable, it also underlines – and this point is of particular importance to our reflection – that if the eucharist is indeed the personal body of Christ, this is as the latter is, following the very correct formula of J.M. Tillard: "enacting the vivification of his ecclesial Body through the Holy Spirit. It gives the personal body, but in the indissoluble link which unites it to the ecclesial Body"[27]. As such, it is impossible to think this body "in itself", independently from the Church! As a body realised by the Spirit, the eucharistic body becomes present only to make the Church itself realised, following the third article of the Credo, by the same Spirit. From this results – as the Fathers have so frequently emphasised – that, following Augustinian vocabulary, the one who is not in the living communion of the ecclesial body receives the body of Christ ritually (*sacramentaliter*), but does not receive it spiritually (*spiritualiter*): one's communion is without fecundity; it is even for one's condemnation (cf. 1 Cor 11). "One should not say that someone eats the body of Christ who is not in the body of Christ" [28].

Finally, let us focus on the *narrative of the institution* itself. The double saying over on the bread and the wine does not only say the body

---

26. In doing this, Vatican II has situated itself in the wake of the Alexandrine tradition. On the other hand and above all, it has wished to avoid to create again difficulties with regard to the "moment of the consecration", which the latin tradition situates in the narrative of the institution, whereas the syrian tradition situates it in the epiclesis following on the narrative of the institution. One can regret that, from this fact, no eucharistic prayer at all of Vatican II has adopted this second point of view, of which one knows that it is just as legitimate.

27. J.M. TILLARD, *Chair de l'Église, chair du Christ*, Paris, Cerf, 1992, p. 64.

28. AUGUSTINE, *City of God* XXI, 35. The Medievals, who knew Augustine well, had not forgotten this truth. For example, BONAVENTURE: "He who wants to approach in a dignified manner the body of Christ must eat it spiritually to chew it (masticet) in this way by the reflection of faith and receive it by the fervour of love. In doing so, he does not transform Christ into him, but it is rather he himself who is projected in his mystical body". ("sed ipse potius traiiciatur in eius mysticum corpus") – *Breviloquium* VI, 9,6.

and blood, but says them as gift "for" (*hyper*). As such, it does not say them as *absolute*, but *relative*. This being-relative, made explicit by the "take and eat from it (or drink from it)" is moreover made visible by the double gesture of "breaking" and of "giving", gestures which have to be considered as "incorporated words". Furthermore, the material itself is the indicator of this relation of gift. Indeed – we will come back to this in a minute – it belongs to the "essential-being" of the bread and the wine to be for their incorporation by the human being. From the phenomenological standpoint, the intentionality of "presence" comes to light in a way from the figure formed by this set of verbal, gestural and material elements. This indicates that the relational "for" is constitutive of the presence of Christ as such. This "for" is not a simple accidental and secondary derivation of it, nor a simple extrinsic finality. This point is of course capital: the eucharistic *esse* is constitutively an *adesse*. Consequently one can never put this *ad* between parentheses, not even during the analysis of the how of the presence.

The latter emerges perhaps with even more strength from the heart of the ritual sequence in three moments which form the breaking of the bread with, just upstream, the sign of peace exchanged between the participants, and just downstream, the communion procession. But we will come back to this point in our final part.

2. *The Pitcher and the Bread*

If one asks – a bit as Heidegger does with regard to the "pitcher"[29] – what is the bread as "thing" (in opposition to the "object")? What is its essence, the *Wesen*?, then it is clear that the latter cannot be reduced to its physico-chemical consistency. It is indeed essential to the bread that it be shared; and this, not in the first place on the scientific level of its value of use (the quantity of calories which it supplies for subsistence), but primarily on the *symbolic* level: the "bread", which one should understand here fully as the *lehem* of the Hebrew Bible, as the "give us our daily bread" of the Our Father, or the "to gain one's bread" of the French proverb (*gagner son pain*) as the symbolic represented of all nourishment (and even more largely of all which the human being needs to be able to subsist), is, by its essence, a socially instituted food. It is made for conviviality. It is essential to it that it is shared with others at a meal. If, for numerous reasons, it is not always handled like that, the bread nonetheless conserves in itself this destination which makes eating,

---

29. M. HEIDEGGER, *Essais et Conférences*, trans. A.P. Préau & J. Beaufret, Paris, Gallimard, 1958, pp. 202-205.

for the human subject, not reducible to a utilitarian act. This is why the bread, the bread-meal, is mediation of maintenance of the word as much as of biological life. It is nourishment of the desire (or of the heart) as much as of the body. In the Heideggerian problematic of the Fourfold (*das Geviert*), one notes thus that it "contains" heaven (sun, rain...) and earth (the soil where the wheat has germinated, grown and ripened) only in view of sharing these with the other "mortals" in an "offering" which permits them to "enter-tain" each other. But it also happens that the bread is presented to God as the highest word of gratitude of humans: recognition *of* God as the one who gives the bread, and through it, exis-tence itself – recognition-as-gratitude *towards* God. Let us think here of the ritual offertories or of the sacrifices of communion which the large majority of religions know. Like the "pitcher" of Heidegger, the bread never manifests its being of bread as well as in this act of religious obla-tion where, fruit of nature (earth and heaven) and fruit of history (the labour of people), it is recognised as a gracious gift of God, and where, sharing it as such (i.e. as gracious gift of God), people nourish them-selves from it. There is nothing more bread than this bread. Sharing this "essential" bread and nourishing themselves from it, they enter-tain their filial connection with their God and they enter-tain themselves mutually as believing subjects in a fraternal communion founded in the communion of all with their God. It is indeed there, in any case, that the bread fully realises its essence of bread.

The preceding reflection of course constitutes only an approach of the mystery of eucharistic presence. There is indeed an *abyss* between the affirmation according to which the bread is never bread except in the religious act where it is recognised as gracious gift from God and the affirmation of the Christian faith according to which this bread is the gracious self-giving (*l'auto-donation gracieuse*) of God Himself in Christ. While this is simply an approach, this reflection is nonetheless interesting. Would not the keeping of a distance between the confession of faith and the result of phenomenological mediation be in fact the con-dition for the eucharist not to become an idol?

3. *The Idol and the Icon*

Indeed, Catholic teaching insists on the fact that the presence of Christ in the eucharist gives itself in the mediation of a *sacramentum* which has the triple characteristic of materiality, of exteriority and of precedence. Because it happens in the sensible materiality of bread and wine, and gives itself as exterior to the faithful, as in front of them and as anterior to the use which they make of it in communion, this presence constitutes a kind of abutment upon which the temptation to reduce the mystery of God or of Jesus Christ to that which Christians say, think or experience of Him comes to vanish. It acts in this way, in its sensible materiality itself, as the highest figure of the defence against idolatry which is imposed on them; it inscribes before them the absolute alterity of God and the impossibility of all seizure of him.

If such is the case, we are in a full paradox. Indeed, on the one hand, among the propositions of faith, the affirmation of the presence of Christ in the eucharist is probably the one mostly threatened by an idolatrous, even fetishistic drift – and this because of the triple characteristic of the *sacramentum* mentioned above. But, from an other point of view, and for the same reasons of materiality, of exteriority and of precedence, to which could be added the non-figurative character of the bread and the wine, we say here that this affirmation can be understood to the contrary as the highest symbolic figure of the defence against idolatry. Let us recall at this point that idolatry resides in the reduction of God to the conditions of the experience which one says to have gained of Him. The eucharistic body of Christ, in its materiality and exteriority, represents well, in this perspective, the most resistant dam against such idolatrous reduction: the mystery of Christ and of the Gospel resists the multiple imaginary attempts to reduce it to what is said or experienced of it. Hence, would not a gesture like inclination or genuflection in front of the consecrated bread be carrying an intentionality which would catch up with the "meta function" evoked before, but expressed this time in a mode of attitude – and not simply of discourse – and of confessing attitude? Would we not face there the symbolic expression of this "always greater" or rather of this "always more other" which the apophatic tradition has attempted to express on the theoretical level by affecting its affirmations on God by a negative petitioner of supra-eminence? One is then brought to think that, far from coming under the status of the idol, the eucharist comes under that of the icon, being understood that this latter intends to preserve the alterity of what it yet wants to allow to be seen. One must not forget, however, that if the distinction between idol and icon is clear on the theoretical level, it is far less so in the facts. A bit like the distinction between "religion" and "magic", one has concretely to do rather with a polarity than with a clear border: all "iconic" representation can function as idol, just like all "religious" behaviour can drift towards "magical" conduct. Consequently, in contrast to the very ideological suspicion which leads to perceiving idolatry only with "the others" (the Catholics with their eucharist, the Protestants with their Bible, the Orthodox with their cult of sacred images, etc.) we recall here that there is, in fact, only one step between the idol and the icon. This step nevertheless crosses an abyss. This is why, without reducing the theology of the eucharist to the theology of the icon – for the link between the signifier and the signified is not at all the same in both cases – we can grant to eucharistic presence a status of icon in difference from the status of idol. In this way we are theoretically on guard against all imaginary holds on the presence of Christ.

4. *A Presence in the Mode of Openness*

Presence as Arrival

The alterity which the icon preserves is moreover inseparable from the concept of "presence". This latter is indeed not of a cosmological, but of an anthropological order, and we have known for a long time now that it designates something other than the simple factuality of subsisting beings which spread themselves before our eyes here and now in this room. The *adesse* of presence is of a different order from the simple *esse* of a mundane thing. Nothing is more present to us than the other in the other's very alterity, so from the fact that the other escapes us and that moreover, because the subject is "breach", one escapes to oneself: it is always "*as an other*" that each and every person apprehends "*oneself*"[30]. So as a concept, presence is constitutively crossed by the mark of the "absence". This does not mean only that the link presence/absence would be like the one, being dialectical, of recto to verso. Such a representation is insufficient, for it in no way prevents us from imagining the presence in the "full" way of a saturating transparency or of an unfailing given. To say that there is no presence unless crossed by absence is precisely to refuse the representation of such a saturation. This, for sure, does not weaken the reality of the aforementioned presence, but qualifies it for what it is: *human* presence. Hence, such presence can only be advent; in its very essence, it is "arrival". Who says "presence" thus says "coming-into-presence".

The Breaking of the Bread

To this first opening is added a second with regard to the presence of Christ in the bread and the wine of the eucharist. This second opening refers precisely to the preposition "in" which was just used. The

---

30. The reference is to the work of P. RICŒUR, *Soi-même comme un autre*, Paris, Seuil, 1990.

scholastics had learned from Aristotle that there are multiple ways for an ordinary being to be "in" a place and those of the 13th century had in this respect criticised the too material image of Hugo of Saint-Victor who had compared the sacraments to "vessels" containing a remedy. Moreover, Thomas among others had recalled that the glorified body of Christ in the eucharist cannot be localised because the localisation is itself accidental. It remains nevertheless that the critique of the representations is always to be taken again, probably because these representations are tied to the desire of "seeing", with all of that this seeing can capture, when it concerns the consecrated host. From this point of view, we have seen to what degree the pre-scholastic theories of eucharistic presence were restricted by the immediacy of this seeing. Moreover, still today is not the exposition of the holy sacrament in a radiant monstrance for adoration suspicious of playing on this highly ambiguous register? I do not intend to say that the praxis of the adoration of Christ in the eucharist – even if it has been developed only in the Latin Church and from the Middle Ages on – would not be theologically legitimate whenever it is lived, in the way Vatican II reminded, in the wake of the eucharistic action, with its large dimension of eating the Word of God, of thanksgiving, of offertory, of supplication... I simply want to recall that in the domain of ritual practices the signifiers or the symbolic figures are more determinating than the ideal signifiers.

The rite of the breaking of the bread is of primary importance in this respect, in that it manifests that if the presence of Christ is indeed inscribed in the bread and the wine, it is not circumscribed there. Moreover, the biblical tradition insists on this: God is indeed present among his people; more precisely, He is present in his Temple, in the Holy of Holies, on the propitiatory which covered the arch of the covenant. Yet this propitiatory constituted a space delimited by two Cherubim with jointed wings ("you who are seated between the Cherubim"), i.e. an open space. From the phenomenological standpoint, this opening manifests that God cannot be assigned a residence. With regard to this matter, one thinks back of the strength with which the prophet Ezekiel castigates the people of Israel who, like the idolatrous, believes to be able to manipulate its God: the glory of God will leave the Temple of Jerusalem to go and join the exiled in Babylon (Ezek 11). The presence of Christ in the eucharist can of course not be enclosed in an intra-mundane being, for the reason of the concept of presence as well as for the reason of its eschatological and pneumatic character. Yet, it is easy to let oneself be taken to fantastic representations in this domain: the believing subject lets him/herself then be deceived psychologically by this instance of the psyche which has been convened to call with Lacan the "imaginary" and which is always willing to attain the obscure Object of the desire. This deception is linked to the symbolic material itself of the eucharist: the bread is indeed a compact and closed reality, where it is easy to imaginarily assign Christ his residence. On top of this, its eating and its assimilation in communion inevitably bring in motion oral fantasms of destructive agressivity and loving assimilation, so of domination and possession.

Against the risks of regression, it is important to recall what has been released from the preceding reflection: the bread never displays as well its essence of bread as in the act of its presentation to God in honouring and of its being shared as presence of God with the other. There it comes to its essential truth. In this perspective, the gesture of the breaking of the bread is a fundamental rite of Mass. It is this for reasons of tradition firstly – as is shown by the narratives of the Last Supper and the words of Luke and Paul – but it is this even more originary way for the reason which we come to say. Through the breaking, a void is hollowed out of the bread. To be sure, not a simple physical void, but a symbolic void, because this is about a sharing, i.e. a void "for", of which the intentionality is communion with the other. No more than the act of pouring out the wine, in the Heideggerian meditation on the pitcher, can be assimilated to a utilitarian flow of drink – for it is "offering" or "offertory" to the other (*schenken, Geschenk*) – can the void here be reduced to a simple physical necessity. In its being made in the presence or in the name of God and in favour of the other, it indeed manifests the very essence of the bread.

Of course, here again the properly theological, i.e. confessing discourse, will immediately forward its difference. First, what is broken is not broken only in the presence and in the name of God, because for the Christian faith the bread has become Christ himself as the bearer of divine life itself. Next, and as a consequence, the communion created by the sacramental participation in Christ is quite more than a simple conviviality. "One bread, one body": the Pauline formula (1 Cor 10,16) requires to be understood in a strong sense. We intend to say that here the metaphor of the body must be granted the strength which the function "meta" gives to it and which "carries it beyond" the simple image.

Hence, the fundamental *sacramentum* of the presence of Christ in the eucharist is the bread, but as broken (or destined to be broken). As such, the bread, in its essential-being of bread, is not as a closed and compact thing, but as reality-for-sharing. The void-for-the-other of the breaking appears in this way as the major sacramental figure of the presence of Christ: it is from this void that the latter arises in some way. This void, as void-for-the-other, produces among the faithful the very figure of the kenosis of Christ "emptying himself" of himself (Phil 2,7) to rekindle the covenant of God with and between humans. So the eucharistic presence of Christ can never be untied from the relation to the other as an effective or potential member of his body. This is brought out with particular power, as announced before, by the ritual sequence formed by the breaking of the bread in its relation to the gesture of peace which immediately precedes it, and the communion procession which follows it. Each of these three rites displays a double dimension of relation to the risen Christ himself and of relation between the participants. The first gesture, the one of exchanging peace, is primarily centred on the second dimension: the people welcome each other there as brothers and sisters; but they do so "in the charity of Christ". The third, the one of communion, is to the contrary centred on the first dimension: it is indeed the risen Christ (and not the brothers/sisters or the Church) who is received there, but one cannot do this in truth without having received each other beforehand as brothers/sisters. As for the central gesture, the one of the breaking, it expresses the two preceding dimensions at the same level: on the one hand, what is shared is the body itself of the risen Christ; but this eucharistic body of the Christ Head is inseparable, even if distinct, from his ecclesial body built by the sharing of the same bread. We have already mentioned the theological reason for this: it is the personal body of Christ which comes into presence in the eucharist, and not the body-Church; but it is the personal body of Christ "handling the vivification of his ecclesial body through the Holy Spirit".

In the wake of the problematic which has just been developed, the best way of thinking the mystery of eucharistic presence, so it seems, is to make the Augustinian theology of the *Christus totus* echo, as it enunciates the truth (here, the *res* of the eucharist) under a metaphorical mode without reducing it for all that to a simple "image". One knows with regard to this the famous formula of Augustine on the eucharistic body: "be what you see and receive what you are". The truth which is uttered there is irreducible to a simple literary metaphor while being no less inseparable from the metaphorical form which mediates it and which precisely "carries it beyond" all representation. The eucharist is the symbolic or sacramental figure which says at the same time the impossibility of confusing the Body of the risen Christ and his ecclesial body (only differences are symbolised) and the impossibility of separating them. It is the realisation of what the author of the letter to the Ephesians calls, at the end of a superb meditation, the *mega mystèrion* (v. 32), namely the indissoluble covenant of Christ and the Church[31].

Institut Catholique de Paris   Louis-Marie CHAUVET
21 rue d'Assas
75270 Paris
France

---

31. This article has been translated by Stijn van den Bossche and John C. Ries.

OFFERED PAPERS

THOMAS AQUINAS: POSTMODERN

I. Introduction: The Two Tyrannies

A major thesis of Jürgen Habermas's *The Philosophical Discourse of Modernity* is that the philosophical conversation of the last two hundred years has been dominated by the battle against two tyrannies, that of the supreme being and that of the supreme ego. The struggle against the first tends to characterize modern thought while the struggle against the second is a key motif in post-modern thinking. Thus modern philosophers from Descartes to Marx wonder how the existence of a domineering supreme being is reconcilable with full human flourishing, morally, politically and intellectually. The solutions to this problem range from Cartesian theological minimalism to Deism and finally to the outright atheism of Feuerbach. It was Sartre who gave perhaps clearest expression to this modern concern in his aphorism that we cannot be fully free as long as God exists. In short, a key project of modernity is the solving of the problem of the competitive supreme being, either through its marginalization or its elimination.

Of course, as the supreme being decreases, its opposite number, the supreme ego, increases. The trajectory is obvious, in seminal form, in Descartes's distantiation of God and his elevation of the *cogito* to a god-like position, at least epistemologically. But the transition from supreme being to supreme ego is most obvious in Hegel's apotheosis of the self-conscious subject, which many have taken to be the full flowering of Enlightenment confidence in the powers and prerogatives of the human person.

But what post-Hegelian thinkers from Kierkegaard and Nietzsche to Foucault and Derrida have noticed is that the new supreme being is hardly an improvement on the old one. Overconfident, arrogant, unaware of its limitations of vision, oblivious to ethical demand, the self-grounding and self-justifying ego sought to master its world. At the end of this most tragic of centuries – marked by world war, nuclear disaster, attempted genocide, technological tyranny and the rape of nature – we are only too aware of the dangers posed by an unlimited, apotheosized human ego. What so many post-modern thinkers have helped us to see, in short, is that this marauding subject is just as much a threat to our freedom and well-being as was the supreme being of classical religion. Accordingly, they critique any attempt to anchor our thought in foundations either theological or anthropological, saying to God-centered and to human-centered philosophy, "a plague on both your houses!"

One of the last thinkers that we would expect to support such a program is Thomas Aquinas, that paragon of pre-modern classical theism. What I want to argue in the course of this paper is that Aquinas's theological program is in fact curiously post-modern precisely inasmuch as it centers around a radical *mise en question* of both the supreme being and the supreme ego. I want to show that Thomas's account of God and the creature assuages both the modern fear of a domineering and competitive supreme being and the post-modern anxiety concerning the aggressive and self-important subject.

II. Thomas and the Supreme Being

What I shall endeavor to demonstrate in this section is that Thomas Aquinas's God is not the competitive supreme being that haunts the imaginations of modern philosophers, that in fact Thomas's account of God represents a sort of systematic dismantling of the mythology of the *ens summum*. Were God competitive with creation, there would have to be a common ground upon which both God and the world stand to fight, a shared background against which both are visible. It is precisely this univocal understanding of the divine and the non-divine that Thomas consistently denies.

Confusion is possible on this point because Thomas does, from time to time, refer to God as *ens* (a being) or the highest *ens*. For example, at the end of the fourth argument for God's existence in the second *Summa* we find: "there is therefore something which is truest and best and most noble and consequently highest being"[1]. And in the *Contra gentiles* we find "something which is highest being and this we call 'God'"[2]. But a far more common designation for the divine is the phrase found frequently in Thomas's writings: *esse ipsum subsistens*, the subsistent act of to-be itself. And in the eleventh question of the *Summa theologiae*, there is a passage that serves as a helpful hermeneutical key for the

---

1. "Est igitur aliquid quod est verissimum et optimum et nobilissimum et per consequens maxime ens." T. AQUINAS, *Summa theologiae*, Ia, Q. 2, a. 3.
2. "Esse aliquid quod est maxime ens et hoc dicimus Deum ." T. AQUINAS, *Summa Contra Gentiles*.

sorting out of this ambiguity concerning God language: "There is a highest being which is not determined in its existence by any nature that comes to it, but which is the subsistent act of to-be itself in no way determined"[3]. It seems clear from this text that even when Thomas, on relatively rare occasion, speaks of God as *ens summum* or *maxime ens*, he implies *ipsum esse subsistens*.

Thus it is now incumbent upon us to determine precisely what he means by this somewhat enigmatic phrase. I would suggest that we look to the detailed and highly nuanced disputed question *De potentia Dei*, a late text of the master, probably dating from the mid 1260's. In question seven of the *De potentia*, Thomas explores the problem of the divine simplicity, and in article two of that *quaestio*, he wonders whether God's essence is the same as his existence. The *Respondeo* here is of great interest, both because it sheds light on the uniqueness of God's mode of being and because it constitutes an indirect argument for the existence of a creator God.

Thomas begins by observing that sometimes several causes, producing a variety of effects, give rise, nevertheless, to one effect in common. To illustrate his point, he uses the homely example of cooking: a group of elements – pepper, ginger, etc. – each making a unique contribution to the flavor of a dish, come together in producing heat. But this phenomenon can be explained, Aquinas tells us, only through recourse to some one superior cause, namely fire, which has, as its proper effect, the common effect in question. In the second part of the *Respondeo*, he applies this general principle to a particular case:

> All created causes have one common effect which is being, though each one has a particular effect which distinguishes it from the others. Thus heat makes something to be hot and a builder makes the house to be. Therefore they have in common the fact that they cause being although they differ inasmuch as the fire causes fire and the builder causes the house. There must therefore be some cause superior to all others in virtue of which all cause being and whose proper effect is being. And this cause is God[4].

3. "Est enim maxime ens, in quantum est non habens aliquid esse determinatum per aliquam naturam cui adveniat; sed est ipsum esse subsistens, omnibus modis indeterminatum." T. AQUINAS, *Summa theologiae*, Ia, Q. 11.

4. "Omnes autem causae creatae communicant in uno effectu qui est esse, licet singulae proprios effectus habeant, in quibus distinguuntur. Calor enim facit calidum esse, et aedificator facit domum esse. Conveniunt ergo in hoc quod causant esse sed differunt in hoc quod ignis causat ignem et aedificator causat domum. Oportet ergo esse aliquam causam superiorem omnibus cuius virtute omnia causant esse et eius esse sit proprius effectus. Et haec causa est Deus." T. AQUINAS, *De potentia*, Q. 7, a. 2.

Since all natural causes, despite their striking variety, unite in producing to-be in some form, there must exist "behind" them a cause whose proper effect is to-be. But, continues Aquinas, the proper effect of a cause is expressive of the very substance or nature of that cause. Therefore there must exist a primordial and unifying cause of causality itself, whose very nature corresponds to that which it produces, viz. the act of to-be.

Now this analysis discloses three important things: God's actual existence, the unique mode of God's existence as that in which essence and *esse* coincide, and the fact that God is the cause of created being in general, what Thomas often calls *ens commune*. Understanding the relationship between the second and third points is of great moment, for one of the commonest misinterpretations of Aquinas on this score is that God – that which exists through itself – is simply conflated with the "force" of being that runs through all finite things or with the totality of created existence. We find evidence of this conflation in forms of Gnostic and pantheistic thinking from ancient times to the present day. Thomas disallows such an interpretation precisely by insisting that the to-be evident in finite things, in all of its intensity, complexity and multiplicity, is itself nothing more than a creature. This distinction between God's form of existence and being in general emerges in the play between the fourth objection and response. The objector argues that that which is absolutely common to all things, viz. *esse*, cannot be the ground for distinctiveness and that we therefore fall into incoherence if we say that God's distinctive essence is that by which nothing can be distinguished from anything else[5]. Thomas responds with his usual laconicism: "the divine to-be which is his substance is not being in general but is a to-be distinct from any other to-be. Therefore by his own to-be God differs from any other being"[6].

The difference of God's being comes to even clearer expression in article three of this same question seven. The issue is whether God can be contained in any genus. It is, of course, one of the marks of Aristotelian science to categorize objects according to genus and species, naming things through comparison and contrast with others. What emerges in the course of this discussion is that God is in no ordinary sense comparable to or contrastable from any of the things in the world.

5. T. AQUINAS, *De potentia,* Q. 7, a. 2.
6. "...esse divinum quod est eius substantia non est esse commune sed est esse distinctum a quolibet alio esse. Unde per ipsum suum esse Deus differt a quolibet alio ente." *Ibid.,* Q. 7, a. 2, ad. 4.

Thomas offers three arguments in support of the proposition that God cannot be contained in a genus, and I shall consider the third, which proceeds from the supreme perfection of God who is the sheer act of to-be. As simply and absolutely actualized, God must contain with himself the perfections of all genera. Were he confined to a particular genus, he would be limited by the restrictions of that category and would be, consequently, only conditionally perfect. As the most intense reality, God must transcend the limitations of any "division" of being:

> Thus it is also evident that God is not a species nor an individual, nor is there any difference in him; nor can he be defined, since every definition is in terms of genus and species[7].

It is here that we see, perhaps most clearly, the questioning of the theology of the supreme being that takes place throughout Thomas's writings. When Aquinas laconically tosses off the observation that God is not an *individuum*, he announces the radicality of the Christian conception of the sacred. God is not a supreme reality in, above or alongside of the world. As that reality which simply *is*, God is prior to the splits that characterize less dramatic expressions of being. God is, in no ordinary sense, above or below the world, precisely because he is, literally, incomparable. He is not a being among beings, nor is he to be, in the strict sense, contrasted to any finite thing. In denying a "thing-like" quality to God, Thomas anticipates Nicholaus Cusanus who spoke of the divine as the *non-aliud*, the not-other.

Of course, a key implication of this metaphysic is that *esse* is a term that can be applied only analogically of God and creatures. Because finite things come from God and are stamped by his creative power, they bear a resemblance to the divine reality and hence both God and creatures can be described with the term "being." But because there is an infinitely great modal difference between that which exists through itself and that which exists through another, the word *esse* is ascribed to God and creatures in only the most cautious and qualified way. And it is most important to note that this analogy between God and creatures is not predicated on the basis of their varying resemblance to some absolute of existence that precedes them, but rather on the participation of all finite things in the unparticipated to-be which is God.

We could summarize by saying that God is to be distinguished from the world, but in a non-competitive manner. The otherness of God can

---

7. "Ex hoc ulterius patet quod Deus non est species, nec individuum, nec habet differentiam, nec definitionem: nam omnis definitio est ex genere et specie." *Ibid.,* Q. 7, a. 3.

be expressed in terms of ontological intensity or modal differentiation: with regard to the world, God is not so much somewhere else as *somehow* else. Thomas Aquinas could never be accused of identifying the creator and the created. But the non-competitiveness of this differentiation appears when we realize that there is no common frame of reference for God and the world, no field that they share, no "ground" for which they are fighting, no genus in which they are both contained.

In emphasizing this non-competitive transcendence of the divine, Thomas is pulling out the implications of Anselm's famous "definition" of God as *id quo maius cogitari nequit*. If God is that than which no greater can be thought, it must follow that God + the world is not greater than God alone. Were that the case – as it would be in a classical philosophical or mythological framework – then God would not be, in himself, that than which none greater can be conceived. But if the universe in its totality adds nothing to the intensity and perfection of God's to-be, if after creation there are more beings but not more perfection of being, then God in no sense needs the world[8]. And this implies, furthermore, that neither God nor the world "threaten" one another. The very incommensurability of created and non-created existence is what allows for their intense but peaceful co-existence. A supreme being – generically the same as other existents – would necessarily threaten, compete with, dominate the "lesser" beings in league with it.

If we were to search out the deepest roots of this claim, we would have to examine Thomas's texts on the Incarnation, for the compatibility and non-competitiveness of the divine and human natures in Jesus is the revealed source of this metaphysical speculation. And if we were to follow this insight, we would find it everywhere in the writings of Aquinas, for it is, I would maintain, a kind of hermeneutical key to the Thomistic world. Whether the issue is the rapport between nature and grace, the relationship between providence and human freedom, the play between supernatural and natural causality, the clarifying principle – sometimes stated, sometimes assumed – is just this non-competitive transcendence of God. The dismantling of the false theology of the *ens summum* is at the very center of Thomas Aquinas's project.

Now if the *mise en cause* of the competitive supreme being is central to the theology of the most important thinker of the medieval Church, how comes it that so many modern philosophers are preoccupied with just this problem? To answer this question, we must turn our gaze to the

8. R. SOKOLOWSKI, *The God of Faith and Reason. Foundations of Christian Theology*, Notre Dame, University of Notre Dame Press, 1982, pp. 41-43.

period between the death of Aquinas and the dawn of the modern age, an epoch that witnessed what was, in many ways, the undermining of the radical Thomistic metaphysic.

Some of the first cracks occur just after Aquinas in the writings of the Franciscan theologian John Duns Scotus. Consciously breaking with Thomas, Scotus maintains the univocity of the concept of being, thereby drawing God and the world under the selfsame linguistic and ontological category. According to this conception, the divine and the non-divine are each instances (however infinitely different in "quantity") of the same shared power of existence. As a result, *ens commune*, which Thomas took to be a creature of God, now becomes a sort of framework in which both God and creatures subsist. Whereas Thomas insisted that God cannot be fit into any genus, Scotus says unambiguously that "God is understood only in the category of being"[9]. The consequence of this radical reconfiguration is obvious: God and the world, now drawn into too close a metaphysical intimacy, emerge as competitors. Sharing the same ontological background, God and creatures now become "beings" necessarily pitted against one another antagonistically. The supreme being has replaced *ipsum esse subsistens*.

The fissure, opened up by Duns Scotus, only becomes wider in the late scholasticism of Suarez. In the great Aristotelian tradition, Suarez specifies that the proper object of the science of metaphysics is "being as being," but then makes an application that is Scotist rather than Thomist. He says that this notion of being is "prior to the nature of God," that is to say, more elemental than and inclusive of the divine nature. And he states, even more baldly, that "the adequate object of this science (metaphysics) must include God"[10]. Both of these claims are intelligible only in the context of a univocal conception of being, as Suarez readily admits: "the being about which we are now speaking is common to both created and uncreated being"[11]. In the framework of Thomas's participation metaphysics, all of these assertions would, of course, be inadmissible. As that which cannot be placed in any genus, even the most general, as that which causes *ens commune*, God could never, for Thomas, be subsumed under any science or brought side-by-

9. "Deus non intelligitur nisi sub ratione entis." J. DUNS SCOTUS, *Ordinatio* I d. 3, Q. 3, n. 126 et 139. Cited in J.-L. MARION, *Saint Thomas d'Aquin et l'onto-théo-logie*, in *Revue Thomiste* 95 (1995) 31-66, p. 40.

10. "...objectum adaequatum hujus scientiae debere comprehendere Deum." F. SUAREZ, *Disputationes metaphysicae*, I sect. 1 n. 26.

11. "Ens, de quo nunc loquimur, commune est enti creato et increato." *Ibid.* II, sect. 2, n. 11.

side with similar beings for analysis. *Ipsum esse subsistens* could never be facilely manipulated and "comprehended" in this Suarezian fashion.

It is, it seems to me, of no small importance that Descartes was trained by Jesuits formed in Suarezian tradition. The founder of modern philosophy, the thinker who bequeathed to modernity the problematic of the competitive supreme being, had, most likely, misconstrued the subtle analogy of being that stands at the heart of the Thomistic synthesis. And this misconstrual, when its implications are fully developed, can be seen in the defensive atheism of Feuerbach, Marx, Sartre and Freud, as well as in the more nuanced critique of onto-theology in Heidegger. What these thinkers miss is that Thomas Aquinas was every bit as suspicious of the supreme being as they. Whereas their primary concern was the fostering of human freedom, Thomas's was the protection of the transcendence and majesty of God. But such protection was, for Aquinas, perfectly correlative to the defense of human dignity and freedom, for he knew that the worship of a false god conduces ultimately to a shrinking of the soul. Perhaps what modern thinkers tended to miss is something that Thomas would have taken as axiomatic: the glory of (the true, non-competitive) God is the human being fully alive.

III. THOMAS AND THE STATUS OF THE CREATURE

We recall that once modernity had marginalized the supreme being, it became a preoccupation of post-modernity to de-throne its successor, the supreme ego. What I will attempt to argue in this section is that Thomas Aquinas does not enter into such a zero-sum calculation, whereby the less we give to God the more we give to the creaturely. On the contrary, he will claim that the proper correlate of the God who is not a supreme being is the creature who does not cling to its independence and ontological prerogatives. If I may state it boldly, Thomas seems to hold that the non-being of God corresponds to the non-being of the creature.

At the heart of Thomas's puzzling teaching on creation is the idea that creation is not like any of the changes or relationships that occur in or between finite things. And this is precisely because it is a rapport, not with the supreme being, but with *ipsum esse subsistens*. The ordinary way to understand a causal relationship is in terms of the substance-to-substance rapport; but such an understanding must be set aside in the case of creation.

In order to explore the Thomistic doctrine of creation, I recommend that we stay with the *De potentia*, since it is in the context of the discussion of the divine power that Thomas offers by far his most thorough and penetrating analysis of creation. The discussion is spread out over 19 carefully argued articles in question three: *de creatione quae est primus effectus divinae potentiae*. Article one raises the obvious question "whether God can create something out of nothing?" Thomas's affirmative response hinges upon the fullness of God's active potency. Every finite agent – even the most elevated – is only partially actualized and therefore can produce effects only through some sort of influence on a pre-existing substance. God on the other hand is fully actual, that is to say, his causal efficacy is unlimited, and he is thus capable, not only of modifying what already exists, but of bringing something from total non-being into being:

> Consequently, through his action, he produces all of subsisting being, without a pre-supposition, as the one who is the principle of being... And for this reason, he can make something from nothing. It is this act of his that is termed "creation"[12].

The qualitative difference between this type of causality and that encountered in the world is made clear in the play between the first objector and the response. The objection is that nothing can go against the common conceptions of the mind, one of which is that *ex nihilo nihil fit*, nothing comes from nothing. Thomas retorts that this is indeed a valid principle but only in regard to finite things that influence one another through motion but that it does not apply in regard to the agent who produces *ens commune* itself.

What I would like to signal at this point is not only the novelty but also the radical non-violence of the causality being described here. In any causal relationship between finite things, there is some sort of intrusion of one being upon another, some influence that comes from the outside. And given the mutual exclusivity characteristic of finite realities, this influence, even when gentle, moderate or welcome, involves a kind of rupture or invasion. The act by which God brings the totality of the universe into existence is, on the contrary, completely non-invasive, non-disruptive, peaceful, since there is, literally, nothing that opposes or resists him. In all mythological or purely philosophical accounts of creation (there is even an overtone of this in Genesis) God or the gods wrestle some force of opposition – another god, matter, chaos – into submission, thereby establishing the order which is the cosmos. The

---

12. "...unde per suam actionem producit totum ens subsistens, nullo presupposito, utpote qui est totius esse principium... Et própter hoc ex nihilo aliquid facere potest; et haec eius actio vocatur creatio." T. AQUINAS, *De potentia*, Q. 3, a. 1.

creative act that Thomas Aquinas describes is neither the violent ordering of the chaos nor the subduing of opposing forces, but the absolutely
sovereign and gentle calling into being of the world[13]. Again, the non-
competitiveness of God and the world is highlighted, especially when
we bear in mind that this creative act is not sequestered simply at the
beginning of time, but is rather a continual act of sustenance in being.
The uniqueness and non-violence of creation is further described in the
exchange between the 17th objection and its response. The objector
maintains, sensibly enough, that if God makes something from nothing,
he *dat esse* (gives being). But that which receives this being which God
gives is either something or nothing. If it is nothing, then nothing is
made (there being no proper recipient); if, on the other hand, it is something, it is outside of the creative act of God, since nothing can be,
simultaneously, both recipient and that which is received. Thus it seems
to follow that God must make the world from something pre-existing,
that creation, in the strict sense, is an incoherency.

Thomas's response to this powerful objection is beautifully under-
stated. In two lines, he signals the overthrow of generally accepted
ontology:

> God, giving being, simultaneously produces that which receives being.
> And thus it does not follow that his action requires something pre-exist-
> ing[14].

We remark the almost Zen-like language: that which receives being is
the being that it receives; that into which the gift of being goes is itself
a gift of being. In denying that there is any substrate to or proper recipient of the influx of creative energy, Thomas is once again denying that
the substance-to-substance rapport is the model for this relationship.
God, as we have seen, is not *a* being, and his creativity does not go out
to *another* being, so as to influence it. To presume so is to assert, *per
impossibile*, that some form of finite existence stands independent of the
creative causality of *ipsum esse subsistens*.

But all of this implies something remarkable, viz. that the creature *is*
the act by which it is created. It seems as though a principal conceit of
Aristotelian metaphyiscs, the view that substance is fundamental and
relationship accidental, is overturned in this context. It appears as though
the relationship between creator and creature is what is primary and

---

13. In this context see J. MILBANK, *Theology and Social Theory: Beyond
Secular Reason,* Oxford, Blackwell Publishing, 1990, pp. 389-390.

14. "...Deus simul dans esse producit id quod esse recipit; et sic non oportet
quod agat ex aliquo praeexistenti." T. AQUINAS, *De potentia*, Q. 3, a. 1, ad. 17.

elemental whereas the "substances" involved – God and the world – are derivative, metaphysically secondary. The giver/receiver language, inextricably tied to a metaphysic of substance, cannot be applied to the act by which finitude itself is constituted. In question 7, Aquinas had shown that God is not a "thing," not an *individuum*; in this response to objection 17 he hints at something just as radical, viz. that the creature too is not a "thing" but a sheer relationship.

The precise ontological status of the creature is the subject of the third article of question three: "whether creation is something really in the creature." What Thomas searches out here is the "location" of the relational act which is *creatio*, whether it is in God, in the creature or somewhere in between. In order to get at this problem, Aquinas invites us first to distinguish between the active and passive senses of creation. In the active sense, *creatio* designates the act by which God makes the world, and this act, as such, is identical to the divine essence. But inasmuch as it involves no dependency of God on the world, it is not said to be "really" in God. In other words, the *operatio* by which God constitutes the universe *is* God, but the *relatio* to the creature which follows from this *operatio* is in God only logically.

But taken in the passive sense, "creation" designates, not a change in the creature, but a relation to the creator, and a relation that belongs to the very to-be of the creature:

> Creation cannot be taken as a movement of the creature prior to its reaching the terminus of its movement but must be taken as an accomplished fact. Consequently, creation itself is not an approach to being, nor a change brought about by the creator, but only the beginning of being and the relation to the creator from whom the creature has its being. And thus creation is nothing other than a certain relation to God, with freshness of being[15].

With this key passage, we come to the heart of Thomas's teaching on creation. Not a change of something pre-existing, creation is the absolute *inceptio* (beginning) of existence in the creature. And because time is itself a creature, we cannot construe this *inceptio* in a chronological sense, as though there were some "time" prior to the moment of creation. Rather, it is the permanently necessary "beginning" that takes place at every instant of a creature's existence. Presupposing nothing,

---

15. "Creatio autem... non potest accipi ut moveri quod est ante terminum motus sed accipitur ut in facto esse; unde in ipsa creatione non importatur aliquis accessus ad esse nec transmutatio a creante sed solummodo inceptio essendi et relatio ad creatorem a quo esse habet; et sic creatio nihil est aliud realiter quam relatio quaedam ad Deum cum novitate essendi." T. AQUINAS, *De potentia*, Q. 3, a. 3.

building upon nothing, requiring no substrate, creation is the sheer "beginning" in which the finite being finds its reality from God. And therefore, precisely as *inceptio* creation is a permanent *relatio* to God, an act of utter dependency.

Now if we link these formulations to the findings of the previous articles we have studied, we come to the following conclusion: the creature cannot be some thing which *has* a relation or which experiences *inceptio*; rather the creature is nothing other than a beginning, nothing other than a relation, nothing but the sheer openness to the inpouring of the divine causality. In a word, the creature *is* what Thomas calls "passive creation," *is* this *quaedam relatio* which involves "freshness of being." In one of his best-known poems, Gerard Manley Hopkins speaks of the "dearest freshness deep down things." This, it seems to me, comes close to what Aquinas means by the creature-constituting act of God which is creation.

As usual, the objections reveal a naturalist, Aristotelian unease with the radicality of creation metaphysics. The third objector, for instance, argues that everything that is is either a substance or an accident. But creation is not a substance, since it is neither matter nor form nor some combination of the two. Nor is it an accident, since an accident follows upon a substance, and creation, as the grounding act by which a thing is, is prior to substance. Thus, *creatio non est aliquid in rerum natura* (creation is not some actually existing thing). What this objector realizes is what we signalled earlier: the overturning of the usual relationship between primary and secondary substances.

Thomas's response is a beautiful example of the breaking of classical metaphysical language involved in describing the novelty of creation:

> This relation (creation) is an accident and, considered in its being, inasmuch as it inheres in a subject, is posterior to the created thing... If however we consider it insofar as it arises from the action of the agent, then this relation is, somehow, prior to its subject, as the divine action itself is its proximate cause[16].

From a purely Aristotelian standpoint, Thomas is speaking nonsense here. Creation is, at one and the same time, prior and posterior to the subject; it is, simultaneously, "super-substance" and accident, both the cause and a derivative modality of a thing. Like a contemporary physicist

---

16. "...illa relatio accidens est, et secundum esse suum considerata, prout inhaeret subjecto, posterius est quam res creata... Si vero consideretur secundum suam rationem, prout ex actione agentis innascitur praedicta relatio sic est quodammodo prior subiecto, sicut ipsa divina actio est eius causa proxima." T. Aquinas, *De potentia* Q. 3, a. 3.

describing light as both wave and particle, Thomas is trying to describe a reality which transcends the limitations of ordinary language and conventional conceptuality. In speaking of the "accidental" nature of the act of creation, Thomas is attempting to defend the ontological integrity of the creature, its modal differentiation from the divine to-be, but in insisting on the non-accidental quality of creation, he is trying to signal the unmitigated dependence of the creature upon the outpouring of the divine generosity. A created thing is surely other than God, but not as one substance is distinguished vis-à-vis another substance.

I hinted above that the deepest inspiration for Thomas's doctrine of the non-competitive transcendence of God is the Incarnation, the co-operative play of the two natures in Jesus. Christ can be seen as well in the background of this creation teaching. When Thomas speaks of the humanity of Christ, he places stress on the obedience of Jesus vis-à-vis the Father, his absolutely radical openness of will and mind to the promptings of the divine. This obedience constitutes the "co-operation" between the natures. In the measure that Jesus' humanity is an *instrumentum* of the divine power, divinity shines forth in him. Now this is the hinge: Jesus' humanity is not compromised in this act of total obedience, just the contrary. But its integrity can be maintained, even in radical obedience, precisely because God is not a competitive supreme being. God's refusal to cling to his substantiality is correlative to a similar creaturely refusal. I would argue that the humanity of Jesus becomes, for Thomas, the metaphysical paradigm of creation in general: Christ's human receptivity is the revelation of the deepest to-be of the creature, just as his divinity is the disclosure of the sheer non-competitive generosity of God.

IV. Conclusion

We might conclude with the observation that "substantiality" is the problem named by both modernity and post-modernity, in the first case the substantiality of God and in the second the substantiality of the ego. When God is hardened into the supreme substance, set apart from the world, *totaliter aliter*, displayed against the backdrop of *ens commune*, God necessarily becomes an oppressor and competitor. And when the ego is hardened into a supreme substance, it inevitably degenerates into imperialism and violence.

But when God is construed, not so much as the *ens summum* as *ipsum esse subsistens*, he emerges as the generous ground of being and freedom, and when the ego is conceived, not so much as a supreme being, but as a supreme letting-be, then its essentially non-violent nature comes into the light. One might argue that the blocky universe of substances (supreme and otherwise) set antagonistically against one another is the projection of a sinful consciousness, of a mind that has forgotten the simplicity of God and the peacefulness of creation.

University of St. Mary on the Lake   Robert BARRON
Mundelein Seminary
1000 E. Maple Ave.
Mundelein, IL 60060
USA

INCARNATION AND IMAGINATION

Catholic Theology of God between
Heidegger and Postmodernity

The Christian tradition is fundamentally a history of effects and receptions, a *Wirkungsgeschichte* as defined by Hans-Georg Gadamer[1]. It is constituted from the occurrence of revelatory events within already interpretation-laden contexts, the ongoing receptions of these events, and the further new meanings generated by these receptions. These effects and receptions are always "interpreted experiences"[2] and form theology's historical horizon. Catholic theology must therefore always be hermeneutical and heed the effects and receptions which not only influence its ability to reflect upon the long history of Christian belief and practice but also affect its success in communicating the truths of revelation which pertain to the nature and active presence of God.

Catholic theology's contemporary situation is strongly influenced on the one hand by the reception of Martin Heidegger's critique of metaphysics and on the other by the continuous critique of modernity carried out by the various types of "post-" which have announced modernity's exhaustion or bankruptcy. This contemporary situation is complex. It influences the search for a viable contemporary theology of sacramental presence, which in turn depends on the refiguration of the theology of God. And new opportunities for discourse about God and God's gracious actions have arisen. David Tracy, for example, has noted the "strange return of God" after modernity's difficulties with divinity. He optimistically suggests that "God enters postmodern history not as a consoling 'ism' but as an awesome, often terrifying, hope-beyond-hope...." God is revealed "in hiddenness: in cross and negativity" and above all in the sufferings of those marginalized by "the grand narrative

---

1. H.-G. GADAMER, *Truth and Method,* trans. J. Weinsheimer & D.G. Marshall, New York, Crossroad, 1989, p. 300 ff.

2. See E. SCHILLEBEECKX, *Interim Report on the Books "Jesus" and "Christ"*, trans. J. Bowden, New York, Crossroad, 1981, pp. 2-19 & ID., *Church: The Human Story of God,* trans. J. Bowden, New York, Crossroad, 1990, pp. 1-45.

of modernity"[3]. But recent discussions of "postmodernism and God" have proposed other challenging discourses of transcendence as well. Some of these bracket or even submerge God altogether while claiming a more emancipatory understanding of religious experience than anything offered by the religious traditions. To such different understandings of divine transcendence, how should Catholic theology react? How should contemporary Catholic theological reflection upon God relate both to the present epoch and to the long Christian tradition of belief and practice in which theology participates as one of the effects?

I wish to examine three temporally-situated effects which should exert a profound influence on theology. The first is the already-mentioned "irruption" of Heidegger's thought. His analysis of ontotheology marks the history of the Catholic theology of God, periodizing it: the character of Catholic reflection on the reality of God after Heidegger's call for the overcoming of metaphysics looks fundamentally different from what came before. The second effect is the current multi-voiced critique of modernity along with the call to purge theology of all "modern" commitments. In the light of these critiques, the Catholic theology of God must re-examine its relation to all previous epochs within the Christian tradition and discern the redemptive and redeemable aspects of each, including modernity. The third effect is ancient – so seminal that it can be considered Christianity's "founding effect", over against which all other effects and receptions must be understood. This is the advent of the Kingdom of God in the life, death, and resurrection of Jesus Christ. Theology must heed the ways in which the arrival of God's Kingdom affects not only our image of God but also the character of time and being.

At the conclusion I want to sketch a program for an authentic Catholic response to the convergence of these effects. By grasping their implications in a foundational way, a contemporary Catholic theology will be better able to mediate for our time and place the pattern of incarnation and sacramentality to which Catholicism is committed and contribute to a new theological paradigm of sacramental presence.

I. THE PERIODIZING EFFECT OF HEIDEGGER'S CRITIQUE

The influence and deep reception of Heidegger's critique of both metaphysics and ontotheology have only recently begun to be made

---

3. D. TRACY, *The Return of God in Contemporary Theology*, in ID., *On Naming the Present: God, Hermeneutics, and Church* (Concilium Series), Maryknoll, Orbis – London, SCM, 1994, pp. 42-43.

clear[4]. One mark of this reception is obvious: Heidegger's *Überwindung* destabilized the traditional identification of God with Being and forced a re-evaluation of the role of metaphysics within Catholic theology, especially the theology of God and Christology[5].

Heidegger claims that philosophy's intrinsic identity as metaphysics is revealed in its obsessive search for the unifying ground of beings[6]. The objectifying representation of Being as a being, an ignorance of the fundamental phenomenality of beings (their sheer givenness as modes of presencing), and the persistent misunderstanding of reality in terms of dualistic oppositions (e.g., Being as "ground" over against beings as "grounded") all add up to the fatal flaw of metaphysical thinking: despite its totalizing claims, it misses the "ontological difference," the very condition which makes the differentiation between Being and beings possible. Thus, rather than metaphysics' two fundamental elements, there are *three* which become apparent to thought: Being (the process of presencing), beings (which are present and take their stand within our field of attention), and the differentiating process which simultaneously connects them and holds them apart[7].

Metaphysics compounds its errors by representing the ultimate unifying principle as the "highest being," the divine ground. Here, Heidegger argues, is where metaphysics becomes ontotheology. "When metaphysics thinks of beings with respect to the ground that is common to all beings as such, then it is logic as onto-logic. When metaphysics thinks of beings as such as a whole, that is, with respect to the highest being which accounts for everything, then it is logic as theologic"[8]. God enters philosophy having been identified with Being, with the unifying Ground of the perduring of beings. However, this God is thereby inscribed within an all-encompassing metaphysical schema which is "bigger" than God. This schema employs God as part of the dualistic formatting

4. For example, see S.K. WHITE, *Political Theory and Postmodernism*, Cambridge – New York, Cambridge University Press, 1991, and G. WARD's editorial introduction to *The Postmodern God: A Theological Reader* (Blackwell Readings in Modern Theology), Malden, MA – Oxford, Blackwell, 1997, pp. xv-xlvii.

5. See A.J. GODZIEBA, *Ontotheology to Excess: Imagining God Without Being*, in *Theological Studies* 56 (1995) 3-20; ID., *Bernhard Welte's Fundamental Theological Approach to Christology* (American University Studies, Series VII, 160), New York – Bern, Peter Lang, 1994.

6. M. HEIDEGGER, *The End of Philosophy and the Task of Thinking*, in ID., *On Time and Being*, trans. J. Stambaugh, New York, Harper and Row, 1972, p. 56.

7. See *The Onto-Theo-Logical Constitution of Metaphysics*, the second essay of HEIDEGGER's *Identity and Difference*, trans. J. Stambaugh, New York, Harper and Row, 1969, pp. 42-74.

8. *Ibid.*, pp. 70-71.

of experience. God rests in the grip of the differentiating process which is always already there ahead of the God who is distinct from beings. This God, in Heidegger's famous description, is "the god of philosophy. Man can neither pray nor sacrifice to this god... can neither fall to his knees in awe nor can he play music and dance before this god"[9].

What are the consequences of Heidegger's critique of ontotheology in the light of the ontological difference? Some recent commentators would read Heidegger's critique in an extremely unilateral and even immanentist way, as rendering *every* image of God illegitimate, *all* theistic discourse impossible, and *all* faith in God suspect because of its alleged totalizing tendencies. But such extreme readings are mistaken if they claim to explain Heidegger's intent. He recognizes the legitimacy of belief and of theistic discourse; indeed he points toward an experience of God which reaches back beyond the image of God constructed by ontotheology and philosophical theology to the God before whom one can indeed "play music and dance". The critique of ontotheology is Heidegger's way of clearing the decks, saying in effect that human reason's attempts to use the idea of God to gain the highest metaphysical vantage-point and thus make the whole of being intelligible are rather betrayals of the divine God who is beyond "the God of philosophy".

A close analysis of Heidegger's comments on faith, philosophy, and ontotheology demonstrates that the extreme readings are unsupported by Heidegger's texts, whether early or late. Heidegger can be interpreted as having developed a Pascalian project of protecting the experiential content of faith (the "what" of our God-talk) from any sort of theoretical distortion (the "how" of our God-talk)[10]. This project has its clear sources in Heidegger's early lectures on the philosophy of religion, in which Heidegger presented a phenomenology of faith derived from his reading of Paul and Augustine, a reading very much influenced by Luther and Kierkegaard. His later critique of the metaphysical reification and dissolution of "the divine God" was a development of an explicitly Lutheran view of faith's relation to theology which he laid out in the 1920s[11]. This

9. *Ibid.*, p. 72.
10. See M. WESTPHAL, *Overcoming Onto-Theology*, in J.D. CAPUTO & M. SCANLON (eds.), *God, the Gift, and Postmodernism*, Bloomington, IN, Indiana University Press, 1999, pp. 146-169.
11. See M. HEIDEGGER, *Phänomenologie des religiösen Lebens* (Gesamtausgabe, II. Abteilung: Vorlesungen 1919-1944, Band 60), Frankfurt a. M., Klostermann, 1995, especially the lectures on the phenomenology of religion (1920-21, which include the Pauline interpretations) and on Augustine and neo-Platonism (1921). See also HEIDEGGER'S 1927 lecture *Phenomenology and Theology* in ID., *The Piety of Thinking,* trans. J.G. Hart & J.C. Maraldo, Bloomington, Indiana University Press, 1976, pp. 10-11.

longer-range context leads one to conclude along with Merold Westphal that the critique of ontotheology "is not directed toward the God of the bible or the Koran, before whom people do fall on their knees in awe, pray, sacrifice, sing, and dance." Rather, it is directed at "the 'metaphysical' tendency, whether found among philosophers or theologians, to imprison theological discourse within a primacy of theoretical reason under the rule of the principle of sufficient reason"[12]. Heidegger thus recognized the legitimacy of belief and of theistic discourse, and intended to open the way toward other possibilities of meaningful discourse about God.

The periodizing and destabilizing nature of Heidegger's critique of ontotheology marks a clear dividing line. No Catholic theology of God after Heidegger can be un-reflectively metaphysical; rather, it must present a rigorous argument which demonstrates how its fundamental conception of being escapes the Heideggerian definition of metaphysics as objectifying, controlling, stultifying representationalism. But no Catholic theology of God can simply follow Heidegger's subsequent path and take up his rather diluted apophatic notion of *das Heilige*. Recently, Jean-Luc Marion and Walter Kasper have offered sympathetic readings of Heidegger which challenge his project as well. Marion believes that what he calls "iconic thought" – our response to the revealed "excess" of God who gives the difference and whose presence is disclosed as gift rather than as idolatrous projection – "outwits" Being by getting beyond the categories of Being which, for Marion, still set the conditions for Heidegger's attempt to think God "beyond metaphysics", despite Heidegger's disclaimers[13]. Kasper, for his part, criticizes any "substance" metaphysics and any thinking which would objectify the transcendent horizon of experience[14]. Rather, freedom (and following this, person and relation), not substance or "self-contained being", is the true overarching category by which the pivotal revealed meaning of the mystery of God as self-communicating love can be apprehended[15]. Freedom is not itself the foundation of Kasper's Trinitarian theology.

12. M. WESTPHAL, *Overcoming Onto-Theology* (n. 10), pp. 148, 160.

13. J.-L. MARION, *God without Being: Hors-Texte*, trans. T.A. Carlson, Chicago, University of Chicago, 1991, pp. 40-43, 84-85, 100-101. See also Marion's explanation of the phenomenological basis for this argument in *Metaphysics and Phenomenology: A Summary for Theologians*, in G. WARD, *The Postmodern God* (n. 4), pp. 279-296.

14. W. KASPER, *The God of Jesus Christ*, trans. M.J. O'Connell, New York, Crossroad, 1984, p. 100.

15. *Ibid.*, pp. 153, 310. See also KASPER's essay *Revelation and Mystery: The Christian Understanding of God*, in ID., *Theology and Church*, trans. M. Kohl, New York, Crossroad, 1989, pp. 30-31.

Rather, he always appeals to the more primordial revelation of "the living God of history who has disclosed himself in a concrete way through Jesus Christ in the Holy Spirit"[16] and to the living, incarnate tradition of faith and discipleship which gives witness to this revelational experience. The two elements – revelation on the one hand and the overarching category of freedom on the other – stand together in a reflective and mutually interpretive equilibrium. Thus Kasper recognizes Heidegger's determinative insight while at the same time remaining faithful to the incarnational logic of the Christian tradition.

II. The Contemporary Situation as Modern and Postmodern

In the present-day Western debate over modernity and postmodernity, to characterize theology's present situation simply as "modern", "postmodern", or "contemporary" without explanation invites only ambiguity. These terms are notoriously difficult to define; they represent not only disputed historical "periods" but also diverse ideological judgments regarding the fundamental presuppositions of these periods. The culture of the modern period cannot be reduced simply to "the Enlightenment"; rather, there are a variety of "modernities" with different, even conflicting attitudes. Similarly, "contemporary" and "postmodern" cannot be reduced to a simple definitions, nor is one term a mere substitute for the other.

Some clarity can be reached if one turns to critical receptions of postmodern theory and culture which are more broadly based in social and cultural theory as well as philosophy[17]. Many of these acknowledge the positive results of the postmodern critique, such as the decentering of autonomous rationality and an openness to legitimate claims of difference. But postmodern culture is seen to manifest as well a paradoxical logic which undermines difference and plurality and which objectifies all "reality" into interchangeable stylish images and cash commodities which are then presented as the truly real. Such commodification imposes a debilitating sameness on life and erases the criteria for ethical evaluation and social and political critique[18].

---

16. W. Kasper, *The God of Jesus Christ* (n. 14), p. 315; see also p. 309 (regarding the mystery of the Trinity).

17. E.g., D. Harvey, *The Condition of Postmodernity*, Oxford, Blackwell, 1990; F. Jameson, *Postmodernism, or the Cultural Logic of Late Capitalism*, Durham, NC, Duke University Press, 1991; B.S. Turner (ed.), *Theories of Modernity and Postmodernity* (Theory, Culture and Society), London – Newbury Park, CA, Sage, 1990.

18. See R. Kearney, *Ethics and the Postmodern Imagination*, in *Thought* 62 (1987) 39-58; Id., *The Wake of Imagination: Toward a Postmodern Culture*, Minneapolis, University of Minnesota Press, 1988, pp. 359-397.

The social theorist Bryan Turner offers a particularly persuasive analysis. He views contemporary culture as the time and place of contention between still-vital modern values and a flourishing postmodern critique; each side has religious roots, but both sides have become secularized in their values and practices[19]. Modernity is a way of life based on fundamental values which were encouraged by the Reformation: individuality, rationalism, and asceticism. Postmodernity represents "an oppositional movement against the rationalizing tendency of the modern project" and against "grand narrative", teleological views of history; it is in fact part of a longer series of oppositional social movements which include the Counter-Reformation and the Baroque. Already present within modernity, then, were elements of its own critique, movements which promoted practices and values (such as the non-rational, the mystical, the location of truth in the absolute, the artistic illusory) as alternatives to the one-dimensional emphasis on the rationality of the individual subject[20].

This oppositional aspect of postmodernity has been appropriated by many who seek to find a voice for Christian theology in contemporary culture. For example, Graham Ward claims that postmodernism undermines "modernity's secular theology" and clears the way for a post-secular, non-foundational theology which "reads metaphysical questions… critically in terms of a theological agenda"[21]. In fact, many of those whom Ward cites as raising the issue of God in postmodernity (e.g., Marion, Levinas, Girard, Kristeva, Milbank) do so by appealing to premodern concepts, metaphors, and apophatic traditions. This oppositional character also holds true for the current deconstructive approach to religion, spurred on by Jacques Derrida's radicalization of Heidegger's "ontological difference" into *différance* and undecidability. The direction of deconstruction's religious discourse can be seen in John Caputo's *The Prayers and Tears of Jacques Derrida,* where any desire for a determinate image of God is dismissed as the remnant of "an excessively Hellenistic frame of mind". Religion – that is, any species of the "determinable faiths" – is declared irrelevant and surpassed by a faith which leaves undetermined whether that faith is a passion for justice or for God[22].

19. B.S. TURNER, *Religion and Social Theory,* 2d ed., London – Newbury Park, CA, SAGE, 1991, pp. ix-xxiv.

20. *Ibid.,* pp. xvii-xix.

21. G. WARD, *The Postmodern God* (n. 4), pp. xxi-xxii, xliii.

22. J.D. CAPUTO, *The Prayers and Tears of Jacques Derrida: Religion Without Religion,* Bloomington, Indiana University Press, 1997, pp. 338-339.

How does a Catholic theology of God react to "the return of God" in ways such as these described by Ward and Caputo? David Tracy's optimistic evaluation of the postmodern portrayal of God, as noted above, may be correct in some respects[23]. But it seems a somewhat hasty and inadequate conclusion in light of the plurality of postmodern images of God. A Catholic theology, with commitments to faith and reason and incarnation, will dialogue with these positions and may eventually come to accept some of them as part of its self-understanding. But in the end it will need to critique and surpass them as well.

For example, Caputo's deconstructive discourse is awash in prophetic metaphors from the Hebrew scriptures. But as his book's subtitle ("Religion without Religion") and subsequent discussion make clear, he rips the flesh and the history from God and from religion, and allows philosophy to position theology and to determine what kind of God-talk allowed. Here undecidability is the sole transcendental condition; it alone determines which speech is possible and establishes a rather dualistic and metaphysical either/or: *either* the univocally negative estimation of specific religious traditions *or* the undecidable idea "God/justice". This amounts to a kind of "atheistic Lutheranism": a negative judgment is delivered against human religious constructs, but the intentional referent for the word "God", if there be one at all, is undecidable – indeed, under the Derridean edict it is forbidden to conceive it.

But this *soi-disant* apophatic emphasis is not a postmodern strategy at all, but rather a replication of the Enlightenment search for *das Wesen der Religion*. There is little difference between this particular deconstructive philosophy of religion and Enlightenment philosophy's pursuit of a "natural" religion cut loose from history and supposedly prior to any specific religious traditions. This quest for the ahistorical essence of religion-in-general distorts the authentic character of the religions, namely, that they are specific ensembles of practices embedded in lived traditions and that their truths have an intentionality which is unknowable when abstracted from those traditions and turned into pure theory. While welcoming any postmodern retrieval of the apophatic dimensions of faith, Catholic theology must contest any over-emphasis on the apophatic which erases affirmation and mediation and thus eliminates the intelligibility of God. In Caputo's case, God remains as extrinsic to human concerns as any modern (i.e. post-Nominalist) philosophical conception of God, while the desire for transcendence takes on the character of an unfulfilled projection by an autonomous subject.

---

23. D. TRACY, *The Return of God* (n. 3), pp. 41-43.

A similar critical appreciation should be extended to arguments which style themselves as "post-secular". Despite Graham Ward's protest that such arguments are not exercises in anti-modernism, he complains that "modernity hijacked the theological, the premodern" and identifies postmodern Christian theology as that which seeks "another city, a heteropolis" which differs from and rejects the modern, secular space[24]. Catherine Pickstock has extended this rejection of modernity even further by claiming that modernity's foremost characteristic is necrophilia. She argues that modern culture, gripped by a fear of death and nothingness and by anxiety over the apparent perpetual non-fulfillment of human desires, compensates by equating "life" with permanence and repetition. Modernity thus reduces life to "the deathliness of equivalence" and covertly posits death as the condition for the possibility of meaning[25]. For Pickstock, the alternative to this "evacuative" theory of signs and language is a theology of the Eucharist and a consequent theory of signs grounded in the medieval liturgy of the Roman Rite and above all in the medieval theology of transubstantiation[26].

Certainly Catholic theology would welcome the dismantling of the secular theodicy of modernity as well as the productive retrieval of the great pre-modern Christian traditions. But this case of postmodern theologians reaching back over a scorned modernity in order to retrieve pre-modern insights leaves modernity unredeemed and too easily portrayed as univocally negative, corrupt, or at least unretrievable. "Modernity" has been reduced to one definition: an epoch characterized by nothingness and absolute rupture, representing the complete suppression or collapse of the living Christian tradition. Along then with the deconstructive strategy, this post-secular discourse displays a distaste for and a delegitimation of modernity as a locus of meaning and of theological truth. These kinds of discourse might be considered varieties of a *Theologie des Trotzdem,* an "in-spite-of" theology. Bernhard Welte coined this phrase for the extrinsicist Catholic Neo-Scholasticism which

---

24. G. WARD, *The Postmodern God* (n. 4), p. xlii. Ward here echoes the arguments (and style) of J. MILBANK, *Theology and Social Theory: Beyond Secular Reason* (Signposts in Theology), Oxford – Cambridge, MA, Blackwell, 1990. Regarding Milbank, see my discussion in *Augustinian Studies* 28 (1997)2, 147-158.

25. C. PICKSTOCK, *After Writing: On the Liturgical Consummation of Philosophy* (Challenges in Contemporary Theology), Oxford – Malden, MA, Blackwell, 1998, pp. 103-105; cf. ID., *Necrophilia: The Middle of Modernity. A Study of Death, Signs, and the Eucharist,* in *Modern Theology* 12 (1996) 405-433.

26. "The event of transubstantiation in the Eucharist is the condition of possibility for all human meaning", C. PICKSTOCK, *After Writing* (n. 25), p. xv.

engaged in a polemic against modernity and retreated into a repetition of the past which itself was ironically modernist[27]. It applies very easily to these particular postmodern arguments as well.

But in a way similar to the theological critique mounted against Neo-Scholastic extrinsicism earlier in this century, a Catholic theology of God must vigorously contest any claim which marks a period of time as devoid of the touch of God and unclaimed by God's salvific will. Particularly relevant here is the fundamental theological principle of the "dangerous memory" of the passion and resurrection of Jesus. Johann Baptist Metz has developed and applied this principle to the situation of the forgotten dead who have been victims of the history of suffering, in order to understand how they too are included in the salvation offered by Christ. In the passion, death, and resurrection of Christ, God has revealed both the promise of the resurrection of all the dead and the rejection of the belief that suffering, meaninglessness, and death have the final word[28]. This principle applies as well to the present case and helps us determine the true status of any historical period which has been judged dead and Godless. The incarnation, death, and resurrection of Jesus Christ testify to the absolute initiative of God to enter into history and into solidarity with all humanity, in every place and time, with no one excluded. God's power of reversal, made manifest in the cross and resurrection of Jesus Christ, guarantees that *no one* and *no time* get left behind, that all persons and all times have access to eschatological transformation[29]. Therefore, the Catholic understanding of God's incarnation in history demands that we practice a positive retrieval of modernity with its testimonies to complex and varied experiences of God and its proper signs of grace and redemptive liberation. Catholic theology should not exercise a critique which would identify modernity as merely the "other city" which enshrines pagan and anti-Christian values.

Such a retrieval will disclose a multi-layered "modernity" far more complex than some theological commentators allow, composed of a variety of cultural and religious histories and numerous indications

---

27. B. WELTE, *Zum Strukturwandel der katholischen Theologie im 19. Jahrhundert*, in ID., *Auf der Spur des Ewigen: Philosophische Abhandlungen über verschiedene Gegenstände der Religion und der Theologie*, Freiburg, Herder, 1965, pp. 397-399.

28. The resurrection provides the basis for the Christian hope in universal eschatological justice, "a hope in a revolution *for all men,* including those who suffer and have suffered unjustly, those who have long been forgotten and even the dead" (J.B. METZ, *Faith in History and Society: Toward a Practical Fundamental Theology*, trans. D. Smith, New York, Seabury – Crossroad, 1980, p. 76 [my emphasis]).

29. Cf. *ibid.*, pp. 113-114.

which contradict the claim that modernity is in essence dead or Godless. The history of Catholic spirituality during the modern period documents any number of movements and styles which reflected the basic belief that the created material world mediates God's presence. One example is the spirituality which is at the heart of Counter-Reformation religious art and architecture[30]. Works such as Caravaggio's *Supper at Emmaus* (the London version), Bernini's *Saint Teresa in Ecstasy,* or Andrea Pozzo's ceiling fresco for Sant' Ignazio in Rome are hardly works of spatial stasis symbolizing closure and death. On the contrary, the ceaseless human desire for divine transcendence is provoked by the sensuous and sumptuous affects we see played out before us. The boundary between the viewer and the work is broken, and the viewer is urged both to savor these worldly appearances and to see past them in order to encounter the inexhaustible divine grace which they mediate[31]. These representations invite the viewer to experience the presence of God in prayer and to participate in the church's sacramental life and performance of good works which, as post-Tridentine Catholicism strongly argued, are authentic bearers of grace.

Another example would be the tradition of French Catholic spirituality during the seventeenth, eighteenth, and nineteenth centuries which emphasized the sacramentality of everyday life. This spirituality does not counsel a flight from the world or a "heroic" life of prayer as the prerequisite for holiness. Instead, it emphasizes that the ordinary actions of everyday experience can mediate the presence of God, that holiness is possible for those dealing with the demands of everyday life. Jean-Pierre de Caussade, for example, calls the availability of God within human everydayness "the sacrament of the moment" and claims that "the actions of created beings are veils which hide the profound mysteries of the workings of God"[32]. Thérèse of Lisieux is part of the same tradition. Her diary entries relating her crisis of faith, though certainly less placid than de Caussade's, are firmly grounded in the same belief that everyday

---

30. Cf. H.O. EVENNETT, *The Spirit of the Counter-Reformation,* ed. J. BOSSY, Notre Dame, University of Notre Dame Press, 1970; K.P. LURIA, *The Counter-Reformation and Popular Spirituality,* in L. DUPRÉ, D.E. SALIERS & J. MEYENDORFF (eds.), *Christian Spirituality: Post-Reformation and Modern* (World Spirituality, Vol. 18), New York, Crossroad, 1989, pp. 93-120.

31. See K. HARRIES, *The Bavarian Rococo Church: Between Faith and Aestheticism,* New Haven, Yale University, 1983, esp. pp. 120-195.

32. J.-P. DE CAUSSADE, *Abandonment to Divine Providence,* trans. J. Beevers, Garden City, Image – Doubleday, 1975, p. 24 ("the moment"); p. 36 (the extended quotation). F. DE SALES subscribes to a very similar "sacramental" understanding; see his *Introduction to the Devout Life,* trans. J.K. Ryan, New York, Doubleday, 1982.

life is graced by God's love and offers the resources necessary for our faith in God, even in the most extreme circumstances where God seems to be absent[33]. Although recent studies have demonstrated the presence of a strong streak of *contemptus mundi* and fear of eternal punishment in much mainstream modern Catholic piety[34], this particular type of Catholic spirituality resisted the rejection of self and world and instead exemplified an equally strong commitment to creation's ability to mediate God's loving presence and plan for salvation. In other words, one does not experience the presence of God *in spite of* everyday life, but *while embracing* everyday life.

As such examples show, theological arguments which simplistically dismiss modernity as devoid of meaningful religious experience or as completely overrun by a purely secular theodicy in fact distort the evidence and assume a definition of modernity which is far too narrow. The vision and practices of Christianity during the modern period demonstrate quite the opposite. They remain important, retrievable resources for the theology of God. The types of theology and piety which supported Counter-Reformation religious art and the optimistic forms of Catholic spirituality explicitly recall the biblical narratives of creation and incarnation. Both the art and the spirituality sought to translate the life-affirming meaning of these narratives in distinctively modern ways, while a continuity with the original "incarnational impulse" in the life, death, and resurrection of Jesus Christ was maintained.

What Metz has called the "practical" and "irritating" character of the idea of God is grounded precisely in this incarnational impulse[35]. God's incomprehensible presence shatters any exclusive fascination with or absorption in neatly-packaged theoretical solutions to the problem of the relationship between God and history. And this includes postmodern solutions. The postmodern God who is approached in *apophasis* is not "other than" the modern God who is approached in terms of grace. Each is an image of the one God, and a theology of God must strive to retrieve all those varied images in a systematic unity.

---

33. T. DE LISIEUX, *Story of a Soul: The Autobiography of St. Thérèse of Lisieux*, trans. J. Clarke, 2d ed., Washington, ICS Publications, 1976, esp. pp. 211-214 (Thérèse's crisis of faith).

34. See J. DELUMEAU, *Sin and Fear: The Emergence of a Western Guilt Culture, 13th-18th Centuries*, trans. E. Nicholson, New York, St. Martin's Press, 1990; S. TUGWELL, *Ways of Imperfection: An Exploration of Christian Spirituality*, Springfield, IL, Templegate, 1985, pp. 208-232, esp. p. 220.

35. J.B. METZ, *Faith in History and Society* (n. 28), p. 51.

III. The Effect of the Kingdom

This emphasis on incarnation leads directly to the final effect to be considered, the Kingdom of God. It is the foundational effect, the "classic" which conditions all subsequent effects and receptions[36].

In the gospels, the revelation of God's "kingly rule" through the words and actions of Jesus is portrayed as the transformation of situations of negativity, suffering, and dehumanization into situations of positivity, joy, and human flourishing beyond any human achievement. The witness of the New Testament is unanimous in claiming that such a fundamental reversal of circumstances could be accomplished only by God, Jesus' Abba. As suggested by Jesus' parables, God's kingly rule makes the offer of love and reversal open to all without qualification and, in doing so, surpasses human expectations and standards. That this reversal of negativity and restoration of human well-being is truly God's salvific will is confirmed by the resurrection of Jesus which is the definitive reversal, the reversal of death into life.

Klaus Hemmerle has offered a fundamental theological analysis which describes the substance and meaning of this Kingdom of God more precisely. The arrival of the Kingdom in Jesus signaled no less than "a total revolution" in human thought and existence, a new understanding of temporality and of being in the light of a Trinitarian ontology[37]. Here, the decisive dawning of God's saving power which had been thought to lay far off in the future had now moved, by the sheer initiative of God, into the midst of the present[38]. Our normal expectations regarding the meaning of life and time are challenged and even shattered by God's revelatory self-giving in love in the incarnation. God's full, radical identification with humanity in the person of Jesus signals God's willingness to enter "the constraints of human speech, thought, and time". Jesus' horrific death reveals how human finitude, loss, and meaninglessness "to the point of a cry of God-forsakenness" are the surprising constitutive factors of "God's most

---

36. For the meanings of "kingdom of God" *(basileia tou theou)* as used by Jesus, see J.D.G. DUNN, *Jesus' Call to Discipleship* (Understanding Jesus Today), Cambridge, Cambridge University Press, 1992, pp. 6-31.

37. K. HEMMERLE, *Thesen zu einer trinitarischen Ontologie* (Kriterien, 40), Einsiedeln, Johannes Verlag, 1976; ID., *Das problematische Verhältnis von Philosophie und Theologie: Theologische Perspektiven,* in *Philosophisches Jahrbuch* 84 (1977) 228-241. All translations are mine.

38. K. HEMMERLE, *Das problematische Verhältnis,* p. 230: "here on the terrain of our existence and thought ... God is no longer the horizon, but the center: this is a radical reversal, a radical change".

extreme solidarity with us, in which the Kingdom reveals itself as pure and radical love"[39].

This revelation also discloses the triune mystery of God and a Trinitarian ontology. The very being of God as a communion of persons in love enters into all aspects of creation and transforms them by "the rhythm of self-giving" and by the invitation to participate fully in divine life. The Trinitarian transformation of the human – and indeed the cosmic – condition compel us to re-read the nature of reality as open-ended and relational rather than static. These revealed mysteries urge us to understand anew the possibilities of temporal reality as possibilities which God has chosen in love to make God's own. This particular theology is Hemmerle's direct response to Heidegger's refusal to link God and being; in fact, Hemmerle places his Trinitarian ontology squarely within the tradition of the overcoming of metaphysics[40]. The self-giving at the heart of the Trinitarian mystery of God ensures that God cannot be construed as a divine object governed by the principle of sufficient reason. Rather, a fundamentally relational understanding of being, which cannot be deduced but only revealed, breaks the constraints of metaphysics. God's love has ontological and eschatological consequences: the experience of God as love is one that is both present and anticipated, since it is of the character of love to increase in the act of loving[41]. In Trinitarian ontology, being and time are linked.

The presence of the Kingdom of God gives rise to what Hemmerle calls theology's "double apriori": a commitment to the revelational starting point whose fundamental content is determined by God's self-giving in love within creation (the theological apriori), and a commitment to explore all the conditions and possibilities of the reality which God has freely chosen as the grammar of revelation (the philosophical apriori)[42]. Thus, on the one hand, Catholic theology is committed to the image of God is revealed in scripture and in its ongoing reception in the life of the church: a Trinitarian communion of persons in love who bear that love into human history and reveal the fundamental complexion of reality to be relational and open-ended. On the other hand, continual conversion to the Kingdom of God demands a discipleship which mirrors and mediates this all-encompassing love of God to others and to the world. Discipleship implies the performance of Kingdom values

---

39. *Ibid.*, pp. 232-233.
40. See K. HEMMERLE, *Thesen zu einer trinitarischen Ontologie* (n. 37), pp. 53-54.
41. *Ibid.*, pp. 44-46, 54, 59-60.
42. K. HEMMERLE, *Das problematische Verhältnis* (n. 37), pp. 238-239.

in the world, as well as a positive estimation of materiality and temporality as valid sources for our knowledge of God. Catholic theology commits itself to a construal of reality which declares no aspect of reality off-limits to God's saving power, since in the person and message of Jesus "God himself enters into a relationship with us, and thus what we are and where we are and how we are become a *locus theologicus*"[43].

A contemporary Catholic theology of God by implication commits itself to the same full-blooded version of incarnation to which God is committed, to the availability of God within creation, to the on-going disclosure of God's character in the performances of Kingdom values, and to the hoped-for eschatological fulfillment of that disclosure.

IV. CONSEQUENCES FOR A THEOLOGY OF GOD

I have characterized Heidegger's periodization of thought about God, the contemporary as both modern and postmodern, and the implications of the arrival of the Kingdom of God as effects which have changed the complexion of the present-day status of the Christian tradition. At the outset of this paper I indicated that one could derive a program for an authentic Catholic response to the issues they raise, and that is what I wish to sketch in this final section.

With the critique of ontotheology, Heidegger discovered "a complex topology of the world of faith that can never be fitted into the horizons of metaphysical theology"[44]. The effect of this discovery should be to force the theology of God to avoid abstract starting points and to drive theology back to its sources, to the events and experiences which give rise to faith. The theologian could then discover precisely why there is such a "lack of fit" and thereby uncover the dimensions of the revelatory experience of God which burst the constraints of metaphysical conceptualities.

Where would one look for such excess which would determine theology's portrayal of God? For Catholic theology, Heidegger's critique gives little help for determining the next move. In fact, Christian belief makes a claim which stands in fundamental tension with Heidegger's emphasis on divinity's contemporary "default" and concealment[45]. Metz

43. *Ibid.*, p. 230.
44. J.S. O'LEARY, *Religious Pluralism and Christian Truth*, Edinburgh, Edinburgh University Press, 1996, p. x.
45. For a summary of Heidegger's position, see B. WELTE, *God in Heidegger's Thought*, trans. W.J. Kramer, in *Philosophy Today* 26 (1982) 85-100.

provides the real clue: "this practical structure of the idea of God is the reason why the concept of God is basically narrative and memorative"[46]. That is, the sources of our understanding of God are found in the on-going history of lived witness to the God of Jesus Christ and in the presence of the Holy Spirit who inspires the praxis of the believing community of Christians for the duration of its journey through history. The identity of God is revealed primarily in the continuing relationship of God with all creation and particularly with human beings, a relationship understood within a narrated history stretching from ancient Israel through early Christianity into the present. The identity of God as love has taken a specific historical shape and is present within history in a substantial, transformative way[47].

Christianity's emphasis upon the specific "worldly" mediation of revelation makes it clear that one never has any "pure", atemporal, context-free experiences of the divine, nor could one postulate what such experiences might be. Rather, these experiences are always situated within particular historically-constituted traditions of religious practice and reflection. Even our simplest attempts to name the transcendent object of our experience would be of questionable meaning without the horizon of a tradition of interpreted experiences and the narrative context which such a tradition generates[48]. That narrative, when told and remembered, becomes the effective catalyst for new experiences.

A contemporary Catholic theology of God, then, is always involved in a double hermeneutic where both revelation and theology are contextualized: on the one hand, the identity of God is mediated to faith by means of historically-constituted and temporally-contingent images of God, and on the other contemporary theology recognizes that its own analyses are situated and contingent. Here is where the theology of God will remain in constant tension with those postmodern analyses of religious experience which seek what amounts to the modern fictional ideal of the "essence of deity" or the notion of "transcendence" prior to all religious traditions.

None of this rules out an apophatic approach to the nature of God. Indeed, it is demanded by the fundamental structure of the incarnation, by the sufferings and death of Jesus, and by the intrinsic poverty of

---

46. J.B. METZ, *Faith in History and Society* (n. 28), p. 51.
47. See *ibid.*, pp. 51-52, where Metz discusses "the primacy of praxis".
48. See J.S. O'LEARY, *Religious Pluralism and Christian Truth* (n. 44), pp. 160-161: "The event of naming is a narrative event. To name 'God' without such narrative context is a helplessly vague gesture at some unthinkable ultimate. Only stories, explicit or implied, taking the form 'the God who …' give the proper name its bearings".

human thought and language. But an *exclusively* apophatic approach, as advocated by certain forms of postmodern religious thought, distorts the character of the Christian tradition. The examples I have cited from modernity are important instances of the *kataphatic* side of this tradition. Indeed, they emphasize the role of affectivity in mediating divine presence, a role with biblical warrants (e.g., Isa 66,13, 1 Jn 4,16-21). The affective responses prompted by Counter-Reformation religious art and by modern French spirituality may have differed in their intermediate goals, and as expressions of Catholicism both stood in tension with the predominantly objective approaches taken by Baroque scholastic theology. But these spiritualities are important resources. They form part of a larger narrative which recalls in a particularly modern way (e.g., by emphasizing the value of individual conversion and the spiritual discernment of one's personal state before God) the revelation of the love of the Triune God, and the possibility of a relationship with God in the midst of everyday circumstances and in the context of the believing community's sacramental praxis and care for others.

One way for Catholic theology to include both the kataphatic and the apophatic is to model itself after Jesus' revelation of the character of the Kingdom of God. His proclamation of the advent of God's reversal contains a promise that life *can* be otherwise than it is and that God *wills* that it be otherwise – a "difference" which begins in the present and is fulfilled in the future. The symbol of the Kingdom of God is Jesus' imaginative reconstrual of the world as God sees the world, as the arena for the action of incarnate grace which promotes the positive and humanizing, overcomes the negative and brutalizing, and refigures our expectations in the direction of eschatological fulfillment. This alternative understanding of reality is ultimately grounded in the otherness of God and entails a critique of purely human plans and power. Our ability to respond to and to conceive this "difference", this fulfillment of desire which exceeds our "normal", rational expectations, is an example of what the philosopher Richard Kearney has termed the "poetic imagination" – that is, a way of thinking by which one can "begin to imagine that the world as it is could be *otherwise*"[49]. The poetic imagination is both a realistic response to contemporary situations and a direct probing of the new possibilities for existence which those situations present. "Thinking otherwise" beyond the status quo – the retrieval of historical consciousness and of hope in transcendence – restores both a belief that

---

49. R. KEARNEY, *Ethics and the Postmodern Imagination* (n. 18), p. 44 (his emphasis).

the present is neither circular nor absolute, and a hope in newly imagined possibilities for a different and better future, a future which exceeds our present abilities and expectations. *Thinking* otherwise is the catalyst for *acting* otherwise with the confidence that the transformation promised by these new possibilities can be appropriated through action.

This framework of the "otherwise" provides a way of bringing the Catholic commitment to incarnation and sacramentality into direct conversation with a postmodern culture that is suspicious of meta-narratives. Christian religious practices and beliefs can be understood as the believing community's activation of its poetic imagination. The community responds to the revealed "excess" of God and of God's grace and probes situations for new possibilities of existence in the light of God's relationship with humankind and with the cosmos. Christianity's "oppositional" nature, animated by the revelation of God in Jesus Christ, announces that life *can* be otherwise than an unending cycle of desires and the commodified images that fulfill them, and that God *wills* that it be otherwise: an "otherwise" which is life-enhancing, beginning in the present and fulfilled in the future. Such an active refiguration of the world toward eschatological fulfillment becomes meaningful for us within our act of faith in God – that is, by our imagining as possible the power of God to transform seemingly hopeless situations and the suitability of the world to mediate such transformation. This response of imagination to the revealed mystery of divine love is the first step toward hoping in and participating in its ongoing actualization. In other words, conversion to God implies putting into practice the values of the Kingdom of God.

Theology's commitment to both kataphatic and apophatic methods as well as its awareness of its hermeneutical situation give rise to a final task which could be considered a legitimate extension of the "philosophical apriori". A contemporary Catholic theology of God must continue the tradition of the rational reflection upon faith, even while heeding the postmodern critiques of modern reason's foundationalist pretensions. Theology cannot offer merely a naive repetition of biblical and traditional materials or an internal apologetic. An "external apologetic", justifying the claims of the particularly Christian understanding of God and God's relation to reality, is still necessary in the thick of the contemporary context where so many stories of ultimacy and transcendence jostle for attention.

This is particularly true in the period after Heidegger's critique of ontotheology. The more extreme interpretations have gone beyond Heidegger's own intention to argue, in various ways, that it is "difference" itself which is the primal condition which conditions God. It is understandable, then, why Marion and Kasper attempt to answer this challenge directly. Their responses fulfill a portion of the tasks outlined here, but each reveals an inadequacy as well. For Marion, charity is the primal condition which conditions even difference; if God is love, then God is the all-determining condition, even of being[50]. But in pursuing this he tilts too far in the direction of the apophatic. Indeed, he has been criticized for reducing the history of divine disclosure and donation to one moment (the death of the crucified Jesus) which seems to bear no relation to the life-history which precedes it[51]. Kasper, for his part, argues that the primal condition is freedom-in-love revealed in the mystery of the Trinity[52]. But he neglects the important resources which spirituality and popular piety offer, and only superficially treats the political and emancipative consequences which flow from considering God in terms of "freedom" and "relational being". As I have tried to show here, a truly contemporary Catholic theology of God should display the rigor seen in the arguments of Marion and Kasper, while acknowledging that the field of evidence for authentic images of God is wider than some contemporary theologies are willing to grant.

If a contemporary Catholic theology of God, mindful of its commitment to incarnation and sacramentality, is to take advantage of these opportunities and respond to the challenges of other discourses which claim legitimacy in speaking about God, it must understand its place within a history of effects which is both intellectual and ecclesial. By retrieving a redemptive history of God from all parts of history and by responding out of the depths of its tradition with an eye toward new possibilities of expression and existence, Catholic theology will be able to provide a more adequate explanation of the revelation of the God of Jesus Christ and a more detailed description of its implications. In doing so, it itself may become an incarnation of the very Kingdom values which reveal God's mysterious reversal of negativity and suffering.

50. J.-L. MARION, *God without Being* (n. 13), pp. 100-105.
51. See T. SANDERS, *The Otherness of God and the Bodies of Others,* in *The Journal of Religion* 76 (1996) 572-587, pp. 579-580; see also J.S. O'LEARY, *Religious Pluralism and Christian Truth* (n. 44), pp. 185-191 and his remarks on Marion's tendency to bypass the historical contingency of our names for God.
52. W. KASPER, *God of Jesus Christ* (n. 14), pp. 303-311, esp. p. 310 (citing Hemmerle); see also p. 153-157. Cf. E.A. JOHNSON, *She Who Is: The Mystery of God in Feminist Theological Discourse,* New York, Crossroad, 1992, pp. 222-223.
53. This essay is a revised version of *Prolegomena to a Catholic Theology of God between Heidegger and Postmodernity,* in *The Heythrop Journal* 40 (1999) 319-339.

It would thus provide, while performing its speculative duties, an ecclesial ministry which is practical and pastoral, and contemporary as well[53].

Villanova University   A.J. GODZIEBA
Department of Theology & Religious Studies
800 Lancaster Avenue
Villanova, PA 19085-1699
USA

AFTER HEIDEGGER: TRANSUBSTANTIATION

Introduction

Why should the question of transubstantiation arise 'after Heidegger'? Is it because, in the light of what Heidegger might have to say about substance, saying what transubstantiation needs to say becomes easier? Does it become easier to think the kind of rupture of the physical that transubstantiation is, *after* Heidegger? Surely the postmodern, with its easy talk of ruptures, breaches, aporia, and so on, invites such a re-engagement? But is it not rather, that transubstantiation stands as a kind of embarrassment, from which Heidegger might free us? This rupture of the physical did not appear in the postmodern, but for us theologians at least, from the beginning. The rupture of the body of Christ present in bread and wine, present on our altars, pre-dates the postmodern, and appears in a cosmos otherwise pretending to be seamless. It is the very *embarrassment* of the rupture of transubstantiation itself that makes it demand to speak again, after Heidegger.

I

How does transubstantiation embarrass us? Herbert McCabe says that "[t]he Council of Trent did not decree that Catholics should believe in transubstantiation: it just calls it a most appropriate (*aptissime*) way of talking about the Eucharist, presumably leaving open whether there might not be other, perhaps even more appropriate ways of talking"[1]. John Macquarrie similarly and routinely refers to transubstantiation as a 'theory' or a 'very good attempt to elucidate the eucharistic mystery'[2]. For St. Thomas, however, and for his antecedents, transubstantiation names something that happens, and is known to happen, to the substances of bread and wine in virtue of their consecration[3].

---

1. H. McCabe, *Eucharistic Change*, in *Priests and People* 8 (1994) 217-221.
2. J. Macquarrie, *Paths in Spirituality*, London, SCM, ²1992, p. 88; Id., *Thinghood and Sacramentality* (Essex Papers in Theology and Society), Colchester, University of Essex, 1995, p. 23 ff.
3. For a summary of earlier uses of the term, see D. Power, *The Eucharistic Mystery*, Dublin, Gill & Macmillan, pp. 244-246.

A further source of embarrassment is summed up well by Catherine Pickstock – that transubstantiation "pushes... Aristotelian categories to breaking point"[4]. Pickstock uses precisely this view to instate her own defence of transubstantiation. In fact transubstantiation indicates the extent to which St. Thomas' re-inscription of Aristotle's physics is total, so that it very naturally concurs with everything else St. Thomas has to say in this regard. Where does Aquinas push Aristotle to breaking point and why? Aquinas breaks company with Aristotle in the matter of the eternity of the world, which for St. Thomas cannot be, since "in principio creavit Deus caelum et terram"[5]. He re-casts the whole of Aristotle's physics, for whom motion in things is eternal, and so for whom the unmoved cause of motion is not a *temporally* prior cause. Transubstantiation does not, strictly speaking, work within an Aristotelian frame at all, rather it depends on an already Christian conception of the cosmos. For St. Thomas, the accidents of the bread and wine remain and are held explicitly by the unlimited power (*infinitam virtutem*) of God[6]. This power, however is exercised because "... Deus... est prima causa substantiae et accidentis"[7], and *not* in virtue of transubstantiation itself. It is for this reason that transubstantiation is not in any way according to nature, and yet in no way disturbs nature: it is not according to local motion and so does not disturb (Aristotle's understanding of) place

---

4. C. PICKSTOCK, *After Writing: On the Liturgical Consummation of Philosophy*, Oxford, Blackwell, 1998, p. 259. She is here herself citing Marion. What she describes here, of the substance of the bread being 'taken up' (p. 260) into the substance of God, because God is more truly substance rather misses the point – in fact as a resolution of transubstantiation Aquinas explicitly rules this out by use of the verb mutare, rather than tollere. (*Summa Theologiae*, IIIa, Q. 75, resp.) St. Thomas actually says that in the sacrament it is 'as if' the substance of bread and wine remains, but this is by a special kind of event which exceeds even the miraculous. He expressly does not want a hierarchy of substances such that a lower is subsumed by a higher, since this would profoundly disturb both the theology of the incarnation and that of the divinisation of the human person. Pickstock's understanding of transubstantiation has the effect of proposing that all bread is potentially the body of Christ ("all bread is on its way to figuring the Body of Christ" [p. 260]), a suggestion St. Thomas explicitly rules out in the Commentary on the Sentences (In IV Sententiarum, *De Sent*. 11, Q. 1) and which he reinforces in the Tertia Pars at question 75, a. 8 (resp.): "non dicitur... panis possit esse corpus Christi". This is explained precisely because there is no continuity of subject or being between bread, and bread which by similitude only has become the body of Christ. Thus no bread is on the way to being the body of Christ until God makes it so, which is a rupture, not a continuity in nature.

5. St. Thomas says on more than one occasion that the opinion of Aristotle that the world is from eternity is false. (Cf., for example, In II Sententiarum, *De Sent*. 1 Q. 1 resp. 5).

6. T. AQUINAS, *Summa Theologiae*, IIIa, Q. 77, a. 1, resp.

7. *Ibid*., IIIa, Q. 77, a. 1, resp.; cf. T. AQUINAS, *Summa Contra Gentiles*, Lb. 4, Cap. 65.

(*topos*)[8]. Central to this is Aquinas' reconfiguration of Aristotle's understanding of causation, so that the conception of first cause as a temporal
initiation stands over against Aristotle's causality (which requires immediate contiguity or entire continuity of the cause of a thing with what it
is caused by)[9]. The first cause is, at least theoretically, remote. This theoretical remotion of causation of things *ab initio* from God is actually
seen to be overcome in the body of Christ, *through* transubstantiation,
because St. Thomas' definition of it indicates the immediacy of God to
the cosmos, by a miraculous means which must both be seen, and known
to be. It requires faith in order to see, and so know, its objectivity.

In this sense, transubstantiation becomes the marker, not for a rupture
of physics, but for the redemption of the physical whose origin is in
God. Transubstantiation is the mark, the point, at which Aristotelian
physics is both preserved and disrupted: preserved, inasmuch as the language of place, motion, category, substance and accident hold; disrupted, inasmuch as this description of the cosmos is now entirely
dependent on Divine power. The point of preservation and disruption is
the body of Christ as such, inasmuch as it is either human alone, or
redemptive (human/divine). Moreover, Aquinas has produced a body
which is *without* Aristotelian place (*locus*, *topos*)[10], entirely *within* the
Aristotelian cosmos. A Christian understanding of the cosmos is here
entirely co-incident with its pagan description, brought to light by the
very body of Christ itself, every time that body itself is repetitiously and
sacramentally made present to the cosmos, and insofar as I have to
'know' to know what transubstantiation makes to be known, this
redeemed cosmos is understood to exist entirely in consequence of (my)
intellection: I am the proper locus of its existence[11].

---

8. *Ibid.*, IIIa, Q. 75, a. 2, resp. "Manifestum est autem quod corpus Christi non incipit
esse in hoc sacramento per motum localem." [It is clear that the body of Christ does not
begin to be in this sacrament by local motion.]

9. ARISTOTLE, *Physics*: IV, 4, 211a31-34; V, 3, 226b34-227a9. See especially *Physics*
VII, 2, 243a3-10.

10. T. AQUINAS, *Summa Theologiae*, IIIa, Q. 75, a. 4, resp., "... cum in hoc sacramento sit verum corpus Christi, nec incipiat ibi esse de novo per motum localem; cum
etiam nec corpus Christi sit ibi sicut in loco...".

11. T. AQUINAS, *Summa Theologiae*, Q. 75, a. 1, resp. "... verum corpus Christi et
sanguinem esse in hoc sacramento, non sensu deprehendi potest, sed sola fide, quae auc-
toritati divinae innititur." The Blackfriars translation of 1920 (*Summa Theologica*, London, Benziger, 1920) says "cannot be detected by sense, nor understanding". This is
clearly wrong, since there is no mention of detection "intellectu" in the Latin, neither in
the Leonine nor the Busa editions. Faith is not opposed to intellect in St. Thomas, indeed,
faith is what would bring intellection to a higher conformity with the divine. Intellection
is necessarily involved in truth, even those truths known by the faith alone, since for

This brings us to a post-conciliar embarrassment, which criticises transubstantiation as an over-fixity on the species of the eucharist. For St. Thomas at least, this is entirely outside transubstantiation's intentions, because transubstantiation enacts an intellection: in undertaking a certain to-be-made-known, it requires that intellection itself is the way in which the redemption in Christ is known *to be*. The real transubstantiation is enacted in the intellect of the believer, yet not in consequence of his or her will, but entirely in consequence of God's power[12]. For St. Thomas, this is because what is true is primarily in the mind, and only secondarily in things, even things which are themselves divine[13].

When in 1277 the Averroists were condemned for limiting the power of God, because they claimed that in Aristotle the relation between place and body was such that not even God could transgress it, Duns Scotus repaired the damage to natural physics itself by showing how a possible body (a rock) could be created by God apart from the earth and held there[14]. A rock (*sw'ma*) which, being apart from the earth, would be 'naturally' held in a place (*topos*) which would not be its proper place, according to Aristotle. But in transubstantiation Aquinas had already performed this feat without naturalising it, by making demonstration of the infinite power of God dependent, not on an inert rock, but on the living and redemptive body of Christ. Transubstantiation installs a body that is not in its proper place. In contrast to St. Thomas, Scotus has been forced by the condemnation of Averroism to produce a conception of the cosmos that, as Helen Lang notes "is strikingly similar to that of Descartes"[15]. Lang implies, and I am convinced she is right, that the condemnation of Averroism in 1277 leads directly to the necessity for what finally becomes Newtonian physics, a claim also made (independently) by Heidegger[16].

St. Thomas reason is the condition under which the truths of faith could be understood. (Cf. T. AQUINAS, *Quaestiones Disputatae: De Veritate*, Q. 10).

12. Hence the importance of the question in the mediaeval schools, "quid sumit mus?" with its concomitant answer, the mouse does not consume the body of Christ.

13. T. AQUINAS, *Quaestiones Disputatae: De Veritate*, Q. 1, a. 2, resp. "Res autem non dicitur vera nisi secundum quod est intellectu adequata; unde per posterius invenitur verum in rebus, per prius autem in intellectu." ["A thing is not called true, however, unless it is conformed with intellection; truth therefore is only subsequently in things and primarily in the intellect.]

14. J. DUNS SCOTUS, *Ordinatio 2*, dist. 2, pars 2, q. 2, par. 231. I am indebted to Helen Lang for this example and her analysis of it. (H. LANG, *Bodies and Angels: The Occupants of Place for Aristotle and Duns Scotus*, in *Viator*, Vol. 14 (1983) 245-266.)

15. H. LANG, *Bodies and Angels* (n. 14), p. 256, n. 41.

16. This is exactly the form of Heidegger's critique of Newton in 1936. In M. HEIDEGGER, *Die Frage nach dem Ding: zu Kants Lehre von den transzendentalen Grund-*

Understood like this, transubstantiation stands as the refusal of a saturation of the cosmos with the Christian God, which Newtonian physics enforces, by constructing the universe as needing to have a beginning. Because the sacred species alone demonstrate the creative power of God *ab initio*, they prevent a pre-emptive redemption of the universe so that it must be received as already redeemed by every unbeliever – where even the unbeliever is forced to accept that there was a beginning to the cosmos, and to construct his or her physical conception of being itself on that basis[17].

sätzen (Gesamtausgabe 41), ed. P. JAEGER, Frankfurt, Klostermann, 1984. Freiburg, winter semester 1935/36. First published as *Die Frage nach dem Ding*, Tübingen, Niemeyer, 1962. Translated as *What Is A Thing?*, trans. W.B. Barton & V. Deutsch, South Bend, Regnery, 1967. Heidegger notes "Das neuzeitliche Denken ist nicht mit einem Schlage da. Die Ansätze regen sich im 15. Jahrhundert in der Spätscholastik.... Erst im 17 Jahrhundert vollziehen sich die entscheidenden Klärungen und Begründungen. (p. 59)... Die Natur oder der Kosmos gelten aber seit der Herrschaft des Christentums im Abendland als das Geschaffene, nicht nur im Mittelalter, sondern auch durch die ganze neuzeitliche Philosophie hindurch. Die neuzeitliche Metaphysik seit Descartes bis zu Kant, und über Kant hinaus auch die Metaphysik des Deutschen Idealismus, ist ohne die christlichen Grundvorstellungen nicht zu denken. Das Verhältnis zum dogmatischen Kirchenglauben kann dabei sehr locker, sogar abgebrochen sein. (p. 84 ff.) [Modern thought does not appear all at once. Its beginnings stir during the later Scholasticism of the fifteenth century... Only in the 17th century are the decisive clarifications and groundings accomplished.... However, since the ascendancy of Christianity in the West, not only throughout the medieval period but also through all of modern philosophy, nature and universe were considered as created. Modern metaphysics from Descartes to Kant, and also the metaphysics of German Idealism after Kant, are unthinkable without the Christian ideas that underlie them. Yet the relation to the dogma of the Church can be very loose, even broken.] In a similar vein, Lang points out "Newton's [conception of] nature is Christian in important ways, eg. God's action in it is indispensable... for Aristotle, natural things have an immediate orientation to their actuality. H. LANG, *The Order of Nature in Aristotle's Physics: Place and the Elements*, Cambridge, Cambridge University Press, 1998, p. 154. It is no accident that both Heidegger and Lang point out the extent to which Aristotle's *Physics* are the wholly neglected underpinning of any serious understanding of Aristotle. (Cf. M. HEIDEGGER, *Platon: Sophistes* (Gesamtausgabe 19), ed. I. SCHÜBLER, Frankfurt, Klostermann, 1992. Marburg, winter semester 1924/25. Translated as Plato's *Sophist*, trans. R. Rojcewicz & A. Schuwer, Bloomington, Indiana, 1997, §12 (c). When the Aristotelian background to Heidegger's thought is understood, it becomes entirely possible to explain his irascible and hostile remarks concerning faith and creation, in M. HEIDEGGER, *Einführung in die Metaphysik* (Gesamtausgabe 40), ed. P. JAEGER, Frankfurt, Klostermann, 1983. Freiburg, summer semester 1935. First published as *Einführung in die Metaphysik*, Tübingen, Niemeyer, 1953. E.T.: *An Introduction to Metaphysics*, trans. R. Manheim, New Haven, Yale, 1959, pp. 6-7.

17. Finally, for St. Thomas, unity of myself with God in Christ is an embodied union, which must be repeated through continual sacramental activity. It is the conjoining of my body with the body of Christ that will both unite me to God and save me. The Christianity of the Newtonian cosmos is undertaken through an act of reason, moreover, as Heidegger has shown over and over again, but above all in characterising ontotheology, a reason that is always in advance of me, and into adequation with which I must always bring myself, and which, far from being repeatable, is always in consequence of a singularity, a single deduction.

II

There have been various attempts to reinstate transubstantiation by appeal to Heidegger's elaboration of *das Geviert*, the 'fourfold'. The temptation to turn to this idea as a resolution of the embarrassments I have named is well summarised by Louis-Marie Chauvet in his monumental work *Symbole et Sacrement*, and can be found in the work of John Macquarrie as well.

In Heidegger's *das Geviert* the worlding of world can be turned out towards divinity, or the earth, mortals or sky. This divinity is not, however, necessarily the Christian God, not because Heidegger is not (or even is) a Christian, but because what in metaphysics was derived as divinity under the sway of reason itself, is, through the worlding of world, to be understood the other way about. World is not now already given in advance by God, as its reason, its being-already-created. Rather, world presses out towards God insofar as it does, to indicate, hint, wink and nudge towards what of the world is divine. Heidegger abolishes all causality in the fourfold, both the causality of Aristotle, and at the same time, the consequences for the physical cosmos of the Newtonian causality, the origin of the cosmos in God. At the centre of unfolding the fourfold is *das Ereignis*, the event of being. Johannes Lotz points out "Das Ereignis hingegen enthält ein Verhältnis, das nicht Kausalität ist, und ein Geben, das nichts mit Machen zu tun hat"[18].

As Chauvet recognises, "Cette voie symbolique est évidement *insuffisante* pour exprimer la portée de la présence eucharistique"[19]. Chauvet is almost at a loss to resolve the embarrassments of transubstantiation, and is left emphasising that, re-reading the decree and canons of the thirteenth session of the Council of Trent, "on doit ne plus dire: «Ce pain n'est plus du pain» which commits us to the terrain of "substance métaphysique" but, in the light of the excoriating critique which is ontotheology in which "le verbe «*être*» n'a originairement plus le même statut du fait que le *Sein* est inséparable du *Da-Sein* humain", that the bread of the eucharist becomes essential bread and mystery: "Ceci est LE pain"[20].

---

18. J. Lotz, *Martin Heidegger und Thomas von Aquin*, Pfullingen, Neske, 1975, p. 181. "Das Ereignis, however, contains a relation that is not causality, and a giving that has nothing to do with power."

19. L.-M. Chauvet, *Symbole et Sacrement: une relecture sacramentelle de l'existence chrétienne*, Paris, Cerf, p. 408. "This symbolic approach is obviously insufficient for expressing the significance of the Eucharistic presence." Author's emphasis.

20. *Ibid.*, p. 410. "One must no longer say 'this bread is no longer bread'… the verb 'to be' no longer has the same status it had at its origin because the Sein is inseparable from the human Da-Sein… This is THE bread."

This does not resolve Chauvet's loss, for it says that after the critique of ontotheology, this (consecrated) bread now throws all other bread into relief. How is this different from Catherine Pickstock's argument that all bread is on the way to being the body of Christ? This bread becomes the breadness of all bread. Bread becomes a Form. And yet, Chauvet has almost grasped the nettle, for the issue here does indeed concern the being of the bread.

For the bread to 'be' it must be 'there', it must eventuate *Dasein*. The problem is that the being of the bread is being read as the breadness of the bread, which resolves nothing. Whatever the bread (and wine) eventuates (*sich ereignet*), it eventuates *for* and *as Dasein*. So if the bread and wine are the body and blood of Christ, and known to be such, they will eventuate *Dasein* as the body and blood of Christ. And for transubstantiation as such, nothing has been said here at all: in commenting only on bread (not even on wine) the question of substance has been overlooked entirely.

III

The appearance of the word 'transubstantiation' in the work of the gender theorist Judith Butler and her co-locutor Slavoj Žižek is an extraordinary event[21]. Moreover, its appearance acts as a renewed source of potential embarrassment. Butler does not spare us: her use appears in 1993 in relation to her reading of the film *Paris is Burning* whose subject matter is pre- and post-operative transsexuals. I do not want to get carried away by the subject matter. Transsexuals explicitly rely on an essentialisation of the 'natural' difference between male and female in order to exist. It should become immediately clear, therefore, why Butler has selected this word to undertake a reading of what this film is about. Moreover, the principal figure to whom the word is applied is a pre-operative transsexual: again, not coincidentally. In her reading of the film, it is only *we who are in the know* that know both what this character, Venus Xtravaganza, 'really' is (there has been no formal transmutation at the hands of the surgeon), and that what Venus really is, is the matter of *our* intellection. As Butler points out, someone who, taking Venus for a 'natural' woman, murders her upon discovering that he has taken her all too literally, and who therefore does not make the transubstantiation we make.

---

21. I do not propose to look in detail at Slavoj Žižek. Žižek's use of the term appears in 1997 (S. Žižek, *The Plague of Phantasies*, London, Verso, 1997).

Slavoj Žižek has also used the term. Writing five years later than Butler, he argues:

> Freud's notion of castration anxiety has any meaning at all only if we suppose that *the threat of castration* (the prospect of castration, the 'virtual' castration) *already produces real 'castrating' effects*. This actuality of the virtual... has to be connected to the basic paradox of power, which is that symbolic power is by definition virtual, power-in-reserve, the threat of its full use which never actually occurs.... The consequence of this conflation of actual with virtual is a kind of transubstantiation: every actual activity appears as a 'form of appearance' of another 'invisible' power whose status is purely virtual[22].

Do these re-uses of transubstantiation connect with a theological use?

In the first place, the question of perspective is radically altered. Butler's use of transubstantiation is more complex than it at first seems. *Paris is Burning* is a film, in which the transubstantiating thing is not, strictly speaking, seen at all. Venus Xtravaganza, the transsexual, is not the thing to be transubstantiated: Venus, rather, is the one seeking the effect of the transubstantiation. Venus seeks a kind of redemption which only the camera (and we who watch from behind, and so in a sense *as*, the camera lens) can confer. Butler notes that "the camera acts as surgical instrument and operation, the vehicle through which the transubstantiation occurs"[23] But the transubstantiation is virtual, not real. Venus desires a form of redemption – we are told: "... Venus speaks her desire to become a whole woman, to find a man and have a house in the suburbs with a washing machine"[24]. The banalized beatitude of this vision of redemption masks its real force (itself a marker of its most postmodern yearning, that surgical castration is predicated on a yearning, not for so much, but so little): the lens alone effects the redemption: it is the transubstantiated thing.

In Žižek's case transubstantiation exposes the 'real' power relations that persist through their tangible appearances. His use of the term "power-in-reserve" exactly corresponds to Heidegger's use of *der Bestand*, the "standing reserve" that is the character of power itself *through* or in the essence (*das Wesen*) of technology[25]. Heidegger notes

22. S. ŽIŽEK, *Cyberspace, or, the Unbearable Closure of Being in The Plague of Fantasies*, New York, Verso, 1998, p. 150.

23. J. BUTLER, *Gender is Burning: Question of Appropriation and Subversion,* in ID., *Bodies that matter: On the Discursive Limits of Sex*, New York, Routledge, p. 135.

24. *Ibid.*, p. 133.

25. Heidegger's elaboration of der Zustand, der Bestand, die Bestandsicherung can be found in M. HEIDEGGER, *Beiträge zur Philosophie (Vom Ereignis)* (Gesamtausgabe 65), ed. F.-W. HERRMANN, Frankfurt, Klostermann, 1989. Original (and incomplete) text worked out between 1936 and 1938, §§256-7, in the Bremen lectures published as *Das*

that "Denn es gehört zum Wesen des Willens zur Macht, das Wirkliche, das er be-mächtigt, nicht in *der* Wirklichkeit erscheinen zu lassen, als welcher er selber west"[26]. Transubstantiation here names that point at which something comes to be seen for what it really is, *despite appearances*. Let us not be distracted by the tantalising mentions of power, gender, and optical configuration, except to say that these are the very structures of the postmodern world. This world is in a forceful confrontation with the Newtonian universe, but it is as it is in consequence of Nietzsche's death of God: it is already drained of God. Transubstantiation must therefore appear in it as parodic of its origins. For both Butler and Žižek, transubstantiation represents a certain 'being taken into the know': what St. Thomas would have understood by 'intellection', but devoid of God. Transubstantiation is for them a 'point at which' something which can be taken for one thing is in fact *known* to be another, *but could still be taken for what it was taken for at first*.

Conclusion

Both Butler and Žižek articulate transubstantiation almost without reference to the two things which would appear to concern the term most: substance, and God. I do not believe that there is a 'natural' or 'ordinary' use of the term: without its appearance in the Christian tradition, it would not otherwise appear. Precisely because it forces us to confront the fact that it has no 'natural' usage (its very power to embarrass us), it enacts not only itself, but its genealogy. As a troubled term, its usage continually highlights and draws attention to areas of difficulty. It is for *precisely* this reason that its reappearance outside a specifically Christian discourse is of significance: unless we bring the genealogy itself to light, we will fail entirely to understand the relations operating between theological and non-theological discourse. Or, are we simply to take our own speaking as discrete from any other, particularly in areas that embarrass us. In this case, we speak to none but ourselves, and not even

---

Ding and *Die Kehre* in M. HEIDEGGER, *Bremer und Freiburger Vorträge: 1. Einblick in das was ist; 2. Grundsätze des Denkens*, ed. P. JAEGER, Frankfurt, Klostermann, 1994; in M. HEIDEGGER, *Die Frage nach dem Technik* in ID., *Vorträge und Aufsätze. 1936-53* (Gesamtausgabe 7), Pfullingen, Neske, 1954 and in *Zur Seinsfrage* in ID., *Wegmarken* (Gesamtausgabe 9), Frankfurt, Klostermann, 1976. 1919-61. First published as ID., *Wegmarken*, Frankfurt, Klostermann, 1967. Translated in full and edited as ID., *Pathmarks*, trans. & ed. W. MCNEILL, New York, Cambridge University Press, 1998.

26. M. HEIDEGGER, *Zur Seinsfrage* (n. 27), p. 390. "For it is part of the essence of the will to power not to permit the reality which it has power over to appear in that reality in which it itself exists".

then – for I do not constitute the entirety of the world which worlds for me by theological language alone.

I have argued that Chauvet's and Pickstock's attempts to restore the term for non-embarrassed use mirror each other, and precisely by avoiding the troubled issue of intellection, fail to show how bread and being belong together. This is because they take the metaphysics of substance to refer (in the mater of transubstantiation) to bread and wine. Butler cites Michel Haar's critique of Nietzsche as the origin of the phrase 'metaphysics of substance', which she argues "constitute the artificial philosophical means by which simplicity, order, and identity are effectively instituted... according to Haar, the critique of the metaphysics of substance implies a critique of the very notion of the psychological person as a substantive thing"[27]. What Haar discusses is not Nietzsche, but Heidegger's critique of Nietzsche[28]. Butler's entire phrase "metaphysics of substance" is a marker for precisely the critique of ontotheology that Chauvet also refers to in his reference to "substance métaphysique"[29]. In this sense Butler writes *after* Heidegger, that is, after the critique has been carried out and is operative within discourse[30].

And yet she does know, more than Chauvet, that the issue here is about the *locus*, the place, the *topos*"of transubstantiation, for which a thing, the thing said itself to be transubstantiated, effects a change in the one who knows the change to have taken place. Metaphysics of subjectivity is a name for what Heidegger names, almost untranslatably, as "Subjektität", the coming about and powerful enacting of power as hegemony, which orders all other configurations to it, as a 'rulership' of subjectivity – what Butler herself names as subjection. He notes in *Identität und Differenz* that being (*das Sein*) will finally come to be thought as "Substanz und Substanzialität" which is the "Subjekt in seiner absoluten Subjektität"[31]. Commenting on Jünger's *Der Arbeiter*, he argues that this same 'subjecticity' now is no longer understood as "Ichheit" of individual subjectivity, but as a ruling form of the will to power will take on the form of "die vorgeformte gestalthafte Praesenz eines

---

27. J. BUTLER, *Gender Trouble: Feminism and the subversion of identity*, New York, Routledge, 1990, p. 20.

28. Which Haar is well aware of and on which he has commented at length. See for instance M. HAAR, *Le Chant de la terre: Heidegger et les assises de l'Histoire de l'Être*, Paris, Éditions de l'Herne, 1987, §§VI-VII.

29. L.-M. CHAUVET, *Symbole et Sacrement* (n. 19), p. 410 (see §II above).

30. Even though she does not know the effect of his critique as such. She is not 'in the know' about it. She has not, to my knowledge, read Heidegger's critique of Nietzsche.

31. M. HEIDEGGER, *Identität und Differenz*, Neske Pfullingen, 1957, p. 37. "Substance and substantiality... [the] subject in its absolute subjecticity".

Menschenschlages (Typus) bildet die äußereste Subjektität, die in der Vollendung der neuzeitlichen Metaphysik hervorkommt"[32]. This being confronted with an already-formed subjectivity into which I must always inscribe myself in order to 'be' at all, in which way 'bodies' (sw'ma) matter (i.e. take on a 'form' that has a 'look') is exactly the critique that Butler advances. She does this in virtue of herself, or rather she does this in the person of one who does not matter (within the heterosexual, masculinist, matrix she critiques), and therefore knows what must be undertaken to effect a transubstantiation, a change in substance which both saves the outward appearances and can be 'known' to have been effected. The change in question is effected in the self as a self-intellection in virtue of something from *without*, but it is effected through (her-)self

Here for the first time we can catch a glimpse of what is really at issue for Butler (and for Žižek) in transubstantiation. Transubstantiation, for them, names a change in the self which is effected through an intellection which is not willed. Theologically thought, this means that the substance of the bread and wine is not strictly speaking at issue (though they are not annihilated): the being of the bread and the wine is eventuated (*sich ereignet*) in a particular way which must entail and effect a change in *me*. I am re-*materialised* as 'in Christ' in a way that I did not will, but rather that has enacted me *as* such. *I* am the proper locus, *topos* of transubstantiation. The body of Christ in me is a body both within, and outside, its proper place.

Heythrop College
University of London
Kensington Square
London W8 5HQ, UK

Laurence Paul HEMMING

---

32. M. HEIDEGGER, *Zur Seinsfrage* (n. 27), p. 396. "the pre-formed formlike presence of a species of men (type) forms the most extreme subjectivity which comes forth in the fulfilment of modern metaphysics".

THE CONCEPT OF 'SACRAMENTAL ANXIETY'

A KIERKEGAARDIAN LOCUS OF TRANSCENDENCE?

Encounter with human creatures is given us through the sense of presence.
Encounter with God is given us through a sense of absence.
Compared with this absence, presence becomes more absent than absence.
Simone Weil – *Notebooks*

The present, however, is not a concept of time, except precisely as
something infinitely contentless, which again is the infinite vanishing.
S.K. – *Three Discourses on Imagined Occasions*

I. INTRODUCTION

Although I would contend that Søren Kierkegaard himself was neither
a postmodern nor a sacramentologist as such, his work nonetheless displays peculiar affinities to these, and can be intriguingly germane to the
question of "sacramental presence" in a postmodern setting.

While at first sight, the curious, even labyrinthine, nature of
Kierkegaard's own writing would hardly seem a promising point of
departure to speak about "sacramental presence", I contend that his
"style" or way of writing seeks to circumscribe a "locus of transcendence", a place wherein something from "outside," might actually break
into one's life, a place wherein a sense of absence may come to be truly
present, a place that may come to be full of grace. Circumscribing such
a "locus", however, could hardly be thought of as an easy affair; indeed,
it is itself a rather a peculiar task, for it lay woven in the enigmatic contours of human existing. Indeed, as Kierkegaard's multi-faceted work
has repeatedly and insistently shown (as well as being reflected in and
through his curious "style"), human existing is not some 'thing' which
can be straightforwardly analyzed and/or explicated. Instead, the 'no-
thing-ness' of human existing is a problematic in which one is already
and inescapably entangled and as such can neither be viewed objectively

nor designated metaphysically. To do so, as Kierkegaard and his various pseudonymous authors have repeatedly and pointedly displayed, misses precisely what it thinks to have conceived/grasped. In short, because the contours of one's own existence are primarily felt rather than seen, a matter of passion [*Lidenskab*] rather than *theorein*, the work of Kierkegaard's writing style is to bring the reader to feel and engage the contours of existing's 'no-thing-ness', for it is precisely "there" where transcendence might break in, where absence may come to be truly present, where the human may come to be touched by the divine.

It is my contention, not unlike Kierkegaard, that whatever a 'locus' of transcendence might be, and however such a "thing" may be *present*, it can only be found in the enigmatic contours of human existing. In terms of "sacramental presence", this means that "Being" and "metaphysical presence" cannot but miss the point since sacramental presence could only come to be "present" in the existential "be-coming" from the groundless no-thing-ness of human freedom. One way of exploring such a "Kierkegaardian" locus of transcendence is through the concept of 'sacramental anxiety', a concept which can emerge through a reading of Kierkegaard's *The Concept of Anxiety*[1] and *Three Discourses on Imagined Occasions*[2]. The first, written pseudonymously, unravels the 'concept of anxiety', unfolding a kind of philosophical anthropology which attempts to make room for faith – in what might be termed a *present absence*; the second, written in his own name, muses upon three sacramental occasions (i.e. a confession, a wedding, and at a graveside) wherein the divine may come to be encountered, reflecting a theological anthropology which also makes room for faith – but now in what might be termed an *absent presence*. The point of reading these two works

---

1. Originally published: Vigilius HAUFNIENSIS, *Begrebet Angest. En simpel psykolo-gisk-paapegende Overveielse i Retning af det dogmatiske Problem om Arvesynden*, København, C.A. Reitzel, 1844. Presently in: *Søren Kierkegaard. Samlede Værker*, Bind IV, eds. A.B. DRACHMANN, J.L. HEIBERG & H.O. LANGE, Copenhagen, Gyldendal, 1901-06. English translation in: *Kierkegaard's Writings VIII: The Concept of Anxiety: A Simple Psychologically Orienting Deliberation on the Dogmatic Issue of Hereditary Sin*, ed. & trans. R. THOMTE, Princeton, Princeton University Press, 1985. Future references will be to *The Concept of Anxiety* and followed by the location in the first edition of the collected works [*SV IV*].

2. Originally published: S. KIERKEGAARD, *Tre Taler ved tænkte Leiligheder*, København, C.A. Reitzel, 1845. Presently in: *Søren Kierkegaard. Samlede Værker*, Bind V, eds. A.B. DRACHMANN, J.L. HEIBERG and H.O. LANGE, Copenhagen, Gyldendal, 1901-06. English translation in: *Kierkegaard's Writings X: Three Discourses on Imagined Occasions*, eds. & trans. H.V. HONG & E.H. HONG, Princeton, Princeton University Press, 1993. Future references will be to *Three Discourses on Imagined Occasions* and followed by the location in the first edition of the collected works [*SV V*].

side-by-side, however, neither intends to determine a hierarchy nor derive some synthesis herein, but to tease out a resonant thread of human and religious existing, without pretending or even desiring to wholly tie up its loose ends[3]. Not only would such a "tying up" seem incongruous to the tenor of Kierkegaard's own way of authoring, the very "tone" of these works clearly thwarts any such direct/straight-forward "cross-reading", while at the same time creating alluring echoes and an evocative resonance.

The concept of 'sacramental anxiety' which can emerge through a "resonant reading" of these rather different works, then, is my way of indicating that a (Kierkegaardian) locus of transcendence is fundamentally, but likewise importantly, peculiar. If the divine and the human are to "touch" – which would seem to be at the very heart of 'sacramental presence' – and yet their essential difference/asymmetry be preserved – which would seem fundamental to the Judeo-Christian sense of a 'transcendent God' –, then the "locus" of transcendence will itself have to "be" rather peculiar, that is be simultaneously permeated with absence and presence. I believe that the 'sacramental occasion', with its pervading and disquieting 'anxiety', reveals precisely such a "con-tentious" locus.

II. PRESENT ABSENCE – *THE CONCEPT OF ANXIETY*

In *The Concept of Anxiety*, the pseudo-nym Vigilius Haufniensis is philosophically vigilant in his deliberation of hereditary sin[4], a deliberation that struggles to come to an understanding of human freedom *in concreto*. Herein, he discloses the paradoxical crux of such existential freedom: one's own freedom has no bottom, no-thing to ground it, yet in existing one must actually bring forth something new, "break ground"

---

3. Indeed, to do so would be to ignore a vital difference in the "author-ity" of these texts. The difference between works written pseudonymously and those in his own name are not merely a matter of true or false names, but draw attention to the "voice" in which something is being said. Herein Kierkegaard's diverse authoring is fundamental to the issues and points of the particular work. As such, I have sought to avoid a direct "cross-reading" of these works while at the same time listening for a resonant thread.

4. See especially his "Introduction", *The Concept of Anxiety* (n. 1), pp. 9-24 [*SV IV*, 281-296]. It should be noted that Vigilius explicitly and repeatedly points out that his deliberations are not theological as such, but only seek to circumscribe the necessary conditions of the possibility of sin, which as a matter of freedom can never actually be explained. Because sin is "something that withdraws deeper and deeper", for reflection "a category that lies entirely beyond its reach has appeared" (*The Concept of Anxiety*, p. 19 [*SV IV*, 291]). In short, it must be remembered that Vigilius' deliberations deal with anxiety, the condition of possibility of sin, as something outside the realm of necessity but within the realm of *existential* freedom.

by making a history, indeed one's very own history[5]. That there is nothing which corresponds to freedom's bottomlessness (or ever could be) means that concrete freedom is felt as anxiety, a fear of no-thing, of the very possibility of possibilities[6]. Such bottomlessness, however, is not mere emptiness, for "freedom's possibility announces itself in anxiety [*Angest*]"[7]. Anxiety is felt as a "dizziness" [*Svimmelhed*] of freedom that "disquiets" [*ængster*] since it stems from an awareness of one's own unfathomable possibility. Still, it must be remembered that human freedom is never *in abstracto*, but always *in concreto*, and as such "it is *entangled freedom*, where freedom is not free in itself but entangled, not by necessity, but in itself"[8]. At the heart of freedom, then, lies an existential question which one must answer for oneself, requiring a "qualitative leap" of self-becoming that cannot be explained from or grounded in what 'is' (the "given"), yet must be answered in and through what 'is'. As such, the experience of freedom's no-thing-ness is "present" – "anxiety's nothing is actually something"[9] – what I here term a "present absence".

By this I mean to emphasize two aspects of freedom's no-thing-ness. First, "absence" indicates that such no-thing-ness is already and essentially a question of "time" (and not some timeless/metaphysical description). Second, and bound to such absence, it is inextricably "present" as anxiety, albeit it taking diverse forms[10].

While many other issues are at stake in Vigilius' deliberation – issues not immediately relevant for my point here – what is particularly germane in his analysis of anxiety is that all its varied forms originate from freedom's groundlessness and the (existential) question of time. While "time has no significance at all for nature", human freedom is precisely an issue of time, or more precisely "the moment" since "only with the

5. See, for example, *The Concept of Anxiety* (n. 1), pp. 17-18 (note), 49, 111 [*SV IV*, 289-291, 320, 379-380]. Whenever speaking about human freedom, Kierkegaard persistently demonstrates (whether in his own voice or displayed through a pseudonym) that human freedom is never simply the infinitely open possibility of choice, a *liberum arbitrium*, but rather inherently entails concretely engaging reality in actuality by "making a history" for oneself, which is precisely how one comes to be one-self. This theme of making a real beginning in actuality ('repetition'), recurrent through out Kierkegaard's multifarious works, is perhaps most pointedly "demonstrated" through Constantine Constantinus' *Repetition*, to which Vigilius himself makes explicit reference (*The Concept of Anxiety*, pp. 17-18 (note), 21 (note) [*SV IV*, 289-291, 293].

6. *Ibid.*, p. 42 [*SV IV*, 313].
7. *Ibid.*, p. 74 [*SV IV*, 343].
8. *Ibid.*, p. 49 [*SV IV*, 320] (my emphasis).
9. *Ibid.*, p. 111 [*SV IV*, 379].
10. For example: the anxiety of innocence, of fate, of guilt, etc.

moment [*Øieblikket*] does history begin"[11]. The time of freedom, then, is not merely a passage of events, a logical unfolding of the eternal, of what has always already been. Such (metaphysical) time, while typically referred to as "past, present, and future" is merely a spatialized kind of time, a sort of timeless time since eternity simply "is", rendering past, present, future to be essentially accidental. The "time of freedom", however, is not a mere unfolding of the eternal, but a groundless origin wherein the eternal *comes to be*. Herein past, present and future are no longer accidental to time but essential to their "touching" in what Vigilius calls 'the moment':

> The moment is that ambiguity [*Tvetydige*] in which time and eternity touch one another, and with this the concept of *temporality* [*Timelighed*] is posited, whereby time constantly intersects eternity and eternity constantly pervades time[12].

Indeed, as Vigilius points out time and again, history is "momentous" precisely because it is a matter of an actual beginning, of something *coming to be*, of what Augustine would call *initium* rather than *principium*[13]. As such, time is vitally pivotal for the individual, for it is in and through temporality – "momentous time" – that an individual be-comes *who* one is. Still, the moment is no-where to be found, and yet can take place anywhere... leaving the individual with the persistent and pressing presence of an absence he/she can never actually fill, i.e.; anxiety.

While Vigilius' examination of anxiety circumscribes "the moment" philosophically, carefully refraining from entering the "dogmatic issue" as such, it nonetheless "situates" the locus of transcendence in the domain of freedom, in the ambiguity of anxiety's present absence. Accordingly, while this work surely bears a philosophical tone and an attentiveness to making "place" for faith, its irony and intimations should not be missed. Briefly, it becomes evident in the course of Vigilius' study that, despite its title, one does not so much grasp/conceive anxiety as one is in its grasp. Instead, he comes to recognize that anxiety ultimately discloses that human freedom must be concretely engaged in such a way that neither the question of freedom's unfathomable bottomless nor the decisiveness of the moment would be eclipsed. Through such a concrete engagement of freedom, anxiety stands as a constant, penetrating imperative wherein one's very self is caught in the question of time – i.e. temporality – by having to engage it in the moment through decision and action.

---

11. *The Concept of Anxiety*, p. 89 [*SV IV*, 359].
12. *Ibid.*, p. 89 [*SV IV*, 359].
13. See Augustine's distinction between *principium* and *initium* in *De civitate Dei*, XI.

While anxiety must surely be undergone by each and all, the present absence of freedom's possibility stands as an inward journey that must be undertaken *in the right way*:

> In one of Grimm's fairytales there is a story of a young man who goes in search of adventure in order to learn what it is to be in anxiety. We will let the adventurer pursue his journey without concerning ourselves about whether he encountered the terrible on his way. However, I will say that this is an adventure that every human being must go through – to learn to be anxious in order that he may not perish either by never having been in anxiety or by succumbing in anxiety. Whoever has learned to be anxious in the right way has learned the ultimate[14].

Because freedom's possibility is a pressing but bottomless existential question, undertaking the journey of anxiety can become "absolutely educative", for it consumes all finite ends while at the same time decisively involving one in one's own infinitude[15]. It is precisely here in such anxiety, in the present absence of the moment, that there is a "place" for faith, a locus wherein a human may come to be touched by a God transcendent.

In this regard, it is important to see that, from the very beginning, even the pseudonym Vigilius has undermined his "author-ity" (and presumably doubly so for the pseudonymously writing Kierkegaard), ultimately keeping his own reflective deliberations "ungrounded" in the domain of freedom, and left as tangled questions for the reader to decide on his/her own[16].

III. ABSENT PRESENCE – THE SACRAMENTAL OCCASION

The concept of 'sacramental anxiety' as a locus of transcendence that I am attempting to draw out here is given a more concrete form in Kierkegaard's *Three Discourses on Imagined Occasions*. Although these discourses are not on any sacrament as such, they nonetheless point to a

---

14. *The Concept of Anxiety*, p. 155 [*SV IV*, 421].
15. *Ibid.*, pp. 155-156 [*SV IV*, 422].
16. In his preface, Vigilius points out that he himself is "an author without any claims", "a layman who indeed speculates but is still far removed from speculation" (*The Concept of Anxiety*, p. 8 [*SV IV*, 280]). His introduction emphasizes how his deliberation is limited to anxiety as the condition of the *possibility* of sin, and not the *actuality*, which must lay outside the scope of even the most astute explanation. Throughout his work Vigilius continually deliberates in such a way that he ultimately undermines his "author-ity", leaving the matter for his reader to work out. Moreover, Kierkegaard's writing this and other works *pseudonymously* is already a "style" which expresses a kind of present absence. In Kierkegaard's work, the pseudonymous author persistently undermines his/her authority and so is present precisely in/through his vanishing.

"place" or "locus" where the divine and the human *might* come to touch, but now to what I would call "sacramental occasions." The imagined occasions of the discourses are a confession, a wedding and at a graveside, each of which displays and deepens the question of "momentous" time, but now with a more distinctively – indeed pointed – religious tone. First, however, it should be kept in mind that these are not written as a theology, much less sacramentology, but are closer to inspirational discourses, reflections that speak to their reader evocatively on an existential level, for – as Kierkegaard's preface forewarns the potential reader – "the meaning lies in the appropriation"[17]. Still, even if these discourses are written in a quite different tone from his pseudonymous works, a certain resonance with the present absence of anxiety can be heard.

In these occasional discourses a pervading absent presence is at work. In and through the imagined occasion, each discourse turns its reader inward to probe one's own self. While God is clearly not present as the "object" of these discourses – and could never be since this would only be a God of one's own making – the pervading "shadows" of a transcendent God can hardly be missed. Again here, the locus of transcendence is not a physical place as such, but a time, a particular (though imagined) *occasion*. The temporality of the occasion means that "something" might come to happen here, something decisive in what is to follow. In each occasion he explores how the "momentous" character of freedom is felt in anxiety and calls for a fidelity wherein the question of existential freedom is engaged in such a way that one is truly "opened" and can be genuinely changed, in and through the most profound – indeed bottomless – seeking.

1. *On the Occasion of a Confession*

In his first discourse, Kierkegaard understands confession to be a "biding place" wherein one is brought to turn inward, to self-examination:

> The confessor seeks God in the confession of sins, and the confession is the road and is *a biding place on the road* of salvation, where one pauses and collects one's thoughts[18].

---

17. S. KIERKEGAARD, *Kierkegaard's writings X: Three Discourses on Imagined Occasions* (n. 2), "Preface", p. 5 [SV V, 175]. Moreover, in each of the discourses he reiterates that "the discourse is without authority" and is simply offered to its reader as an opportunity for self-engagement.

18. *Ibid.*, p. 15 [SV V, 182] (my emphasis).

This turning inward, however, is not mere introspection, for confession moves beyond deliberations on freedom's possibility and requires an accounting of *actual* freedom, and *before* God. Such an accounting calls forth an underlying question that lies at the heart of such an occasion: "what it means to seek God". Kierkegaard's discourse aspires to unfold this question, and to do so in such a way that the reader feels the profound anxiety of its probing *in*quiry and the decisiveness of the moment at hand.

Since God ultimately transcends one's grasp – "being" absent – the confessor's seeking reaches out into the "unknown" [Ubekjendte]. This unknown, however, is not simply some-thing not yet known, nor some supreme idea (*eidos*). Rather, the unknown is sought after as the highest good beyond all names and designations, a good that inspires wonder [*Forundringen*]. Insofar as "wonder is immediacy's sense of God and is the beginning of all deeper understanding"[19], the seeking of God places the confessor on a road toward a destination unknown, beyond one's own determination and control. Still, because the unknown summons one at the deepest of levels, "awakes the wonder of the whole person", one must seek it out, continually striving after "an enormous being that exists when it is gone, that is and is not"[20].

As such, wonder is a deep sense/awareness that the transcendent ("when it is gone") unknown can never simply "be" present. Instead, this unknown is an "absent presence" which underlies and calls into question the confessor's seeking of God. Put in other terms, the seeker will never come to possess that which is sought as present before oneself; instead, one will "have come to be alone with the Omni-present One"[21]. To be alone before God, then, entangles the individual in oneself in such a way that one becomes acutely aware of the decisive depths of one's bottomless freedom – in all its anxiety – realizing that at bottom one must come to be changed:

> to seek means that the seeker oneself is changed. One is not to look for the place where the object of one's seeking is, because it is right with one; one is not to look for the place where God is, one is not to strive to get there, because God is right there with one, very near, everywhere near, *at every moment everywhere present*, but the seeker must be changed so that one oneself can become the place where God in truth is[22].

19. *Ibid.*, p. 18 [SV V, 185].
20. *Ibid.*, pp. 23, 20 [SV V, 189, 186].
21. *Ibid.*, p. 25 [SV V, 190].
22. *Ibid.*, p. 23 [SV V, 189] (my emphasis). See also: "But the decision, the dangerous moment of collecting himself when he is to withdraw from his surroundings and become alone before God and become a sinner – this is a stillness that changes the

Still, so as not to lose the sense of anxiety that inherently lies in matters of existential freedom, Kierkegaard's first discourse ends without concluding. Rather, the reader is left alone to work out one's own confession in wonder. He only points out that the thorough self-transparency required of confession means that one must neither escape nor succumb to anxiety, opening oneself to its probing inquiry, and that the moment for such an occasion lies right before one: "this very day"[23]. In this way, the locus of transcendence, the place where God may truly come to be "omni-present", lies in that *anxious moment* of confessional stillness when one's bottomless freedom is acutely felt and deeply probed.

2. *On the Occasion of a Wedding*

While surely speaking to a different occasion, Kierkegaard's reflections on "a wedding" once again resonate with the anxiety that stems from the question of time and its decisive moment. He explains that "first love" is surely a gift, but that this gift cannot to be taken for granted. The very nature of love is that it does not leave the individual unchanged; indeed, love entails an imperative to be given reality – we might say "incarnated" – in and through "momentous time".

A wedding is the occasion when one – responding to love's imperative – indeed begins by "giving word" to the "indefinable wealth of mood"[24]. This, however, is not simply a matter of naming what is in fact the case, but is a true beginning of love in and through its speaking for the future, i.e. making a promise. The making of such a promise shows how the realization of love begins by a "resolution in freedom" which intends a "covenant for eternity"[25]. In this way love becomes a duty to engage time and make a history, requiring both decision and action:

> Indeed, the wedding ceremony is like a wreath of eternity, but love weaves it, and duty says it must be woven; and love's delight is to weave it, and duty says it must be woven – *every day from the flower of the moment.*

ordinary just as the storm does. He knows it all, knows what is to happen to him, *but he did not know the anxiety that grips him when he feels himself abandoned by the multiplicity in which he had his soul*; he did not know how the heart pounds when the help of others and the guidance of others and the standards of others and the diversions of others vanish in stillness...in short he had no conception of *how the knower is changed when he is to appropriate his knowledge"* p. 37 [200] (my emphasis).

23. "–And there is indeed a place for this, my listener, and you know where; and there is indeed an opportunity, my listener, and you know how; and there is indeed a moment, and it is called: this very day [*endnu idag*]". *Ibid.,* p. 36 [SV V, 199].

24. *Ibid.,* p. 43 [SV V, 204].

25. *Ibid.,* p. 43 [SV V, 204-205].

> Here eternity is not finished with time, but the covenant is eternity's begin-
> ning in time; the eternal resolution and the duty for eternity must remain
> with the wedded pair in the union of love *through time*"[26].

Kierkegaard points out that such a weaving of the eternal from the
moment can only begin in and through earnest resolve, in this case: "Love
conquers [*overvinder*] everything"[27]. As a resolution, this is neither a
metaphysical claim made *sub specie æternitatis* nor a factual/descriptive
claim made at the end of time, but rather a venture, a way of making of
a true beginning in freedom which understands that time must be
earnestly and constantly engaged – "woven" – in such a way that love's
eternity comes to be in and through overcoming every-thing.

While "only the resolved person can dare to say love conquers everything at the beginning", this "daring" is not simply a question of "self-
determination" but a way of "venturing" time[28]. As such, this resolve
that 'love conquers everything' forms "love's abiding place" which
inspires and sustains the individual in his/her daily, concrete weaving of
the eternal reality of love. To *under*take such a resolution – and not
merely state it – requires one "to *will* to have *true conception of life and
of oneself*", which at bottom "already implies the second great requirement, which is just like the first: *a true conception of God*"[29].

This double requirement of marital resolve – which pointedly shows
itself on the occasion of a wedding – ultimately stems from an understanding of oneself as a bottomless yet decisive question of freedom that
must be continually answered in and through time. Like the one seeking
God on the occasion of a confession, the one who promises with resolve
does not escape anxiety's grasp, but engages it in the right way by decisively yet humbly venturing. For the venturer understands the journey as
a continual task – a "weaving" – that one must undertake in all earnestness, radically opening one to the new/unknown. As such, the conception of God is not "an incidental addendum to the conception of life
and of oneself", for with out a true conception of God, any*thing* that
would be taken as grounding the resolution (such as happiness, fate, the
great prize, etc.) is "to idolize"[30]. Accordingly, marital resolve does not
– indeed cannot – dispel anxiety as such, but is the way in which the
individual, in Vigilius' terms, learns to be anxious in the right way, and

---

26. *Ibid.*, p. 45 [SV V, 205].
27. *Ibid.*, p. 46 [SV V, 206].
28. *Ibid.*, pp. 52-63 [SV V, 212-220].
29. *Ibid.*, pp. 52, 63 [SV V, 212, 221] (Kierkegaard's emphasis).
30. *Ibid.*, pp. 63, 64 [SV V, 221].

so learns the ultimate. With its resolve 'love conquers everything', the occasion of the wedding is fundamentally sacramental, for it is at bottom a "godly invitation" which opens one in such a way that the flower of love can indeed bloom eternal.

3. *At a Graveside*

Kierkegaard's final discourse stands at the graveside. In some respects, this might be thought a rather odd – if not morbid – place from which to reflect. As Kierkegaard himself points out, "Then all is over!... in the grave there is no recollection, not even of God"[31]. In the end, death itself offers nothing, only an impenetrable silence. Still, death has its own earnestness – is indeed "the schoolmaster of earnestness" – insofar as being along side a grave brings the thought of death to focus upon one's own death. At this place, at the edge of the silent grave, the thought of death is far from the cunning contemplation of death by which one forgets this to be one's own lot:

> the cunning contemplator places himself on the outside; but even if the contemplation of death uses pictures of horror to describe death and terrifies a sick imagination, it is still only a jest if he thinks of it as the human condition but not as his own.
> ... Earnestness is that you think death, and that you are thinking it as your lot[32].

Insofar as one draws one's attention upon one's own death – and not death in general or of another – the thought of death cuts through the constant danger of illusion and self-deception. As such, the earnestness of the thought of death is not found in some mood (which only remains esthetic), but lies precisely in its impact, in how the individual's inner being is grasped hold of.

The point of this discourse, then, is to ponder "death's decision" from the graveside. Kierkegaard attempts to do so – recognizing that this earnestness can only be learned by oneself[33] – by reflecting upon three facets of 'death's decision': its decisiveness, indefinability, and inexplicability.

Kierkegaard believes that the *decisiveness* of death's decision merits repetition, for unlike anything else death's "all is over" comes unabated,

---

31. *Ibid.*, p. 71 [SV V, 226].
32. *Ibid.*, pp. 73, 75 [SV V, 228, 230].
33. "Death is the schoolmaster of earnestness, but in turn its earnest instruction is recognized precisely by its leaving to the single individual the task of searching himself so it can then teach him earnestness as it can be learned only by the person himself.", *Ibid.*, pp. 75-76 [SV V, 230].

entirely outside one's deliberations, interpretations or power. What makes this finality a matter of earnestness, however, is that this decisiveness is thought and thought at a graveside:

> That death can make a finish is indeed certain, but the challenge of earnestness to the living is to think it, to think that all is over, that there comes a time when all is over. This is a difficult thing, because even in the moment of death the dying person thinks that he still might have some time to live...[34]

But when thought *at a graveside*, the cunning deception of postponement and diversion is revealed; there is no reflective "perhaps". Here a lucid awareness of death's decisive "now all is over" brings one to genuinely feel the imperative of time's scarcity, the "momentousness" of "this very day". Such thought could never be a matter of speculation, but calls for action:

> Earnestness does not waste much time in guessing riddles; it does not sit sunk in contemplation, does not rewrite expressions, does not think about the ingeniousness of imagery, does not discuss, *but acts*[35].

In this way, death's earnestness is a "life force" which makes one acutely appreciate the need to engage time here and now. By producing a scarcity of time, death provides "the right momentum in life" directing one to "grasp the present this very day", for "with the thought of death the earnest person is able to create a scarcity so that the year and the day receive infinite worth"[36].

In reflecting upon the *indefinability* of death, we once again – from a different angle – are confronted with the anxiety of momentous time. Death surely makes everything equal – in the end, all will lie side by side, grave by grave – where differences no longer make a difference. (Indeed, "the mirror of death" does not flatter or allow one to distract oneself in one's dissimilarities from the others, as the mirror of life sometimes flatters us.) But death's equality should not be understood in such a way that one forgets that "death takes each one separately"[37].

---

34. *Ibid.*, p. 79 [SV V, 233].
35. *Ibid.*, pp. 82-83 [SV V, 236] (my emphasis).
36. *Ibid.*, pp. 83-84 [SV V, 236].
37. "Whatever conception you want to have of your life, yes even its significance for the eternal, you do not talk yourself out of death, you do not make the transition to the eternal in the course of a speech and with one breath... *behold, death takes each one separately* – and he becomes silent. Whatever difference you want to imagine in the one living, death makes him just like the person whose dissimilarity did not make him distinguishable. To the vain person, the mirror of life sometimes depicts his dissimilarity with flattering faithfulness, but the mirror of death does not flatter; its faithfulness shows all to be identical; they all look alike when death with its mirror has demonstrated that the dead person is silent", *Ibid.*, pp. 83-84 [SV V, 236] (my emphasis).

Instead, earnestness understands the equality of death as "the empty space," "the equality of annihilation" before which one "shudders [*gyser*]", a shudder that impels the life of spirit[38]. As such, equality does not define death as such – death in its absolute silence remaining utterly indefinable – but is more akin to an existential uncertainty within which one learns to think death's certainty. In this way the earnest thought of death's equality brings one back once again to "this very day" in all its anxious-filled momentousness:

> Earnestness, therefore, becomes the living of each day as if it were the last and also the first in a long life, and the choosing of work that does not depend on whether one is granted a lifetime to complete it well or only a brief time to have begun it well[39].

The point of death's equality, then, is to impel one to engage time – one's own time – in all earnestness.

Finally Kierkegaard's reflections upon death's decision concern its *inexplicability* [*uforklarlig*]. Once again the reflections turn the question concerning death's decisiveness back upon the one who would think death at a graveside. Indeed, while "death itself explains nothing", its inexplicableness comes to probe the inquirer:

> See, this inexplicableness certainly needs an explanation. But the earnestness lies just in this, that the explanation does not explain death but discloses the state of the explainer's own innermost being[40].

What is decisive about such an explanation, then, is not something that can be given to or be applied by another, but instead that the explanation "acquires retroactive power and actuality in the life of the living person" – i.e. a retroactive power that "comes to penetrates one's life and transforms it" – death thereby becoming one's teacher in earnest[41].

In case a reader would still be persistent in explaining the inexplicability of death in such a way that one evades death's decisiveness for oneself, Kierkegaard points out that this is not only a fundamental misunderstanding, but a sort of madness:

> not only is that person mad who talks senselessly, but the person is fully as mad who states a correct opinion if it has absolutely no significance for him.

In the end, the aim of this discourse – not unlike the others – is not to teach something, to disseminate true opinions, but to bring a reader to

38. *Ibid.*, p. 89 [SV V, 241].
39. *Ibid.*, p. 96 [SV V, 247].
40. *Ibid.*, p. 97 [SV V, 248].
41. *Ibid*, pp. 97-98 [SV V, 248-249].

reflect inwardly, to have who one is called into question. The crucial point is *how* the truth is had and what difference this makes.

> ... Alas, yet it is so easy, so very easy, to acquire a true opinion, and yet it is so difficult, so very difficult, to have an opinion and to have it in truth[42].

So what then is a reader to make of Kierkegaard's reflections? In and through the imagined occasion, are they not mirrors which have taken away every opinion so that a reader is brought back to oneself as an ever-anxious question to be answered in and through time? Do not the occasions of a confession, a wedding and standing at a graveside immerse one in this bottomless but decisive anxiety wherein one may come to learn the ultimate?

IV. THE CONCEPT OF 'SACRAMENTAL ANXIETY'

By reading these two irreducibly differing works of Kierkegaard side by side, hearing a resonance without conflation, I believe that a fruitful tension comes into play between the present absence of anxiety and the absent presence of an (imagined) sacramental occasion. What I have termed the concept of 'sacramental anxiety' is a way of thinking about 'sacramental presence' as a locus of transcendence without falling into idolatry. As such, the sacramental occasion could never be a secure or explanatory enterprise (except perhaps in superstition and systematic thinking), but inherently entails 'anxiety', i.e. the perils of freedom, the need to act, and the wonder of the unfathomable. A sacramental occasion, then, is momentous insofar as it requires one to venture oneself in what might be called the adventure of anxiety: in confession one must "become open/opened in honesty" by embracing responsibility (past, present and future) so as to begin a new history; in marrying one must resolutely promise for an unknown future; and at a graveside one must feel the silence of one's own death; and in each be decidedly changed/transformed. Herein the presence of God is neither a secure anchor nor an overwhelming power, but an *absent* presence calling one ever-deeper into one's bottomless freedom, to what might be termed the occasion/moment of grace. Of course, insofar as these discourses concern merely *imagined* occasions, it is once again left for a reader to actually bring the occasion to such reflections.

Here I have tried to draw out the "concept of sacramental anxiety" as way of indicating the locus – or better "the moment" – wherein transcendence might break into human existence. Still, it would seem that as

---

42. *Ibid.*, p. 99-100 [SV V, 250].

such any theologizing would be inextricably "occasional," meaning that a theologian would be caught in the awkward position of claiming no author-ity (something like Kierkegaard) or risk missing transcendence by having "locating" it, rather than be questioned by it.

Faculty of Theology   John C. RIES
Katholieke Universiteit Leuven
Sint-Michielsstraat 6
B-3000 Leuven

GOD DOES APPEAR IN IMMANENCE AFTER ALL

Jean-Luc Marion's Phenomenology as a New First Philosophy for Theology[1]

I. A Theologian's Line of Approach in Reading a Strict Phenomenology

As an introduction to this contribution I want to delimit my theological perspective in reading Marion's monograph *Étant donné*[2]. As such, I shall do nothing more than to present Marion's study *Étant donné* in function of its Christian-apologetic and theological implications. While on the one hand this is a limited approach, it is at the same time precisely in these implications that the major importance of Marion's phenomenological study for the philosophy of religion after Nietzsche and Heidegger – and certainly for theology as well – comes to the fore, particularly for sacramentology as the discipline within theology that asks among other things *how* God appears in reality.

My option for this line of approach implies that I will not pursue other interesting possibilities here. More specifically, I will not exhaustively present the whole study – which consists of five very technical 'Books'. Neither shall I deal with the critiques on Marion's position, which, as he himself recognises, represents as yet a minority position in

---

1. It was quite a pity that Jean-Luc Marion – together with Louis-Marie Chauvet a protagonist of a postmetaphysical fundamental-sacramental theology – though invited as keynote speaker, could not attend the conference of which this study reports. Yet it seemed useful to add his challenging perspective to the debate. Therefore, as I prepared at that time my Ph.D. in sacramental theology on the topic of the conference – sacramental presence in a postmodern context – and because Marion's phenomenology is of prevailing importance in it, I was asked to present Marion's thinking in this volume, so as to offer to the reader also this perspective of thought, that intends to provide theology with nothing less than a new first philosophy to support its claims. See e.g. J.-L. MARION, *Eine andere "erste Philosophie" und die Frage der Gegebenheit*, in J.-L. MARION & J. WOL-MUTH, *Ruf und Gabe. Zum Verhältnis von Phänomenologie und Theologie* (Kleine Bonner Theologische Reihe), Bonn, 2000, pp. 13-34.

2. J.-L. MARION, *Étant donné. Essai d'une phénoménologie de la donation*, Paris, PUF, 1997, 452 pp. (English translation is in preparation.)

phenomenology. Nor shall I take a philosophical stance as Marion himself does by being very explicit that he precisely does *not* write any theology in this study, but only phenomenology[3].

But precisely because Marion indicates a place in reality that can on the one hand be perceived by reason (phenomenologically), and where on the other hand God, if He becomes present at all, manifests Himself in phenomenality, because in other words he does not need God in advance to indicate the possibility of His appearance in reality, Marion becomes an ally of the theologian in search of a *theologia rationalis*, i.e. a reasonable account of what the believer believes from his/her faith surrender. I hope that this paraphrase of my point of departure will have gained some clarity by the end of this contribution.

What This Is – or Continues to Be – All About: Continuity and Discontinuity between 'Marion I' and 'Marion II'

I can resume the theological question at stake here in this: how does God become *present*, as the really *Other* than we, who radically differs from us and hence is not in the prolongation of our differentiating gaze? Within ontology such an encounter with God does not seem to happen: the relational or what something is for me (*ad-esse*) can never become the absolute or what something is as such (*esse*). Being cannot escape the subject-object relation. The classical 'models of distance'[4], like cause-effect, substance-accidents, or signified-signifier, never bring the other present, except through some 'leap' already within faith; analogy is as much linked to onto-theology as it is set free from it. But such analogy no longer functions. And here we can situate the crisis of monotheism in Western culture: is God limited to what we call God, is He not there outside our gazing or naming?

In the perspective of this very broad question, something must be said about the previous history of *Étant donné*. Although, compared to what came before[5], *Étant donné* (1997) and also already *Réduction et*

---

3. See already *Étant donné*, p. 11, at the end of the *réponses préliminaires*, where Marion in connection to this addresses an ironical plea to the 'benevolent reader' not to put into his mouth what he does not want to have said. See further on *passim* in the whole study.

4. As Marion called them at a sacramentology conference in Rome in May 2000. The text of this conference will appear as J.-L. MARION, *The Sacrament and its Phenomenality: Being and Donation*, in N. REALI (ed.), *Il mondo del sacramento. Filosofia e teologia a confronto*, Milano, 2001.

5. I refer mainly then to J.-L. MARION, *L'idole et la distance: cinq études*, Paris, Grasset, 1977 and ID., *Dieu sans l'Être*, Paris, PUF, 1982. Marion's investigations in the history of philosophy can remain outside our scope here. See for a division of his work

donation[6] bring such a new sound in Marion's thinking that we can make mention of a 'Marion I' and 'Marion II', there is on closer inspection also a great deal of continuity between both. Indeed, whoever seeks to understand the intention of *Étant donné* must keep in mind the intuition that apparently never let go of Marion: the distinction between the idol and the icon[7]. In the idol humans install an absoluteness to which each and everything can be related (or be made relative), a ground on which all the rest can stand, in short an *instituting* god who passes on an order, a 'why' and a 'what for', to the *instituted* reality. And in this idol-god humans mean to encounter God – which means immediately that the idol deserves respect: it is the best humans can make of God. In metaphysics-as-ontotheology (as Heidegger describes it), which through thinking defines God or Being in reality, as a result the *concept* of God or of Being, conceived by humans, is such an idol too. But also this kind of idol appears – as already the Greek *eidoolon* indicates, to be only a mirror: the gazing gaze of the transcendental Ego – the Ego that like the god (read: in the installation of the god) builds the bridge to transcendence – this gaze contemplates in the idol only the Ego itself, or its own thoughts, assembled in a concept. Idolatry is always self-idolatry, and by the time the idol becomes unmasked, one knows oneself alone again, in an existence that is ultimately groundless. At the end of the era of metaphysics the believer sees him/herself then referred back to a kind of fideistic position: the belief in God has not become impossible, but it can in no way be made accessible rationally nor argued for, for every indication of God in reality means idolatry. Here traditional apologetics falls into trouble; it could never deliver a *proof* of God, yet did demonstrate for reason the *possibility* of God's existence, in such a way that beyond all reason's arguments only a person's will had to decide about faith in God[8].

In all his works now, whether they deal with Descartes, philosophy of religion, phenomenology or theology, Marion tries to demonstrate that we have to change the direction of gazing: there are indeed no gods in reality – idols are human-made – but that (entire) reality has itself an *iconic* character: reality is a screen (*écran*) through which an Other

---

by Marion himself in the area's of history of philosophy, the border between theology and philosophy, and phenomenology: J.-L. MARION, *De l'histoire de l'être à la donation du possible*, in *Le débat. Histoire, Politique, Société* 72 (1992) 179-189.

6. J.-L. MARION, *Réduction et donation. Recherches sur Husserl, Heidegger et la phénoménologie*, Paris, PUF, 1989, 312 pp.

7. See mainly: J.-L. MARION, *Dieu sans l'Être* (n. 5), pp. 15-38.

8. For an account of Christian apologetics by Marion, see J.-L. MARION, *L'évidence et l'éblouissement*, in ID., *Prolégomènes à la charité*, Paris, 1986, pp. 69-88.

gazes at us. Reality has a given character, and whatever we do, we always respond to what has first been given to us. In this way, Marion gives the theologian words to what belief in creation means. The problem, however, is that theology cannot be used as a (believer's) argument in philosophy, and yet this is what 'Marion I' is doing. In his study *Dieu sans l'Être*, theology appears to be the crown on philosophy. For only theology no longer speaks about the one Whom we think to see (metaphysical presence, figure of the idol), or Whom we think not to see (metaphysical absence, all the same figure of the – now unmasked – idol). Only theology lets the gazing towards reality no longer start with our gazing, but with the one *Who sees us*: the Other who is gazing at us through the screen of Being (theological-analogical presence, figure of the icon)[9]. At the end of the 'deconstruction' of metaphysics which Marion carries out in this study, when reality is in front of us only as a series of data, without any transcendental starting point, he opts for a Giver who precedes all that is given, even if he recognises that he violates the thinking of Being in so doing[10]. Here Marion in fact leaves the path of (modern?) philosophy; in *Étant donné* he admits this and calls *Dieu sans l'Être* in fact a kind of negative theology[11].

In the meantime, however, Marion has not sat idle. He continued searching more particularly in phenomenology – 'Marion II' – for a way to indicate the 'other', and hence the iconic face of reality, *without* having to make an appeal to a theological claim – which immediately implies that this other will no longer have to be God, but will belong to immanence[12]. Or more correctly, the immanent other – other is here to

---

9. A clear synthesis of this apophatic theology via a 'third way' alongside metaphysical presence and absence is found in J.-L. MARION, *In the Name: How to Avoid Speaking of "Negative theology"*, in J.D. CAPUTO & M.J. SCANLON (eds.), *God, the Gift and Postmodernism* (The Indiana Series in the Philosophy of Religion), Bloomington – Indianapolis, Indiana University Press, 1999, pp. 20-41. See also the discussion 'On the Gift' with J. Derrida that follows (p. 54-78.)

10. J.-L. MARION, *Dieu sans l'Être*, p. 152. As the text makes clear, the reference of violation is to the Heideggerian claim that Being unfolds itself in the data as beings. Marion replaces the scheme of the self-unfolding of Being in beings with a scheme of a radically Transcendent Giver who gives the things given included Being.

11. J.-L. MARION, *Étant donné* (n. 2), p. 16, footnote 1. Marion is even clearer on the shift in his thinking in *Auf der Suche nach einer neuen Phänomenologie*, in J.-L. MARION & J. WOLMUTH, *Ruf und Gabe* (n. 1), p. 46.

12. I want to put the largest possible emphasis to this 'without any theological claim'. This does not mean that Marion would have abandoned his faith, nor even his theological agenda. It does mean, however, that he does not need God to indicate the structure of givenness in phenomenality. And precisely in this 'laying down' of theology as laying down a kind of immanent alterity (see further on) in phenomenality a radical shift in Marion's thought is executed. This shift means not only a change of position compared to

be understood as what does not come up only with *my gaze* – thus not belonging to my gaze - is then the *possibility* of God's immanence, even if we can never find out whether this immanence of otherness would also correspond to a Transcendence, which can only *de facto* grant it a divine character. Therefore we talk about the phenomenological 'laying down' of theology: Marion lays down theology, by laying down otherness (from my gaze), and possibly the invisible presence of God, in immanence. As such, he finds back beyond the post-metaphysical fideism the traditional apologetic standpoint of the Catholic Church: as the radically Other, God is nevertheless observable for reason (in immanence), but it demands the leap of faith (in God's transcendence) to then call what/Who one sees 'God'. In this regard, Marion quotes Augustine's famous confession of God as *interior intimo meo*[13]. He wonders whether phenomenological reduction (see further) – which indeed has to put between parentheses all transcendencies – also erases this radical immanence of God from perception. Throughout the study this is the sometimes hidden theological-apologetic agenda of *Étant donné* – which does *not*, however, in itself submit the phenomenology to theology: Marion's laying down of theology means at the same time its deposition in phenomenality – as nothing more but also nothing less than a rational possibility.

And with this we have arrived *in medias res*. Throughout the five 'Books' of his study *Étant donné* Marion develops his immanent-iconic perspective. Book I deals with givenness as fundamental principle of phenomenology: a pure, i.e. a completely reduced, phenomenon is *given*. Book II demonstrates how this givenness can occur within the historical: a pure given or a *gift* is a phenomenon. Book III deals with the qualities of the phenomenon as given in phenomenality. Book IV focuses on the gradations in givenness in the given, and leads up to the 'saturated phenomenon' as the calibration of all phenomena[14]. It is here

---

Dieu sans l'Être, as well all phenomenological articles preparing *Étant donné* – especially wherever the saturated phenomenon (see further) is considered – have after the publication of this study been superseded to a certain point, because Marion in these articles still let the appearance of givenness be accompanied by the appearance of the divine or *theophany*. This theophany is replaced in *Étant donné* by the *self*-giving of what is given. And as I shall show, precisely this self-giving is what constitutes Marion's phenomenology as a first philosophy.

13. See J.-L. MARION, *Étant donné* (n. 2), p. 106, footnote 1: "(...) or il se trouve précisément que la théologie révélée définit Dieu aussi bien par l'immanence que par la transcendance: ainsi, selon saint Augustin, Dieu se découvre-t-il comme "interior intimo meo" (*Confessiones*, III, 6, 11)".

14. An explanation of what 'saturated' means, will follow. We can suffice here by pointing to the excessive in it: it means enough, turning into *more* than enough (*satis*).

too that the narrative Jesus Christ appears to be the historical paradigm of the phenomenon of revelation. Finally, Book V explores the position of humans within a phenomenology of givenness: humans no longer appear to be a subject but still hold a special seat as the ones to whom something is given, i.e. the *adonné*[15].

Below we first stand still at Books I and II, in which the structure of givenness is established. Subsequently, we will direct ourselves mainly to Book IV. In it Marion clarifies on the one hand the new element he brings into phenomenology – the 'saturated phenomenon' – and thinks through his phenomenology up to revelation-as-possibility. Of course this does not mean that the other Books would be less important. But it is my intention to introduce only a sufficient number of elements, which will allow me to present some theological implications of the phenomenology of givenness.

II. BOOK I: GIVENNESS AS A NEW PRINCIPLE FOR PHENOMENOLOGY

According to Marion, phenomenology is a contra-method. Science as a method *demonstrates*. Ultimately this is what also metaphysics does as a first philosophy: to lead back to the foundation with the purpose of finding indubitability, order and certainty. Phenomenology, on the contrary, only 'monstrates' or shows. It wants to receive what appears as it manifests itself – and therefore phenomenology is by method atheistic; it does not occupy itself with what precedes immanence, in which things appear to us[16]. Phenomenology studies only the appearance of the thing in its phenomenon. But phenomenology wants even 'more', which is in fact 'less'. As long as phenomenology manifests, it still reduces the thing to an appearance, and maintains the privilege of perception and subjectivity over manifestation. The transition from demonstrating to 'monstrating' should therefore be continued in a transition of letting the

Jean Greisch in his remarks on *Étant donné* describes this 'more' very well. At the annual fair banquet his grandmother would encourage her grandchildren: "Mes enfants, mangez jusqu'à plus faim, *et un peu plus*". See J. GREISCH, *Index sui et non dati*, in *Transversalités* 70 (1999) 27-54, p. 42.

15. *Adonné* seems very difficult to translate. I have struggled with it in Dutch (*begaafde*), and also Marion's German readers have not found a good term. To their question about this, Marion replies that the English trial 'addicted' is not very successful, but suggests no alternative. In German he tries with *ein Zugegebener*. See J.-L. MARION & J. WOLMUTH, *Ruf und Gabe* (n. 1), p. 64.

16. Marion's extension of phenomenology then consists in this: he extends immanence into an invisible level, where reality 'gives itself' before it appears. According to him, this invisible level can nevertheless be observed phenomenally, so phenomenology must pay attention to it.

thing show *itself*. Only then does the thing show *itself* in the phenomenon. In this transition, however, the paradox of phenomenology is situated. For the *knowledge* of the (intended *self-*)manifestation of the thing always comes 'from me': "Le paradoxe initial et final de la phénoménologie tient précisément à ceci qu'elle prend l'initiative de la perdre"[17]. Phenomenology takes the initiative to join the thing in its auto-manifestation and drop every contribution of itself in doing so.

The difficulty of this paradox explains the continued discussions on the method of phenomenology since it arose with Husserl. We speak then about reduction, wherein the phenomenological method seeks for indubitable meaning, not following *a priori* conditions of knowledge, but for the meaning that the phenomenon indubitably gives to itself. By taking the initiative, phenomenology unavoidably constitutes the phenomenon, but it does this in the way that it only wants to recognise the meaning that the thing attributes to itself in its appearing. In the application of the reduction phenomenology clears all obstacles for the thing itself to manifest itself. Reduction means to take away all pseudo-foundations (let us say: God or the Ego) that prevent the thing from manifesting *itself*. Reduction prepares the scene for the forthcoming of the phenomenon, by taking away all scenic elements, until the thing appears in an auto-staging. So the method of phenomenology is the method that directs itself against every method, included its own watching: it is contra-method. Phenomenology guides the manifestation of the phenomenon as a police-officer guides a manifestation: preceding the manifestation to clear the space, but not directing it.

A discussion with Husserl and Heidegger leads Marion now to his own '*a posteriori*-principle': the more reduction, the more givenness. Husserl reduced every given in reality to a given *object* that appears before the subject (transcendental reduction). Heidegger reduced to a given *being* that is 'of Being' (existential reduction), but that via the detour of Being still appears before a kind of subject (the *Dasein*). So in Husserl and Heidegger we do not see anything outside ourselves. Reality starts at ourselves, we nowhere encounter a real 'other' than ourselves. It seems then that an encounter with God as the Other cannot be thought rationally. But according to Marion the given is not an object, nor a being, but the object and the being are … *given*. His own, third reduction limits the appearing to what in it is truly givenness, and so to the strictly appearing, the given itself. In this way the phenomenon shows *itself* and receives the primacy of reality. The principle of givenness thus does not

17. J.-L. MARION, *Étant donné* (n. 2), p. 15.

set the rules within which the phenomenon appears in advance, but determines only after the appearance of the phenomenon, via the reduction, its status as given phenomenon. Therefore it is not just a principle, states Marion, but *the* ultimate principle of *all* phenomenology[18]. Whoever does not accept the principle 'the more reduction, the more givenness' for phenomenology, deprives the phenomenon of the possibility to show *itself*, and blocks again the breakthrough that phenomenology wants to bring about in philosophy: to let reality show itself, or to let the other appear independent of the subject.

Illustration: An Ordinary Painting

Do we see the other than ourselves? Does the phenomenon ever show *itself*? And how can we understand Marion's abstract answer to this question: the phenomenon shows *itself*, not as an object, not as being, but as given? An example of such a phenomenon Marion finds in an ordinary painting. This painting offers itself to the gaze in the simplest way, as an object and a being without anything more. If it can be further reduced to the visibility of a given that is merely given, *before it becomes an object or a being*, then one can already largely suppose that every phenomenality can be reduced to givenness. So the question about the mediocre painting is: "Quel phénomène m'est ainsi donné, ou plutôt en quoi ce qui m'apparaît relève-t-il de la donation – se réduit-il à un donné?"[19] Three further reductions can be successively applied: two of the reduction of the painting to the level of the object (here Marion uses Heidegger's critique of Husserl), and one of its reduction to the level of the being (here Marion criticises Heidegger's own position).

Firstly the reduction of the painting to an object *'present-at-hand'* (*Vorhanden*) can be further reduced. That in which the painting is present-at-hand as an object does not do justice to its phenomenality. We can change or take away the frame around it, we can replace the canvas, even replace the painting pigments point by point, etc. When eventually all material elements of the painting have been changed, the being present-at-hand of the painting will be completely changed, even if never disappeared; yet the phenomenality remains the same. The phenomenality appears *in one or another* present-at-hand, but this specific present-

18. *Ibid.*, p. 30: "Dès lors la donation devient moins une option phénoménologique parmi d'autres, que l'on pourrait accepter ou récuser selon son humeur ou son école, que la condition non fondatrice et pourtant absolue de la montée du phénomène vers sa propre apparition".

19. *Ibid.*, p. 62.

at-hand apparently does not belong to the phenomenality of the painting. The actual phenomenality of the painting, its appearing, resides elsewhere.

A second answer urges itself now: maybe the painting can be reduced to an object that can be handled and used, so to a kind of implement 'ready-to-hand' (*zuhanden*). In the present-at-hand there is probably something else to see than this present-at-hand. The showing up of the painting requires, beyond seeing its present-at-hand, the (subjective) looking at the painting as an act. The phenomenality of the painting would start then by the looking-as-acting of the looker; the painting is 'present-at-hand for somebody' or 'ready-to-hand'. Yet, Marion replies, on closer inspection looking at the painting is not a 'handling' of it, whereby the painting would appear only when we make it function by our gaze. The painting could then be described as an object of the esthetical *enjoying* of the gaze that makes it function by finding it pleasant, or as object of *evaluation* by a trader who makes it function by according a trade value to it, or as object of a critical *judgement* that makes it function by applying a canon of beauty. But in these three legitimate examples of handling the painting, a limitation simultaneously comes to the fore which occurs in the use of the category of 'handling': each time the painting is handled *in a specific way*, by a specifying limitation of 'the painting itself' to an object of enjoyment, trade value and doctrine. The painting can be handled only according to criteria introduced by the one who looks, which redefine it functionally and hence do not belong to the phenomenality of the painting itself. The three lookers already see three different things, *behind which* each time the painting appears, that thus appears loose of its way of functioning. But how does it appear then?

A third answer follows: the phenomenon of the painting appears ultimately reduced as a being (*ein Seiendes*). In the further reduction of this – Heideggerian – reduction we arrive precisely at the new moment in Marion's phenomenology: even as a being the painting does not yet appear *itself*. The beautiful of the painting (as the specificity of art) does not belong to the 'object' of the canvas (neither as 'present-at-hand' nor as 'ready-to-hand'), but can no longer be pointed at via reason, can hardly even be put into words, and remains intangible. We can never say adequately what the beautiful about the painting *is*. This becomes clear (among other things) from this, that the painting does not appear in as far as it *is*, but because it is *exposed*. A private collection turns out to be rather a depriving collection, it prevents the painting from appearing. For all aspects of the painting that can be subsumed in categories of being, that can be stored and communicated, all books about it, do not suffice for it to come into visibility *itself*: in order for us to be able to find it beautiful, we must *see* the painting. And finally, even the possibility of looking at the painting does not suffice yet to see: many people leave the museum without having seen. To see, we must ultimately see that the painting exposes, reveals *itself*.

Here we arrive at the core of givenness: time and again I can go and look at the painting, but I can only hope that it 'will give itself to me', so that I see what cannot be uttered in words, *what is not, yet does appear*. Considered like this, the exposition of the painting to the visitor in fact rather offers the chance to expose the visitor to the painting that will perhaps give itself to him/her: this piece of art speaks to me, it does something to me, I find it beautiful… The ordinary painting then *has addressed* the visitor, in a way that cannot be brought into words. Whatever the visitor will say about the painting later on (categories of being), this is not that in which the painting *gives itself to a person*, and makes one an *adonné*, an whom is given, an addressed, a called person – on a strictly phenomenological level. The painting 'speaks', shows *itself*, or gives *itself*. Therefore, just like a piece of music does not simply want to be heard, but to be heard each time again, so must we not simply see the painting, but see it each time again. From this it becomes clear again that the painting does not consist in its being (which can be stored in memory), but in its very appearing, always new again at every visit (maybe…). The painting appears whenever the gaze exposes itself to its event, its coming to light, its it-self-giving appearance. To give itself comes first, only then follows the looking.

How then can we describe this event of the painting, as the paradox of a non-object and a non-being that nevertheless appears? To do this Marion leans on descriptions of artists themselves. For example, Baudelaire notices: "… la plupart de nos jeunes coloristes manquent de mélodie"[20]. Baudelaire appeals here to an analogy with sound because 'what' he wants to express about the painting does not belong to the painting as a being, hence cannot be expressed in painter's terms. That 'what' that young painters lack does not belong to the real visibility of the painting. In and through the pictorial object and being, the painting itself must still appear, must give something, must speak in its 'melody'. Paul Cézanne calls this melody the *effect*, that which the painting effects in

    20. C. BAUDELAIRE, *"Salon de 1845"*, in Y.-G. LE DANTEC & C. PICHOIS (ed.), *Oeuvres Complètes*, Paris, La Pléiade, 1966, p. 863, quoted in J.-L. MARION, *Étant donné*, p. 72.

the one who looks. When the painting is (not yet) finished, the artist leans back, looks at it and asks him/herself 'what does it give'. What does the painting give more than its real, visible components? Its effect, the 'what' it effects, never comes into visibility itself[21]. When do I really see (the phenomenality of) the painting? When I see 'what it gives'. The painting ultimately appears as given, in the effect that it gives. The painting *is* not; when everything about it is reduced (*tout étant réduit*) it *gives*. And this invisible core of the painting is traced by putting in parentheses all in this phenomenon that does not grow from pure phenomenality: its character of 'object' and 'being'. A further reduction is not possible, because in the painting as given there is nothing left to reduce: no object and no being. In the end, this is the reason that those phenomena which can be reduced most easily to their givenness are the least objective and the least being. To these belong, among others, respectively to give time, to give one's life, to give one's word, to give (grant) peace, to give meaning, to give death/kill (*donner la mort*). Here the indicated is already spontaneously reduced to the phenomenally given. These expressions do not give an object or a being; they have only an effect: that to which each phenomenon has to be reduced if it wants to appear in an absolute way, so without a preceding intervention of the subject[22].

III. Book II: A Pure Gift as Touchstone for Givenness

But if a painting gives itself, does this not in fact betray a causal relationship? In givenness – that we trace by further reducing the thing as being or object, to a given – do we not all the same run into a kind of metaphysical transcendence once again (so that givenness stands again for an instituting idol that institutes the given)? Does the painting really give *itself*? In other words: does a pure gift exist? In Book II on the gift, Marion examines, starting from the deconstruction of the gift by J. Derrida, whether such a self-gift exists: a gift without a reason or a cause outside itself, in short a gift that also on closer examination appears to be nothing more than a gift. This gift then should not enter

---

21. As an esthetic experience, Marion dwells longer on this in his essay *La croisée du visible*, Paris, Ed. de la différence, 1991.

22. What we describe here, Marion will nuance in Book V of *Étant donné*, where he will claim that the phenomenon is *given* outside the subject, but does not *appear* without anybody to whom it appears. So the subject is still needed, but comes in the dative and ablative instead of the (transcendental) nominative. The subject has epistemic priority, but the phenomenon has logical priority. We will not be able to elaborate this point more extensively here.

into the causal-economic scheme of the *do ut des*, which will make it no longer a pure gift, but an exchange, something exchanged for some wage.

The hypothesis of such a gift according to Derrida implies that firstly no donee (*donataire*) nor donor (*donateur*) should intervene in the gift (*don*), for both recompense (hence: economise) the gift. As soon as the *donee* receives the gift (to refuse it is also a way of receiving), the donor receives the donee's receiving (the (in-)gratitude) in exchange for what is immediately no longer a gratuitous gift, but an exchange. And the *donor* receives, by his/her always (also) narcissistically coloured self-awareness as donor: he/she receives his/her self-esteem in exchange. But even the *given gift* (*don donné*) itself cannot intervene in a pure gift, for as soon as it appears, it is gazed at by the donor and the donee, who by this very fact start intervening and land in the economical position, as we have just observed. In short, a pure gift seems to be something impossible, and in that case givenness is not self-giving, but a causal construction. Marion, however, will apply to the gift what he made clear about the painting: just as the painting showed itself phenomenally as that which did not belong to its character of 'object' or 'being', so the gift remains absent from what goes together with it on the level of object and being. Marion's complex reasoning to arrive at this, can be more or less recognised in the experience of giving and receiving a present[23]. What is (a) present in the object that I receive and all that this object 'is', precisely escapes to this character of 'object'/'being'. As soon as I start evaluating the present in its object value or in what it is, I no longer see it as a present (gift). We say then: "That is not what matters here; what really counts here is the gesture (the gift)". The present does not belong to the thing and what the thing is; indeed, it is there *in spite of* this thing[24]. As such, Marion turns Derrida's conclusion on the non-existence of the gift upside-down, into an argument in favour of the gift. According to Derrida the present (the gift) cannot become present in presence. Indeed, Marion replies: the present (the gift) *gives itself* without presence. So Derrida's deconstruction of the gift as object/being offers to Marion the paradigm of the pure gift: the gift is not, and so gives itself.

In the part of Book II that follows, Marion specifies the gift – which he here defined negatively as non-object and non-being – in positive

---

23. The word 'present' (= gift) of course already indicates the new – non-metaphysical – presence Marion is looking for.

24. Therefore, when we visit e.g. somebody ill, the visit itself can become the present, without any-thing – and this to me seems in fact the sacramental heart of each pastoral visit: self-giving in immanence, in which for the believer God becomes 'present'.

terms. He does this by showing in an extensive analysis that in a *histor-ical* gift the donor, the donee and the given gift can be reduced or 'bracketed', so that in the end in *reduced* immanence a pure gift occurs, set free of all its transcendentals or conditions, which would drag it immediately into the logic of economy. Marion then concludes that givenness, in which the thing gives *itself* and so appears without becom-ing visible, does not introduce a new transcendence, and so does not install an idol. Givenness is then corroborated phenomenologically, as becomes clear in the gift.

And on this precise point is situated, in my opinion, the transition from Marion I – apologete and sometimes crypto-theologian – to Mar-ion II – apologete-phenomenologist. The thesis of *Dieu sans l'Être* (i.e. God gives being without entering being) is adopted here in a phenome-nological translation: God without Being becomes Givenness outside being. The theological crown on being as gift is replaced by the phe-nomenal givenness of being; theology is laid down in phenomenology, where thus God's presence in immanence appears as a rational *possibil-ity*. In a theological reflection on this step we can contend via givenness: God's grace as the *relation* of the transcendent Giver to what is given in immanence, is pointed at phenomenologically, without this 'what is pointed at' adopting an onto-theological status, for it does not appear in being (hence before the transcendental subject), but it remains 'Mys-tery', invisibility, just like what the painting gives cannot be described except through analogy. The difference between the believer and the non-believer will then consist in this: that the believer grants to given-ness in its *intern* or immanent aspect of 'giver' as giving itself (hence strictly without any transcendental character), that the believer will grant to this giver *also* a transcendent character of *Giver*. Only this last step – which by no means necessarily follows from the phenomenological scheme – leads us into theology. Thus we observe here the possibility that God – Who as radically transcendent Giver stays outside imma-nence – *also* appears within immanence, even if He does so without entering visibility or being. From this move it becomes evident that God becomes 'rationally possible', that He can be indicated in immanence at a level preceding the differentiating human gaze, hence without His appearance reducing Him to an idol, i.e. a god installed by the human gaze. And the dynamite of this apologetic claim resides in this, that this immanent 'outside being' – thus the possibility of a non-idolic God – becomes observable phenomenologically, and under this condition is no longer a strictly fideistic confession of a Mystery that can never be pointed at.

IV. BOOK IV: THE PHENOMENON GIVING AND SHOWING ITSELF:
THE SATURATED PHENOMENON

But what in fact happens when a phenomenon like the painting gives itself? In what manner does it give *itself* and does it not appear only in answer to the gazing gaze of the subject? How does the painting succeed in giving *itself*? This is the basic question of Book IV.

In metaphysics the phenomenon always appears in front of a horizon and a transcendental, that in the end come together in the Ego: the object or being appears before a subject. Husserl adopts this presumption *mutatis mutandis* in his phenomenology: the phenomenon appears within a horizon and before a subject. Yet in a phenomenology of givenness these limitations need to be suspended, because, as we saw before, there the phenomenon gives itself without any causal or other antecedent. So Marion begins a search for phenomena that turn the limits upside-down by crossing the horizon instead of inscribing themselves in it, and that reverse each and every condition to their appearance by leading the Ego to itself instead of letting themselves as phenomena being reduced to it. As such, both limits do not disappear, but such phenomena unfold themselves as phenomena in a paradoxical way, by contradicting the limits and playing with them.

How would such a phenomenon look? To answer this question Marion appeals to the phenomenological duo of intuition and intention. In the Husserlian tradition the phenomenon is characterised – according to Marion – by a *lack* of intuition. In a stream of impressions the person never experiences the whole phenomenon at the same time – just like we never see all sides of a cube simultaneously; we have of this cube only an 'intuition' (*Anschauung*) of maximally three sides in which the phenomenon cube gives itself to us in perception. Hence the phenomenon as *die Sache selbst* never lets itself be known in its 'intention' (the 6 sides). The subject must therefore define – through subjective completion – the intention of the phenomenon in a concept of it. Or put in other words, for the thing to appear itself, the intuition of it (the part observed) must *idealiter* coincide with the intention (the whole cube). For Husserl, such a thing almost never occurs. The only exceptions here are mathematics and formal logic, i.e. the degree zero of phenomenality. This makes Marion wonder why precisely these 'empty' phenomena have to be the model for all phenomena. The right to appear is denied to the real phenomena, in their calibration to these empty phenomena (adaequation intuition – intention): for real phenomena always suffer a lack of intuition to keep pace with intention.

And having arrived at this point Marion once again reverses the direction of gazing from 'idol' to 'icon'. There is one possibility which phenomenology has not taken into consideration so far:

> Au phénomène supposé pauvre en intuition, ne peut-on pas opposer un phénomène saturé d'intuition? (...) la possibilité d'un phénomène où l'intuition donnerait *plus, voire démesurément plus*, que l'intention n'aurait jamais visé, ni prévu?[25]

The phenomenon is then no longer calibrated to mathematical abstraction, in which intuition and intention coincide because both are zero. Rather, *every* phenomenon should be calibrated to the saturated phenomenon with its surplus of intuition over against intention: in what appears there, more *gives itself* than any intention of the phenomenon which I can imagine. Over against the limited number of faces of the cube stands here then the cubist painting, in which the faces of the cube multiply endlessly in always more faces and always more cubes: the experience saturates all conceptual framing, intuition as what gives itself outdoes intention as what constitutes the phenomenon into an object. Here the phenomenon truly gives itself, always exceeds our subjective, conceptualising gaze, and always stays ahead to our gazing.

Marion describes this model of the saturated phenomenon more in detail by reversing the four Kantian categories by which we judge and know phenomena, so the whole way in which we know reality: quantity, quality, the relational and the modality or manifestation before the Ego[26]. An extensive analysis leads him to the following set of four saturated phenomena.

> The *event* is the prototypical example of a phenomenon that according to *quantity* exceeds endlessly what we can survey.
> The *idol* is the prototypical example of a phenomenon that according to *quality* endlessly exceeds what our gaze can support.

---

25. J.-L. MARION, *Étant donné* (n. 2), p. 276-277. In a footnote (p. 276, note 1) Marion explains why, in spite of the reversal, he does not speak about a *saturating*, but still about a *saturated* phenomenon: intuition saturates the phenomenon as a concept of meaning, and this "(...) uniquement au nom de la donation: le phénomène saturé l'est d'abord de donation".

26. For the analysis that follows, it is important to keep well in mind that Marion does not introduce new epistemological categories according to how they do (not) fit him, but goes on thinking with the ones of Kant. More in particular, when Jesus Christ appears to gather all four kinds of saturated phenomena in his person, it might seem as if Marion would in fact deduce the saturated phenomenon from the biblical data, and then would reverse this construction to make it philosophically-apologetically acceptable. Yet this is not the case: the four kinds of saturated phenomena are strictly four reversals of the Kantian categories of judgement, and that they can be retrieved in the New Testament descriptions of Christ does not mean then that they were therefore 'invented' there.

> The *chair* (flesh, *la chair*) is the prototypical example of a phenomenon
> that appears without any relation to something else, so in an absolute way.
> The *icon* is the prototypical example of a phenomenon that cannot be gazed
> at, because from the very beginning it constitutes the Ego into its witness,
> instead of submitting itself to that Ego.

Jesus Christ: Revelation-as-Possibility

We cannot deal here with Marion's more extensive description of this
reversal and the resulting four types of saturated phenomena, but will
concretise the types immediately from the historical paradigm that
appears to gather them all four in itself: Jesus Christ. But before we can
do that, we must push the present, abstract structure to its fulfilment, in
the phenomenon of revelation-as-possibility.

Let us imagine a phenomenon, Marion suggests, in which (a) an endless number of branches (b) each give themselves maximally. Such a
phenomenon appears to be a doubly (a + b) saturated phenomenon, *in
which the whole reality appears as purely giving itself*: here we face the
phenomenon of revelation-as-possibility.

Put into a scheme, the following structure now appears:

Satur. phenom.   ⟶ 1) to quantity: that cannot be surveyed – event

2) to quality: that cannot be supported – idol

(saturation of horizon)   3) to relation: absolute – chair

(saturation of Ego) ⟵ 4) to modality: that cannot be gazed at – icon

       maximal phenomenality
       revelation
       historical paradigm: Christ

saturation (2ⁿᵈ degree)

       of the saturation (1ˢᵗ degree)

            of phenomenality

On closer inspection it becomes clear that Jesus Christ is, in the biblical
narratives that witness to him, circumscribed as the one who cannot be
surveyed, who cannot be supported, who is absolute and who cannot be

gazed at. In other words, his person saturates the four Kantian categories of judgement. Conclusion: in Jesus of Nazareth the possibility of a phenomenon of revelation gives itself in the historical. Jesus is the historical paradigm of the phenomenon revelation-as-possibility. Jesus Christ appears to be this paradigm of revelation, because his manifestation occurs following the four saturation types of the paradox, i.e. the saturated phenomenon. We can now make this more concrete.

1) According to quantity, He gives himself as an entirely unsurveyable event (*invisable*). One cannot frame Jesus, one can never 'spot' him. To the question who he is (Mk 8, 27-31), no complete answer follows. He always remains the Coming (Jn 1, 15.27), who cannot be determined. He was sent, 'from the Father and to the Father'. Therefore also Christ himself does not fore-see the end of the world, no more than the ones who expected Him could fore-see Him. These things, the unfore-seeable, only the Father knows. And for mortals this double unforeseeability means that they must give up fore-seeing, calculating and determining, and must expose themselves to expectation. "La veille et l'attente inversent la prévision"[27]. The figure of Christ thus obtains a character of a perfectly unforeseeable paradox: in it intuition saturates each preceding concept according to quantity.

2) According to *quality*, humans cannot support the true Christ (*insupportable*). In the figure of Christ intuition arrives at and most of the time exceeds what the gazing gaze can withstand: "I have yet many things to say to you, but you cannot bear them now" (Jn 16,12). Unbearable appears thus far to be the excessively visible: Jesus's clothes become excessively white, and the voice from the other world 'from the cloud' frightens the disciples present. (Lk 9,34-35; Mt 17,5-7). The unbearable follows here from the unveiled seeing of Jesus. Therefore: as soon as Jesus says "I am he"[28], the soldiers shrink and fall on the ground. And also the women present at the tomb "and they said nothing to anyone, for they were afraid"(Mc 16,8). To experience Jesus is beyond each quality of experience: the women are "filled with fear and great joy" (Mt 28,8). Intuition in the

---

27. J.-L. MARION, *Étant donné* (n. 2), p. 330, with quotes from Mk 13,13; Mt 24, 42; Jn 1,15.

28. Marion notes the link between "I am he" and the "I am who am" (Exod 3,14); see *Ibid.*, p. 331, note 1.

experience of Jesus also saturates beyond touching (Thomas) and not
touching ("do not hold me" (Jn 20,17)), beyond reunion (I am with
you always (Mt 28,20)) and departure ("While he blessed them, he
departed from them, and was carrie up into heaven" (Lk 24,51)).
Whoever sees the true Christ no longer sees him qualitatively, but by
an excess of seeing.

3) According to *relation*, Christ appears as an absolute phenomenon,
that annuls each relation as dependency from something else in this
reality. Jesus saturates each horizon in which a relation might take
him. Not only does his 'hour' escape the time of the world and his
face the space of the earth[29], but "my kingship is not of this world"
(Jn 18,36). Jesus Christ is, like the phenomenon of the type of the
chair (my chair is my unicity), absolutely different. Therefore Christ
becomes really visible only when Jesus departed: "Truly, this was
the Son of God" (Mt 27,54). And at the same time, Jesus escapes
each plurality of phenomenal horizons; he cannot be related to anything, which John expresses thus: "But there were also many other
things which Jesus did; were every one of them written, I suppose
that the world itself could not contain the books that would be written" (end of the gospel, Jn 21,25). His royal title appears in three
languages, (at least) four evangelists try in mutual difference to write
about what they have seen but what they can neither conceptualise
nor completely put into words; many are the literary genres in the
Scriptures; and of all titles for Christ not one renders Him completely. And then there is still the multiplication of spiritualities in
the imitation of Christ.

4) Finally, according to *modality*, Christ appears as a phenomenon that
cannot be gazed at by the transcendental Ego, because as an icon He
gazes (first) at the Ego, and constitutes this into his witness. For this
reversal of the gaze, many quotations could of course be mentioned
(e.g. the vocational narratives). Marion opts for the narrative of the
rich young man (Mk 10,17-22). In his kneeling down, the young
man already implicitly recognises Christ's primacy. After this Jesus'
goodness must show him the way that he can go. But Jesus refuses
to let himself be called good, and restricts himself to listing the

---

29. Both without a quote in Marion. We think respectively of Jn 2,4b where maybe in
all its hardness the 'without relation' of Christ's being absolute comes to the fore: "Of
woman, what have you to do with me? My hour has not yet come"; and of the transfiguration on Mount Tabor, or of the face on Veronica's cloth.

commandments of the Law, that ask in fact respect for the other as other. And the young man recognises the iconic character of the Law that defines him: "Teacher, all of these I have observed from my youth". Then Jesus applies the Law to himself: He institutes the young man radically by gazing at him with a loving gaze, and thus changes the Ego into his witness.

5) And here also happens the raising to the square of saturation. Jesus asks for a saturation (sell everything and give it to the poor) of the saturation (the respect for the 'first' other); the respect for the poor as others turns into a *giving oneself* to the poor, and so to the first among them ("and come follow me"). Precisely this second saturation (the more than the Law) of saturation (the Law rules my life) is what the young man refuses.

We can accordingly conclude: Jesus Christ is the historical paradigm of the maximal self-giving of the whole of reality, or of the phenomenon of the type of revelation. This phenomenon does not add a fifth type to the four saturated phenomena as reversals of the Kantian categories of judgement, but bundles these four and saturates them in the second degree. And in this phenomenological figure of revelation, the *possibility* of Revelation is realised: either God cannot manifest Himself in phenomenality, as in metaphysics and in phenomenology up to Husserl – which Marion considers to be an unquestioned *a priori* position – or in phenomenology the possibility should be extended to the possibility of the manifestation that asks the question of God.

V. To Conclude: Some Theological Reflections about the Position of Marion II

I am aware that this summary presentation of *Étant donné* does not do full justice to the richness and above all the stringent logic of Marion's study. The same counts for some consequences that I derive now, and in which I want to show the major importance of this study. As such they probably remain rather sketchy. I only hope to offer here some impulses for further reflection, and to raise the reader's interest in Marion's thoughts.

Firstly, in and through givenness Marion undermines the thinking of difference that since Nietzsche and Heidegger has manoeuvred reason into the impasse of 'the end of philosophy-as-ontology' or of the impossibility of finding truth (unity, presence, identity...) in seeing reality 'as it is', and not coloured by our subjective way of looking. These authors

indeed demonstrate that no transcendent instance can be shown by reason that could utter a meta-judgement. The particular – even revolutionary – character of Marion's phenomenology consists in this: truth in it
adopts a strictly *immanent* character, and hence need no longer be
founded by a transcendent God or one of His transcendental surrogates.
Marion does not remove difference at the beginning of ontology (subject–object-relation), but discloses before all this givenness. We find
immanent truth then in observing (1) *that* things are (being) given to us
'from elsewhere' (this now means: not from our gazing gaze) and (2)
that they eventually give *themselves* to us, by which we come to stand in
the position of *adonné* or responding to what is given. We can indeed
say and do what we want to, but all this is always already a response to
that which has first been given to us. It is correct that this truth preserves
a strictly mysterious character in the area of *what* we have to say and do;
within ontology the subject keeps the first word. But whatever we say or
do, there is always the fact *that* we already respond. Finding the truth, as
it were from Life itself, is then situated on the path of not denying *that*
we respond, so in giving up our autarky. In reflecting further on this
logic of love or logic of (from) the encounter of the other, Marion continues his intellectual pilgrimage after *Étant donné* (also Book V already
broaches this). But in any case, autonomy must surrender here rationally
to heteronomy.

That autonomy must surrender to heteronomy, has for theology far-
reaching consequences. First this means the being right of monotheism
over against other religions as different faces of idolatry: God does not
belong to the 'self' of our reality, but is the radically Other. But even
more importantly, theological rationality – including Christian metaphysics as 'theo-ontology' – in which humans receive their meaning
from the other than themselves (figure of the icon) seems then to be right
rationally over against autonomous reason that lets humans give meaning to themselves (figure of the either installed or unmasked idol). Theological reason *is* universal reason, it is intellectually right. What was
considered thus far as the religious figure of thinking, appears to be the
only correct way of thinking. Of course this does not solve all the problems of the world. But it situates their 'solution' in a (forever unfinished) correct hermeneutic of biblical logic or monotheist tradition,
which is the logic 'from the other'. Here Heidegger's sigh that only a
god (real otherness) could save us, is met: in the structure of givenness
the immanence of God is 'laid down' in reason.

The foregoing paragraph immediately implies that the ultimate truth
of the Christian confession depends solely upon resurrection. For the

logic of Christian faith keeps upright strictly within immanence, or *dies-seitig*-oriented, which means: without God. So Marion's truth is immanent, but precisely for that reason not self-justifying. As God's immanent presence can be thought henceforth without a divine character, we need to invoke Him from now on only as the *also* Transcendent, Who liberates us from the mortality of *all of* immanence: including givenness in which immanent reality gives *itself*, and including immanent truth, which can find ultimate justification only in resurrection. And this in fact is not a theological iconoclasm, but a very traditional Christian claim: our truth holds on the level of ontology, even if it receives its justification from faith.

Marion thus solves – perhaps for the first time – the age-old conflict between *theologia rationalis* and *theologia revelata*, or, in the words of Pascal, between the God of philosophers and the God of Abraham, Isaac and Jacob[30]. Marion makes these two ways of thinking to each other's exact reverse side. Starting from philosophical thinking, Marion finds the figure of revelation as possibility in the reversal of the Kantian categories of judgement. Starting from the data of biblical revelation, he finds in the narrative Jesus Christ the same figure of revelation. Both, reasonable phenomenology and revealed theology, thus find the same God, be it respectively as a reasonable possibility and as a fact for faith. And Marion can achieve this because, in contrast to metaphysics where the person points to (*one's idea of*) God, his phenomenology succeeds in letting the phenomenon of God-as-possibility[31] manifest *h/Himself* to the person.

All the foregoing can in fact be theologically synthesised in this: Marion lets God, remaining the Invisible, appear for reason. In this he comes back finally to the position of Vatican I on the 'natural knowledge of God'[32]. According to this council, the *natural* (i.e. non-believing) light

---

30. Marion hides this a bit in *Étant donné*, because he wants to defend himself from the suspicion of ontotheology, and hence claims that if he is not doing phenomenology, then he is doing *theologia revelata* and not *theologia rationalis*. He however fully recognises to have brought both together in the aforementioned discussion with Derrida *On the Gift*: "I suggest that revelation – of course, for me, the revelation of Christ, but any kind of revelation, if there are other claims to revelation – can acquire phenomenological status and match other kinds of phenomena. In that precise sense, the distinction between the field of philosophy and the field of theology, the 'limits' between them in the meanings of Kant and Fichte, could be bridged to some extent". (See *God, the Gift and Postmodernism*, p. 63.)

31. In some unguarded moments in *Étant donné*, Marion identifies the phenomenon of revelation to God (as possibility), hence showing his own believing interpretation of the phenomenon of revelation.

32. In a long interview with Marion at the age of 24 (!), this question was already asked of him: How far can the believer go with Heidegger without running into conflict

of *human* (i.e. non-theological) reason can contemplate the *invisible essence* of God. And yet faith is required to call what one sees then – a kind of ontological presence – God, the theological Present. This onto- logical and theological presence, both belonging to metaphysical dis- course, Marion has now replaced with respectively the intrigue of given- ness or the self-giving of reality, and the Giver or Creator. To conclude, we can link this to Marion's fundamental intuition of idol and icon. If from the figures of idol and icon two mutually irreducible ways of gaz- ing at reality result, and so two radically conflicting phenomenologies out of which one cannot but choose, then it is not reasonably shown that the way of gazing in which God sees us, is correct. The believer can then no longer say that his/her rationality is 'reasonably true'; it is only true *within faith*. As a result, Marion I had to put a theological presence as a crown to reason; in the other case he should have to recognise that the whole encounter with God and the truth discourse derived from this encounter, only take place *within* human speech, within the *option* of faith. But if God appears only within human speech, he does not appear at all...[33] This difficulty of an obligatory theological usurpation of rea- son Marion II has solved, by 'laying down' theology into phenomenol- ogy: God does appear in immanence after all[34].

Katholieke Theologische Univ. Utrecht   Stijn VAN DEN BOSSCHE
Heidelberglaan 2
NL-3584 CS Utrecht
The Netherlands

with Vatican I? (See J.-L. MARION and A. DE BENOIST, *Avec ou sans Dieu? L'avenir des valeurs chrétiennes* (Carrefour des jeunes 3), Paris, 1970, esp. pp. 27 and 126.) In my opinion, 'Marion II' – i.e. *Étant donné* – is the answer to the very basic critique in this question to the position of 'Marion I', a critique holding also for most of theology and philosophy that does not want to think as if Nietzsche and Heidegger had never been.

    33. Compare the title of Derrida's essay denouncing *la différance* before the installa- tion of the Name: *How to avoid speaking...* According to Derrida we cannot not speak.

    34. This essay was completed shortly before the appearance of Marion's *De surcroît. Études sur les phénomènes saturés* (Perspectives critiques), Paris, PUF, 2000, 208 pp. In *De surcroît* Marion extends and elaborates the reflections on saturated phenomena appearing in *Étant donné*. The french *surcroît* means '(in) addition' and in Marion's usage refers specifically to the excess of intuition over concept and meaning, as occurring in the saturated phenomena. But the expression 'de surcroît' also means 'moreover', and thus also refers to the fact that in *De surcroît* Marion further pursues and clarifies the four types of saturated phenomena defined in *Étant donné*. The interested reader will find in it numerous forceful arguments for the notion that this phenomenology goes beyond the structure of intentionality.

A GENEALOGY OF PRESENCE

Elite Anxiety and the Excesses of the Popular Sacramental Imagination

I. Introduction

Critiques of naive assumptions of presence, such as those offered by Chauvet and Marion, have contributed much to theology in general and sacramental theology in particular. They have employed Heidegger's critique of metaphysics productively to highlight the perennial temptation within Christianity to control God, to turn from the searing ambiguity of God's presence to comforting idols of our own construction. The relevance of such accounts of our narcissistic inclination to deny and obliterate what we cannot comprehend is beyond question at this *fin de siècle mal*. However, these critiques and talk of "sacramental presence in a postmodern context" raise the question of the correspondence between erudite debates concerning presence and popular experiences of such. What is the relationship between intellectual problems such as the univocity of being or onto-theo-logic and the concrete experience of presence among believers? As Terry Eagleton has noted, idealist or "culturalist" assumptions about the causal relationship between ideas and practice often lurk beneath postmodern theoretical perspectives that would disavow them to the end[1]. Examples abound, from Chauvet's linking of ontotheology with ecclesial triumphalism to Radical Orthodoxy's assignment of all modern evils to Duns Scotus. An extreme example can be found in John Caputo's assertion that any determinate belief system inevitably "spills blood, doctrinal, confessional, theological, political institutional blood, and eventually, it never fails, real blood"[2].

Michel Foucault has persuasively argued that ideas and meanings can be illusory distractions from the power dynamics that construct persons

---

1. T. Eagleton, *Ideology: an Introduction*, London, Verso, 1991, p. 36 ff.
2. J. Caputo, *The Tears and Prayers of Jaques Derrida*, Bloomington, Indiana University Press, 1997, p. 6.

and culture. Power goes about its work quietly as, in the words of one commentator, "ideology babbles on"[3]. If this is the case, then the critique of ideas may be equally illusory. Critiques of presence must attend not only to the particular notions of presence active in a given religious culture, but also to their symbolic and ritual expression and to the material infrastructure and power relationships that construct and constrain them. There is a well-established attempt to describe such a broad cultural experience of presence – the concept of the Catholic "sacramental imagination." It is helpful for locating debates concerning presence within a cultural horizon but, as we will see, many uses of the concept suffer from their own idealist abstraction. As a remedy, this paper will employ methods of cultural analysis that situate culture and meaning within concrete infrastructures of power and material culture, namely those of Foucault, Bourdieu, Certeau and Asad.

This analysis will be undertaken in the form of a Foucaultian genealogy, that is, as a "history of the present" that aims to unearth the power dynamics, rooted in the past that structure contemporary culture and consciousness. It will show that, whatever the legitimacy of postmodern anxiety concerning presence in light of this century's *leitmotif* of ideologically driven atrocity, this anxiety has a long and less laudable history. Issues of presence and theological imagination have been a perennial site of struggle between elites and the *populus* in Christianity (a struggle that dates at least to the initial syncretistic conflicts between Christianity and the Germanic and Mediterranean religions of Europe). It continues today in ways that resist easy ideological mapping. Zygmunt Bauman's argument that postmodernism is an expression of the anxiety of intellectuals in the face of cultural production and consumption which they no longer control is consonant with this genealogy[4]. I will argue that far from being an innocent analytical inadequacy, the ignorance of power dynamics in these various narratives occults this power struggle within Christianity as well as the theologian's role in it. For this reason, awareness of this dynamic is profoundly relevant to contemporary theological practice.

This essay will proceed in three parts. In the first, I will survey uses of the term "sacramental imagination" and note their shortcomings. In

---

3. M. DE CERTEAU, *The Practice of Everyday Life*, trans. S. Randal, Berkeley, University of California Press, 1984, p. 46.

4. Z. BAUMAN, *Is There a Postmodern Sociology?*, in ID., *Intimations of Postmodernity*, London, Routledge, 1992, pp. 93-113. I am grateful to A. Godzieba for introducing me to Bauman's thesis. See A. GODZIEBA, *Ontotheology to Excess: Imagining God without Being*, in *Theological Studies* 56 (1995) 3-20.

the second, I will outline a method that will allow a more precise analysis of the culture of presence in Catholicism. In the final section this method will be applied to two moments formative for contemporary Catholicism: the Reformations of the 16th century and the Liturgical Renewals of the 19th and 20th centuries. We will examine how the power struggles within the Christian community were enacted in changes in visual and ritual culture. These struggles and their cultural manifestations have profound consequences for the experience of presence in Catholicism. The paper will conclude with reflections on the contemporary continuations of these conflicts and their implications for the practice of theology.

II. THE SACRAMENTAL IMAGINATION

"The Catholic sacramental vision 'sees' God in all things (St. Ignatius of Loyola): other people, communities, movements, events, places, objects, the environment, the world at large, the whole cosmos. The visible, the tangible, the finite, the historical – all these are actual or potential carriers of the divine presence"[5]. So Richard McBrien defines the principle of sacramentality, which he lists first in his sketch of the characteristics of Catholicism. Attempts, such as his, to sketch the broad spirit of the tradition date at least to the 19th century. This desire is present in the works of Möhler and Newman, both of whom situated particular doctrines within a broader organic whole[6]. Similar concerns are evident in the work of their 20th century heirs: Karl Adam, Yves Congar, and Romano Guardini (whose position at Berlin, in addition to philosophy of religion, was Catholic *Weltanschauung*). Congar's writings on tradition are illustrative. Desiring to transcend scholastic propositional understandings of doctrine, Congar argued that the "monuments" of tradition could not be reduced to the Bible, patristic sources and Denzinger. They included as well: liturgy, worship, gestures, and the lifestyle of believers[7]. Here, form and content are united. The desire to sketch the broad mediations of tradition is an expression of a sacramentally informed theology that presumes such mediations are broad. The notion of the sacramental imagination is a commonplace in contemporary theology. It can be found in works in ethics, feminist theology, homiletics,

5. R.P. McBrien, *Catholicism*, New York, Harper Collins, New Edition 1994, p. 10.

6. J.A. Möhler, *Einheit in der Kirche*, Cologne, Jakob Hegner, 1957. *Symbolik*, Cologne, Jakob Hegner, 1960, ²1961; J.H. Newman, *Essay on the Development of Doctrine*, Notre Dame, University of Notre Dame Press, 1989.

7. Y. Congar, *Tradition and Traditions: An Historical Essay and a Theological Essay*, trans. M. Naseby & T. Rainvorough, New York, MacMillan, 1966.

sacramental theology and systematics[8]. David Tracy's work is by far the most influential expression of this concept. Building upon Paul Tillich and Langdon Gilkey, he sketches the tension between the analogical and dialectic traditions within Christianity[9]. The "analogical imagination" is marked by open, trustful anticipation of God's sacramental, incarnational presence in the world. It presumes the fundamental continuity between the human and divine, without confusing the two. Tracy considers this imagination's comfort with ambiguity and its ability to conceive similarity without suppressing difference a geneal resource for religious belief in a pluralistic world.

This broad expectation of presence corresponds with the concrete attributes of Catholicism: an emphasis on mediation and communion manifest in a robust conception of church office, a rich architectural and artistic heritage, a complex liturgical practice, an aesthetics fascinated with sensuality and extravagance and a fundamentally communal anthropology.

The term is used in non-theological discourse as well. Although Andrew Greeley is a figure hard to characterize as non-theological, he has made significant use of the concept in his professional contributions to the sociology of religion. In Tracy he found the crystalizing insight for his decades long attempt to sketch Catholicism as a Geertzian cultural system that could be analyzed through the methods of quantitative sociology. He identifies the sacramental imagination as a "non-propositional tradition" to which Catholics remain faithful even when they disagree profoundly with church leaders. His quantitative studies attempt to

---

8. For ethics see D. HOLLENBACH, *A Prophetic Church and the Catholic Sacramental Imagination,* in J. HAUGHEY (ed.), *The Faith that Does Justice,* New York, Paulist, 1977, pp. 234-263. M. DALLAVALLE argues that sacramentality marks Catholic feminist anthropology in its greater openness to embodiment and willingness to posit a relationship between sex and gender. M. DALLAVALLE, *Neither Idolatry Nor Iconoclasm: A Critical Essentialism for Catholic Feminist Theology,* in *Horizons* 25 (1998) 23-42. For the same reason, feminists are ambivalent about this characteristic of Catholicism, see E. SCHÜSSLER-FIORENZA's observation that sacramental forms of Christianity are those most opposed to ordaining women, *Feminist Spirituality, Christian Identity, and Catholic Vision,* in C. CHRIST and J. PLASKOW (eds.), *Womanspirit Rising: A Feminist Reader in Religion,* New York, Harper, 1979, p. 144 ff. For a use of the term in homiletics, see M.C. HILKERT, *Naming Grace: Preaching and the Sacramental Imagination,* New York, Continuum, 1997; for sacramental theology, see L-M. CHAUVET, *Symbole et Sacrement,* Paris, Cerf, 1987, and S. Ross, *Extravagant Affections: A Feminist Sacramental Theology,* New York, Continuum, 1998.

9. D. TRACY, *The Analogical Imagination: Christian Theology and the Culture of Pluralism,* New York, Crossroad, 1984; P. TILLICH, *The Dynamics of Faith,* New York, Harper and Row, 1957; L. GILKEY, *Catholicism Confronts Modernity: A Protestant View,* New York, Crossroad, 1975.

show its correlations with political and lifestyle choices, while his polemical and fictional writings contain an effusive evocation of this culture[10].

The notion of the sacramental or Catholic imagination also appears in studies of Catholic literature. From William Lynch's classic *Christ and Apollo: The Dimensions of the Literary Imagination* to its dissemination in contemporary cultural studies approaches to Catholicism, it has provided a hermeneutic for recognizing the Catholic horizon of texts which do not address explicitly theological or ecclesial themes[11]. Una Cadegan traces the emergence of this interpretive category in Catholic literary critics to their attempts to reconcile dogmatic fidelity with the iconoclastic aesthetics of modernism. The recovery or recognition of the Catholicism of great modernist writers required redefinition of orthodoxy as "a particular imaginative stance consonant with Catholicism as a world view, not simply a doctrinal formulation"[12].

Discussions of the sacramental imagination speak of several overlapping sources and mediations of this culture. The first of these is doctrinal. Central doctrines such as the incarnation and creation portray matter and created reality as intrinsically good. Whether or not it is appropriate to speak of Aquinas as having a "doctrine" of analogy (and whether subsequent scholastic uses of this concept were adequate to his insights), his articulation of the analogical nature of religious language and the *analogia entis* are a classic locus of this insight in Catholicism. This, however, raises the question of the demographic reach of these doctrines. Familiarity can be assumed in learned circles but certainly not for most contemporary Catholics, let alone the generations before widespread literacy.

A second mediation of this imagination is the liturgy. The sensuality and complexity of Catholic ritual are frequently contrasted with the more austere forms of Protestant worship. As Cadegan notes, however, there is a striking absence of concrete references to liturgy in the reflections of

---

10. A. GREELEY, *The Catholic Myth: The Behavior and Beliefs of American Catholics,* New York, Charles Scribner, 1990; ID., *Theology and Sociology: on Validating David Tracy,* in *Journal of the American Academy of Religion* 51 (1991) 643-652; ID., *Religion as Poetry,* New Brunswick, NJ, Transaction Publishers, 1995; ID., *Catholics, Fine Arts and the Liturgical Imagination,* in *America* 174 (1996) 9-14.

11. W.F. LYNCH, *Christ and Apollo: The Dimensions of the Literary Imagination,* New York, American Library, 1960. Lynch's contribution is little acknowledged. He used the phrase "analogical imagination" decades before Tracy but, to my knowledge, is not cited by him.

12. U. CADEGAN, *Cultural Work and Catholic Literature,* in *U.S. Catholic Historian* 17 (1999) 3, p. 28.

Catholic authors on the inspiration for their work. Although it is invoked in the abstract, along with a generalized sense of ritual, the effects of particular liturgical practices are more often presumed than demonstrated[13].

Another frequently invoked mediation of the sacramental imagination is artistic culture. Examples range from classic artists such as Dante, Caravaggio and Mozart, to more modern figures such as Bernanos, Chesterton, Rouault and Flannery O'Connor. In general, such references are to high culture. Several problems result. First, while such art draws from the well of broader culture and, thus, may be illustrative of a Catholic mentality (and of an artistic mentality which does not define itself in opposition to tradition), it certainly cannot bear the demographic burden of maintaining this culture. Second, artistic and literary elites are much more likely than others to possess a sophisticated knowledge of theology and doctrine. To take just one example, O'Connor was a devout reader of both Aquinas and Teilhard de Chardin. It is, therefore, no surprise that she wrote with a keen sense of sacramentality and spoke of the fiction writer's need for an "analogical vision"[14]. The value of these great works notwithstanding, Catholics have produced an enormous amount of art and writing that is seldom awarded the designation "literature" let alone "great" art. While cultural studies has found much of interest in low culture and "kitsch," theology struggles with its embarrassment with the popular (at least close to home). Popular culture does appear in the penumbra of narratives on the sacramental imagination. One finds reference to devotions, the veneration of saints, and practices such as the Rosary. But such invocations are seldom central to these descriptions. Of this much more will be said.

Of the various mediations mentioned, the theological/ doctrinal is the most developed. Here lies a fundamental problem. A category derived from particular doctrines is transformed into a description of culture. Evidence is then culled from heterogeneous aspects of Catholic culture and history to fill in this predetermined narrative outline in a manner akin to proof-texting. There is, indeed, much in the breadth of the tradition to support it, but the historical range of evidence cited and the deductive logic employed leave the particularities of this imagination unexplored. Does the Catholic imagination really find God in *all* things? Is it biased toward some realities and against others? Examples abound.

13. *Ibid.*, p. 30.
14. R. LABRIE, *The Catholic Literary Imagination*, in *U.S. Catholic Historian* 17 (1999) 3, p. 12. The quotation is from F. O'CONNOR, *Mystery and Manners*, New York, Farrar, Straus, and Giroux, 1969, p. 159.

Red wine, bread, and oil signify in a way that vodka, shellfish and yoghurt do not. Clearly the particular narratives and liturgical rituals of the tradition shape this imagination on the level of symbols. What else does?

This deductive construction of the sacramental imagination also leads to an overestimation of the correspondence between doctrine and practice. Another way to consider this problem is to ask whether narratives of the sacramental imagination are normative or descriptive statements. If they are descriptive, a concrete analysis will likely illuminate ruptures and non-correspondences in the tradition. Hence, the central question being pursued by this study: whose imagination is being discussed? Most literature on the sacramental imagination has precious little to say about either the activity of imagining or the person imagining[15]. For this reason, the term "sacramentality" used by some is more appropriate. Our interest here is imagination. How do these various accounts of presence (postmodern concern for its excesses, romantic Catholic evocations of a culture of sacramentality) relate to the actual experience of presence by the Christian masses? Before venturing to answer these questions, we must first develop a method adequate to them.

III. METHOD

The intellectual contributions of those branded "postmodern" are not limited to critiques of ontotheology. They include as well, insights into the construction and intractability of discourse that foreground the location of human experience within a structuring linguistic heritage. These heritages are inevitably as limiting as they are empowering, as marked with contradiction and elision as with coherence. Michel Foucault has shown that these linguistic formations are not purely ideational realities. They are not simply two dimensional systems of signs in relationship – *discursive formations* – whose emphases and blind-spots are mediated solely through language; but *discursive regimes* deployed in human space; structured in relationships of power, technologies and rituals. This provides a more adequate model for conceiving the cultural particularities of presence, and a more specific set of mediations or structuring elements to analyze[16].

15. Exceptions include Hilkert, Lynch and Tracy (n. 8, 9, and 11). D. Power discusses the prayer of the community as imagination in *Sacrament: The Language of God's Giving*, New York, Crossroad, 1999, pp. 172-176.

16. For Foucault's reflections on the genealogical method see *Nietzsche, Genealogy, History*, in D. BOUCHARD (ed.), *Language, Counter-Memory, Practice*, Ithaca, Cornell University Press, 1977, pp. 139-164; as well as his two extended genealogical works:

Questions concerning the role of ritual and power in the constitution of the sacramental imagination might suggest a mimetic analysis. Such a view would conceive rituals as practices of objectification, performances that enact the power hierarchy within the community. One need not reduce ritual to the miming or allegorizing of doctrine to conclude there is much to be said in this regard[17]. Early Christianity adopted the symbolism and ritual of Roman Imperial spectacle and the Basilica as a worship space. Its subsequent development reinforced this hierarchical division, whether one speaks of the Iconostasis in the East or the separation of the chancel from the Choir in the West. This essay, however, will pursue a different analysis. Emphasizing the agency implicit in imagination, it will explore its construction in Foucault's sense of "genealogy," as a historical account of the derivation of the power relations at work in the present. Before beginning the historical portion of this analysis, we must specify the definition of imagination that will guide it.

IV. IMAGINATIVE AGENCY AND CULTURAL CAPITAL

Although imagination cannot be adequately understood without reference to a horizon of understanding, attention to the agency of imagination is equally essential. For this reason, discussions of the sacramental imagination in terms of the constellation of Christian doctrines that suggest sacramentality must be balanced with attention to the active elements of the imagination: the power or prerogative to conceive mediations of the divine. It is not simply a question of believing that God can be present in all things but of the freedom and power to engage in such imaginative activity. It is the difference between assigning sacral aura to wine because of its liturgical use and finding God in one's everyday activities.

Pierre Bourdieu's notion of "cultural capital" is illuminative in this regard, especially his distinction between its objectified and internalized

---

M. FOUCAULT, *Discipline and Punish*, New York, Pantheon, 1977; ID., *The History of Sexuality*, Vol. 1, New York, Pantheon, 1978. The use of Foucault here is derived from the more extensive reflections offered in V. MILLER, *History or Geography? Gadamer, Foucault and Theologies of Tradition*, in G. MACY (ed.), *Theology and the New Histories*, Maryknoll, Orbis, 1998, pp. 56-85.

17. For criticisms of this form of analysis see F. JACQUES, *From Language Games to 'Textual Games'. The Case of the Religious Rite*, in *Liturgy and the Body*, Concilium 31 (1995) 3, 1-21; C. BELL, *Ritual Theory, Ritual Practice*, New York, Oxford, 1992, pp. 182-223. An example of such a mimetic analysis can be found in P. Cobb's ecclesiological analysis of the contrasting hierarchies of liturgical space in the East (vertical–relativizing the entire community) and West (horizontal–enacting differences within the community). P. COBB, *The Architectural Setting of the Liturgy*, in *The Study of the Liturgy*, New York, Oxford, 1992, pp. 534-535.

dimensions[18]. As objectified, cultural capital refers to objects that require interpretation to be consumed. For our concerns, this applies to the varieties of images, sculptures, rituals and spaces to which believers have access. As internalized, cultural capital refers both to knowledge of cultural goods and the resultant facility in their interpretive appropriation. With such facility comes a sense of authority to creatively engage cultural goods. Although this distinction is not a strict separation, it illuminates two important dimensions of the sacramental imagination as agency. The sacramental imagination requires both concrete materials on which to operate and a sense of competence and authority to do so. Both dimensions are contested in the cultural struggles of Christianity.

Bourdieu developed his notion of cultural capital to address questions of the role of the educational system in class reproduction in Modern France. He tended, therefore, to emphasize canonical interpretations of cultural goods and the power derived from such knowledge. This is inadequate for our purposes because we want to attend to more unruly and dynamic exercises of interpretive activity. Michel de Certeau's various reflections on the practice of everyday life, bricolage and the "rhetoric of walking," address these concerns. A post-structuralist *par-excellence*, Certeau augmented Foucault's insights into the constructive power of discourse with an account of the ways in which individuals and groups engage discursive regimes; turning them to serve their own needs and desires. In his words, cultural consumers are "unrecognized producers, poets of their own acts, silent discoverers of their own paths in the jungle of functionalist rationality." Their actions "trace out the ruses of other interests and desires that are neither determined nor captured by the system in which they develop"[19].

Combined with the concept of cultural capital, this provides a perspective that attends to both the complex and unpredictable ways in which cultural symbols, rituals and spaces are appropriated, as well as the power dynamics implicit in this process. Certeau's attention to the creative agency of consumption is essential for this analysis because it provides a more complex understanding of the power potential of objectified cultural capital. While the question of whether cultural expression

18. P. BOURDIEU, *The Forms of Capital*, in J.G. RICHARDSON (ed.), *Handbook of Theory and Research for the Sociology of Education*, New York, Greenwood Press, 1986, pp. 241-258. See his more extended reflections of cultural capital in ID., *Distinction: A Social Critique of the Judgement of Taste*, trans. R. Nice, Cambridge, MA, Harvard, 1984.
19. M. DE CERTEAU, *The Practice of Everyday Life*, Vol. 1, trans. S. Randal, University of California Press, 1984, p. xviii.

in the church is "democratic" or not is undoubtedly significant, this model gives a more refined account of the complex politics of cultural production. In addition to the question of whether or not a group or individual is able to engage in production (e.g., artistic creation, oral and written expression etc.), one must also investigate how subaltern groups relate to cultural products not of their own making, and to the availability of material that can be so engaged.

An example can be found in the various Afro-Christian religions of Latin America (Santeria, Candomble, Voudou, etc.). Enslaved peoples, forcibly torn from their land and civilization, creatively appropriated a hegemonically imposed religious culture. What looked on one level to be obedient acceptance, was in fact a much more complex ruse of the oppressed that preserved not only Yoruba cultural and religious traditions but also the cultural agency of the slaves. The model being employed highlights the importance of cultural material in this dynamic. The "stuff" of European Catholicism – narratives, images, statues, worship spaces, rituals – provided the basis for this complex cultural bricolage. A more austere religious system, such as those of the radical reformation, would not have provided such material, and the result would likely have been quite different. There are no Afro-Unitarian Religions. The outcome was determined as much by the presence of cultural material for appropriation as it was by more strictly defined power inequalities. Here, culture and power merge.

Significant suspicion is necessary to explore the power dynamics in Catholic culture surrounding the issue of presence and imaginative agency, because the sacramental imagination functions as a relatively undisputed *bon mot* in theological discourse. Michel de Certeau's influential essay on popular culture, aptly named "The Beauty of the Dead," can serve as a tutor for our suspicions[20].

Certeau recounts how the emergence of the study of popular culture in France in the 18th and 19th centuries, was premised on the very demise of its object. Scholarly discourse on popular culture has often been the retrospective romanticization of a vanquished foe. It both rests upon and represses the historical violence of elite subjugation of the masses. "Anesthetized" of its revolutionary and disruptive power, peasant culture could be safely displayed and interpreted by academic museum keepers. In addition to this repressive effect, there is an ongoing, fundamental

---

20. M. DE CERTEAU, D. JULIA & J. REVEL, *The Beauty of the Dead: Nisard*, in *Heterologies: Discourse on the Other,* trans. B. Massumi, Minneapolis, University of Minnesota Press, 1985, pp. 119-136.

contradiction at the heart of even the most well intended discourses on popular culture. Certeau finds in such scholarship a dialectical oscillation between "voyeurism and pedagogy." "The gaze of the *docti* can present itself as neutral, and – why not? – even kindly. The most secret violence of the first folklore wave was to have camouflaged its violence. This brings us up to the present day"[21]. The root of the problem lies in the fact that "popular culture can only be grasped in the process of vanishing because, whether we like it or not, our knowledge requires us to cease hearing it, to no longer know how to discuss it"[22]. It is not simply a matter of developing a method adequate to a particular object, but of a fundamental power inequality, where the culture of those studied is appropriated for the scholars production. In the words of Brazilian theologian Ivone Gebara:

> [I]t is necessary to recall that observers already have power: the power of knowledge and that of possessing analytical tools. Furthermore, they make their observations, do their interpretations, and publish their results with precise objectives in mind, even if those objectives *happen to be the improvement of the life situation of those observed....* Anyone who carries out a study does so from a position of power over those studied[23].

Academic study of the popular removes this discourse from its lived context, censoring its voices so that it may be used as a resource for academic production. This "ethnographic" method is a fundamentally violent appropriation of culture[24]. Here we find something akin to Bauman's sketch of the relationship between the intellectual and the masses. We will return to this topic in the conclusion. Let us now explore this relationship in the history of Christianity.

V. EXCESS AND ANXIETY: A GENEALOGY OF
THE SACRAMENTAL IMAGINATION

A history of issues relevant to the sacramental imagination reveals a combination of romanticization and repression strikingly similar to Certeau's account. Narratives of the progressive clericalization of Christianity are well known and need not be repeated here. In addition to the

---

21. *Ibid.*, pp. 125-126.
22. *Ibid.*, p. 131.
23. I. GEBARA, *A Feminist Perspective on Enigmas and Ambiguities in Religious Interpretation*, in T. BAMAT & J-P. WIEST (eds.), *Popular Catholicism in a World Church*, Maryknoll (NY), Orbis, 1999, p. 258. Emphasis added.
24. M. DE CERTEAU, *Ethno-Graphy. Speech, or the Space of the Other: Jean de Léry*, in ID., *The Writing of History*, trans. T. Conley, New York, Columbia University Press, 1988, pp. 207-243.

more obvious issues of anxiety concerning the religious excesses of the *populus* and the variety of programs undertaken to control them, our model of agency and cultural capital allows us to focus on the equally important changes in ritual, space and material culture. There is a wealth of material to cover in this regard, from architectural issues such as the adoption of the Basilica as a worship space, the separation of the Chancel, and the emergence of pews in the 17th century, to linguistic ones, such as the emergence of vernacular which rendered the Latin of the liturgy accessible only to the learned. Our analysis will focus on two movements: the reforms of the 16th century and the liturgical renewal of the 19th and 20th centuries.

1. *The Reformations*

Any discussion of romanticization in Christianity must address the construction of Medieval and rural Christianity as an organic plenum, a culture of faith. Evocative stereotypes of the faithful peasant abound – whether walking in the illumination of the stained glass at Chartres, immersed in a symbolic expression of faith unhindered by illiteracy, or pausing amidst work in the fields to pray the Angelus with the tolling of the cathedral bells. Jean Delumeau (among others) has argued that such idealizations of the Middle Ages tell us more about the presumptions of later generations wrestling with dechristianization and secularization, than of the epoch they propose to describe[25]. Outside of the major towns, beneath a nominal Christian veneer, rural Europe remained effectively pagan until the reforms of the 16th century. As Jedin noted more than four decades ago and contemporary historiography of the Early Modern period confirms, the Protestant and Catholic Reformations of the 16th century are best considered as parallel movements with similar motivations[26]. Historians have described these reformations as programs of "acculturation" that sought to address perceived inadequacies of faith and practice[27]. Positively, through a variety of catechetical techniques, and negatively, through the suppression of whatever religious leaders "were coming to perceive as 'superstitious,' 'pagan,' immoral or simply

25. J. DELUMEAU, *Sin and Fear: The Emergence of a Western Guilt Culture, 13th-18th Centuries,* New York, St. Martins, 1990.

26. H. JEDIN, *Katholische Reformation oder Gegenreformation? Ein Versuch zur Klärung der Begriffe nebst einer Jubiläumsbetrachtung über das Trienter Konzil,* Luzern, Josef Stocker, 1946.

27. C. HARLINE, *Official Religion – Popular Religion in Recent Historiography of the Catholic Reformation,* in *Archive for Reformation History* 81 (1990) 239-262, p. 245ff.

indecorous"[28], the doctrines and practices of a clerical elite were imposed on the "living, active, dynamic popular culture" of the peasantry[29].

Clearly, such a dichotomous and essentializing account glosses over differences within these groups and understates commonalities among them. The term "popular" is notoriously ambiguous, and it is worth noting that "local" religion outside of the towns was not necessarily popular. Rituals and devotions were (not surprisingly) disproportionately influenced by the aristocracy and clergy. While evidence is not lacking for outright suppression of cultural practices and the literal destruction of artefacts in the reformations, the notion of power implicit in the acculturation thesis misses the nuanced negotiations that marked these cultural transformations. The reformers appropriated and reinterpreted popular practices as much as they repressed them and the laity were often enthusiastically involved in the reforms[30].

The reforms need not be violent to be significant to our thesis. Overtly violent or coercive actions are seldom effective. They tend instead to engender resistance. Effective exercises of power involve negotiation; they elicit the compliance of their subjects by "guiding the possibility of conduct and putting in order the possible outcome" and by constructing particular freedoms that empower the subject[31]. Thus, even the more nuanced tactics of the Catholic Reformation (there are, of course, plenty of examples lacking nuance) were exercises of power that channelled popular religiosity into orthodoxy.

Examples of such negotiated appropriation can be found in many dimensions of culture. Instead of suppressing popular practices such as processions, Borromeo and other Catholic reformers turned them toward more orthodox focus[32]. There are many such examples, here we will

28. P. BURKE, *Popular Piety*, in S. OZMENT (ed.), *Catholicism in Early Modern History*, St. Louis, St. Louis University Press, 1982, p. 118.

29. R. MUCHEMBLED, *Popular Culture and Elite Culture in France, 1400-1750*, trans. L. Cochrane, Baton Rouge, Louisiana State University Press, 1985, p. 5.

30. J. O'MALLEY, *Catholic Reform*, in S. OZMENT (ed.), *Catholicism in Early Modern History* (n. 28), p. 309; P.T. HOFFMAN, *Church and Community in the Dioceses of Lyon, 1500-1789*, New Haven, Yale, 1984, pp. 136-137.

31. M. FOUCAULT, *The Subject and Power*, in ID., *Beyond Structuralism and Hermeneutics*, eds. H. DREYFUS & P. RABINOW, Chicago, University of Chicago Press, ²1983, p. 220.

32. Processions are significant for the active role and access to the consecrated Eucharist that they afforded the laity. An account of events surrounding a popular procession in 17th century Paris is illuminative. The laity enthusiastically supported a tradition of carrying the sacrament to the vineyards to combat the insects that threatened their crops. The higher clergy, uncomfortable with the practice, suggested instead a rite of

focus on a dimension of culture that was central to the controversies of the reformations: images. The politics of images are particularly relevant to our concerns because of the relationship between images and imagination. The literature on the visual dimension of Christianity is vast. A critique of the ocular piety that dominated the second millennium of Western Christianity was central to the liturgical renewal, which associated it with the passive role of the laity[33]. This equation of the gaze with passivity has been seriously questioned. Western thinkers through the Reformation held that hearing was the more passive sense. This is evident in Eckhart's and Luther's assertions that hearing, not sight was the proper mode of faith because it implied passivity. Prior to the 13th century, with significant survivals into the 16th, vision was understood to be a profoundly active sense, akin to touch[34]. For this reason, issues of visual perception and the role of images are profoundly important for our reflections on imagination and power, as the gaze was understood in a way intrinsically linked with agency.

Hans Belting has argued that Reformation iconoclasm belies the power images held at the time[35]. In the era "before art" (whose end was contemporaneous with the reformations), images were understood as receptacles of the holy, presences of divine power. Their authenticity was legitimated by narratives of divine or miraculous origins. Innovation in reproduction was considered an obstacle to this presence that only faithfulness to the original could guarantee. The reformers' theologies, whether the extremes of Protestant iconoclasm, the more moderate views of Luther, or the defensive stance of Trent, all rejected – either in theory or practice – this iconic understanding of the image. While the intensity of the iconoclasts may confirm the vestigial power of images at the time, the programs of the moderates were defined by the emerging problematic of art: the understanding of images as objects of human contrivance. Luther did not reject the religious use of art outright. He held that it could function as an allegorical illustration of the content of scripture; a view given classic expression in Cranach the Elder's various renditions of *Law and Gospel*. The polysemy of the image, however, was to be made subservient to the proclaimed Word. The predella of

exorcism–a ritual which they controlled. See P. BURKE, *Popular Piety* (n. 28), p. 122. Citing J. FERTE, *La vie religieuse dans la campagnes parisiennes, 1622-95,* Paris, Vrin, 1962.

33. See J.A. JUNGMANN, *Pastoral Liturgy,* New York, Herder and Herder, 1962; L. BOUYER, *Liturgy and Architecture,* South Bend, Notre Dame, 1967.

34. M. MILES, *Image as Insight,* Boston, Beacon, 1985, p. 96 ff.

35. H. BELTING, *Likeness and Presence: A History of the Image before the Era of Art,* trans. E. Jephcott, Chicago, University of Chicago Press, 1994, pp. 458-490.

Cranach's *Wittenberg Altarpiece* portrays this relationship. An image of Crucifix hovers between the congregation and Luther, who, expounding the Gospel from the pulpit, gestures toward the image with one hand, the other placed firmly on the biblical text. A similar subordination of the image characterized the Catholic reformation. Instead of destroying images, it transformed them. Frontal images of saints, perhaps functioning as fetishistic mediations of power, were replaced with side views that served more didactically as examples of graced action[36]. (If space allowed, a full treatment of the cultural politics of the Catholic Reformation would have to address the somewhat surprising irruption of the Baroque and the significant ways in which it subverted the rational administration of Tridentine Catholicism[37].) Trent's defense of the adoration and veneration of images rejected their iconic, fetishistic function. It justified them instead in terms of the emergent artistic paradigm of reference. They are to be revered "not because some divinity or power" abides within them but because of their "similitude" to their subjects – to whom reverence and devotion are referred[38]. With this language, the Counter Reformation legitimated the preservation of images from a previous era, whose function was clearly much more cultic than its definition could embrace. The practical preservation of these images paralleled this theoretical dynamic. While their continued power was evident in struggles over their location and control, these iconic images were

36. P. BURKE, *Popular Piety* (n. 28), 124, citing M.-H. FROESCHLÉ-CHOPARD, *La religion populaire en Provence orientale au XVIIIe siècle*, Paris, Éditions Beauchesne, 1980; H. BELTING, *Likeness and Presence* (n. 36), p. 80 ff.

37. The didactic character of much of the Baroque, and the fact that it was undeniably the production of an elite, suggest continuity with dynamics sketched here. From the perspective of objective cultural capital, however, its exuberant excesses of organic, fleshly imagery and texture provided copious material for imaginative engagement within worship space. Its didactic portrayal of the natural and human world as a topos of plenitude and grace likewise can be understood as a legitimation of the everyday sacramental imagination. For a discussion of the subversive character of the Baroque see Godzieba (n. 4), 16-17, where he draws from the work of B. TURNER, *Recent Developments in the Theory of the Body*, in M. FEATHERSTONE (ed.), *The Body: Social Process and Cultural Theory*, London, Sage, 1989, p.199-217.

38. Council of Trent, 25th Session, 1563, *On the Invocation, Veneration, and Relics, of Saints, and on Sacred Images*, in N. TANNER (ed.), *Decrees of the Ecumenical Councils*, Washington D.C., Georgetown University Press, 1990, pp. 774-776. Note the shift from Second Nicea's (787) use of *hypostasis* to Trent's "likeness." Here Belting's narrative coincides with Marion's. The era of art expresses the values outlined by Marion in his phenomenology of the idol. It is concerned with representation and knowledge and contains nothing more than what is put into it by the artist. Belting's history of the precursors and emergence of the Christian icon would however render Marion's account problematic. J.-L. MARION, *God Without Being: Hors-Texte*, trans. T. Carlson, Chicago, University of Chicago Press, 1991.

housed in ciboria, altarpieces, frescos and indeed entire chapels that
framed them interpretively within the instrumental, didactic art of the
reformation[39].

This interpretive appropriation of popular practices and images is one
of the oft-cited, ingenious traits of Catholicism: its ability to embrace
symbols and practices from diverse cultures and turn them to its own
use. Conventional narratives of the sacramental imagination would
interpret this positively as a manifestation of the optimism concerning
presence in Catholicism. The counter-narrative we are pursuing here
suggests a different interpretation – not as a comfort with mediation –
but as anxiety manifest in the desire to control and limit it. These negotiated appropriations of the Catholic Reformation were quantitatively,
but not qualitatively different from the iconoclastic extremes of the
Protestant one. Both presumed the inadequacy of popular religious
practice and belief, and, for this reason, undertook efforts to recast them
in orthodox form. Belting considers the emergence of interpretation a
conquest of the power of images by theologians and artists. It reveals
not only the power of images, but also the power at stake in their interpretation. The miraculous claims made about holy images were direct
challenges to clerical authority. These images mediated the divine without need for hierarchical consecration. When re-authorized in artistic
terms, images were safely reduced to human artefacts. The administration of their proper meaning was reserved for the competence of intellectual and artistic elites whose authority was legitimated in the
process[40].

This strategy of intentionalization of ritual and image has affinities
with Foucault's account of the emergence of disciplinary power. Not
content with the limits of bodily control, penal technology aimed at controlling thought as well[41]. Foucault believed that the modern notion of
interiority was created in this process. This creation of interiority has
affinities with Belting's association of interpretation and depth
hermeneutics with the era of art[42]. The Catholic reform desired more
than simply determining which rituals would be practiced or the artistic

39. H. BELTING, *Likeness and Presence* (n. 36), pp. 484-490.
40. *Ibid.*, p. 7.
41. M. FOUCAULT, *Discipline and Punish: The Birth of the Prison,* trans. A. Sheridan,
New York, Vintage, 1979, p. 29.
42. Much more could be said here the relationship between this ecclesial policy and
the rise of representation as a concern in the West. See M. FOUCAULT, *The Order of
Things,* trans. A. Sheridan, New York, Pantheon, 1970; and M. DE CERTEAU, *The Scriptural Economy* in *The Practice of Everyday Life,* Vol. 1, ed. S. RANDAL, Berkeley, University of California Press, 1984, pp. 131-153.

environment of worship space, it wanted to guide the interpretation of rituals, gestures and images in order to control their meaning, to contain their polysemy within the bounds of orthodoxy. When the sacramental imagination is conceived as a doctrinal horizon of understanding, such administration of interpretation seems an appropriate exercise of pastoral oversight. When the issue of imaginative agency is raised however, it appears quite differently: as a direct disempowering of the masses through the elite appropriation of cultural capital. The emergence of "the proper meaning" or even meaning itself as a category delegitimates the interpretive activity of non-elites. Talal Asad argues that this association of meaning with practice is a fundamental characteristic of Christianity, indeed that it is the very "standpoint of theology"[43]. Asad's analysis is particularly helpful for the tension it elucidates. Meaning, power and culture are bound together in a way that resists easy differentiation. The reading of meaning into action and ritual is both fundamental to the Christian understanding of practice and a power strategy that has all-too-often been used repressively. There is a seemingly intractable tension between maintaining orthodoxy and maintaining the agency of the *populus*.

2. *The Liturgical Renewal*

This account of the reduction of the agency of the laity could be developed and nuanced with evidence from any number of other periods. We will turn to an example drawn from later Modern Catholicism that further illuminates the intractability of the tension between meaning and imaginative agency: the liturgical renewals of the 19th and 20th centuries. This movement has both dissimilarities and continuities with the reformation period. While its desire for the "full, conscious, and active" participation of the congregation in the liturgy is consistent with our concern for imaginative agency, this grounded a program of communicating the proper meaning of liturgical action to the participants that continued the dynamics of the reformations[44]. The Eucharistic liturgy was emphasized as the central ritual mystery of the Church. Anything that was perceived to detract from this focus — whether the practice of devotions, architecture or artwork — was stripped away. In this regard, its massive undertaking of historical retrieval notwithstanding, the liturgical renewal was consonant with the ethos and forms of modern architecture and

---

43. T. ASAD, *Anthropological Conceptions of Religion: Reflections on Geertz*, in *Man* 18 (1983) 237-259, p. 245.
44. *Sacrosanctum Concilium*, 14 and *passim*.

drama[45]. Josef Jungmann exemplified this combination. He believed religious art and architecture were held in thrall by the subjective vision of artists and the reified categories of various art forms. Thus, they alienated the worshipping community because they were not expressions of their faith. Influenced by the Abbot of Maria Laach, Ildefons Herwegen, Jungmann envisioned ancient Christianity as an organic harmony where the faith of the community as a whole was expressed in the "unified idiom" of textual, ritual and artistic expression[46]. This sense of lost fullness inspired Jungmann's historical retrieval, a move paralleling the modernist turn to primitivism[47]. The turn to minimalist aesthetics aimed to return the sacralized ritual of the sacraments to their original ground in the sacramentality of the everyday – the simplicity of "washing in water, soothing with oil, sitting at table"[48].

There is much to be said for this program. It engendered a shift from a sense of mystery that was in fact mystification – an aestheticized experience of incomprehension – to a more theologically adequate understanding of mystery as experience of the transcendent God who is nevertheless present in the community gathered, re-membering Jesus. From the perspective of imaginative agency and cultural capital however, this program continued the dynamic of the reformations: the control and attenuation of presence. The paring away of para-liturgical devotions was as much a loss of rituals in which the laity could actively participate as a recentering on the Eucharist[49]. The simplification of liturgical space (which often enough involved the elimination of inferior art) was equally an elimination of other mediations that decentered the

45. P. Cobb notes that the proscenium arch and chancel arch disappear simultaneously. P. COBB, *Architectural Setting of the Liturgy*, in *The Study of the Liturgy* (n. 17), p. 538.

46. M. WEDIG, *The Defeat of Visual Aesthetic Arianism* in *Source and Summit: Commemorating Josef A. Jungman*, Collegeville, Liturgical Press, 1999, p. 214, n. 8. Wedig develops at length the parallels between Jungmann's and Belting's thought as well as elite anxiety over the imaginative activity of the masses. See Jungmann's essay *Liturgy and Church Art*, in *Pastoral Liturgy*, New York, Herder and Herder, 1962, pp. 357-367. For a discussion of the tensions between the Vatican II liturgy and the sensibilities of "popular" Catholicism see M. AMALADOSS, *Toward a New Ecumenism: Churches of the People*, in T. BAMAT & J.-P. WIEST (eds.), *Popular Catholicism in a World Church* (n. 23), p. 279.

47. *Ibid.*, p. 218-219.

48. D. POWER, *Sacrament* (n. 16), p.146.

49. See N. Mitchell's account of the emergence of Eucharistic devotions as an attempt by the laity to reclaim the Eucharist against progressive clericalization from the 9th through 12th centuries. N. MITCHELL, *Cult and Controversy: The Worship of the Eucharist Outside Mass*, New York, Pueblo, 1982. See also S. Ross's similar account of the empowering function of devotions for women. S. ROSS, *God's Embodiment and Women*, in C. LACUGNA (ed.), *Freeing Theology*, San Francisco, Harper, 1993, p. 190.

presider[50]. Finally, the turning of the celebrant to face the people and the Biblical homily further established the ritual as an intentional communication, suggesting again the congregation's responsibility to derive the proper meaning from these practices. The combined effects of these reforms drastically reduced the space, time and material available for the laity to actively exercise imagination. This circumscribed the enormous potential of the shift to the vernacular for a return of cultural capital to the laity. Thus, a program designed to communicate the meaning of the liturgy in order to renew the life of the Church on all levels, is shown to have consequences in direct conflict with its professed goals because of its underlying structural effects[51].

VI. CONCLUSION

This essay has argued that the question of presence is not purely an ideational one. As its importance in sacramental theology would suggest, the experience of presence is constructed in rituals, spaces and images. The politics of presence are inseparably linked to this infrastructure. This makes theological analysis and constructive proposals much more complex. As our examination of the liturgical renewal has shown, it is not simply a matter of what we mean or intend to bring about. The material infrastructure of culture can have effects directly

50. S. White documents the commercialization of "tasteless, mass-produced" church art as early as the 1920's. S. WHITE, *Art, Architecture and Liturgical Reform*, New York, Pueblo, 1990, p. 170. Note however, that according to the analysis of cultural capital, the quality or origin of cultural goods is not determinative, as whatever their quality they provide material on which to exercise imagination. D. Freedberg argues that the emergence of standardized woodcuts in the 16th c. lead to an increase in presence due to the greater familiarity which convention introduced into devotional and catechetical images. D. FREEDBERG, *The Power of Images: Studies in the History and Theory of Response*, Chicago, University of Chicago Press, 1989, p. 177 ff.

51. In the U.S., these transformations in worship space accompanied the exodus of Catholics to the suburbs, which exacerbated these attenuations of cultural capital. The neighborhood parish ceased to exist, and with it went the geographical sense of the parish, which could serve to relativize clerical sacralization of church space (as did the practice of processions which likewise depended on the urban scale of parish boundaries). The decline of the neighborhood parish also brought a decline in the generational hierarchy in the worship space. The presence of community elders in the Eucharistic assembly provided an alternative mediation of authority in worship space. R. Orsi has spoken of an "iconostasis of black clad" matriarchs framing the celebrant in mid-century New York Italian parishes. Clearly this relativized the celebrant's authority, but it also provided an opportunity for the community to imagine itself as a mediation. (Orsi's comments were made at the 1995 meeting of the Roman Catholic Studies Group at the American Academy of Religion Annual Meeting in Philadelphia. See R. ORSI, *The Madonna of 115th Street: Faith and Community in Italian Harlem, 1880-1950*, New Haven, Yale, 1985).

contrary to our avowed goals. For this reason, theological reflection must take them into account.

This essay began with the assumption that postmodern suspicions of presence are valuable; they have important practical and political consequences for the practice of theology. This remains the case, but this analysis has added another strata to these suspicions. We have uncovered a history of conflict over the power of cultural production and interpretation beneath this postmodern anxiety.

The conflict between popular and erudite knowledges continues (among other places) in progressive theology today. There is a fault line between an ethical and perhaps pneumatological desire to respect popular religion and a conflicting desire, of similar inspiration, to channel, appropriate or instrumentalize popular religiosity so that it may issue in ethical praxis. This essay has shown how such laudable desires are frequently enacted in ways that are in fact repressive. Here we encounter the enormous (hopefully not intractable) problem of the political conflict that is inherent to our location as academic elites. Certeau is particularly valuable because he makes Bauman's characterization of the postmodern intellectual reflexive. The study of popular culture

> informs us less about popular culture itself than about what it means for a progressive academic to speak of popular culture today. This brings us back to the ubiquitous problem we must try to answer: *Where does one speak? What can be said?* But also, Where do *we* speak? This makes the problem directly political, because it makes an issue of the social – in other words, primarily repressive – function of learned culture....Where are we, outside of learned culture[52]?

Certeau's further conclusion is based upon an analysis that takes the political location of knowledge seriously: "[W]e cannot ignore the fact that it is impossible for a *written* act (ours), an ambition...to seriously purport to found a new kind of relation"[53]. That requires a political act.

In order to avoid this category error of confusing the act of concluding an essay with resolving a political tension, I offer an example of this tension in the contemporary moment in *lieu* of a conclusion. The *Hermita de la Caridad del Cobre* in Miami, Florida, a shrine to Our Lady of Charity, the Patroness of Cuba, is a hybrid and contested site if ever there were one. It is important to wealthy Cuban expatriates and to later immigrants on the margins of the economy, to practitioners of Catholicism, Santeria, and those whose beliefs and practices lie somewhere

---

52. M. DE CERTEAU, *The Beauty of the Dead* (n. 20), p. 135. Emphasis original.
53. *Ibid.*, p. 135-136.

between the two. The iconography and ritual surrounding the Caridad bear a striking resemblance to that of Oshun, an *Orisha* in the Yoruba pantheon[54]. There is tension between the official Church's desire to suppress practices and beliefs that manifest the Yoruba genealogy of the cult and devotes who do not make such sharp distinctions. The line between the Afro-Cuban and Catholic elements of the site, much to the delight of postmodern sensibilities, is profoundly difficult to draw. Oshun is associated with gold and light, and it is a common practice to make offerings to the Caridad of yellow flowers. Another Santeria practice – that of offering food to the deity is evident in the plates and urns which can be seen – through a hazy flotsam of yellow rose petals – lying at the bottom of the bay outside the Shrine. Inside, a sign exhorting visitors to instead leave donations to provide food for the poor is surrounded by a mountain of yellow roses.

Department of Theology   Vincent J. MILLER
Georgetown University
120 New North
37th & O Sts.
Washington, DC 20057-1135, USA

54. For a discussion of the political-religious contestations at the Shrine, see T. TWEED, *Our Lady of the Exile: Diasporic Religion at a Cuban Catholic Shrine in Miami,* New York, Oxford University Press, 1997. For an analysis of the relationship between *La Caridad del Cobre* and *Oshun*, see J. MURPHY, *Santeria: An African Religion in America*, Boston, Beacon, 1988.

"UNTITLED"

ON DENOTING SACRAMENTAL PRESENCE

I. RITES AS A CASE OF A FUNDAMENTAL THEOLOGY

Sacramental presence is a subject which – 'normally' – not has been situated in the field of fundamental theology, which is the field of theology in which I am working. Nevertheless, in this contribution I will raise some considerations about sacramental presence in this regard, i.e. a perspective of fundamental theology. And herein I will choose an aspect of the Christian praxis as my point of departure. In a widely secularised society as it exists in my country, the Netherlands, many people no longer understand that I participate in liturgical rites. In particular, they would not understand it if I would do so on behalf of old traditions only, only on behalf of the authority of social institutions or un-reflected habits in my personal life. Referring to this sociological question – the so-called implausibility of Christian belief in a secularised society – I want to make clear that the subject of sacramental presence implies a problem which concerns fundamental theology and that this problem arises from concrete participation in liturgical rites.

Which problem do I mean? Which problem arises when I want to explain to my neighbours and to my friends, even to my children, that I participate in liturgical rites? Which problem arises when I try to justify that I am really interested in it and that I like it? I do not mean the usual explanations of biographical and psycho-sociological art. My neighbours, friends and children do not ask me about my childhood, my education nor even about my work as a theologian at the Catholic University of Nijmegen. Rather, the question which arises refers to my longings. They ask me about choices and drives. They ask which position and relevance liturgical participation has between other choices and drives. The question which arises, is: what kind of longing is hidden in these rites?

Why does this question belong to the field of fundamental theology? Of course, the question of longings can be understood as a psychological question. But I do not mean to reflect on rites as structures of our human psychic energy[1]. Perhaps you will consider that 'longings' do not belong to facts like rites, and that rites eventually could be considered to be an object of our human longing or an incentive of it, but that they do not possess subject-like qualities. Rites do not hide something like longings and talking in this way is only metaphorical language. Perhaps you wonder why I use this phrase: what kind of longing is hidden in these (liturgical) rites I participate in. I will attempt to comment on this.

Using this phrase, I want to recall a beautiful booklet of the Dutch religious psychologist Jacques Janssen, *Nederland als religieuze proeftuin* [Netherlands as an experimental garden in religion][2]. At the end of his final essay, he quotes *Paul Valéry*: religion offers words and rites, gestures and considerations in those moments people do not know what to say or what to do. Janssens refers to the motto *cache ton Dieu* [hide your God] *(Valéry)*. He remarks that this motto is connected with a quest-spirituality which is widespread in the Netherlands. Therefore, he gives the following definition of religion: religion is a disinterested and continuous quest for a kernel[3]; a kernel of reality in his opinion.

So, when I ask what kind of longing is hidden in rites I participate in, I refer to a Dürkheimian concept of rites. Rites and their symbolism are collective behaviour which cannot be reduced to a sense or a content that can be fully cleared up in a rational way. There is something strange in it, something magical. Janssen quotes the anthropologist Tambiah, saying that the logic of religious language is neither understandable nor communicative. So, in my perception, rites hide a disinterested and continuous quest for a kernel, a quest which is not fully understandable in a rational way because the desired kernel is in the end magical.

But, you could ask, why do you use the concept of longing? I owe the concept of longing to Fergus Kerr's book *Immortal Longings. Versions of Transcending Humanity*[4]. In this book he studies conceptual elements, tracks of religion in recent Western philosophy and literature. The core question of this book is whether they contain elements of an unusual concept of immortality? The word 'unusual' is meant with regard to theologies. Kerr looks for unusual concepts. In the theology, he argues, usual concepts of immortality refer to an ideal of perfection. In theological traditions, we are accustomed to think about the ultimate, redemptive reality as a reality which reconciles us with God and with each other

---

1. Cf. M. Van Uden, *Rouw, religie en ritueel,* Baarn, Ambo, 1988.
2. J. Janssen, *Nederland als religieuze proeftuin,* Nijmegen, KSGV, 1998, pp. 94-95
3. J. Janssen, *Nederland als religieuze proeftuin,* p. 95.
4. Cf. F. Kerr, *Immortal Longings. Versions of Transcending Humanity,* London, SPCK, 1997.

because this redemptive reality is supposed to be the perfection of our lives and histories. It is assumed that the redemptive reality delivers us from finitude and individuality, delivers us from contingencies and from our body. As such, Kerr searches for unusual concepts. His core question could be formulated in another way: how can a theology enter into dialogue with concepts of immortality which do not refer to the idea of perfection? Is it possible (in theology) to interpret theological traditions without referring to the idea of perfection? Is it possible to turn theological traditions around in a different direction, reading them in a direction downwards, reading them as a descent into the mundane realities of an everyday world?

What kind of longing is hidden in rites I participate in? What kind of disinterested and continuous quest for a kernel is offered by these rites? Do they offer a kernel which is magical in the end? And is it possible to interpret this quest as a descent into mundane realities of an everyday world?

These questions belong to the field of fundamental theology. For in this field the research is about the analysis and interpretation of cultural-religious *idiomata* from a perspective of a philosophical theology[5]. In this paper my attention is focused on the ritual dimension of this idiomata, especially the concept of *sacramentum*.

Originally, the theological category 'sacrament' was used by Tertullian. Sometimes, he used this category to interpret the Pauline expression *mystèrion* (e.g. Eph 3, 8-9)[6]. According to Tertullian, the mystery of Christ, his 'economy of salvation', is the reality which is meant by St. Paul as a reality which is veiled, obscured. Therefore, Tertullian uses the concept *sacramentum*. In his idiom, it expresses something which is *obumbratum de significatis, occultum in deo ab aevis. Sacramenta* are: figures, *enigmata*, allegories which are necessary *in medio patio saeculorum*. These figures have a dispersion in time and an orientation towards God. *Sacramenta* thereby both reveal and hide the economy of the *sapientia Dei*.

What kind of longing is hidden in rites I participate in? In my Christian tradition, these rites are called *figures 'in medio patio saeculorum'*, *enigmata* which are *obumbrata de significatis*. Therefore, I have entitled my paper with the word 'Untitled'. I owe this expression to many

5. Cf. T. VAN DEN HOOGEN, *Ernstige lichtzinnigheid. Een theologisch essay over hedendaagse cultuur als taal van God* (UTP-katern, 21), Baarn, Gooi & Sticht, 1998, pp. 13-54.

6. Cf. D. MICHAÉLIDES, *Sacramentum chez Tertullien*, Paris, Études Augustiniennes, 1970, pp. 323-326.

modern artists who use it to emphasise that their images reveal something that is beyond the borders of our language. What continuous quest for a kernel is hidden in the *figures 'in medio patio saeculorum'* I participate in? And can it be revealed, denoted and interpreted as a quest for an economy of salvation, an economy of God's wisdom in the mundane realities of the everyday world?

II. *QUAESTIO DISPUTATA*: WHAT IS THE SIGNIFIER OF SACRAMENTAL PRESENCE?

Is it possible to reinterpret sacramental presence in a direction downwards, as a descent into the mundane realities of an everyday world? Can I reinterpret my participation in the *figures 'in medio patio saeculorum'*, this quest for an economy of salvation, as a quest for God's wisdom in the mundane realities of the everyday world? My hypothesis about the turning around of theology that we have to accomplish, is that one of its conditions is to change our linguistic programme.

What is a linguistic programme and why is it so important? A linguistic programme is a function which categorises a network of combinations and disintegrations of linguistic signs and which performs figures[7]. These figures have a functional dimension. The linguistic programme arranges signifiers and their significations in a hierarchical order. But these figures also have a substantial dimension. The relation between signifiers and their significations is limited; it cannot be open to all directions. We have to configure our confrontation with reality time and again by defining constraints and by pushing back frontiers.

A linguistic programme is important because it makes clear that our confrontation with reality is a linguistic affair which we try to analyse and to understand by reconstruction of various processes of denoting. A linguistic programme makes clear that these processes of denoting linguistic signs reveal histories of communication. Accordingly, within a hermeneutical project of the theology attention needs to be paid to linguistic programmes, i.e. to the reconstruction of processes of denoting[8].

Having the intention to reinterpret my quest for an economy of salvation as a quest for God's wisdom in the mundane realities of an everyday world, I aim at a hermeneutical project of the theology. Therefore, I have to pay attention to the process of denoting which is present in Tertullian's word *sacramentum*. According to Michaélidès, *sacramentum*

7. U. Eco, *Semiotik und Philosophie der Sprache*, München, Wilhelm Fink Verlag, 1985, pp. 39-40.

8. T. VAN DEN HOOGEN, *Ernstige lichtzinnigheid* (n. 4), pp. 150-164.

denotes that someone who violates the oath, one's word of honour to which one is consecrated, becomes *sacer*, i.e. left to the anger and punishments of the gods[9]. As such, *sacramentum* has two main significations, a juridical (military and civil) one and a religious one and a signifier which appears in those different domains, i.e. a vow, a pledge, a word of honour. When Tertullian uses this word (*sacramentum*), he changes the signifier. In discussion with Gnostic philosophers, he wants to express the character of the Christian concept of reality which is present in the act of faith. Christian faith, Tertullian wants to say, does not regard *enigmata* which are fundamentally ambiguous because they refer to a silent mystery. Christian faith refers to the wisdom of God which is present in the *mustèrion euaggeliou*[10]. And within this context, the *mustèrion euaggeliou* appears in a polemic sense, in an opposition between (Gnostic) heresy and (Christian) truth. Referring to St. Paul's concept of *mystèrion*, Tertullian wants to avoid every 'mysterious' suggestion. Tertullian wants to stress the undoubted reality of God's wisdom and the undoubted real nature of the relation of faith towards this wisdom. According to Tertullian, the signifier of *sacramentum* is God's wisdom and our faith in it. In accordance with St. Paul, this signifier has the character of an economy of salvation. That economy of salvation is the object of the consecration. That consecration is founded in a real history, so Tertullian, for the wisdom of God is expressed in prophetic signs and sacramental rites, i.e. rites which affirm the strong connection between faith and sign[11].

The linguistic programme of Tertullian is an example of a strong linguistic programme. In a strong linguistic programme, words are signs which refer in an equivalent and analogous way to reality, the reality of God's mystery, the economy of salvation. This reality is present in the act of faith and therefore, the act of faith is sacramentally confirmed in its dynamic realism. The reality of God's mystery is the signifier of the act of faith. Because Tertullian has a sacramental concept of the act of faith, he can emphasise that there is nothing 'mysterious' in this signifier. Signifier and signs are 'public'.

Whereas Tertullian develops here an example of the strong linguistic programme in a case where the 'public' dimension of Christianity is at stake, Augustine does so in a case where the 'inner' dimension needs clarification.

---

9. D. MICHAÉLIDES, *Sacramentum chez Tertullien* (n. 5), pp. 31-32.
10. *Ibid.*, p. 317.
11. *Ibid.*, p. 340.

Augustine is a theologian who understood theology as a spiritual quest. His concept of the *sermo de Deo*, as he defined theology, is a concept of wisdom. Theology is a rational effort to explain the Word of God he reads in the Bible as an expression of the wisdom of God. Brian Stock, in his study *Augustine the Reader. Meditation, Self-Knowledge and the Ethics of Interpretation,* puts forward that Augustine was deeply rooted in a culture of eloquence and developed a theory, a philosophy of mind, which has its core in the idea and the imagination of the self of the reader. Understanding God's wisdom is the result of a mental re-reading of stories of past events which are stored in our *memoria*. As Stock writes: "Scripture offers the reader… a privileged medium, through which God's will, framed in narratives, can be internalised and directed outwards as ethically informed action"[12]. Stock stresses that this reading process is conceived by Augustine as an 'odyssey' which permits the individual to ascend through a metaphorical 'infancy' and 'adolescence' to a certain level of 'maturity'[13].

A beautiful example of this 'odyssey' is offered in Book 11 of Augustine's *Confessions*. The 'odyssey' to maturity is, from the beginning, conceived as an 'odyssey' towards God.

In Book 11, Augustine puts the question of how temporal extension is experienced. How do we measure such extension? When we sing the hymn *Deus creator omnium*, he argues, then I do not measure the syllables which pass by but something in my *memoria*, something that fastens itself in it and continues. Measuring time is measuring the endurance of one's *memoria* and comes along with the awareness of contrast with the multitude of impressions. The *memoria* is Augustine's expression for what we could – perhaps – define as our subjectivity, that kernel inside us that is the power of our human being.

According to Augustine, a human being can distinguish his quest for the wisdom of God with the *memoria*. Indeed, Augustine's reflections about *memoria* and time are *confessions*. In his reflection, he creates – so to speak – his Other, his partner in dialogue. This partner in dialogue makes his reflections possible. This partner in dialogue is always present because this partner awakens Augustine's reflections. His reflections have the configuration of a prayer. Augustine's 'odyssey' is an 'odyssey' towards God. And through this journey he becomes mature.

12. B. STOCK, *Augustine the Reader. Meditation, Self-Knowledge and the Ethics of Interpretation,* Cambridge – London, Belknap Press of Harvard University Press, 1996, p. 12.
    13. *Ibid.,* p. 17-18.

This kind of theology is a fine example of the idea that the Christian is a human being who can realise oneself by transcending one's finitude and contingency. This kind of theology is characterised by what *Umberto Eco* described as a strong linguistic programme. Obviously, words are signs of a reality that is present in these signs. There is a relation of equivalence and analogy between sign and reality. Augustine is aware of the distinction between temporal reality which passes by and is corruptible, and eternal reality which holds on and is the basis for truth and trust. Of course, eternal reality is God's reality, reality which is God's creation. So, there are words which are signs which refer to our corruptible reality and there are words which refer to Gods creation, to eternal reality. Accordingly, Augustine makes a distinction between words of the Scripture – heard by the external human ear – and the words of God in these words – heard by the internal ear.

> The external ear reported these words of Thine, which were made for time, to the prudently reasoning mind whose internal ear is attuned to Thy eternal Word. But this mind compared these words which sound in time with Thy Word, eternal in its silence, and it proclaimed: 'It is different, it is far different.' These words are far below me; they do not even exist, for they are fleeting and transitory: 'But the Word of My God endureth above me forever'[14].

"It is different. It is far different." Augustine refers in this text to different approaches to time which are essentially different approaches to reality. In the first approach, he measures time through a reflection on his sensorial perceptions. In the second approach, he mirrors this reflection on God's creative silence. In both approaches, the relation of equivalence and analogy between sign and reality fades away. In the first approach, he discovers that our sensorial perceptions in their multitude of impressions suppose something else, the *memoria*. In the second approach, he discovers that *memoria* does not endure forever. In both approaches, the equivalence between sign and reality fades away. It slips between our words.

Augustine writes here – every bit a theologian – in a cultural context of eloquence and he tries to explore his almost mystical depths. As the Dutch theologian *Van Bavel* has put it[15], Augustine accomplishes his

---

14. *Conf.* XI, vi,8, transl. by Vernon J. Bourke, *Fathers of the Church. A New Translation, Writings of Saint Augustine*, Volume 5, New York, Fathers of the Church Inc., 1953, p. 335.

15. T.J. VAN BAVEL, *Spreken of zwijgen over God bij Augustinus* [*Affirmation and Negation in our Talk of God according to Augustine*], in *Tijdschrift voor Theologie* 37 (1997) 132-148.

thinking in the mystery of the Infinite One. He looks reluctantly for a path between Platonism and Christian faith. In confrontation with the mystery of the Infinite One, he gives in to this mystery.

This is also an example of a strong linguistic programme. The distinction between the external ear and the internal ear supposes that words are signs which refer in an equivalent and analogous way to reality, the reality of God's mystery.

In reading Augustine's *Confessions*, I realise that theology is challenged to change its linguistic programme. Precisely, when I am longing for a spiritual quest like Augustine, I can no longer refer to the idea of perfection. To denote the signs which are hidden in the texts of Scripture or in the rites of liturgy, I can no longer refer to the signifier, the real presence of God's mystery in its economy of salvation. Thinking about my confrontation with the longings which are hidden in liturgical rites and in the texts of Scripture, I have to turn theology around, because theology is challenged today to interpret this quest for God's wisdom as a descent into mundane realities of the everyday world. Hence, theology is challenged to review its linguistic programme. Theology has to ask if and how the idioms of Christian rites and texts can provide signifiers of the reality of God's wisdom. But theology usually looks for its 'case' in the opposite direction. Theology usually supposes its signifier (God's wisdom) to be present in a transcendent and perfect realm "out there"; theology usually continues its traditional structure of *exitus et reditus.* Even in a century during which many theologians developed a clear awareness of the necessity to do theology in a contextual way, this traditional structure and its linguistic programme are widely present. But the question of Fergus Kerr is a question which encourages us to leave behind this classic way of doing theology. Is it possible to turn theological traditions around in a different direction, reading them in a direction downwards, reading them as a descent *into* the mundane realities of the everyday world?

As a theologian, I participate in this factual, Western culture and in its history. I try to do so in a way that is critical towards the ideologies which are produced by this culture. I wonder if theology has to change its linguistic programme because theology is deeply rooted in a linguistic programme which supposes that the Christian is a human being which can realise oneself by transcending one's finitude and contingency. So, when I – within my secular culture – ask what kind of longing is hidden in rites I participate in, I have to review my linguistic programme in order to interpret the spiritual quest as a descent into the mundane realities of the everyday world.

III. VERSIONS OF GOD'S PRESENCE

In theology today, it is common sense to do theology with a Christological bias. I try to understand this bias by saying that reflections about the *logos* of God always have a reference in the *Geschichte* of Jesus. Without reference to Jesus of Nazareth, theology cannot denote the logos of God. One of my masters in the theology, Piet Schoonenberg, used to say that God becomes God-for-us in the *Geschichte* of Jesus' human 'genesis'. In this way, he explained why theology cannot denote the logos of God without reference to Jesus of Nazareth.

The position of Schoonenberg refers undoubtedly to a far-reaching transformation of traditional Christology. Schoonenberg is one of the theologians who have transformed the classic Logos-centred Christology by meditating the consequences of a historical and critical exegesis and new insights in Patristic thought. He develops a christological theory about the traditional Christian dogma about Jesus Christ and puts forward that God becomes God-for-us in the personal existence of this human being. This christological theory is characterised by a hermeneutical approach. According to Schoonenberg, an expression of the Christian dogma about Jesus Christ demands this approach.

Nevertheless, the history of Schoonenberg's theological thought makes clear that a hermeneutical approach of the Christian dogma about Jesus Christ can be characterised by different linguistic programmes.

In a first period[16] of christological reflections, Schoonenberg wants to reinterpret the neo-chalcedonian model or paradigm of theological speculations about the dogma of Chalcedon (451)[17]. This paradigm wants to express that the unity between creation and redemption has its signifier in the unique person of Christ. The dogmatic expression of the uniqueness of Christ is explained by a model of his divine childhood. This model explains the divinity of Christ by stating that the human nature of Christ is present in an *anhypostatic mode* in the son of God who is the subject of Christ and who is present in his human existence in an *enhypostatic mode*.

Schoonenberg declares that this neo-chalcedonian paradigm has to be revisited, although it is traditional and very powerful in the theological tradition of Christianity. For, this paradigm continues several aporias concerning the humanity of Christ. One of them is that the humanity of Christ is approached without reference to the particular economy of

16. I don't want define the different periods of Schoonenberg's theological development. I only want to distinguish two major stages in his christological thought.

17. Cf. P. SCHOONENBERG, *Hij is een God van mensen. Twee theologische studies,* 's-Hertogenbosch, Malmberg, 1969, pp. 49-195.

salvation. According to Schoonenberg, this economy of salvation is the signifier of the humanity of Christ – in the Scripture of the New Testament as well as in the formulas of Chalcedon. Because of this signifier, Schoonenberg proposes a new explanation of the christological dogma of Chalcedon. In his explanation, the signifier (the economy of salvation) demands that our faith in God be honest about the unity and completeness of a human person. Theological Christology has to meditate about the unique presence of God's economy of salvation in the unity and completeness of the human person of Jesus Christ.

Obviously, in this period the linguistic programme has a strong character – in the relation between signifier (economy of salvation) and signification (uniqueness) as well as in the explanation of the relation between God's presence in the humanity of Christ (christological signifier) and God's presence in the humanity of humankind (soteriological signification).

During a later period[18] of christological meditations, Schoonenberg meditates that God becomes God-for-us in the *Geschichte* of Jesus' human 'genesis'. Thus, he explained why theology cannot denote the logos of God without reference to Jesus of Nazareth.

According to Schoonenberg, this implies some radical new theological concepts. Herein he says that we in the theology can leave behind the concept of God's *essence* because it is not denoted by Jesus' being God-for-us. Indeed, God's presence is denoted by God's relations to our human history. God's presence is involved in time. God's presence is the history of the proximity of our world to God as well as the history of God's proximity to our world. According to Scripture, God's existence is the history of God's relating to the world and this process is the very core of God's being God. The Holy Scripture talks about the Word and about the Spirit to express two main characteristics of this history of God's relating to the world. The symbol of the Word expresses that God's relating implies difference and transcendence. God is dedicated to our world and *near to* our world. The symbol of the Spirit expresses that God's relating implies indwelling and immanence. God is *present in* our world.

In the *Geschichte* of Jesus' human 'genesis', a really new incarnation of God's relating to the human world is recognised in his personal existence. God's Word is expressed in the proximity to the sacrifice of this man, and God's Spirit is present in his suffering love. Jesus denotes God's transcendent being-for-us preferably as immanence in everything and

---

18. Cf. P. SCHOONENBERG, *De Geest, het Woord en de Zoon. Theologische over-denkingen over Geest-christologie, Logoschristologie en drieëenheidsleer*, Averbode – Kampen, Altiora – Kok, 1991.

everybody who is worthless, worthless regarding the *sophia tou kosmou*, as St. Paul said (1 Cor 1,20). According to this interpretation, Jesus denotes God's *kenosis*. God becomes temporal in a lasting dedication to every creature which is as a matter of fact non-existent. God becomes temporal by a descent to these kinds of mundane realities. God becomes God-for-us by losing its deity, one could say with help of a distinction I have learned from Eckhart.

In the second period, the linguistic programme goes through important variations. First of all, the signifier changes. Instead of the economy of salvation, Schoonenberg puts forward the history of God's becoming God-for-us. The signification changes also. Human beings can become a person, esp. those human beings who are 'non-existent'. Secondly, the explanation of the relation between God's becoming God and our becoming human undergoes variations. The christological signifier becomes unique in his 'kenosis' and the soteriological signification is conceived of as God's streaming out in our world.

IV. LONGING FOR SACRAMENTAL PRESENCE

When the concept of presence undergoes important variations, the concept of sacramental presence will likewise change. Therefore, the question is whether it is possible to reinterpret sacramental presence in another linguistic programme.

In theology, the classic shape of the linguistic programme is the strong linguistic programme. As can be observed in the writings of Tertullian and Augustine, the signifier and its significations are related to each other in an equivalent and analogous way. So, when I participate in liturgical rites, my quest is also characterised by this equivalence and analogy. Although participation in liturgical rites is conceived of as a quest which is not fully understandable in a rational way, this quest seems to be rational as long as we can suppose that there is an equivalent and analogous relation between the signifier (God's wisdom and the economy of salvation) and the salutary significations which are hidden in these signs.

But, what happens when I participate in liturgical rites within a cultural context which no longer supports the supposed equivalence and analogy? I can try to escape this cultural context. I can try to rebuild a world of past rituals and symbols – like happened in the field of architecture when churches were built in a neo-gothic style. So, I could try to direct my longing to a neo-classic liturgy which performs this lost equivalence and analogy. According to my opinion, the factual liturgy in our Christian tradition shows many efforts of this. Participating in this kind of liturgy,

I can hardly explain – not to my neighbours, nor to my friends, nor to myself. For, in the context of our factual society the supposed equivalence and analogy are hardly supported.

I do not want to escape my factual cultural context. I do not want to do it. The main reason for refusing such an escape is not an uncritical overestimation of its technical and economical efforts, nor uncritical self-satisfaction, nor an uncritical reception of its lifestyle. Rather, the main reason for refusing this escape is the affection and attachment to people who give birth to my life, who make me aware of friendship and companionship, who challenge me to meditate on God, happiness and life forever.

Because I refuse to escape my factual cultural context and because I desire to continue participating in liturgical rites – I am every inch a theo-logian – I look for another linguistic programme.

Umberto Eco defines the alternative as a weak linguistic programme. A weak programme arises, when language is approached as a labyrinth, he says. When we approach language as a network which is characterised by endless relations, then we leave the idea of perfection. Preferably, such a system refers to its own immanence.

My question now reads: Can we reread Tertullian's concept *obumbratum de significatiis* and Augustine's *creative silence* with a weak linguistic programme? Is it possible to reinterpret the disinterested and continuous quest for a kernel in terms of a pattern of endless related signs about mundane realities of the everyday world?

I will look for it and try to expound that this is a possibility which refers to the core of Christian belief and Christian liturgical rites. I will look for a possibility which refers to a new interpretation of the concept of sacramental presence.

In the third section, we saw that the concept of presence can undergo important variations. Theological interpretation of the concept of 'presence' implies that the relation of God's reality to our human reality can be defined as pan-en-theistic. Schoonenberg uses this word to express his conviction that God comes towards the world because being *in* the world's creative processes God is the One who is near to it. Because God is, being *in* the world's creative processes, the nearest One to it, God becomes recognisable as the nearest One in relation to everyone who is worthless. God comes to the world by many histories of 'kenosis' and God's being the nearest One is revealed in this way. In the light of Jesus' *Geschichte*, God's presence cannot be recognised in ways of transcendence from our reality. Preferably, it will be recognised by ways "downward", ways of descent into the everyday world. Schoonenberg calls this: God's personalisation, God's becoming related to worthless people.

What is the 'sacrament' of this personalisation of God's pan-en-theistic presence? Augustine would answer that we can attune God's wisdom with our *memoria*. Perhaps we have to say now that we also can attune God's presence in people who slip our mind. Perhaps we become aware of sacramental presence when we are among realities which have been forgotten and among people who are disfigured in their lives and live non-existently. Sacramental presence is a dance around the old Ark (Exod 25) and we are aware of the empty space between the wings of the Cherubs on the wooden top of it[19].

V. SUMMARY

Sacramental presence is a subject which – "normally" – has not been situated in the field of fundamental theology. In this field, research concerns the analysis and interpretation of cultural-religious *idiomata* from a perspective of philosophical theology[20]. In this paper my attention has focused on the ritual dimension of this *idiomata*, especially the concept of *sacramentum*. Is it possible to reinterpret sacramental presence in a direction downwards, as a descent into the mundane realities of the everyday world? My hypothesis about the turning around of theology that we need to accomplish, is that one of its conditions is to change our linguistic programme, from a strong to a weak linguistic programme. Analysing Tertullian's concept of *sacramentum* and Augustine's concept of *memoria*, I try to reinterpret the christological bias of God's presence. God's presence is not recognised in ways of transcendence of our reality. Preferably, it will be recognised by ways downwards, ways of descent into the everyday world. Schoonenberg calls this: God's personalisation, God's becoming related to worthless people. The signifier of God's presence becomes his 'kenosis' and the signification is conceived of as God's streaming out in our world. Sacramental presence expresses a disinterested and continuous quest for this presence as a kernel of reality.

Faculty of Theology   Toine VAN DEN HOOGEN
Katholieke Universiteit Nijmegen
Postbus 9103
NL-6500 HD Nijmegen
The Netherlands

19. Cf. J. POHIER, *Quand je dis Dieu*, Paris, Seuil, 1977, pp. 25-38.
20. Cf. T. VAN DEN HOOGEN, *Ernstige lichtzinnigheid.* (n. 4), pp. 13-54.

INDEX OF NAMES

BIBLIOTHECA EPHEMERIDUM THEOLOGICARUM LOVANIENSIUM

SERIES I

* = Out of print

*1. *Miscellanea dogmatica in honorem Eximii Domini J. Bittremieux*, 1947.

*2-3. *Miscellanea moralia in honorem Eximii Domini A. Janssen*, 1948.

*4. G. PHILIPS, *La grâce des justes de l'Ancien Testament*, 1948.

*5. G. PHILIPS, *De ratione instituendi tractatum de gratia nostrae sanctificationis*, 1953.

6-7. *Recueil Lucien Cerfaux. Études d'exégèse et d'histoire religieuse*, 1954. 504 et 577 p. Cf. *infra*, nᵒˢ 18 et 71 (t. III).   25 € par tome

   8. G. THILS, *Histoire doctrinale du mouvement œcuménique*, 1955. Nouvelle édition, 1963. 338 p.   4 €

*9. *Études sur l'Immaculée Conception*, 1955.

*10. J.A. O'DONOHOE, *Tridentine Seminary Legislation*, 1957.

*11. G. THILS, *Orientations de la théologie*, 1958.

*12-13. J. COPPENS, A. DESCAMPS, É. MASSAUX (ed.), *Sacra Pagina. Miscellanea Biblica Congressus Internationalis Catholici de Re Biblica*, 1959.

*14. *Adrien VI, le premier Pape de la contre-réforme*, 1959.

*15. F. CLAEYS BOUUAERT, *Les déclarations et serments imposés par la loi civile aux membres du clergé belge sous le Directoire (1795-1801)*, 1960.

*16. G. THILS, *La «Théologie œcuménique». Notion-Formes-Démarches*, 1960.

   17. G. THILS, *Primauté pontificale et prérogatives épiscopales. «Potestas ordinaria» au Concile du Vatican*, 1961. 103 p.   2 €

*18. *Recueil Lucien Cerfaux*, t. III, 1962. Cf. *infra*, n° 71.

*19. *Foi et réflexion philosophique. Mélanges F. Grégoire*, 1961.

*20. *Mélanges G. Ryckmans*, 1963.

   21. G. THILS, *L'infaillibilité du peuple chrétien «in credendo»*, 1963. 67 p.
                    2 €

*22. J. FÉRIN & L. JANSSENS, *Progestogènes et morale conjugale*, 1963.

*23. *Collectanea Moralia in honorem Eximii Domini A. Janssen*, 1964.

   24. H. CAZELLES (ed.), *De Mari à Qumrân. L'Ancien Testament. Son milieu. Ses écrits. Ses relectures juives* (Hommage J. Coppens, I), 1969. 158*-370 p.   23 €

*25. I. DE LA POTTERIE (ed.), *De Jésus aux évangiles. Tradition et rédaction dans les évangiles synoptiques* (Hommage J. Coppens, II), 1967.

   26. G. THILS & R.E. BROWN (ed.), *Exégèse et théologie* (Hommage J. Coppens, III), 1968. 328 p.   18 €

*27. J. COPPENS (ed.), *Ecclesia a Spiritu sancto edocta. Hommage à Mgr G. Philips*, 1970. 640 p.

   28. J. COPPENS (ed.), *Sacerdoce et célibat. Études historiques et théologiques*, 1971. 740 p.   18 €

29. M. DIDIER (ed.), *L'évangile selon Matthieu. Rédaction et théologie*, 1972.
    432 p.   25 €
*30. J. KEMPENEERS, *Le Cardinal van Roey en son temps*, 1971.

SERIES II

31. F. NEIRYNCK, *Duality in Mark. Contributions to the Study of the Markan Redaction*, 1972. Revised edition with Supplementary Notes, 1988. 252 p.
    30 €
32. F. NEIRYNCK (ed.), *L'évangile de Luc. Problèmes littéraires et théologiques*, 1973. *L'évangile de Luc – The Gospel of Luke*. Revised and enlarged edition, 1989. x-590 p.   55 €
33. C. BREKELMANS (ed.), *Questions disputées d'Ancien Testament. Méthode et théologie*, 1974. *Continuing Questions in Old Testament Method and Theology*. Revised and enlarged edition by M. VERVENNE, 1989. 245 p.
    30 €
34. M. SABBE (ed.), *L'évangile selon Marc. Tradition et rédaction*, 1974. Nouvelle édition augmentée, 1988. 601 p.   60 €
35. B. WILLAERT (ed.), *Philosophie de la religion – Godsdienstfilosofie. Miscellanea Albert Dondeyne*, 1974. Nouvelle édition, 1987. 458 p.   60 €
36. G. PHILIPS, *L'union personnelle avec le Dieu vivant. Essai sur l'origine et le sens de la grâce créée*, 1974. Édition révisée, 1989. 299 p.   25 €
37. F. NEIRYNCK, in collaboration with T. HANSEN and F. VAN SEGBROECK, *The Minor Agreements of Matthew and Luke against Mark with a Cumulative List*, 1974. 330 p.   23 €
38. J. COPPENS, *Le messianisme et sa relève prophétique. Les anticipations vétérotestamentaires. Leur accomplissement en Jésus*, 1974. Édition révisée, 1989. XIII-265 p.   25 €
39. D. SENIOR, *The Passion Narrative according to Matthew. A Redactional Study*, 1975. New impression, 1982. 440 p.   25 €
40. J. DUPONT (ed.), *Jésus aux origines de la christologie*, 1975. Nouvelle édition augmentée, 1989. 458 p.   38 €
41. J. COPPENS (ed.), *La notion biblique de Dieu*, 1976. Réimpression, 1985. 519 p.   40 €
42. J. LINDEMANS & H. DEMEESTER (ed.), *Liber Amicorum Monseigneur W. Onclin*, 1976. XXII-396 p.   25 €
43. R.E. HOECKMAN (ed.), *Pluralisme et œcuménisme en recherches théologiques. Mélanges offerts au R.P. Dockx, O.P.*, 1976. 316 p.   25 €
44. M. DE JONGE (ed.), *L'évangile de Jean. Sources, rédaction, théologie*, 1977. Réimpression, 1987. 416 p.   38 €
45. E.J.M. VAN EIJL (ed.), *Facultas S. Theologiae Lovaniensis 1432-1797. Bijdragen tot haar geschiedenis. Contributions to its History. Contributions à son histoire*, 1977. 570 p.   43 €
46. M. DELCOR (ed.), *Qumrân. Sa piété, sa théologie et son milieu*, 1978. 432 p.   43 €
47. M. CAUDRON (ed.), *Faith and Society. Foi et société. Geloof en maatschappij. Acta Congressus Internationalis Theologici Lovaniensis 1976*, 1978. 304 p.   29 €

*48. J. KREMER (ed.), *Les Actes des Apôtres. Traditions, rédaction, théologie,* 1979. 590 p.

49. F. NEIRYNCK, avec la collaboration de J. DELOBEL, T. SNOY, G. VAN BELLE, F. VAN SEGBROECK, *Jean et les Synoptiques. Examen critique de l'exégèse de M.-É. Boismard,* 1979. XII-428 p. 25 €

50. J. COPPENS, *La relève apocalyptique du messianisme royal. I. La royauté – Le règne – Le royaume de Dieu. Cadre de la relève apocalyptique,* 1979. 325 p. 25 €

51. M. GILBERT (ed.), *La Sagesse de l'Ancien Testament,* 1979. Nouvelle édition mise à jour, 1990. 455 p. 38 €

52. B. DEHANDSCHUTTER, *Martyrium Polycarpi. Een literair-kritische studie,* 1979. 296 p. 25 €

53. J. LAMBRECHT (ed.), *L'Apocalypse johannique et l'Apocalyptique dans le Nouveau Testament,* 1980. 458 p. 35 €

54. P.-M. BOGAERT (ed.), *Le livre de Jérémie. Le prophète et son milieu. Les oracles et leur transmission,* 1981. *Nouvelle édition mise à jour,* 1997. 448 p. 45 €

55. J. COPPENS, *La relève apocalyptique du messianisme royal. III. Le Fils de l'homme néotestamentaire.* Édition posthume par F. NEIRYNCK, 1981. XIV-192 p. 20 €

56. J. VAN BAVEL & M. SCHRAMA (ed.), *Jansénius et le Jansénisme dans les Pays-Bas. Mélanges Lucien Ceyssens,* 1982. 247 p. 25 €

57. J.H. WALGRAVE, *Selected Writings – Thematische geschriften. Thomas Aquinas, J.H. Newman, Theologia Fundamentalis.* Edited by G. DE SCHRIJVER & J.J. KELLY, 1982. XLIII-425 p. 25 €

58. F. NEIRYNCK & F. VAN SEGBROECK, avec la collaboration de E. MANNING, *Ephemerides Theologicae Lovanienses 1924-1981. Tables générales. (Bibliotheca Ephemeridum Theologicarum Lovaniensium 1947-1981),* 1982. 400 p. 40 €

59. J. DELOBEL (ed.), *Logia. Les paroles de Jésus – The Sayings of Jesus. Mémorial Joseph Coppens,* 1982. 647 p. 50 €

60. F. NEIRYNCK, *Evangelica. Gospel Studies – Études d'évangile. Collected Essays.* Edited by F. VAN SEGBROECK, 1982. XIX-1036 p. 50 €

61. J. COPPENS, *La relève apocalyptique du messianisme royal. II. Le Fils d'homme vétéro- et intertestamentaire.* Édition posthume par J. LUST, 1983. XVII-272 p. 25 €

62. J.J. KELLY, *Baron Friedrich von Hügel's Philosophy of Religion,* 1983. 232 p. 38 €

63. G. DE SCHRIJVER, *Le merveilleux accord de l'homme et de Dieu. Étude de l'analogie de l'être chez Hans Urs von Balthasar,* 1983. 344 p. 38 €

64. J. GROOTAERS & J.A. SELLING, *The 1980 Synod of Bishops: «On the Role of the Family». An Exposition of the Event and an Analysis of its Texts.* Preface by Prof. emeritus L. JANSSENS, 1983. 375 p. 38 €

65. F. NEIRYNCK & F. VAN SEGBROECK, *New Testament Vocabulary. A Companion Volume to the Concordance,* 1984. XVI-494 p. 50 €

66. R.F. COLLINS, *Studies on the First Letter to the Thessalonians,* 1984. XI-415 p. 38 €

67. A. PLUMMER, *Conversations with Dr. Döllinger 1870-1890.* Edited with Introduction and Notes by R. BOUDENS, with the collaboration of L. KENIS, 1985. LIV-360 p. 45 €

68. N. LOHFINK (ed.), *Das Deuteronomium. Entstehung, Gestalt und Botschaft / Deuteronomy: Origin, Form and Message,* 1985. XI-382 p.   50 €
69. P.F. FRANSEN, *Hermeneutics of the Councils and Other Studies.* Collected by H.E. MERTENS & F. DE GRAEVE, 1985. 543 p.   45 €
70. J. DUPONT, *Études sur les Évangiles synoptiques.* Présentées par F. NEIRYNCK, 1985. 2 tomes, XXI-IX-1210 p.   70 €
71. *Recueil Lucien Cerfaux,* t. III, 1962. Nouvelle édition revue et complétée, 1985. LXXX-458 p.   40 €
72. J. GROOTAERS, *Primauté et collégialité. Le dossier de Gérard Philips sur la Nota Explicativa Praevia (Lumen gentium, Chap. III).* Présenté avec introduction historique, annotations et annexes. Préface de G. THILS, 1986. 222 p.   25 €
73. A. VANHOYE (ed.), *L'apôtre Paul. Personnalité, style et conception du ministère,* 1986. XIII-470 p.   65 €
74. J. LUST (ed.), *Ezekiel and His Book. Textual and Literary Criticism and their Interrelation,* 1986. X-387 p.   68 €
75. É. MASSAUX, *Influence de l'Évangile de saint Matthieu sur la littérature chrétienne avant saint Irénée.* Réimpression anastatique présentée par F. NEIRYNCK. *Supplément: Bibliographie 1950-1985,* par B. DEHANDSCHUTTER, 1986. XXVII-850 p.   63 €
76. L. CEYSSENS & J.A.G. TANS, *Autour de l'Unigenitus. Recherches sur la genèse de la Constitution,* 1987. XXVI-845 p.   63 €
77. A. DESCAMPS, *Jésus et l'Église. Études d'exégèse et de théologie.* Préface de Mgr A. HOUSSIAU, 1987. XLV-641 p.   63 €
78. J. DUPLACY, *Études de critique textuelle du Nouveau Testament.* Présentées par J. DELOBEL, 1987. XXVII-431 p.   45 €
79. E.J.M. VAN EIJL (ed.), *L'image de C. Jansénius jusqu'à la fin du XVIIIᵉ siècle,* 1987. 258 p.   32 €
80. E. BRITO, *La Création selon Schelling. Universum,* 1987. XXXV-646 p.   75 €
81. J. VERMEYLEN (ed.), *The Book of Isaiah – Le livre d'Isaïe. Les oracles et leurs relectures. Unité et complexité de l'ouvrage,* 1989. X-472 p.   68 €
82. G. VAN BELLE, *Johannine Bibliography 1966-1985. A Cumulative Bibliography on the Fourth Gospel,* 1988. XVII-563 p.   68 €
83. J.A. SELLING (ed.), *Personalist Morals. Essays in Honor of Professor Louis Janssens,* 1988. VIII-344 p.   30 €
84. M.-É. BOISMARD, *Moïse ou Jésus. Essai de christologie johannique,* 1988. XVI-241 p.   25 €
84A. M.-É. BOISMARD, *Moses or Jesus: An Essay in Johannine Christology.* Translated by B.T. VIVIANO, 1993, XVI-144 p.   25 €
85. J.A. DICK, *The Malines Conversations Revisited,* 1989. 278 p.   38 €
86. J.-M. SEVRIN (ed.), *The New Testament in Early Christianity – La réception des écrits néotestamentaires dans le christianisme primitif,* 1989. XVI-406 p.   63 €
87. R.F. COLLINS (ed.), *The Thessalonian Correspondence,* 1990. XV-546 p.   75 €
88. F. VAN SEGBROECK, *The Gospel of Luke. A Cumulative Bibliography 1973-1988,* 1989. 241 p.   30 €

89. G. THILS, *Primauté et infaillibilité du Pontife Romain à Vatican I et autres études d'ecclésiologie*, 1989. XI-422 p. 47 €
90. A. VERGOTE, *Explorations de l'espace théologique. Études de théologie et de philosophie de la religion*, 1990. XVI-709 p. 50 €
*91. J.C. DE MOOR, *The Rise of Yahwism: The Roots of Israelite Monotheism*, 1990. *Revised and Enlarged Edition*, 1997. XV-445 p.
92. B. BRUNING, M. LAMBERIGTS & J. VAN HOUTEM (eds.), *Collectanea Augustiniana. Mélanges T.J. van Bavel*, 1990. 2 tomes, XXXVIII-VIII-1074 p. 75 €
93. A. DE HALLEUX, *Patrologie et œcuménisme. Recueil d'études*, 1990. XVI-887 p. 75 €
94. C. BREKELMANS & J. LUST (eds.), *Pentateuchal and Deuteronomistic Studies: Papers Read at the XIIIth IOSOT Congress Leuven 1989*, 1990. 307 p. 38 €
95. D.L. DUNGAN (ed.), *The Interrelations of the Gospels. A Symposium Led by M.-É. Boismard – W.R. Farmer – F. Neirynck, Jerusalem 1984*, 1990. XXXI-672 p. 75 €
96. G.D. KILPATRICK, *The Principles and Practice of New Testament Textual Criticism. Collected Essays*. Edited by J.K. ELLIOTT, 1990. XXXVIII-489 p. 75 €
97. G. ALBERIGO (ed.), *Christian Unity. The Council of Ferrara-Florence: 1438/39 – 1989*, 1991. X-681 p. 75 €
98. M. SABBE, *Studia Neotestamentica. Collected Essays*, 1991. XVI-573 p. 50 €
99. F. NEIRYNCK, *Evangelica II: 1982-1991. Collected Essays*. Edited by F. VAN SEGBROECK, 1991. XIX-874 p. 70 €
100. F. VAN SEGBROECK, C.M. TUCKETT, G. VAN BELLE & J. VERHEYDEN (eds.), *The Four Gospels 1992. Festschrift Frans Neirynck*, 1992. 3 volumes, XVII-X-X-2668 p. 125 €

SERIES III

101. A. DENAUX (ed.), *John and the Synoptics*, 1992. XXII-696 p. 75 €
102. F. NEIRYNCK, J. VERHEYDEN, F. VAN SEGBROECK, G. VAN OYEN & R. CORSTJENS, *The Gospel of Mark. A Cumulative Bibliography: 1950-1990*, 1992. XII-717 p. 68 €
103. M. SIMON, *Un catéchisme universel pour l'Église catholique. Du Concile de Trente à nos jours*, 1992. XIV-461 p. 55 €
104. L. CEYSSENS, *Le sort de la bulle Unigenitus. Recueil d'études offert à Lucien Ceyssens à l'occasion de son 90ᵉ anniversaire*. Présenté par M. LAMBERIGTS, 1992. XXVI-641 p. 50 €
105. R.J. DALY (ed.), *Origeniana Quinta. Papers of the 5th International Origen Congress, Boston College, 14-18 August 1989*, 1992. XVII-635 p. 68 €
106. A.S. VAN DER WOUDE (ed.), *The Book of Daniel in the Light of New Findings*, 1993. XVIII-574 p. 75 €
107. J. FAMERÉE, *L'ecclésiologie d'Yves Congar avant Vatican II: Histoire et Église. Analyse et reprise critique*, 1992. 497 p. 65 €

108. C. BEGG, *Josephus' Account of the Early Divided Monarchy (AJ 8, 212-420). Rewriting the Bible*, 1993. IX-377 p.	60 €
109. J. BULCKENS & H. LOMBAERTS (eds.), *L'enseignement de la religion catholique à l'école secondaire. Enjeux pour la nouvelle Europe*, 1993. XII-264 p.	32 €
110. C. FOCANT (ed.), *The Synoptic Gospels. Source Criticism and the New Literary Criticism*, 1993. XXXIX-670 p.	75 €
111. M. LAMBERIGTS (ed.), avec la collaboration de L. KENIS, *L'augustinisme à l'ancienne Faculté de théologie de Louvain*, 1994. VII-455 p.	60 €
112. R. BIERINGER & J. LAMBRECHT, *Studies on 2 Corinthians*, 1994. XX-632 p.	75 €
113. E. BRITO, *La pneumatologie de Schleiermacher*, 1994. XII-649 p.	75 €
114. W.A.M. BEUKEN (ed.), *The Book of Job*, 1994. X-462 p.	60 €
115. J. LAMBRECHT, *Pauline Studies: Collected Essays*, 1994. XIV-465 p.	63 €
116. G. VAN BELLE, *The Signs Source in the Fourth Gospel: Historical Survey and Critical Evaluation of the Semeia Hypothesis*, 1994. XIV-503 p.	63 €
117. M. LAMBERIGTS & P. VAN DEUN (eds.), *Martyrium in Multidisciplinary Perspective. Memorial L. Reekmans*, 1995. X-435 p.	75 €
118. G. DORIVAL & A. LE BOULLUEC (eds.), *Origeniana Sexta. Origène et la Bible/Origen and the Bible. Actes du Colloquium Origenianum Sextum, Chantilly, 30 août – 3 septembre 1993*, 1995. XII-865 p.	98 €
119. É. GAZIAUX, *Morale de la foi et morale autonome. Confrontation entre P. Delhaye et J. Fuchs*, 1995. XXII-545 p.	68 €
120. T.A. SALZMAN, *Deontology and Teleology: An Investigation of the Normative Debate in Roman Catholic Moral Theology*, 1995. XVII-555 p.	68 €.
121. G.R. EVANS & M. GOURGUES (eds.), *Communion et Réunion. Mélanges Jean-Marie Roger Tillard*, 1995. XI-431 p.	60 €
122. H.T. FLEDDERMANN, *Mark and Q: A Study of the Overlap Texts*. With an *Assessment* by F. NEIRYNCK, 1995. XI-307 p.	45 €
123. R. BOUDENS, *Two Cardinals: John Henry Newman, Désiré-Joseph Mercier*. Edited by L. GEVERS with the collaboration of B. DOYLE, 1995. 362 p.	45 €
124. A. THOMASSET, *Paul Ricœur. Une poétique de la morale. Aux fondements d'une éthique herméneutique et narrative dans une perspective chrétienne*, 1996. XVI-706 p.	75 €
125. R. BIERINGER (ed.), *The Corinthian Correspondence*, 1996. XXVII-793 p.	60 €
126. M. VERVENNE (ed.), *Studies in the Book of Exodus: Redaction – Reception – Interpretation*, 1996. XI-660 p.	60 €
127. A. VANNESTE, *Nature et grâce dans la théologie occidentale. Dialogue avec H. de Lubac*, 1996. 312 p.	45 €
128. A. CURTIS & T. RÖMER (eds.), *The Book of Jeremiah and its Reception – Le livre de Jérémie et sa réception*, 1997. 331 p.	60 €
129. E. LANNE, *Tradition et Communion des Églises. Recueil d'études*, 1997. XXV-703 p.	75 €

130. A. DENAUX & J.A. DICK (eds.), *From Malines to ARCIC. The Malines Conversations Commemorated*, 1997. IX-317 p. 45 €
131. C.M. TUCKETT (ed.), *The Scriptures in the Gospels*, 1997. XXIV-721 p. 60 €
132. J. VAN RUITEN & M. VERVENNE (eds.), *Studies in the Book of Isaiah. Festschrift Willem A.M. Beuken*, 1997. XX-540 p. 75 €
133. M. VERVENNE & J. LUST (eds.), *Deuteronomy and Deuteronomic Literature. Festschrift C.H.W. Brekelmans*, 1997. XI-637 p. 75 €
134. G. VAN BELLE (ed.), *Index Generalis ETL / BETL 1982-1997*, 1999. IX-337 p. 40 €
135. G. DE SCHRIJVER, *Liberation Theologies on Shifting Grounds. A Clash of Socio-Economic and Cultural Paradigms*, 1998. XI-453 p. 53 €
136. A. SCHOORS (ed.), *Qohelet in the Context of Wisdom*, 1998. XI-528 p. 60 €
137. W.A. BIENERT & U. KÜIINEWEG (eds.), *Origeniana Septima. Origenes in den Auseinandersetzungen des 4. Jahrhunderts*, 1999. XXV-848 p. 95 €
138. É. GAZIAUX, *L'autonomie en morale: au croisement de la philosophie et de la théologie*, 1998. XVI-760 p. 75 €
139. J. GROOTAERS, *Actes et acteurs à Vatican II*, 1998. XXIV-602 p. 75 €
140. F. NEIRYNCK, J. VERHEYDEN & R. CORSTJENS, *The Gospel of Matthew and the Sayings Source Q: A Cumulative Bibliography 1950-1995*, 1998. 2 vols., VII-1000-420* p. 95 €
141. E. BRITO, *Heidegger et l'hymne du sacré*, 1999. XV-800 p. 90 €
142. J. VERHEYDEN (ed.), *The Unity of Luke-Acts*, 1999. XXV-828 p. 60 €
143. N. CALDUCH-BENAGES & J. VERMEYLEN (eds.), *Treasures of Wisdom. Studies in Ben Sira and the Book of Wisdom. Festschrift M. Gilbert*, 1999. XXVII-463 p. 75 €
144. J.-M. AUWERS & A. WÉNIN (eds.), *Lectures et relectures de la Bible. Festschrift P.-M. Bogaert*, 1999. XLII-482 p. 75 €
145. C. BEGG, *Josephus' Story of the Later Monarchy (AJ 9,1–10,185)*, 2000. X-650 p. 75 €
146. J.M. ASGEIRSSON, K. DE TROYER & M.W. MEYER (eds.), *From Quest to Q. Festschrift James M. Robinson*, 2000. XLIV-346 p. 60 €
147. T. RÖMER (ed.), *The Future of the Deuteronomistic History*, 2000. XII-265 p. 75 €
148. F.D. VANSINA, *Paul Ricœur: Bibliographie primaire et secondaire - Primary and Secondary Bibliography 1935-2000*, 2000. XXVI-544 p. 75 €
149. G.J. BROOKE & J.D. KAESTLI (eds.), *Narrativity in Biblical and Related Texts*, 2000. XXI-307 p. 75 €
150. F. NEIRYNCK, *Evangelica III: 1992-2000. Collected Essays*. 2001. XVII-666 p. 60 €
151. B. DOYLE, *The Apocalypse of Isaiah Metaphorically Speaking. A Study of the Use, Function and Significance of Metaphors in Isaiah 24-27*, 2000. XII-453 p. 75 €
152. T. MERRIGAN & J. HAERS (eds.), *The Myriad Christ. Plurality and the Quest for Unity in Contemporary Christology*, 2000. XIV-593 p. 75 €
153. M. SIMON, *Le catéchisme de Jean-Paul II. Genèse et évaluation de son commentaire du Symbole des apôtres*, 2000. XVI-688 p. 75 €

154. J. VERMEYLEN, *La loi du plus fort. Histoire de la rédaction des récits davidiques de 1 Samuel 8 à 1 Rois 2*, 2000. XIII-746 p.   80 €
155. A. WÉNIN (ed.), *Studies in the Book of Genesis. Literature, Redaction and History*, 2001. XXX-643 p.   60 €
156. F. LEDEGANG, *Mysterium Ecclesiae. Images of the Church and its Members in Origen*. 2000. XVIII-722 p.   84 €
157. J.S. BOSWELL, F.P. McHUGH & J. VERSTRAETEN (eds.), *Catholic Social Thought: Twilight of Renaissance?* 2000. XXII-307 p.   60 €
158. A. LINDEMANN (ed.), *The Sayings Source Q and the Historical Jesus*. 2001. XXII-776 p.   60 €
159. C. HEMPEL, A. LANGE & H. LICHTENBERGER (eds.), *The Wisdom Texts from Qumran and the Development of Sapiential Thought*. 2001. X-486 p. Forthcoming.

PRINTED ON PERMANENT PAPER • IMPRIME SUR PAPIER PERMANENT • GEDRUKT OP DUURZAAM PAPIER - ISO 9706

ORIENTALISTE, KLEIN DALENSTRAAT 42, B-3020 HERENT